THEODORE ROOSEVELT
IN THE BADLANDS

By the Same Author

In the Shadow of Wounded Knee

THEODORE ROOSEVELT
IN THE
BADLANDS

★

A YOUNG POLITICIAN'S
QUEST FOR RECOVERY
IN THE AMERICAN WEST

ROGER L. DI SILVESTRO

WALKER & COMPANY
New York

In quoting text from historic documents, all original spellings were preserved. Very minor and only occasional alterations were made to grammar and punctuation and only for the sake of clarity.

Published by Walker Publishing Company, Inc., New York

All papers used by Walker & Company are natural, recyclable products made from wood grown in well-managed forests. The manufacturing processes conform to the environmental regulations of the country of origin.

LIBRARY OF CONGRESS CATALOGING-IN-PUBLICATION DATA

Di Silvestro, Roger L.
Theodore Roosevelt in the Badlands : a young politician's quest for recovery in the American West /
Roger L. Di Silvestro. — 1st U.S. ed.
p.   cm.
Includes bibliographical references.
ISBN 978-0-8027-1721-4
1. Roosevelt, Theodore, 1858–1919—Homes and haunts—North Dakota—Badlands.
2. Presidents—United States—Biography.   3. Frontier and pioneer life—North Dakota—
Badlands.   4. Ranch life—North Dakota—Badlands—History—19th century.
5. Badlands (N.D.)—Biography.   I. Title.
E757.D585 2010
973.91'1092—dc22
2010044297

Visit Walker & Company's Web site at www.walkerbooks.com

First U.S. edition 2011

1 3 5 7 9 10 8 6 4 2

Typeset by Westchester Book Group
Printed in the U.S.A. by Quad/Graphics, Fairfield, Pennsylvania

FOR MAUDE AND KEN,
who introduced me to America's true West
and left me with countless fond memories

AND WITH THOUGHTS OF MY FATHER,
who first introduced me
to the life of Theodore Roosevelt

Although he was more a tourist and outside investor in the West than a permanent resident, Roosevelt and the West is one of America's great stories. His sojourns in the Dakotas, Montana, and Wyoming had a powerful influence on his outlook and politics. Most of all, his time in the West brought him great joy.

STEPHEN E. AMBROSE,
introduction to *Hunting Trips of a Ranchman and The Wilderness Hunter*

It rains here when it rains an' it's hot here when it's hot,
The real folks is real folks which city folks is not.
The dark is as the dark was before the stars was made;
The sun is as the sun was before God thought of shade;
An' the prairie an' the butte-tops an' the long winds, when they blow,
Is like the things what Adam knew on his birthday, long ago.

From *Medora Nights*

CONTENTS

Preface xi

Prologue 1

1 The Badlands Rancher as a Young Man 5

2 The Lure of the West 26

3 The Bison Hunt 35

4 Love and Loss 59

5 Under Western Skies 70

6 The Ranchman 82

7 The Politician 100

8 A Time of Preparation 109

9 Grizzly Hunt 121

10 Gunfighters and Blaine 139

11 Winter, 1884–85 146

12 Roundup 161

13 At Home in East and West 177

14 On the Trail of Outlaws 198

1 5   Love, Guilt, and City Politics 218

1 6   The Blizzards of 1886–87 235

1 7   Badlands Legacy: From the West to the White House 243

Epilogue 257

Acknowledgments 265

Notes 267

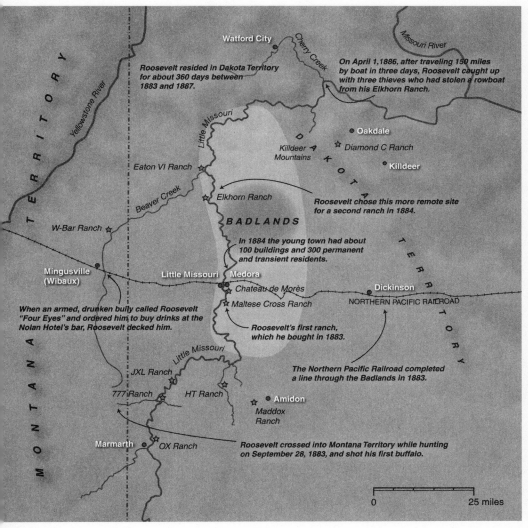

Watford City

Missouri River

Cherry Creek

Roosevelt resided in Dakota Territory for about 360 days between 1883 and 1887.

On April 1, 1886, after traveling 150 miles by boat in three days, Roosevelt caught up with three thieves who had stolen a rowboat from his Elkhorn Ranch.

Yellowstone River

T E R R I T O R Y

Little Missouri

D A K O T A

● Oakdale

Killdeer Mountains

☆ Diamond C Ranch

Eaton VI Ranch ☆

Beaver Creek

☆ Elkhorn Ranch

● Killdeer

Roosevelt chose this more remote site for a second ranch in 1884.

B A D L A N D S

W-Bar Ranch ☆

In 1884 the young town had about 100 buildings and 300 permanent and transient residents.

T E R R I T O R Y

Mingusville (Wibaux)

Little Missouri ● Medora
● Chateau de Morès

Dickinson

☆ Maltese Cross Ranch

NORTHERN PACIFIC RAILROAD

When an armed, drunken bully called Roosevelt "Four Eyes" and ordered him to buy drinks at the Nolan Hotel's bar, Roosevelt decked him.

Roosevelt's first ranch, which he bought in 1883.

Little Missouri

The Northern Pacific Railroad completed a line through the Badlands in 1883.

M O N T A N A

JXL Ranch ☆

☆ Amidon
Maddox Ranch

777 Ranch ☆   ☆ HT Ranch

Marmarth ●   ● OX Ranch

Roosevelt crossed into Montana Territory while hunting on September 28, 1883, and shot his first buffalo.

0   25 miles

oan Pennington)

PREFACE

MORE YEARS AGO THAN I CARE TO RECALL, WHEN I WAS SIXTEEN, A family in the Nebraska Sandhills invited me for an extended summer stay on their cattle ranch, a spread of some six thousand acres of grassland grazed by two thousand Black Angus cattle, a handful of Texas longhorns, and several dozen quarter horses. The ranch lay about thirty-five miles from the nearest town, a compact village of tree-shrouded houses and one- or two-story buildings that was home to 810 residents.

Only dirt roads—actually, roads of the grayish white sand that gave the region its name—led from the town to the ranch, and at least half of those roads were just dual tire tracks cutting across a minimalist landscape of empty, rolling green hills under a generally spotless sky. Some of the hills were scarred by wind-carved blowouts, sandpits that looked white in the distance. Barbed-wire fences trailed over the slopes, and here and there at the base of a hill stood a tree or two. In the wide valleys the glittering blades of windmills spun at the top of tall steel frames, pumping clear, cold water into low, circular tanks. Black cattle drifted along below the hills, grazing or going to the wells. A calf might bawl for its mother, or a bull might bellow to a rival. A skein of pronghorn, white rumps blazing in the sun, might stream across a flat; a mule deer might stand atop a high hill overlooking denim-clad men working in a hay meadow. Hawks often wheeled in the sky, and almost always the melody of western meadowlarks played over the pastures. The terrain itself was more or less unchanged by the inroads of the livestock industry. Native prairie grasses, at least knee high, rippled in the wind, rolling like the surface of the sea; shallow ponds of clear, chill water nurtured families of ducks.

Before I left my suburban Omaha home to go to the Sandhills, on the first day of summer, I wanted to read about what I might expect of ranch life. So I picked up a collection of the writings of Theodore Roosevelt and read his descriptions of ranching in the Badlands of 1880s Dakota Territory. Certainly, ranching had changed in the ensuing decades. Texas longhorns, common commercial livestock in Roosevelt's era, were curiosities kept for ornamentation in my time. Virtually all cattle and horses in the Sandhills were registered animals with long bloodlines. We almost always rode to and from pastures in a pickup truck, and we used a two-way radio for communicating with the house and with neighboring ranchers.

But in critical ways, life in cow country had not changed. Ranching still demanded men and women who did not complain of hardship (the rancher with whom I worked had broken almost every rib in his body over the course of his first forty-five years, having been jumped on by a horse, for example), and the work was still subject to the whims of nature—blizzards and such. Some days, exactly as had Theodore Roosevelt and his crew, we saddled roughly broken horses, which might buck when mounted, and trotted out to distant pastures to move cattle. We rode to the sound of creaking leather, jingling spurs, and clopping hooves muffled by sand; sunlight melted into sweat on the horses' shoulders, and the fragrance of wild grasses sweetened the air. We would round up cows and brand their calves with glowing irons, amidst the odor of singed hair and burning flesh, in the way that disturbed one of Theodore Roosevelt's ranch hands. We kept rifles in a rack over the pickup's rear window and shot occasionally at some poor random beast that was not protected by law—a coyote, perhaps, or a prairie dog. To paraphrase Roosevelt's comment on the open range, we felt the charm of ranch life, exulted in its abounding vigor and its bold, restless freedom, and felt real sorrow for those who would never know what is perhaps the pleasantest, healthiest, and most exciting form of American existence.[1]

Roosevelt's writing helped prepare me for what lay ahead on the first of many prolonged visits to this ranch in the Nebraska Sandhills. I am still surprised at how closely his descriptions matched the world I encountered. For example, he described how curlews—large, long-legged birds with long, slim, down-curved bills—would fly up beside him as he rode horseback through the Badlands, staying always out of gun range but warning away other wildlife with their calls. In this way the bird steers a potentially threatening intruder away from its nest. The day I arrived in the Sandhills, driving down a two-track road along a hay meadow, a curlew flew up beside the car and escorted it for fifty yards or more, calling out its warning—a living memory from Theodore Roosevelt's Badlands.

I have been fortunate in coming full circle with Roosevelt and ranching, enjoying the privilege of writing this book. If I have done the book right, it will give the reader a passageway into the fleeting era of open-range ranching in the Dakota Badlands, when Roosevelt was a young man stricken by tragedy, uncertain of his future, and unsure of his ambitions.

PROLOGUE

WHEN HE DIED AT SIXTY ON JANUARY 6, 1919, THEODORE ROOSEVELT left behind a life of adventure and accomplishment that ranked him among the nation's great leaders and one of its most popular, the only twentieth-century figure to be carved into Mount Rushmore along with Washington, Jefferson, and Lincoln. He had served as an avid reformer and de facto head of the early federal Civil Service Commission, setting the stage for the end of the spoils system. He had helped build up the nation's sea power as assistant secretary of the navy. He had commanded a cavalry unit during the Spanish-American War, which he had help foment, and he had come out of military service a national hero, landing in the New York governor's mansion for an innovative stint as the state's political head.

Two years as governor led him to the vice presidency of the United States in 1901, a position he held for only a few months before the assassination of President William McKinley put Roosevelt in the White House at forty-two—still the youngest man ever to lead the nation. After a presidency during which he won the Nobel Peace Prize for settling the

Russo-Japanese War in 1905, he went on a ten-month safari to East Africa, collecting specimens for the Smithsonian Institution and for the American Museum of Natural History in New York City, which his father had helped found in the 1870s. In the 1912 election he led the Progressive Party, a.k.a. the Bull Moose Party, to challenge Republican candidate William Howard Taft, who had become president in 1909 as Roosevelt's handpicked successor but had not lived up to Roosevelt's expectations. The 1912 race was one of Roosevelt's rare failures: He lost and so did Taft, giving the White House to Democrat Woodrow Wilson, whom Roosevelt despised. Partly in dismay over this development, Roosevelt went off to explore an uncharted river in South America for several months in late 1913 and early 1914, nearly killing himself with hardship. As a result of this trip, a river in Brazil bears his name.

Roosevelt's disdain for Wilson grew as the new president sought to avoid U.S. participation in World War I. After the United States entered the war in 1917, Roosevelt sought the administration's permission to raise an army regiment that he would lead, but he was rebuffed. All four of Roosevelt's sons served in Europe; the youngest, Quentin, was killed when the fighter plane he piloted was shot down. After the war, Roosevelt was widely bandied about as a potential Republican candidate in 1920, a race he might have run had not death found him first.

But before all that, before his career, as he himself put it, "rose like a rocket," before he became the stuff of American myth, legend, and misunderstanding, he was a young man suffering the anguish of a heart that broke on Valentine's Day 1884 when, within hours of each other, his mother and his wife died just two days after his wife had given birth to his first child.

Only twenty-four years old, Roosevelt for the past two years had served in the New York Assembly, where he had been enjoying perhaps the most promising political career in the state. Those twin deaths stunned him, however—friends worried that he would lose his mind—and by autumn he added to his sorrows the conviction that his political career, too, was dead, felled because he had sided with a controversial Republican presidential candidate. Bereft in his home life and bewildered by the downward drift of his career, he sought escape in one of the most remote and rugged places in the United States south of the Canadian border—the

Badlands of Dakota Territory, America's last frontier, a wilderness only then opening to the cattle industry. There he established a ranch, adopted the buckskin garb of the pioneers, and spent generous amounts of time hunting dangerous game, such as grizzly bears and mountain lions. Before his sojourn in the Badlands ended, the West would play as large a role in Roosevelt's personal Manifest Destiny as it did in the nation's. Within two years he would find physical strength and emotional stability, salvaging the wreckage of his life and forging himself into the historical figure who would gaze down in stone from Mount Rushmore. Toward the end of his life he would say that if, for some reason, he had to give up all but one of his memories, out of the many adventures and accomplishments he had achieved and enjoyed, he would keep the memory "of my life on the ranch with its experiences close to Nature and among the men who lived nearest her."[1]

He also said of the Badlands, during a campaign visit as a vice presidential candidate, "here the romance of my life began."[2] This comment may be taken more literally than he probably intended. Love and its loss were motivators for much of what happened to him in the Badlands. Hermann Hagedorn, a biographer who wrote about Roosevelt's ranching years in a book published in 1921, looked back in the 1960s at what he had written so long before, and what he saw gave rise to these thoughts:

The real story of Theodore Roosevelt's ranching days has never been told. It involves Roosevelt's two wives, Alice Lee and Edith Carow, and when I wrote "Roosevelt in the Badlands," almost forty years ago, I was not in a position to tell all I knew and, in fact, I knew only part of the story. In the perspective of almost 75 years, the whole picture is now unfolding, and can be told.

It is a story of a brilliant and successful young man who came out to the Bad Lands in the summer of 1884, outwardly alive and alert but inwardly shattered by the death in childbirth of the young wife he had devotedly loved. He had grown up in a society in which the romantic conceptions of Victorian literature were indisputable realities, and was convinced that, when his wife, Alice, died, happiness for him had forever died with her. Like the familiar heroes of fiction who had loved and lost, he fled to the wilderness, not so much to forget what he had lost but to live his life in its afterglow. His attitude of mind was sentimental, morbid and unreal.[3]

In the Badlands, Roosevelt recovered from that state of mind. He also revived politically and physically. This book is the story of his Badlands years.

I

THE BADLANDS RANCHER
AS A YOUNG MAN

Although Theodore Roosevelt would ride broncos and hunt buffalo in the Dakota Badlands, would stalk grizzlies and shoot elk, would ranch cattle and track down armed outlaws and become renowned during a political campaign as the Cowboy Candidate, he was urban born and raised. In his youth, he lived on West Fifty-seventh Street, just off Fifth Avenue, the most prestigious address in New York City. "Fifth avenue is the fashionable street, *par excellence*, of New York," an 1881 guidebook observed.[1] "To live and die in a Fifth avenue mansion is the dearest wish of every New Yorker's heart." Practical matters reinforced the prestige: Streets near the Hudson and East rivers were among the dirtiest and most vice-ridden, making waterside addresses distinctly undesirable, and Fifth Avenue was as far from either river as possible on the narrow island.[2]

On the northwest corner of Fifty-seventh Street and Fifth Avenue in the 1880s stood a squat, five-story mansion of red brick and limestone with bay windows, recessed arched windows, corner turrets, and a sharply peaked roof punctuated with huge dormers—a Vanderbilt home. Around the corner, Fifty-seventh Street was lined "east and west of Fifth avenue, with palatial mansions, and [was] among the ultra fashionable thorough-fares."[3] The Roosevelt family home stood at 6 West Fifty-seventh, poised, much as Theodore would be throughout his life, between two worlds. South of Fifty-seventh Street the city sprawled across Manhattan, known even in the late 1800s for its urban drive, energy, and bustling pace. One New Jersey man who took a job there after the Civil War wrote a dozen years or more later, "We are all living too fast; we are working too hard. Instead of taking a leisurely stroll to our business in the morning, we rush down town at a furious pace. We grind, grind at our treadmills all day, and grind too hard. We bolt our meals in a fourth of the time we should give to them; we rush back home at night as furiously as we left it in the morning, and our evenings are spent in an effort to keep up the excite-ment of the day. . . . This haste, this furious pace at which we are going, at business, at pleasure, at everything, is the great curse of New York life."[4]

North of Fifty-ninth Street, Manhattan was rural. Goats were so dis-tinctive a part of the region above Central Park that it was called "the goats."[5] On the East Side, along Fifth Avenue, many old estates—such as seventy-acre Jones' Woods, beginning at Sixty-eighth Street—still stood intact. Winding paths led across open lots to isolated homes. Along salt creeks running from the interior of Manhattan, residents caught crabs, eels, mussels, and clams; in the East River they trapped lobsters. Unusu-ally high tides flooded marshes on the East Side from Ninety-second Street north to about 108th and as far west as Third Avenue. Stands of trees punctuated the East Side all the way to the village of Harlem. On the West Side, truck farms formed the margins of Ninth Avenue.[6] "All in all," wrote an 1880s resident, Manhattan above Fifty-ninth "was about as wild and picturesque a piece of wilderness as ever laid outdoors."[7]

Theodore Roosevelt Sr. had moved his family to the city's edge in 1872, when he built the house on Fifty-seventh Street for his wife. Martha Roo-sevelt, called Mittie within the family, was a former southern belle whom Theodore had met during a trip to Georgia in 1850, when he was nine-teen, and she was fifteen. She grew up on a slave-holding plantation in the northwest part of the state, near Roswell; her daughter Corinne contended in a memoir that the slaves were treated like family friends, even though Mittie's half brother shot and killed one during a moment of pique.[8] Mittie was fashionably pale—"more moonlight-white than cream-white, and in the cheeks there was coral, rather than a rose, tint."[9] Her hair was fine and dark with a russet glow. As a mother she was affectionate, Corinne recalled; her "gracious loveliness and deep devotion wrapped us round as with a mantle."[10]

The Roosevelts were Knickerbockers, wealthy people who traced their heritage to Manhattan's first Dutch families—the Roosevelts had arrived in the colonies in the mid-1640s.[11] Despite their prominence, the Knicker-bockers were not free of detractors: "They are clannish, and cling together, looking down with a lofty contempt upon all who cannot show a Dutch ancestor, or produce a long line of family portraits as proof of their descent. Many of these people are highly educated, refined, and would be a credit to any society, were it not for their ridiculous affectation of supe-riority to their neighbors."[12]

In the 1700s, Johannes Roosevelt founded a linseed oil company on Manhattan's Maiden Lane. He diversified into chocolate and flour and undertook general contracting jobs.[13] He also built the foundation of the Roosevelt family fortune by buying land.[14] Johannes' son, Jacobus, born in 1724, followed in his father's footsteps, establishing a hardware business.[15]

Jacobus' grandson, Cornelius Van Schaak Roosevelt—grandfather of the future president—was born in 1794.[16] He was the first man in his branch of the Roosevelt line to take a non-Dutch bride; he also was prob-ably the last to require his family to speak only Dutch at Sunday dinner. He inherited the family talent for commerce, introducing the firm of Roosevelt and Son to finance as well as making it the top plate-glass purveyor in the United States, profiting from sales to rapidly growing New York City.[17] During the financial panic of 1837 he kept a cool head and invested in more New York real estate, becoming one of the city's top ten land investors, with holdings in excess of $1.3 million. He became a director of Chemical Bank.

His youngest son, Theodore senior, joined the family firm in 1851, when he was twenty. Put in charge of the plate-glass division, he made a fortune supplying glass to Chicago when the city was rebuilding after the 1871 fire. Shortly after that incident, Roosevelt and Son gave up import-ing glass and became a banking firm, headed by Theodore's brother James.

Theodore spent much of his time working for philanthropic causes.

His financial support helped create Roosevelt Hospital, the Bellevue Training School for Nurses, and the New York Orthopedic Dispensary for the Deformed and Crippled; he was a major benefactor to the YMCA; he worked with orphan asylums and with mental asylums for the poor. He helped organize the Union League Club, a high-society organization dedicated to civic works, beginning during the Civil War.[18] He was vice president of the State Charities Aid Association, a board member of United Charities and the State Board of Charities, and a founder of the Children's Aid Society, the Society for the Prevention of Cruelty to Animals, the Metropolitan Museum of Art, and the American Museum of Natural History. He also taught Sunday school and served Sunday dinner at the Newsboys' Lodging House.[19] One of the newsboys he helped support later became an Alaska governor.[20]

When Theodore junior was born on October 27, 1858, the total number of millionaires in New York, Boston, and Philadelphia was only around seventy.[21] His grandfather Cornelius stood among them as one of Manhattan's five richest men.[22] This wealth meant that Theodore was born into a comfortable childhood, which began in a large brownstone townhouse on Twentieth Street between Broadway and Fourth Avenue.[23] His childhood, however, included grave challenges. He was subject to bouts of asthma and painful digestive problems.[24] The Roosevelt family called his stomach problem cholera morbus, but today it would be called gastroenteritis or, commonly, stomach flu, though actually it is caused not by an influenza virus but by nervous stress. Attacks can arise rapidly and last up to ten days.

Asthma attacks first struck when Roosevelt was three years old: "I was a sickly, delicate boy, suffered much from asthma, and frequently had to be taken away on trips to find a place where I could breathe. One of my memories is of my father walking up and down the room with me in his arms at night when I was a very small person, and of sitting up in bed gasping, with my father and mother trying to help me."[25]

To relieve the attacks, which generally occurred at night, his parents dosed him with coffee and even made him smoke cigars, which would interrupt the asthma attack by inducing nicotine sickness.[26] His father sometimes bundled him up and took him for fast carriage rides, in the hope that the change in air would help.[27] Roosevelt: "I could breathe, I could sleep, when he held me in his arms. My father—he got me breath, he got me lungs, strength—life."[28] The air in New York may itself have been part of the problem, laden as it was with particulate pollution, such as soot, from the burning of wood and coal for fuel.

As he neared his twelfth birthday, following a summer in which Theodore was as often sick as he was well, a doctor examined him and reported that in addition to fresh air he needed exercise to build lung capacity.[29] With his father's encouragement, young Theodore embarked on a regimen of outdoor activity, gymnastics, and exercise with a professional trainer. His father even turned the upstairs back porch of their house into a gymnasium.[30]

Theodore was so diligent in his fitness program that by 1871 he was much improved. That August he experienced no spells of illness—his longest period of good health in years.[31] But setbacks plagued him. In summer 1872 an asthma attack struck, and his family sent him off alone to the fresh air of Maine's Moosehead Lake. There two boys about his age bullied him. Roosevelt was shocked to find that when he fought back, either boy "could not only handle me with easy contempt, but handle me so as not to hurt me much and yet to prevent my doing any damage whatever in return."[32] After that incident, he signed up for boxing lessons with an ex-prizefighter named John Long.

Within three years, at five feet eight inches tall and 124 pounds, he won a pewter cup for dominating the lightweight division at Long's gym.[33] From August 21 through December 11, 1875, he bested his brother and several male cousins in fourteen of fifteen athletic contests, including running, wresting, boxing, and jumping.[34] His arduous physical training was paying off. He continued boxing, and later wrestling, throughout his life, even in the White House.[35]

Despite his illnesses, Theodore enjoyed summer trips to the Hudson Valley, the Long Island shore, and rural New Jersey and twelve-month family trips to Europe, Egypt, and the Middle East. A special pleasure was Oyster Bay, Long Island, which had been a Roosevelt family retreat ever since Cornelius opened a summer house there. In 1874, Theodore's father rented a country house near Oyster Bay that the family named "Tranquillity."[36] The Roosevelt children rode horses on the empty country lanes and held picnics on Cooper's Bluff, where they read aloud and competed in poetry contests; cousins visited in droves, and Theodore studied natural history and rowed on the bay in the smallest boat during the roughest water.[37] The children also wrote competitive essays on William Wordsworth, Washington Irving, and Plutarch's *Lives*. Theodore would recite Edgar Allan Poe's "The Raven" and "Ulalume" in a "strange, rather weird, monotonous tone . . . Poe's rhythm and curious, suggestive, melancholy quality of perfection affected strongly his imagination, and he placed him high in rank amongst the poets of his time."[38]

Educated by private tutors, Roosevelt was an avid reader. One of his favorite authors as a child was Mayne Reid, who wrote tales of the West, such as his 1869 book *The Boy Hunters, or Adventures in Search of a White Buffalo*, in which he described ways to hunt bison.[39] In his *Autobiography*, Roosevelt wrote that "the novels of Mayne Reid together strengthened my instinctive interest in natural history."[40]

The characters in the *The Boy Hunters* provided a model for Roosevelt. Basil, the hero of the story, "is a 'mighty hunter.' He is more fond of the chase than of ought else. He loves hunting for itself, and delights in its dangers. He has got beyond the age of bird-catching and squirrel-shooting. His ambition is not now to be satisfied with any thing less exciting than a panther, bear, or buffalo hunt."[41] *The Boy Hunters* live in a house with a hallway that "resembled a little museum," with mounted birds, mammals, and insects.[42] It resembled Roosevelt's own childhood collection of natural history specimens, animals he mounted himself after his father hired a taxidermist to teach him.[43]

His zeal for wildlife began early: "While I was still a small boy I began to take an interest in natural history. I remember distinctly the first day that I started on my career as a zoologist. I was walking up Broadway, and as I passed the market to which I used sometimes to be sent before breakfast to get strawberries I suddenly saw a dead seal laid out on a slab of wood. That seal filled me with every possible feeling of romance and adventure. I asked where it was killed, and was informed in the harbor. I had already begun to read some of Mayne Reid's books and other boys' books of adventure, and I felt that this seal brought all these adventures in realistic fashion before me. . . . I had vague aspirations of in some way or another owning and preserving that seal, but they never got beyond the purely formless stage. I think, however, I did get the seal's skull, and with two of my cousins promptly started what we ambitiously called the 'Roosevelt Museum of Natural History.'"[44] As a boy he collected birds for his museum, and during a family trip to Egypt and Palestine in winter 1872–73, when he was fourteen, he shot so many birds—between one hundred and two hundred—that he lost count.[45] However exciting the ruins of ancient Egypt had been to Roosevelt's youthful imagination, he recalled in the years ahead that "this bird-collecting gave what was really the chief zest to my Nile journey."[46] He killed his first big game, a white-tailed deer, in New York's Adirondack Mountains at fifteen or sixteen, using the French shotgun his father had given him for shooting in Egypt.[47]

In 1876 Theodore went off to Harvard with the idea that he might develop a career in the natural sciences. He left New York City for Cambridge, Massachusetts, on September 27 to join the university's 820 other students as one of 246 freshman.[48] He moved into a room on the second floor of a boardinghouse at 16 Winthrop Street.[49] The room was cozy, with a fireplace, a large, carved table for study, a chaise longue for relaxation and reading, a smattering of his stuffed birds under glass, and a fur rug. At Harvard he boxed and practiced "a good deal" with his rifle, walking the three miles to and from the range; he noted in an 1878 letter to his mother that "my scores have been fair, although not very good."[50] He continued to enjoy outdoor shooting sports, making several hunting trips to Maine, where he shot lynx and deer and took strenuous hikes through woods and over mountains.

Fellow Harvardians thought Roosevelt was "quite unrestrained."[51] One Boston debutante remembered him as "studious, ambitious, eccentric—not the sort to appeal at first."[52] He was slightly built, weighing only 145 pounds. Like dandies of the time, he parted his hair high on his head, and his pale blue eyes, in photographs, were piercing, almost fierce. Muttonchops brushed to a froth—a style already unfashionable at Harvard—framed his face. With a voice that bordered on a falsetto, he spoke in rapid, staccato outbursts that often degenerated into stammering. In discussions, he sometimes worked himself into states of such manic animation that he collapsed from nervous exhaustion. He was not much of a dancer, tending to hop, and was too energetic and forceful to be suave. As an aspiring naturalist, he kept various animal specimens not only in his rooms but in his pockets, which did not enhance his appeal. And his hair-trigger temper erupted easily into fistfights, during which he would swing at friends who tried to restrain him.[53]

Nevertheless, he succeeded in cultivating friendships with the only people that he believed counted—the gentlemen minority among the student body—and was invited to join most of the exclusive Harvard clubs. The clubs were critical to a man's career, because membership rosters were watched carefully for potential recruits by New York, Boston, and Philadelphia law firms and brokerage houses. "Investment houses banked on the proposition that social success in college implied occupational success in later life."[54]

In his sophomore year, Roosevelt was one of forty men invited to join the Institute of 1770, Harvard's oldest and largest social club. Institute membership set a student on the pathway to the hallowed Porcellian Club, the most exclusive of the so-called final clubs attained only after a student had worked his way up a hierarchy of lesser groups. He was a member of Delta Kappa Epsilon (DKE), a fraternity created at Yale University in 1844 as an alternative, ironically, to the highly selective clubs. DKE, also called the Dickey, was a secret society within the larger, more respectable Institute of 1770. Some fifty students out of each class were elected in groups of ten.[55] Membership in the Dickey conferred status. "On election nights, many a sophomore lay sleepless in his dark bed, listening. Was that roving midnight chorus, whose progress he could mark in the distance, going to approach and stop beneath his window with its jaunty serenade announcing he was 'in,' and so send thrills of triumph and joy through his young body, or was he destined only to hear it wander and pause beneath luckier windows, and die away? To be left out of the Dickey meant that your social future at Harvard was likely to be in the back seats."[56]

During his junior year, Roosevelt was invited to join the Porcellian, founded in the 1790s with the motto *Dum vivimus vivamus*, "While we live, let's *live*." Nicknamed "the Porc," its emblem was a pig. He also was invited to join the Hasty Pudding Club, founded in 1790 by a Harvard junior with a moniker that smacks of eighteenth-century New England: Nymphus Hatch. The club was named for a traditional American dish that founding members ate at their first meeting and was organized to promote friendship, conversation, and enjoyment, the last generally in the form of parties and entertainments. Roosevelt served as secretary for Hasty Pudding. He also was librarian of the Porcellian; treasurer of another exclusive club, the O.K.; president of the literary fraternity Alpha Delta Phi; editor of the *Advocate*; and vice president of the Natural History Society.

Throughout his Harvard years Roosevelt struggled with choosing a career. The natural sciences beckoned; his father told him that if he went into science he would have to do so seriously, not as a dilettante, and that if he was not going to earn money by going into law or business, he would have to cut expenses.[57] "In other words, if I went into a scientific career, I must definitely abandon all thought of the enjoyment that could accompany a money-making career, and must find my pleasures elsewhere," Roosevelt wrote years later.[58]

He was still mulling over his future when personal tragedy struck. In mid-December his father collapsed. Initially doctors thought he was suffering from peritonitis and did not think his condition life-threatening, but he soon became desperately ill, bedridden in great pain.[59] Corinne wrote in her diary on January 6, 1878: "Three weeks ago tomorrow, Father was taken very ill, the first week was awful, he was in a stupor nearly all the time from the opiates given to still the pain. . . . It is so terrible to see him suffering such agony and not be able to do anything to ease his pain. He is so wonderfully, marvellously patient, never a word of his own suffering, so lovely to everyone. I do not believe there is another man on earth like father. How much he has done for me and how little I can do for him."[60]

On February 9, 1878, young Theodore was summoned home to New York; he took the overnight train, but by the time he arrived his father was dead, felled by cancer shortly before midnight on the ninth. In their diaries, Theodore, Corinne, and Elliott described sharply contrasting reactions. Corinne, February 9, 1878: "Asleep in Jesus. Safe in the arms of Jesus. 'Oh death where is thy victory, oh grave where is thy sting.' 'In that city which hath no need of sun, either of the moon to shine in it, for the glory of God doth lighten it, and the lamb is the light thereof.' My own dear father, I will never love anyone as I love you. I long for you so deeply but I know it is best."[61]

Elliott, February 9, 1878: "As the last struggling breath was drawn

Mother cried out the words of comfort to the girls. 'I expect he is safe in the Arms of Jesus now.' Yes my little bereaved mother. He is."[62]

Theodore seemed too choked with emotion to express his feelings. He wrote only, "My dear Father. Born Sept. 23rd 1831."[63] Nothing more until the twelfth, when he penned a long entry that spanned the pages to the eighteenth:

He has just been buried. I shall never forget these terrible three days: the hideous suspense of the ride on [he probably meant to write "home"]; the dull, inert sorrow, during which I felt as if I had been stunned, or as if part of my life had been taken away; and the two moments of sharp, bitter agony, when I kissed the dear dead face and realized that he would never again on this earth speak to me or greet me with his loving smile, and then when I heard the sound of the first clod dropping on the coffin holding the one I loved dearest on earth. He looked so calm and sweet. I feel that if it were not for the certainty that as he himself has so often said, "he is not dead but gone before," I should almost perish. With the help of my God I will try to lead such a life as he would have wished. He was the most wise and loving father that ever lived; I owe everything to him. It is terrible to think I have never done anything for him not even during his sickness. I never had an unkind word from him, though I was always promptly punished if I did wrong. For the last five years he has scarcely spoken to me reprovingly. He was so unselfish and was so continually making others happy that he was always happy himself; his 46 years of life were, excepting the last two months, happy ones.[64]

On the page dated February 19 he wrote: "It seems impossible to realize I shall never see him again; he is such a living memory. Truly 'he was eyes to the blind, feet to the lame, and a father to the poor.' "[65]

Roosevelt returned to Cambridge on the twenty-third and noted in his diary that his father's will left him capital that would yield about eight thousand dollars annually, "comfortable although not rich."[66] Most of his fellow New Yorkers might have disagreed, as the income by most standards was more than generous and exceeded the annual salary of Harvard's president. An office worker then felt lucky to earn eight dollars a week.[67] Moreover, Roosevelt's eight thousand dollars would go far. Taverns offered porterhouse steak for thirty-five cents—the most expensive item on the menu at the Jim Fisk tavern at about that time.[68] At the Boss Tweed tavern, a customer could have roast turkey and cranberry sauce for eighteen cents, fried eels for a dime, and a quarter of an eight-inch pie for a nickel. The most expensive theater seats were two dollars.[69]

By the twenty-fifth, Roosevelt was boxing again, but on Sunday, March 3, he wrote, "Have been thinking about Father all evening, have had a good square break down and feel much the better for it." A few days later, on the fifth, he wrote that it seemed "brutal to go about my ordinary occupation, but I must keep employed. I can not [begin?] to mix with the fellows yet." On the sixth he added, "If I had very much time to think I believe I should almost go crazy. But I think I can really and humbly say 'Thy will be done.' On Saturday, March 9, he wrote, "It is just one month since the blackest day of my life." The following day he noted, "Had another square break down."

Theodore Roosevelt had had his first meeting with death. He regained his equilibrium during the ensuing months and by autumn was ready to have his first avowed encounter with another of life's great challenges and rewards, love.

He met Alice Lee for the first time during a weekend stay at the home of Richard Saltonstall, a tall young man from Boston's highest social echelon who was Roosevelt's closest friend during junior year.[70] On Friday, October 18, 1878, the two students mounted Saltonstall's buggy in Cambridge, crossed the Charles River, and drove six miles over gently rolling country shaded occasionally by elms and maples ablaze with autumn. They came finally to Chestnut Hill, atop which perched two imposing houses against a backdrop of chestnut trees. One was the Saltonstall mansion. The other, separated from the Saltonstalls' by only twenty yards of upward-sloping lawn and a garden gate, was the family home of Richard's uncle by marriage, George Cabot Lee of the prestigious Boston banking firm Lee, Higginson and Company. The residential arrangement had a tribal feel, with boardwalks laid down among the houses for visits when rain turned pathways into mud.[71] The Lee house—clapboard, lit inside by myriad windows, gabled, and overtopped with brick chimneys—included an adjoining tennis court. The house smelled of fresh linen, waxed floors, and camphor.[72]

With close-cropped white hair and bright blue eyes, George Lee was small, cheerful, and dapper.[73] His wife, originally from New Bedford, had "worried brown eyes" and often retreated to her room to nurse an unspecified ailment called her "turns." She always wore black, even to weddings.[74] Their daughter, seventeen-year-old Alice, was a close friend of Richard's sister, Rose. Theodore may have met Alice on the long sweep of the front lawn that evening as the sun melted into dusk.[75] A little more than a year after the introduction he would write, "As long as I live, I shall never forget how sweetly she looked, and how prettily she greeted me."[76]

Unusually bright and energetic, Alice was called Sunshine by family and friends. Like Roosevelt, she enjoyed a good laugh and was often the life of the party. She was athletic, winning tennis tournaments and taking cross-country hikes in a long, firm stride. Highly literate, she had a taste for Thackeray, Hawthorne, Shelley, Swinburne, and Henry Wadsworth Longfellow, the author of Theodore's favorite poem, *The Saga of King Olaf*. Her hair, said one woman acquaintance, was golden, her eyes dove gray. Her neck was long and slender, her nose upturned, her mouth small. At five feet seven inches, she was only an inch shorter than Roosevelt.

Roosevelt's diaries reveal that on the following day he and she, with Rose and Richard, walked the woods around Chestnut Hill and drove to a neighbor's house for lunch, afternoon tea, and a night of song and dance. On Sunday afternoon, following church, Theodore and Alice went off into the woods alone to collect chestnuts. Roosevelt blithely wrote that she was "a very sweet, pretty girl"—which was how he usually described female acquaintances.[77] But months later, in his entry for January 30, 1880, he would confess that he had fallen in love with her at first sight, that she was "my first love, too."[78] He would add, "I had never before cared . . . a snap of my finger for any girl."[79]

He drove again to Chestnut Hill on November 11, 1878, for a tea that included Alice Hathaway Lee.[80] At Thanksgiving he returned, a guest for the holiday. He spent Thanksgiving Day dancing, walking, and playing lawn tennis with Alice.[81] Alice allowed him to call her by her first name—quite the coup for Theodore, as in this era a first-name basis defined intimate friendship.

The two pages following the diary entry in which he recorded that triumph are torn out—throughout his life Roosevelt censored his journal. A clue to what he had written appears in his entry for January 25, 1880, which indicates that on Thanksgiving Day 1878—scarcely a month after he had first met Alice—he had vowed to himself that "win her I would, if it were possible."[82] And with that vow, as he later told a close Harvard friend, Henry Minot, he had committed himself to the "eager, restless, passionate pursuit of one all-absorbing object."[83]

The pursuit proved long, arduous, and punishing; friends even feared he would lose his mind over it. Alice often edged away without discouraging his advances. In early December she consented to go with him, in the company of Rose, to a photography studio to have pictures taken of the three of them.[84] In his diary Roosevelt confessed that from then on, for the next fifteen months, Alice Lee was on his mind every waking hour. On December 11 he begged God to help him remain as virtuous as his father would have wanted, "and to do nothing I would have been ashamed to confess to him. I am very . . ."[85] But he blacked out the rest.

During the early weeks of 1879, he saw Alice at teas with the Saltonstalls and at dances at her house. He joined her for winter walks and tobogganing. He preened for her in fashionable straight-legged, uncreased trousers, high collars, silk cravats punctuated with cameo pins, and cutaway coats that accentuated his fobbed watch chain. She accepted an invitation to Roosevelt's apartment for a lunch party that involved five other girls and five other college boys, with Mrs. Saltonstall as chaperone. Roosevelt presented Alice with a rug made from a lynx pelt he had collected on a recent hunting trip in Maine.[86]

Spring warmed the air, and Alice seemed to warm to Theodore. He decided to make more frequent trips to Chestnut Hill and accordingly had his horse, Lightfoot, shipped up from New York. With hunting crop and beaver hat—and looking, he thought, "very swell"—he made almost daily trips to see her.[87] They took walks. They played whist. They danced the knickerbocker. He told her ghost stories and taught her the five-step waltz. They attended theater parties and took a trip to New Haven to watch Harvard beat Yale in a boat race. Throughout the spring season he relived in his diary the hours he spent with her, highlighting the accounts with an occasional verbal chortle: "What a good time I am having. . . . I can't conceive of a fellow possibly enjoying himself more."[88]

By June the academic year was winding down, approaching the day when Roosevelt would go back to New York City for the summer, leaving Alice Lee wide open to potential rivals. The remedy, in Roosevelt's view, was to propose to her, which he did in late June.[89] She turned him down but did not leave him hopeless, inviting him to continue his pursuit in the fall.

Back at Harvard toward the end of summer, he drove his new carriage— a sporty, two-wheeled Tilbury—to Chestnut Hill to see her on September 26, 1879, but his diary for that day does not mention her by name. He had not seen her for a month or more, but his only reference to her was to observe obliquely that "the girls are as lovely as ever."[90] She all but vanished from his diary from that date through most of November, except for one reference when he listed her among the guests at an opera party on October 16. Two previous pages have been torn away. What happened between them is perhaps alluded to in a letter he wrote to a relative in 1880, looking back to late 1879: "I did not think I could win her, and I went nearly crazy at the mere thought of losing her."[91] In a letter to his sister Anna in November 1879, he cried: "Oh the changeableness of the female mind!"[92]

The time at which he wrote that letter was one of impending change: After Thanksgiving Alice would come out as a debutante, making her fair game for all suitors. He visited her at Chestnut Hill over Thanksgiving, but she gave him no cause for optimism, though she did flirt with him. Four days later she had the traditional coming-out. Roosevelt suffered. For distraction, he tried to immerse himself in reading and even writing— he started penning a book he called *The Naval War of 1812*. But insomnia plagued him. In his diary entry for January 30, 1880, he would recount what he called "the tortures of the last four months," during which "night after night I have not even gone to bed."[93] Instead, he roamed the wintry Cambridge woods. When, after one foray, he refused to go back to his apartment, an alarmed classmate telegraphed Roosevelt's family for help. Theodore's cousin James West Roosevelt came to the rescue, calming the heartbroken suitor. At about this time, Theodore bought a set of French dueling pistols in case he had to deal with competitors.[94]

When Theodore boarded a train to New York for the Christmas holidays he had not seen Alice for two weeks. But the season brought an unexpected gift. The day after Christmas, Alice arrived in New York, along with other denizens of Chestnut Hill, for a week's visit. She accepted Roosevelt's invitation to stay at 6 West Fifty-seventh Street, and he had "an uproariously jolly time" showing her around town.[95] On New Year's Day 1880 he took Alice and her retinue for lunch and dancing at Jerome Park, a wooded retreat in the Bronx that featured a racetrack as well as a lavish dining room and ballroom. His quarry was finally, and literally, falling into his arms, however erratic his dancing.

Nevertheless, even after the New York City episode she kept him on a string, uncertain, doubtful. Finally he brought the situation to a climax, as he described in his diary on Sunday, January 25, 1880: "I drove over to the Lees determined to make an end of things at last; it was nearly eight months since I had first proposed to her, and I had been nearly crazy during the past year; and after much pleading my own sweet, pretty darling consented to be my wife. Oh, how bewitchingly pretty she looked! If loving her with my whole heart and soul can make her happy, she shall be happy. . . . the aim of my whole life shall be to make her happy, and to shield her and guard her from every trial; and oh, how I shall cherish my sweet queen!"[96]

Various epistles written around this time reveal the fervor of Roosevelt's emotions. A note from Theodore's aunt Mrs. James King Gracie to Alice, dated February 1, 1880: "This morning hardly before I had opened my eyes Theodore came down bubbling over with happiness to inform us that we were to have a new niece and that you dear Miss Alice were to be the one."[97]

A note to Alice from Theodore's uncle James Alfred Roosevelt, writing from 4 West Fifty-seventh Street on February 1, 1880: "Theodore has come back to us in a wild state of happiness, delightful to behold."[98]

Once engaged, Theodore could unleash his pent-up yearnings. On February 23 he confessed in his diary, "When we are alone, I can hardly stay a moment without holding her in my arms or kissing her; she is such a laughing, pretty little witch; and yet with it all she is so true and so tender."[99] A month later he wrote, "It is perfectly impossible to tell how much I love her; it is not merely thinking of her all the time, it is much more than that; she is *always* present in my mind."[100]

The couple embarked on a predictably emotional series of letters that would take them up to the wedding. Roosevelt, in handwriting small and exceedingly clear and controlled, June 8, 1880: "You sweet, pretty darling, I perfectly long to be with you; I perfectly hate to think it will be a week before I shall see you. My own sunny faced Queen, I don't think you are ever absent ten minutes from my thoughts; I know every one of your saucy, bewitching little ways, and every expression of your sweet, bright pretty face."[101]

Alice, June 9, 1880: "Teddy I do miss you so much and long for the 16th so as to have you back again at Chestnut Hill, I love you with my whole heart, and you are always in my thoughts."[102]

But doubts and anxiety crept in, surfacing cryptically in their letters. Alice, October 6, 1880: "Teddykins I know you can make me happy and you must never think it would have been better for me, if we had never met; I should die without you now Teddy and there is not another man I ever could have loved in this world. You are a naughty boy to write me such a blue letter. You must not think that I think you the least exactly, Teddy. I am going to try and be a good wife for you."[103]

Theodore, October 17, 1880: "Oh my darling, I do so hope and pray I make you happy. I shall try very hard to be unselfish and sunny tempered as you are, and I shall save you from every care I can. My own true love, you have made my happiness almost too great; and I feel I can do so little for you in return. I worship you so that it seems almost desecration to touch you; and yet when I am with you I can hardly let you a moment out of my arms. My purest queen, no man was worthy of your love; and I shall try very hard to deserve it, at least in part."[104]

They married on his twenty-second birthday, October 27, 1880. She was nineteen. After two weeks at the Roosevelt summer home on Long Island's Oyster Bay, they moved into 6 West Fifty-seventh Street. Shortly after the wedding he wrote in his diary, "Our intense happiness is too sacred to be written about."[105]

★ ★ ★

Manhattan in 1880 was home to 1,164,673 residents who lived on the threshold of the modern age—already part of Broadway was lit with electric lights, and within two years Thomas Edison's electric company would light the blocks lying among Nassau, Pearl, Spruce, and Wall streets.[106] Within three years the Brooklyn Bridge would open, the first roadway across the East River. The year Roosevelt married, the city telephone exchange served twenty thousand subscribers who each paid a ten-dollar monthly rental fee. Within this modernizing world, Theodore and Alice moved in the best social circles. The evening of Tuesday, January 10, 1881, found him seated at dinner next to Mrs. Astor, New York's society leader; the next day he took Alice sleighing beyond Harlem and attended a "very jolly" theater party that night; the following day, Thursday the thirteenth, found him at the Astors' Great Ball.[107]

Roosevelt pursued his career with his usual vigor. He attended the Columbia College Law School, housed in a formerly private residence at 8 Great Jones Street on the northwest corner of Lafayette Place, and he continued to work on his book, *The Naval War of 1812.* He also decided to go into politics rather than law, business, or science.

His earliest surviving mention of a potential political career appears in his diary entry for August 18, 1879, while he was still at Harvard; ruminating about his future, he concludes, "I shall probably either pursue a scientific course, or else study law, preparatory to going into public life."[108] Apparently he gave up on science as a career in part because Alice did not approve of it, and in part because he found that at Harvard, natural science emphasized lab work rather than field research, and lab work did not appeal to him.[109] He also told a friend that he abandoned science because he became convinced that he could be more useful to the world in public life.[110] He wanted "to try to help the cause of better government in New York."[111] Years later he wrote that, given his financial freedom, he believed he should pursue a course suited to improving the larger world. "I felt that my need for more money was to be treated as a secondary need, and that while it was my business to make more money where I legitimately and properly could, yet it was also my business to treat other kinds of work as more important than money-making."[112]

He began his quest by joining the Twenty-first Assembly District Republican Association, which met at Fifty-ninth Street and Fifth Avenue in Morton Hall—"a dingy, barnlike room situated over a saloon, and furnished severely with wooden benches, many spittoons, and a speaker's table decorated with a large pitcher of ice water."[113] In later years his friend Henry Cabot Lodge observed that the Twenty-first District group "was not an association composed of his normal friends; in fact, the members were not only eminently practical persons but they were inclined to be rough in their methods. They were not dreamers, nor were they laboring under many illusions. Roosevelt went among them a complete stranger."[114]

His political efforts were rejected by his social peers. "The better class of New Yorkers have a holy horror of politics, and all things pertaining thereto. They will not attend the primary meetings or the nominating conventions, and, in too many instances, will not even vote."[115] Wrote one family member, "We felt that his own father would not have liked it, and would have been fearful of the outcome. The Roosevelt circle as a whole had a profound distrust of public life."[116] Politics was considered a low pursuit. Roosevelt: "The men I knew best were the men in the clubs of social pretension and the men of cultivated taste and easy life. When I began to make inquiries as to the whereabouts of the local Republican Association and the means of joining it, these men—and the big business men and lawyers also—laughed at me, and told me that politics were 'low'; that I would find them run by saloon-keepers, horse-car conductors, and the like, and not by men with any of whom I would come in contact outside; and, moreover, they assured me that the men I met would be rough and brutal and unpleasant to deal with. I answered that if this were so it merely meant that the people I knew did not belong to the governing class, and that the other people did—and that I intended to be one of the governing class."[117]

Roosevelt was not, in fact, a lone wolf among his social caste in seeking political office. While he was running for state assembly, William Waldorf Astor was running for Congress, putting out large sums at saloons to buy drinks and get votes—though, admittedly, running for Congress was seen as not quite so unsavory as running for state office.[118] But Roosevelt was not even the first in his family to take an active role in state politics. One of his great-uncles (brother of Cornelius) was a Tammany Democrat who served in the New York State Assembly, in the U.S. House of Representatives, and on the New York State Supreme Court.[119] Another, more distant cousin also served in the State Assembly, in 1835, and published books urging a curb on the powers of the banking industry.[120] Roosevelt's uncle Robert Roosevelt, a Democrat like the others, was the owner and editor of the *Citizen*, a New York literary newspaper that also focused on politics and on exposing civic corruption; in addition, he served in the U.S. House of Representatives and as minister to the Netherlands during the first Cleveland administration.[121]

The negative reaction of at least a portion of Roosevelt's family and peers to his career choice, however, would have been understood by the average New Yorker. "The besetting sin of the people of New York is their lack of public spirit. The race for wealth, the very struggle for existence, is so eager and intense here, that the people think little of public affairs, and leave their city government, and all its vast interests, in the hands of a few professional politicians. They pay dearly for this neglect of such important interests. They are taxed and plundered by rings and tricksters, and are forced to bear burdens and submit to losses which could be avoided by a more patriotic and sensible treatment of their affairs. Business men here regard the time spent in casting their votes at the polls, or in arranging a political canvass so that good men only shall be secured for public officers, as so much time lost. They say they cannot afford to take it from their business. The result is they are put to greater loss by unnecessary and unjust taxes."[122]

In the 1880s, as they had for decades, party bosses maintained political control at all levels by handing out appointive jobs to party faithful. "But now a new generation was springing up, with its leaven of hope and idealism and its intuitive faith in honesty," wrote one observer of the era. "More completely than any one else, Roosevelt embodied to the country the glorious promise of this new generation."[123]

He was nominated to the New York Assembly from the Twenty-first District.[124] On November 5, 1881, he was optimistic enough to write Alice, visiting her parents, that "the canvas is getting on superbly; there seems to be a good chance of my election, but I don't care, anyway."[125] Three days later he was elected by a majority of 1,501 over the Democratic candidate.[126]

When he first joined the other 127 members in the Assembly, the old hands in Albany found him peculiar.[127] After taking note of Roosevelt's upper-crust accent, his glasses, and his first name—at that time, "Theodore" had much the same oddball connotations as "Algernon" or "Percy"—one reporter asked himself, "What on earth will New York send us next?"[128] A fellow legislator recalled a meeting at which, "all of a sudden, the door opened and in rushed Mr. Roosevelt. He made his way up and sat right down at the foot of the chairman of the conference. He had on an enormous overcoat and had a silk hat in his hand. As soon as opportunity was given, he addressed the chairman and he pulled off his overcoat and he was in full dress. He had been to a dinner. He had on his eyeglasses and his gold fob. His hair was parted in the middle and he addressed the chairman in the vernacular of the FFV's of New York. We almost shouted with laughter to think that the most veritable representative of the New York dude had come to the Chamber."[129]

In the legislature, Roosevelt showed political bravery in his commitment to reform. He called for the impeachment of a politically powerful judge. "And for sheer moral courage that act is probably supreme in Roosevelt's life thus far," reported the *Saturday Evening Post*. "He must have expected failure. Even his youth and idealism and ignorance of public affairs could not blind him to the apparently inevitable consequences. Yet he drew his sword and rushed apparently to destruction—alone, and at the very outset of his career, and in disregard of the pleadings of his closest friends and the plain dictates of political wisdom."[130]

His bold stands won widespread support: "I have drawn blood by my speech against the Elevated Railroad Judges, and have come in for any amount both of praise and abuse from the newspapers. It is rather the hit of the season so far, and I think I have made a success of it. Letters and telegrams of congratulations come pouring in on me from all quarters."[131]

By Easter 1882, he had earned the respect of other legislators and of voters across the state. A former classmate at Harvard and Columbia would write of Theodore, "We hailed him as the dawn of a new era, the man of good family once more in the political arena; the college-bred tribune superior to the temptations which beset meaner men. 'Teddy,' as we called him, was our ideal."[132] After seeing him in action on the Assembly floor, his publisher, George Putnam, wrote "Here at last was a man without compromise, of courage and determination, with the extraordinary gift of high ideals and able to put them into being."[133] His legislative career moved at such a rapid pace that in both 1882 and 1883 he was named the Republican nominee for speaker of the Assembly; even though he lost, the nominations placed him among the top party leaders.[134]

His personal life was moving along at a steady pace; in October 1882 he and Alice bought a home of their own, a small brownstone at 55 West Forty-fifth Street. He also was making advances in the literary world. In May 1883 his book *The Naval War of 1812* had just appeared in bookstores.[135] It would sell three editions in two years, become a textbook at several colleges, and by 1886 would be found on every vessel in the U.S. Navy, as required by special regulation. Even in Britain the book would be respected as the definitive text on the 1812 naval war, and it would remain so for nearly a hundred years.[136]

In addition to his political agenda, in spring 1883 Roosevelt was experiencing the fever of another enthusiasm, big-game hunting. His brother, Elliott, helped enflame Theodore's interest in big game. During a bout of bad health in 1876, Elliott had gone to live at Fort McKavett in central Texas, where he hunted bison, the largest North American mammal—bulls weigh up to a ton.[137] The stories Theodore had heard from Elliott, and also from a cousin who had hunted Texas bison, fired his imagination.[138] To top it off, in 1880 Elliott returned from India after a year of hunting tigers and other Asian game. Theodore was left restless with envy, pacing his home like a caged lynx and telling his wife that he was "perfectly happy with her but some time he must go off with his gun instead of pouring over Brown versus Jenkins etc."[139] Three years later, the urge was still unfulfilled.

2

THE LURE OF THE WEST

THEODORE ROOSEVELT ARRIVED AT CLARK'S TAVERN ON WEST Twenty-third Street before sundown on Monday, May 28, 1883, to join a hundred or so other gentlemen for the New-York Free Trade Club's annual dinner, which began at seven-thirty. The setting was convivial and celebratory, with frequent toasts of wine and sparkling amber. Roosevelt was one of several speakers arguing against protective U.S. tariffs.[1]

The members greeted him enthusiastically when he rose to address the club sometime after ten o'clock. He spoke on "The Tariff and Politics," urging club members to be more persistent in fighting for tariff repeal. Exhibiting the independence of mind that had made him a hero among political reformers, he said two or three good friends had told him that public support of free trade would kill him politically. "There is certainly a reaction in public sentiment against our doctrines, but this should not encourage cowardice in the ranks," he said. "It should rather make the advocates of free trade more persistent in their efforts to bring about the desired reform."[2] He also took what might well have been an elitist slap at the average citizen, observing that the benefits of free trade could be explained easily to thinking and educated people, but that the vast majority of Americans, slow to grasp the advantages, would delay progress on tariffs.

During the course of the evening, Roosevelt encountered a former navy officer who had joined the military as a common sailor in 1862 and risen to the rank of lieutenant commander by 1868.[3] About six months before the free-trade dinner, Henry Honeychurch Gorringe had gotten into a dispute with the secretary of the navy that exploded into front-page headlines and led to Gorringe's resignation from the military.[4] Even if the dustup had not occurred, Roosevelt would have known Gorringe by reputation, based in part on the commander's role in bringing to Manhattan a massive, ancient obelisk given to the United States in 1879 by Ismail Pasha, the reigning khedive of Egypt, to celebrate the opening of the Suez Canal. Carved out of a single block of granite from a quarry in Upper Egypt, the obelisk stood sixty-seven feet two inches tall, measured five and a half feet square at the apex, and weighed two hundred tons.[5] William H. Vanderbilt put up the more than one hundred thousand dollars needed to move the obelisk to New York, and Gorringe was dispatched in autumn 1879 to fetch it. The obelisk arrived on July 20, 1880, and Gorringe masterminded its removal to Central Park, rolling it on iron tracks with cannonballs for ball bearings. Erected the following January, the obelisk immediately became one of the park's most popular attractions, dubbed "Cleopatra's Needle" even though it was some fifteen hundred years older than she.

Following that triumph, Gorringe had tried to launch a shipbuilding company but had failed from lack of capital. By the evening of the free-trade dinner, he was working on another investment scheme: He had recently returned from a tour of the West, where he had secured the rights to turn a former military cantonment in the Badlands of Dakota Territory into a private hotel and hunting lodge. He also was preparing to form a cattle syndicate in the same area.[6]

Roosevelt was drawn to Gorringe by their mutual interest in naval power, but it was the commander's western plans that welded a real bond between them.[7] Roosevelt was keen on the West, which was much in the news and much on people's minds. Another of the dinner attendees, Roosevelt's publisher, George Putnam, recently had issued *The Great Northwest*, a book that extolled the virtues of life along the Northern Pacific Railroad line, which cut through the Badlands.[8] In addition, investing in western ranches—in the "beef bonanza"—was something of a fad among easterners; Roosevelt himself had put ten thousand dollars into a Wyoming ranch run by fellow Harvard graduates, and his father-in-law also was investing in cattle.[9] The West and the livestock industry were covered frequently in newspapers, too, where Roosevelt read a letter about the Badlands written by Howard Eaton, a rancher headquartered near Gorringe's Dakota property.[10]

Regional promoters touted the Badlands as a hunter's paradise, the last bastion of the rapidly dwindling buffalo.[11] Dakota newspapers boasted that in 1880, two hunters killed ninety deer and pronghorn and fifteen elk during six weeks of shooting, including eleven elk bagged within about fifteen minutes.[12] When Roosevelt and Gorringe discussed the Badlands at the free-trade dinner, Roosevelt apparently said that he wanted to shoot a buffalo "while there were still buffalo to shoot." Gorringe invited him to the Badlands for a hunt together; Roosevelt readily accepted.[13]

The Badlands bordered the eastern edge of Montana Territory for about 225 miles, starting at the Missouri River in the north and concluding southward toward Wyoming.[14] On average, the Badlands was about fifty miles wide; at its heart lay the snaking bed of the Little Missouri River in a valley generally about three-quarters of a mile wide. The river's course was guesswork on maps; it sometimes flowed ten or fifteen miles from where cartographers showed it.[15] The surrounding area was "a land of magnificent proportions and a weird beauty that gripped one like a spell. From the Missouri to the Rockies was the sweep of a province untamed—as fine a limit of earth as was ever traversed by the shadow of a cloud—clean and primal as if but yesterday it had received the sanction of God at the end of His sixth day's work. You could ride a horse through its expanse for months without striking a furrow or a fence."[16]

Only seven years before Roosevelt met Gorringe, the Badlands had been made dangerous by Indian war parties defending the last of their hunting grounds. In 1883, visitors could still find wheel ruts left by Custer's troops as they moved toward the famous last stand along Montana's Little Bighorn River, perhaps 180 miles to the southwest.[17] The cantonment Gorringe had bought, composed of well-constructed buildings, was an artifact of that hazardous era. The Sixth Infantry had erected it in 1879 on bottomland on the west side of the Little Missouri, midway between the cottonwoods that edged the river and a high range of hills that bordered the river valley. The army stationed some fifty soldiers there to protect railroad construction crews as the Northern Pacific line pushed through on its way to the Pacific Coast.

The cantonment became a gathering place for people coming into the surrounding region. A town grew up nearby, called Little Missouri after the river but known locally as "Little Misery." In spring 1883 it consisted of three or four little houses, the cantonment buildings, a train stop, a hotel, and a collection of saloons that, in addition to alcohol, offered gambling and prostitutes—"the coarse vices that masquerade as pleasures in the various raw frontier towns," as Roosevelt would put it after he became familiar with the place.[18] The nearest sheriff was 150 miles away, the nearest U.S. marshal hundreds of miles to the south.[19] Justice and the law were enforced by the whim or the firepower of local residents. In Little Missouri's early days, for example, a woman "whose character was not above reproach" killed a man; the grand jury "shot craps" to decide whether to hold her or free her, and the dice decreed freedom.[20] In 1882 three men— one of them William Merrifield, who would manage one of Roosevelt's ranches—stopped in at a saloon to chase off would-be desperados who had said they were going to steal horses. "No, there was no court procedure," Merrifield recalled years later, "just a lot of bullets and a notice to get out of town, and you bet they got out of town."[21]

By 1883 the railroad had trains running to Little Missouri. Gorringe that spring was refurbishing the officers' quarters and hospital, opening a store and hotel, and bringing in horses and wagons for his expected clientele, whom he believed would come to hunt deer, pronghorn, elk, bighorn sheep, bears, and other Badlands game.[22] His business had help from the railroads. Hoping to increase passenger traffic, the Northern Pacific publicized the region in travel brochures as "Pyramid Park," a name presumably more appealing than "Badlands."[23]

The animal on which Roosevelt and Gorringe were setting their sights was the bison or American buffalo. Prior to European settlement of the

West, bison streamed in millions across the Great Plains, though their numbers are disputed. Naturalist Ernest Thompson Seton estimated their native population at seventy million.[24] William T. Hornaday, one of the nation's leading wildlife experts at the end of the nineteenth century, put the figure at a low five and a half million.[25] Today, biologists have tended to settle upon an estimate of thirty million plains bison in the mid-1800s.[26] In any event, the grasslands harbored a lot of them. "They were so numerous they frequently stopped boats in the rivers, threatened to overwhelm travelers on the plains, and in later years derailed locomotives and cars, until railway engineers learned by experience the wisdom of stopping their trains whenever there were buffaloes crossing the track."[27]

Bison were slaughtered by commercial, or market, hunters for two products: meat, particularly the tongue, and hides. The market hunters were a special breed. One early Montana cowboy, Teddy Blue Abbott, would recall toward the end of his life that "the buffalo hunters was a rough class— they had to be, to lead the life they led."[28] He added, "The buffalo hunters didn't wash, and looked like animals. They dressed in strong, heavy, warm clothes and never changed them. You would see three or four of them walk up to a bar, reach down inside their clothes to see who could catch the first louse for drinks. They were lousy and proud of it."[29]

In the northern plains, seasoned hunters believed that bison hides were in their best condition from November 15 to December 15, when the thick, cold-season hair was not yet showing wear.[30] These hides were sold hair on as robes; later in the season, the animals were shot for leather. A bison robe was "one of the great comforts of the old trotting horse era," essential for riding in sleighs and for driving public carriages and horse-drawn streetcars.[31] "These robes together with bear skins and kindred domestic hides were found in the equipment of every well appointed stable." Hides sold for sixty-five cents to ten dollars each, but three and a half dollars was the common price.[32] Indians sold bison hides for three or four cups of coffee or sugar.[33] In winter, hunters often killed more bison than their skinners could handle; the carcasses would be left to freeze, which made them impossible to skin. Abbott: "Riding the range, you would find lots of skeletons with pieces of hide still sticking to them. It was all waste."[34]

Bison meat was popular in eastern restaurants that also offered deer, pronghorn, and other game. It sold for only two or three cents a pound when the animals were abundant.[35] Hornaday estimated that a million people could have eaten to satiety on the meat wasted in the buffalo slaughter. "Probably not more than one one-thousandth of the buffalo meat that might have been saved and utilized was saved."[36]

The southern herd, which roamed below the Union Pacific railroad line and which Hornaday estimated at four million animals, was essentially wiped out by 1875, leaving behind perhaps ten thousand stragglers that were mopped up by sport hunters such as Elliott Roosevelt.[37] Market hunters turned next to the northern prairies, including the Badlands. In 1882, an estimated five thousand white hunters and skinners roamed the northern range. In 1883, a herd of perhaps seventy-five thousand bison crossed the Yellowstone River in Montana, pursued by hunters who killed all but five thousand. One famed hunter, Vic Smith, killed 107 buffalo in an hour without changing position.[38]

After the Northern Pacific Railroad came through the Northwest, "buffalo were shot down by the tens of thousands, their hides stripped off, and the meat left to the wolves."[39] From rail stations between Miles City, Montana Territory, and Mandan, Dakota Territory, some fifty thousand robes were shipped on the Northern Pacific in 1881, the first year of major commercial hunting in that region.[40] The following year, about two hundred thousand robes traveled the railway, but the next year only forty thousand, and the year after that only one carload, shipped from Dickinson, Dakota Territory, the last shipment ever made.

Indians, too, played a role in bison destruction. In June 1882, the agent in charge of the Standing Rock (Lakota) Sioux Reservation turned the Indians loose on a herd of perhaps fifty thousand bison that appeared about forty miles east of the Badlands.[41] Six hundred hunters killed about five thousand buffalo in two days. In late summer 1883, a thousand Lakota warriors swept down on America's last large bison herd, some ten thousand animals that had found refuge near the Badlands. The Lakota killed nine thousand. "When we got through the hunt, there was not a hoof left," said Vic Smith, who rode with the Lakota. "That wound up the buffalo in the far west, only a stray bull being seen here and there afterwards."[42]

The buffalo hunters did not realize at first that the last large bison herd was gone, and so in autumn 1883 they outfitted themselves for another winter of shooting, "often at an expense of many hundreds of dollars, and blithely sought 'the range' that had up to that time been so prolific in robes. The end was in nearly every case the same—total failure and bankruptcy."[43] This breakdown was commemorated at least once: Belly-Ups Station, the first stage stop out of Miles City on the route to Deadwood, was named for the buffalo hunters who went belly up in 1883.[44] Market hunters turned to shooting smaller game, selling the meat to hotels and railroad section houses.[45]

In the 1870s, a few western states and territories passed laws to protect bison. One of the first was an 1872 Colorado statute declaring that bison hunters could not leave meat to rot. However, none of these laws was actually enforced. Hornaday: "The western game laws of those days amounted to about as much as they do now [1889]; practically nothing at all."[46]

Some members of the U.S. House and Senate tried to enact federal bison protection laws between 1871 and 1876.[47] One bill made it through Congress, but President Grant let it die in a pocket veto even though proponents pointed out that stopping the bison slaughter made economic sense—the government was paying for beef to feed reservation Indians while market hunters left thousands of tons of buffalo meat to rot each year.[48] Destroying the bison, Hornaday suggested, cost the nation twenty times what conserving it would have cost, "a prodigality and wastefulness which even in the lowest savages would be inexcusable."[49]

By 1876, bison advocates "finally gave up the fight."[50] At the time, the northern herd was still large and might have been saved. Hornaday believed that protecting the animals would have required a "proper code of game laws and a reasonable number of salaried game-wardens, sworn to enforce them and punish all offenses against them."[51] A fifty-cent tax on bison robes would have paid for the game wardens, he contended. The federal government allowed the slaughter to continue in order to destroy the plains Indians by wiping out their source of food and of materials for shelter and tools. Abbott: "And in a way it couldn't be helped. But just the same it was a low-down dirty way of doing the business."[52]

Once the large herds were gone, surviving bison were reduced to a form of ecological poverty. "A few straggling, cruelly harried, terror-stricken bands, mostly hiding away in the more remote and involved fastnesses of the near-by Bad Lands, where they had vainly sought sanctuary from the great Nemesis which had overtaken them, were the last participants in the grim tragedy now being enacted."[53] These were the animals Roosevelt intended to hunt, illustrating Hornaday's contention that "the nearer the species approaches to complete extermination, the more eagerly are the wretched fugitives pursued to the death wherever found."[54]

However eager he was to hunt bison, before Roosevelt could go West he had to deal with his responsibilities for summer 1883, a season that proved difficult for him. He suffered asthma and cholera morbus attacks, the result of the stresses imposed on him in the state assembly and by his efforts to build a massive country house for himself and Alice. Since 1880 he had been buying acres of rolling woodland on Long Island's Cove Neck, flanked on the east by Cold Spring Harbor and on the west by Oyster Bay, which together opened into Long Island Sound.[55] From the site on which he planned to build his house, he could see his family's summer home, Tranquillity. He intended to call his Cove's Neck house Leeholm, after Alice's maiden name. He hired the architectural firm Lamb and Rich of 486 Broadway, known for its country-home designs, and ordered a house with ten bedrooms on the second floor and two on the third, as well as maid's rooms.[56]

Under the pressures of legislation and architecture, by early July 1883 Roosevelt was so sick with stomach pain that his doctor sent him to a Catskill Mountains spa. At Richfield Springs he soaked in hot baths and drank a prescribed concoction that, he claimed, tasted of sulfur matches steeped in tepid water, with a subtle bouquet of kerosene.[57] On July 22 came the kind of news that, throughout much of his life, would bring on digestive and asthmatic attacks: Alice's physician, Dr. Wynkoop, told her that she exhibited "every symptom of having a child" and should plan on hiring a nurse by the fifth of February, as the baby was "very likely to come between that time and the 15th or 20th."[58]

Roosevelt by August was much improved, though still visibly drained, and he went back to buying land and planning a Badlands hunting trip.[59] Toward the end of the month, he left Alice with her family near Boston and readied himself to leave for Dakota Territory on September 3, going alone because Gorringe dropped out. The day before he left, he wrote Alice a letter of mixed emotions: "I have been miserably homesick for you all the last forty-eight hours; so homesick that I think if it were not that I had made all my preparations, I should have given up the journey entirely. I think all the time of my little laughing beauty, and how pretty she is, and how she goes to sleep in my arms, and I love you so. You sweetest of all little wives!"[60] He contended, however, that "the hunting will do me good; and I am very anxious to kill some large game—though I have not much hopes of being able to do so. . . . Goodbye, my own fond darling; a thousand kisses for your sweet lips from Your ever loving husband Thee."

3

THE BISON HUNT

Roosevelt faced a five-day train ride, including a layover in Chicago before boarding another train for a twenty-hour ride to St. Paul, Minnesota, where he would have to contend with a layover as long as twelve hours.[1] But the trains were fairly comfortable, with refreshments served and reading matter for sale as passengers moved along at twenty or thirty miles per hour.[2] Stops on cross-country rides were frequent in the 1880s, however, making progress intermittent—the Chicago–to–San Franciso route, for example, included about 250 stops.

Roosevelt endured the trip well from the very beginning. The day after he left New York he jotted a note on a postcard to his mother: "Slept well last night, ate well today, and am feeling like a fighting cock; the cholera morbus seems like a dream of the past—or, to speak more definitely, a nightmare."[3] Eventually he crossed a bridge over the Red River that took him from Minnesota into Dakota Territory. The flat country beyond the car windows was unbroken hour after hour, a tabletop of grassland and the occasional farm.

On Friday, September 7, Roosevelt boarded the six o'clock train from

Bismarck, in north-central Dakota Territory, and set off across increasingly broken prairie known among locals as Slope Country. "At numerous points were to be seen bluffs and high, serrated ranges of hills, overtopped by an occasional lone butte standing sentinel-like above the surrounding billowy grass country," wrote a traveler who made the trip to Little Missouri in spring 1883.[4] "Railroad stations were few and far between, and these usually consisted of a rough board shed—serving as a telegraph office—an equally rough section house, and a water tank, together with a sparse scattering of shacks in the background." Lakota Indians from nearby Standing Rock Reservation lingered around the train platforms, trying to sell curios to passengers.[5]

The Badlands was still a raw frontier when Theodore Roosevelt journeyed there.[6] Warring Indians had been subdued in the region scarcely six years earlier. The Northern Pacific Railroad had just reached the West Coast, becoming the second transcontinental line. Only hours before Roosevelt crossed Slope Country, a special train decked with flags had passed through, carrying the president of the railroad and former U.S. president Ulysses S. Grant on their way to celebrate the driving of the last stake in the Northern Pacific line.

The coming of the rails was jolting the Badlands out of its wilderness past. As the track had moved westward from Bismarck and facilitated the killing of bison, the grasslands were left open for cattle.[7] Trains also provided a way for Badlands ranchers to ship cattle to Chicago packing houses and to the nation's biggest meat sellers. Partly as a result of that development, 1883 saw the arrival in the Badlands of the first large herds of Texas cattle, triggering the ranching boom that would dominate the region in the 1880s.[8] At the same time, farmers were coming into eastern Dakota. The burgeoning agricultural industry helped boost the territory's population fivefold by 1890.[9] Roosevelt alit just in time to see the close of the last frontier in the states and territories below the Canadian border.

Roosevelt rolled through the region at night, staying up until ten to play whist with "a party of jolly young Englishmen. Then I tumbled into my bunk and at two o'clock tumbled out, at the Little Missouri Station."[10] Had he arrived at midday, he might have found the station a lively place. Lumberjacks in bright red, blue, and striped mackinaws, with hobnailed boots, would gather there to watch trains arrive. They might be joined by coal miners and by long-haired, bearded hunters and trappers in fringed buckskins, by would-be ranchers checking out the region, and even by professional gamblers working the local saloons.[11] But in the predawn hours Roosevelt was greeted only by darkness and bitter cold. The four or five buildings that stood like pale ghosts in the somber night seemed mere shanties.[12] Near the train stop he picked out a small, two-story building with a sign in front that read *Pyramid Park Hotel*. Roosevelt had found Henry Gorringe's haven for hunters.

Lugging his gear, including a .45-caliber Sharps rifle and what was likely a double-barreled British rifle designed for large Asian and African game, he groped his way to the hotel, its every window dark and silent.[13] He began to pound vigorously on the door and soon found himself face-to-face with a short, stocky former riverboat captain with gray whiskers and a bulbous nose red from years of drinking—some locals said he had downed enough booze in his lifetime to float his steamer through a day's run.[14] He was notorious for his swearing and honored Roosevelt with an exhibition of his proficiency. Roosevelt, however, had a letter of introduction from Henry Gorringe, which would have mollified Captain Moore.

Once inside, Roosevelt found that the hotel was crude and unfinished. A corner of the large ground floor served as the manager's office, dominated by a rough desk on which sat a small showcase of brightly labeled cheap cigars. Several rough chairs and benches ranged along walls hung with posters. In another corner stood a makeshift sink with tin basins where guests washed. Towels, shared by all, hung on wall racks.

Captain Moore led Roosevelt up a stairway with no handrails to the second floor, which provided the typical sleeping arrangements of a frontier hotel.[15] About a dozen canvas cots were lined up with heads to the wall in a single large room with no partitions or ceiling, each cot covered with quilts and graced with an uncased feather pillow likely as dirty as if it had been used to shine a stove.[16] Roosevelt wrote Alice that the sleepers who occupied the beds "greeted my advent with any thing but cordiality; but, cold and sleepy, I paid them small heed, turned promptly into a vacant bed and slept soundly till morning."[17] Cost for a night: two bits.[18]

The next day Roosevelt woke up early. After a visit to the shared basin and towels for washing, he joined the general stampede for breakfast. He did not leave behind a description of this gustatory rite of passage, but another guest of the hotel earlier in 1883 did, and his experience would have resembled Roosevelt's: "By the time we got seated, the realization had come to us that eating, here, was purely a matter of business. That it was up to us to get busy or else get left, for the goodly array of edibles on the table was disappearing with amazing rapidity. As usual among a frontier crowd, when eating was in order, talking was not. With the exception of a few of the more recent arrivals from the east, to a man they had their noses down close to their plates and were keeping them right there."[19]

The perfunctory breakfast concluded, Roosevelt went outside for a look around. The town lay in the Little Missouri River valley. Roosevelt: "This, like most other plains rivers, has a broad, shallow bed, through which in times of freshets runs a muddy torrent, that neither man nor beast can pass; at other seasons of the year it is very shallow, spreading out into pools, between which the trickling water may be but a few inches deep. Even then, however, it is not always easy to cross, for the bottom is filled with quicksands and mud-holes. . . . From the edge of the valley the land rises abruptly in steep high buttes whose crests are sharp and jagged. This broken country extends back from the river for many miles, and has been called always . . . the 'Bad Lands.' "[20] The valley flats and the slopes of surrounding hills were grassy, but the domed faces of the bordering buttes were rutted and torn by wind and water, pale in color, bleaching almost to white when the sun stood high, warming almost to gold when the sun lay low, and marked with horizontal bands of black, blue, and red earth.

Across the railroad track the hotel faced three or four rough shacks at the base of Graveyard Butte, named for a cemetery on its slopes. Down the track to the west stood a house and water tank. Nearby hunched a saloon called Big-Mouthed Bob's Bug-Juice Dispensary and the rough-board shanty that served as the train station.[21] Along a flat across the river sprawled a group of white tents and a scattering of buildings under construction. At the north end of this conglomeration lay a complex of interconnected buildings from which rose a tall brick chimney—a slaughterhouse, only two weeks short of completion.

The slaughterhouse and all around it composed the new town of Medora, inaugurated only a few months before by Antoine-Amédée-Marie-Vincent-Amat Manca de Vallombrosa, Marquis de Morès, whom the locals called the "Crazy Frenchman." He was the sort of larger-than-life man that Theodore Roosevelt idolized as a child. Born in Paris on June 14, 1858, the same year as Roosevelt, the dark-eyed, black-haired de Morès was even-featured, wore a rakish moustache with waxed, upturned ends, and stood more than six feet tall.[22] He could shoot prairie chickens on the wing with a Winchester rifle. He was descended from a Spanish family that had held a marquis title since the fourteenth century; his father had married into the French aristocracy. De Morès was raised with nurses and governesses who taught him French, English, Italian, and German by his tenth birthday.[23] He attended St. Cyr, the French equivalent of West Point, from which he was graduated in 1879, whereupon he joined the French cavalry and was sent to Saumur, a distinguished cavalry school where he excelled in both classroom and field studies. He subsequently rode with the Tenth Hussars in putting down an Algerian rebellion; before coming to the United States, he fought two duels, killing his opponents.

He resigned from the military in 1882 and, while frequenting the salons of Paris, met the daughter of a wealthy New York banker, a pale young woman standing only about five feet tall; German by birth, her name was Medora von Hoffman. Like de Morès, she loved adventure. She was skilled with firearms, an excellent horsewoman, spoke seven languages, painted pictures, and played piano.[24] They married on February 15, 1882, and spent the summer in Europe before sailing in August for New York City, where de Morès intended to work in his father-in-law's bank at 50 Wall Street, a leading investment firm.[25] But the Marquis soon was bored with banking and intrigued with stories he had heard from a cousin, Count Fitz-James, about the Dakota Badlands.[26] This interest was stoked when the Marquis met the apparently ubiquitous Commander Gorringe, who trumpeted the profits a man could rake in from Badlands ranching.[27] Having a million dollars of his own, as well as the backing of a wealthy father, a rich father-in-law, and a wife with an income of ninety thousand dollars yearly from securities, the Marquis in early March 1883 set out with his assistant, William van Driesche, for the Badlands.[28]

Initially the Marquis planned to make the town of Little Missouri his headquarters, but conditions there did not please him. After riding around the region with van Driesche, stopping for al fresco lunches of tinned sardines, meat, cheese, bread, and pâté de foie gras with white wine, the Marquis started to scoop up land.[29] He bought four thousand acres across the river from the town of Little Missouri; there he set up a large white tent and started building a town of his own, named Medora after his wife. He also bought a stretch of land on both sides of the river, about five miles wide and twenty to twenty-five miles long, as well as twelve thousand acres of wheat land near Bismarck.[30]

Once he had land, de Morès began buying cattle, some sixteen thousand head from as far off as the Powder River in Montana.[31] He intended to create not only a ranch but also a new way to market meat. In Medora, he started building a massive slaughterhouse and packing plant in which he would process his own livestock, as well as all that he could buy from local ranchers. He would then load the meat onto his own refrigerator cars, cooled with ice cut in winter from rivers and lakes and stored in his chain of warehouses, and sell the meat directly to customers at his own stores in New York. By shipping meat rather than cattle and by cutting out the Chicago packers as middlemen, he could sell beef for three cents a pound less than any conventional competitor. In conjunction with this plan, he opened three stores in Manhattan, painted bright red, where his slogan, "From Ranch to Table," advertised his discounted meat.[32] He also boasted of a plan to plant fifty thousand cabbages that would grow "under glass in some peculiar French manner, and when they have attained a certain size, will be transplanted into individual pots and forced by rich fertilizers, made from the offal of the slaughter-houses and for which preparation he owns the patent."[33]

Despite his ambitions and his free spending on goods and labor, the Marquis was not destined to cut a popular figure in the Badlands. He was standoffish and thought himself better than others, a fatal social mistake in the West.[34] He alienated the cattlemen by bringing in sheep, which he planned to fatten for his packing plant. Roosevelt would later capture on paper the prevailing attitude about sheep in the Medora region: "Cattlemen hate sheep, because they eat the grass so close that cattle cannot live on the same ground. . . . No man can associate with sheep and retain his self-respect."[35]

De Morès also violated the tacit agreement among the ranchers that, except in the immediate vicinity of a ranch house or around some water sources, the land would not be fenced or even legally owned.[36] Virtually all Badlands ranchers were squatters on federal or railroad land to which they held no title. The Marquis compounded the insult of buying thousands of acres by starting to fence it. "Then hell broke loose," especially when he fenced off the only practicable route downriver, long used by hunters with their pack trains.[37] Travelers would cut the fence, and de Morès' men would repair it.

Land disputes, and perhaps some frontier finagling, led to a shootout between the Marquis and three hunters, a confrontation that was the talk of the Medora area for months and that shows how life in the lawless West could be driven by petty politics, greed, and personal animosity.[38] The story of the shootout also would have given Roosevelt some useful instruction about the Marquis' determination and his affinity for gunplay.

The dispute may have started in a rivalry between a market hunter named Frank O'Donald and a local badman named Eldridge G. "Jerry" Paddock. A quarter Cherokee, O'Donald had arrived in the Badlands early enough to name some of the local buttes, including Bullion, Square, and Sentinel.[39] He partnered with two other men. One was Jack or John Reuter, born in Illinois in 1848 and called "Dutch Wannegan" because his parents had come from Germany and because he had come to Dakota Territory on a boat named *Wannegan*.[40] The other partner was Riley Luffsey, with whom Paddock had once guided sport hunters through the Badlands. Luffsey was a tall, lean, good-natured Missourian whose friends thought him "square as a die and dependable in a pinch."[41]

Paddock had lived in the Badlands since the 1860s and resided in a shack or dugout on the edge of town.[42] About five feet eleven inches tall, with broad shoulders and a narrow waist, he sported a black goatee and drooping moustache so long it could be tied under his chin.[43] Although enemies said he was "the damnest thief ever lived" and "the sneakiest man in town, always figuring on somebody else doing the dirty work, and him reap the benefits," those who liked him said that "once [he] was your friend, he was your friend, and that was all there was to it."[44] Inclined to settle arguments with a gun rather than his fists, he was a very good shot, capable of killing a running deer "as a man shoots a bird on the wing."[45] He reputedly killed at least three men. It also was rumored that men to whom he owed money were "opportunely" kicked into oblivion by horses "in a manner that was mysterious to men who knew the ways of horses."[46]

Nevertheless, even honest citizens sometimes partnered with him, and he would eventually hold a position in town government. "We were such a small group of people in a big country that we were compelled to associate with each other right along, regardless of who, what or how."[47]

Though the details are sketchy, the dispute between Paddock and O'Donald apparently began with a marksmanship contest in which Paddock forfeited the bet, a development that somehow started bad blood between them.[48] Later, the three hunters discovered that someone had ripped open their tent; they pegged Paddock the guilty party.[49] By then, Paddock was working for the Marquis, which some residents believed showed a lack of judgment on the Frenchman's part.[50] According to some locals, Paddock, driven by his grudge against O'Donald, persuaded de Morès to lay claim to land that O'Donald and his partners already had picked for themselves, "whereupon the boys were duly notified to evacuate, which of course they naturally refused to do."[51] Faced with de Morès' threat, O'Donald told one rancher friendly to him, "Ever jumps us, jumps from there right into his grave."[52] At least one resident thought this response was not so much brave as stupid. Mrs. Elizabeth Roberts, who came to the Medora area in 1882 when she was ten years old, said the hunters "were considered rather, not very brainy, and kinda dumbbells—that's what we call them now."[53] They stayed on their land despite de Morès and his threats because "they didn't have sense enough to get scared."[54]

Meanwhile, Paddock, goading the situation, was telling de Morès that the hunters were planning to kill him.[55] The trio came into Medora on June 21, drank heavily, and went on a shooting spree. Because Billings County, in which Medora lay, had no court system or law enforcement officers, de Morès at this point traveled to Mandan to ask the judge there what he should do if the hunters came after him; the judge replied that he should shoot back.[56] Back in Medora on the twenty-fifth, de Morès found that the hunters were still shooting and threatening. He wired the sheriff in Mandan to come settle the matter. The sheriff showed up the next day with a posse that had signed up mainly for the train trip to Medora, because "none of them had been up there before."[57] Local opinion of the posse was low: "Didn't know any more than a woman who had never seen any trouble . . . a regular bunch of mosquitoes."[58]

When the posse met the hunters, the trio bluntly refused to be arrested and rode out of town. Anticipating such an escape, de Morès, along with Paddock and other hired men, lay in ambush on the edge of town where the trail narrowed between a bluff and the railway track. As the trio approached, de Morès and his men opened fire, wounding O'Donald and killing Luffsey.[59] The sheriff arrested de Morès and his men, Paddock excepted because he had avoided being seen at the ambush. The judge in Mandan promptly dropped all charges.

Luffsey was buried on Graveyard Butte, and his friends contemplated lynching the Marquis but did not molest him when he returned home. Some residents were inclined to be forgiving. "He was a pretty good sort of a man," said one ranch hand who was with the Marquis for five years. "Of course, he'd get a little blood-thirsty sometimes."[60]

Theodore Roosevelt probably knew little or nothing about the Marquis and his exploits during his first visit to the Badlands, though clearly men of the Marquis' stature and Roosevelt's standing could hardly avoid one another for long in towns as small as Medora and Little Missouri. That morning, however, Roosevelt was still finding his way around. Before he could ride out on the hunting trail he had to hire a guide and wagon and buy supplies; the people on whom he would depend were characteristic of the frontier towns of the American West.

First he met Gorringe's secretary, W. R. Wright, "a wide awake yankee, who received me with the greatest cordiality and got me to at once shift my things over to the company's ranche building, where I have a room to myself and am very comfortable."[61] Wright took him for a ride around the countryside—"a very desolate place, high, barren hills, scantily clad with coarse grass, and here and there in sheltered places a few stunted cottonwood trees." As soon as they returned from the ride, Roosevelt talked with a dark-complexioned man with round, twinkling eyes. Frank Moore was Captain Moore's son and Gorringe's manager. He was in his late thirties and of medium height but so fat that he looked short.[62] As a young man he had worked on his father's steamer on the Upper Missouri River, ingratiating himself with soldiers he met on board and lining up the position of post trader, or sutler, at a fort on the Missouri. Such an appointment offered good business opportunities, because each fort had only one sutler, making the position a monopoly.[63] Eventually he ended up the post trader at the Little Missouri cantonment and, when it closed, partnered with Gorringe in turning the place into a hunters' resort.[64] He installed his father and mother to run the hotel.

Frank Moore was generally well liked in Medora.[65] He could usually be spotted in a bright red mackinaw shirt, fringed buckskin pants, and high-topped boots with a gaudy design on front. He wore the typical wide-brimmed hat of the West and the usual flashy silk kerchief tied round his neck, but he was about the only man in Little Missouri who did not carry a gun.[66] He was famously lax with money. "His cash register was his pocket, and, as long as there was anything in it, why should he worry?"[67] He kept his accounts mostly in his head, which generally was clouded with alcohol.[68] Whatever his shortcomings, he was widely regarded as a "big-hearted" man willing to help people out of difficulties.[69]

In keeping with this reputation, he was happy to offer advice when Roosevelt asked about a hunting guide. He steered Roosevelt toward Joe Ferris, a jack-of-all-trades in his mid-twenties who superintended the cantonment stable.[70]

Husky and square, with a drooping moustache, Ferris had come to the Badlands from New Brunswick, Canada, in 1881 with his brother Sylvane and their friend William Merrifield, taking advantage of the Northern Pacific's largesse in giving potential settlers free rides.[71] Merrifield initially had worked as a professional hunter, collecting meat for railroad construction crews. The Ferrises had made ends meet doing odd jobs, such as cutting wood for the military cantonment. Using the money they earned, Sylvane and Merrifield bought a few head of horses and cattle. They also signed a contract in 1882 with two Minnesota cattlemen, H. B. Wadsworth and W. L. Halley (also spelled Holley and Hawley), to share profits on some 150 head of cattle shipped to Little Missouri, creating one of the first significant ranches in northwestern Dakota Territory.[72]

Joe Ferris, who disdained physical labor such as hunting and ranching, was reluctant to guide Roosevelt.[73] Ferris: "He was a slender young fellow, and I had my doubts whether he could stand the long trip. To be honest about it, I expected to have to take care of him on the trip—saddle his horse, show him the customs of the plains, see that he got his grub regularly and the other little things that come up on a hunting trip of the kind."[74] One Roosevelt characteristic, in particular, put off Ferris, as it initially would almost everyone Roosevelt met in the Badlands: He "had those big glasses on and [they] made him look kinda odd to us fellows out there who wasn't used to those things."[75] However, Roosevelt apparently was persuasive, or perhaps a good fee made the case for him; in any event, Ferris agreed to a buffalo hunt. Roosevelt also wanted to hunt elk, but Ferris said elk were "too uncertain to go after."[76]

Ferris and Moore talked over the best places for finding bison and concluded that the base of operations should be the Gregor Lang ranch, fifty miles upstream.[77] The Ferrises and Bill Merrifield in previous years had shot bison in the area, so it seemed promising.[78] At midday Ferris began to put together a team of horses and a wagon, with blankets and provisions that filled the wagon bed almost to overflowing by the time he picked up Roosevelt at his room.[79]

Roosevelt found time that sunny Saturday to let Alice know that "this afternoon we start for the buffalo range. . . . I will now be away for two or three weeks, and when I come out will at once take the train for the East, so this is the last letter my darling will receive from me till the hunt is over. . . . Good bye my own sweetest love, I shall pray for you every night; good bye my *doubly* dear wife."[80]

As they headed out into the Badlands, Ferris thought they would find a buffalo quickly; then he could hie back to the cantonment.[81] Bison had been plentiful the year before. In the recent past his brother and Merrifield had even spotted six bison along the river near their ranch house; they shot the animals and sold the meat to a hotel keeper.[82]

In the creaking wagon, the hunters headed for a ford across the river but stopped almost immediately when they discovered that Roosevelt's rifle had a defective part.[83] Ferris suggested they borrow a replacement from Jerry Paddock. They found him at home, and he said he was glad to loan a spare part as well as a better buffalo rifle.[84]

That afternoon, swinging southward along the twisting course of the river, Roosevelt and Ferris planned to drive about seven miles to the ranch operated by Sylvane Ferris and Bill Merrifield. Sometimes they rattled along a valley a mile or more wide, and other times buttes rose abruptly from the riverbanks; surrounding hills were capped with tawny grass, ravines were dark with cedars, and the river bottoms were shadowed by cottonwoods. When the trail snaked over the buttes, they could see the Badlands spreading out in a maze of hills and ravines where seams of coal burned for years when struck by lightning, sending up clouds of smoke by day and glowing red in the night, overhung with the smell of sulfur.[85] Left in the ground, the burning coal heated stretches of earth into a red, brick-like substance called scoria. Roosevelt concluded that "when one is in the Bad Lands he feels as if they somehow *look* just exactly as Poe's tales and poems *sound*."[86] In one of his books he would call the Badlands the "devil's wilderness."[87]

They drove past the log house that served as headquarters for the Custer Trail Ranch, founded by investors from Pennsylvania and run partly as a hunting lodge.[88] It was named for Custer because he and his men had camped at that site on the way to the Little Bighorn. Roosevelt and Ferris forded the river a mile upstream and again a quarter mile later. After wending a path through a stand of cottonwoods they entered a wide valley, the buttes retreating on either side, and they spotted a lone peak called Chimney Butte. Below it was the log cabin in which Sylvane Ferris and Bill Merrifield lived and which served as headquarters of their Chimney Butte Ranch, also known as the Maltese Cross after its cattle brand.

Located just off a main wagon road, the ranch compound included a horse corral and a chicken coop behind the cabin.[89] The Canadians, with typical frontier pragmatism, had built the house from lumber they had scavenged from the river—railroad ties that had been cut about twenty-five miles upstream at a place called Short Pine Hills and that had jammed up during low water while floating toward the rail line.[90] The men set the ties into the ground vertically, put on a dirt roof, and chinked the walls.[91] Inside was one room with a table, three or four chairs, a stove, and three bunks. They did not bother to put in a floor.

Sylvane, about twenty-four years old, and Merrifield, four years older, were thrifty, honest, and independent but a bit stolid, imbued with "the circumscribed puritanical atmosphere of their upbringing."[92] Sylvane was shy but frequently exhibited an affable grin, while Merrifield was more reserved, though he had a reputation for grating on people, primarily because of his ego. "Bill . . . had a reputation among the boys of liking the looks of Bill. Furthermore, he liked the ladies and believed himself to have an irresistible way with them."[93] Neither had much to say to the smallish dude from New York until after dinner, when they sat at the lone table and dealt cards for a game of old sledge; then the ice began to melt.[94] They were still playing when frantic squawks from the chickens sent the four men rushing outside to fend off a bobcat raiding the adjoining coop. The cat escaped, but when the men returned to the cabin they were in a more amiable mood and started swapping life stories.

Later in the evening Roosevelt and Joe Ferris made plans for the next day. They faced a forty-five-mile journey to the next stop, and Ferris wanted to make it in the buckboard.[95] Roosevelt had other ideas—he wanted a saddle horse. Merrifield and the Ferrises protested that they had no saddle horse to spare. Roosevelt's persistent plea for a horse, and his declaration that he could not possibly sit still for a forty-five-mile wagon ride, aroused their suspicions. "By gosh, he wanted that saddle horse so bad that we were afraid to let him have it," Joe Ferris recalled years later. "Why, we didn't know him from Job's off ox. We didn't know but he'd ride away with it. But, say, he wanted that horse so blamed bad, that when he see we weren't going to let him have it, he offered to buy it for cash."[96] Money was a form of trust the Canadians understood, and so before Roosevelt curled up to sleep in his blanket on the cabin's dirt floor he was the owner of a buckskin mare named Nell.

Roosevelt mounted Nell at dawn and headed south along the river, with Ferris driving the loaded wagon. They continued across buttes and flats and past the ruins of an abandoned stage stop; they followed the Fort Keogh Trail for a few miles, marked by the deep wheel ruts of army wagons traveling in an earlier era to the fort in southeastern Montana; and they forded the river at least twenty-three times before coming that evening to Little Cannonball Creek. About fifty yards from the mouth of the creek they saw a cabin in a stand of cottonwoods.

Inside the cabin, sixteen-year-old Lincoln Lang and his father, Gregor, were just about to sit down to dinner.[97] New to the Badlands, they had arrived the previous spring because of an oblique connection with Henry Gorringe. Among the investors contemplating a partnership with Gorringe was Sir John Pender, a wealthy London capitalist who had built his reputation in part by funding and laying one of the earlier Atlantic cables.[98] Pender hired Gregor Lang—a Scotsman living in Ireland who had farmed and worked with cattle and had spent a year or more traveling in the United States—to go to Dakota Territory and report on the ranching opportunity. Lang brought with him his teenage son, named after the U.S. president Gregor idolized.

When the Langs stopped in New York City in spring 1883 to visit Gorringe, they sensed that he was not happy to see them—he had wanted Pender to invest in the project without further inquiry. He refused to give them an introduction to his staff at Little Missouri. After two weeks of wrangling, however, he capitulated. In April the Langs boarded a train for the five-day ride to the Badlands.[99] After meeting the friendly but boozy Frank Moore and assessing his shoddy accounting procedures, Lang felt obliged to report these negatives to Pender, who cabled that Gregor Lang should drop out of the Gorringe partnership and set up a ranch on his own.[100] Lang bought the cabin at the mouth of Cannon Ball Creek from O'Donald and Luffsey a short time before their shootout with de Morès.[101]

Now, as the day chilled into night on Sunday, September 9, 1883, the Langs heard a wagon rattling up to their house. Stepping to the door, Lincoln, in the dimming light, was able "to distinguish the outline of a light wagon and team, together with a driver of bulky build sitting in the seat. To the rear, sitting on a pony, with a rifle lying across the saddle in front of him, was a second individual of lighter build."[102] The wagon driver bellowed out, "Hello Link," and the boy recognized the voice of Joe Ferris, for whom he had worked as a stable hand during the period when Gregor was first setting up in the Badlands. The other man he did not recognize, but he could see "that he was a young man, who wore large conspicuous-looking glasses, through which I was being regarded with interest by a pair of bright twinkling eyes. Amply supporting them was the expansive grin overspreading his prominent, forceful looking lower face, plainly revealing a set of large white teeth."[103]

In cow country, unspoken rules insisted that visitors who rode up to an occupied ranch house stay mounted until invited to step down.[104] "Violators of customs like these were rarely shot, but they did create distrust, and distrust was always more or less dangerous in a country where each person was largely dependent upon himself for defense against criminals."[105] The invitation might be "Climb down and eat a bean with us" or "Fall off and stay awhile." Ranchers were expected to feed all visitors. "The law of hospitality on the range was very strict. You had to feed and shelter your worst enemy if he came to your house in a storm, and if you refused him shelter, you had better leave that country."[106] A cowboy could live through the winter by riding from one outfit to another and taking advantage of the "law of hospitality," a process called riding the grub line. "Grub line riders were welcome wherever they stopped, because people who had been shut up all winter were glad to see new faces. They brought the news of the range."[107] A traveler could take food and shelter as needed even if the owner was not home. Etiquette required that the borrower take no more than was necessary and leave a note inventorying what was used, not with any intention of paying it back but to keep all borrowing aboveboard and to show that he had not wantonly robbed the larder.[108]

Accordingly, Lincoln welcomed Ferris with "Glad to see you" and "Light and unhitch. Just in time for supper." Meanwhile, his father—stocky, blue-eyed, wearing glasses and muttonchops—slipped past his son, and Ferris introduced the Langs to Theodore Roosevelt.[109] When they were inside the cabin, Roosevelt presented the elder Lang with a letter of introduction from Gorringe, who harbored no animosity over the broken deal with Pender and was, in fact, taking Lang's advice at that very time, seeking to replace Frank Moore as his manager.[110]

Despite having arrived in the Badlands only two days earlier after days on a train and having traveled nearly fifty miles by horse and by wagon over the past thirty hours or so, Roosevelt talked with Lang into the late hours, while Ferris slept and Lincoln tried to stay awake listening. The New Yorker and the Scot hit it off, as both were men of intellectual acuity with a yen for talk and a shared admiration for Abraham Lincoln.[111] Moreover, Lang had thoroughly researched the local cattle industry and could serve as a fount of knowledge. The bison hunt now offered an unexpected bonus: evenings of discussion about ranching.

As luck would have it, Roosevelt woke the next morning to pouring rain, rare at that time of year. Rain was more than an inconvenience; it could prove dangerous, making the Badlands gumbo clay as slippery as grease. Ferris suggested they put off the hunt until the weather cleared, and the Langs backed him up, pointing out the risks, but Roosevelt would not give up. "He had come after buffalo and buffalo he was going to get in spite of hell and high water."[112]

The hunters rode out at six in the morning, eastward across the Little Missouri and over miles of defiles and divides and precarious ground.[113] Rain fell all day. The only game they saw: two or three mule deer at a distance, and later a lone buck that they stalked to within two hundred yards. Roosevelt took a shot and missed. Ferris put a bead on the fleeing deer, impossible though the shot seemed, and fired once; down went the buck. Roosevelt slammed his rifle to the ground and shouted: "Godfrey! I'd give anything in the world if I could shoot like that!" Witnessing the Roosevelt rage (Roosevelt rarely swore; the strongest oath Joe Ferris heard from him was "By Godfrey"), Ferris almost regretted that he had pulled off the difficult shot.[114]

They saw no buffalo, though, and returned to the Langs' plastered from head to horse with mud. That night Ferris went early to bed, but Roosevelt stayed up for more talk with Gregor Lang. And so it went for several days: the hunt in unrelenting rain, the evenings when Joe Ferris collapsed into bed and Roosevelt talked with Lang, staying up at least one night until two in the morning. Still, Roosevelt rose at dawn, and the hunters pressed on. Lincoln Lang: "He nearly killed poor Joe. He would not stop for anything."[115] More than once Ferris was on the point of caving. "But could he lie down to a tenderfoot? Hardly. So he was obliged to keep going while trying to look as if he enjoyed it."[116]

By then Ferris realized that he had misjudged Roosevelt: "He was able to do for himself at every turn. Where he learned to ride horseback I don't know, but I do know that he rode as well or better than I did and could stand more knocking about than I could. Where he didn't know of the ways of the West he learned by observation—and he paddled his own canoe from the start."[117]

Nevertheless, Roosevelt's confidence in the hunt was beginning to flag. In a letter to Alice he sounded as if he were on the verge of giving up: "I have been out a week now, nearly, and though it is good game country, yet, by Jove, my usual bad luck in hunting has followed; I haven't killed anything, and am afraid the hall will have to go without horns, for this trip at least."[118] On the seventeenth, via a hunter returning to Little Missouri, Roosevelt sent Alice another letter lamenting his lack of success: "My ill luck in hunting has followed me steadily. For the first five days I shot very badly, missing everything; for the last three days, I have hit almost everything I fired at, but have somehow managed to lose it."[119] He had wounded a deer but lost it in a thicket. "Still, though buffalo are too scarce for me to hope to get one, yet I still think I will bring you home one or two pair of deer antlers." He added, "I am now feeling very well, and am enjoying the life very much. I am every day and all day long on horseback, scrambling over the almost inconceivably rocky and difficult hills of the 'bad lands,' or galloping at full speed over the rolling prairie or level bottom." He signed off, "Good bye, my blessed little love, you are never out of my thoughts, and I love you more and more all the time."

The talks with Lang turned increasingly to the cattle business, until one night, several days into his stay, Roosevelt said that he felt the outdoor life was the only one for him, that he loved the Badlands and wanted to be in and of it, and that he believed ranching was a good business in which to invest.[120] What, he asked, would Lang advise?

Lang said he had every confidence in the future of the cattle industry but did not want to assume the responsibility of counseling the young New Yorker.

Meanwhile, the sun finally appeared, much, it seems, to the relief of Joe Ferris, who later declared, "I'm telling you, after a week he was fresh as a daisy, and I was dead beat."[121] Ferris was even more shocked when Roosevelt said that in 1880 his doctor had warned him that he had a weak heart and should avoid even such mild exertion as running up stairs.[122] Roosevelt had responded that he was not only going to ignore this advice but do the exact opposite. Roosevelt: "When I was twenty-one, I promised myself that I would live my life up to the hilt until I was sixty, and to be prepared for anything that happened after that."[123]

The day grew warm as the hunters rode eastward for about ten miles across the broken country, spotting two or three deer before they came across a fresh bull bison track.[124] On wet ground the track was easy to follow, but on earth already drying the hooves left barely a mark. For half an hour they rode up a ravine, following the buffalo. When they passed the mouth of a side branch, or coulee, they heard an animal plunging through brush and saw the bull galloping along the base of a butte and out of sight so quickly that they did not have time to shoot. They spurred their horses into a gallop.

The bull reappeared speeding agilely up the slope of another butte about a quarter of a mile away. Reaching the top, the animal stopped and looked back at them; "while so doing he held his head high up, and at that distance his great shaggy mane and huge fore-quarter made him look like a lion. In another second he again turned away and made off." They followed his track for miles but lost him on hard ground and never saw him again.

Giving up, they rode over the flat prairies that began far from the river. Such flats were broken by ravines up to thirty feet deep and a dozen wide or were edged with cliffs or rounded buttes. Some ravines held pools of water, and at ten that morning they stopped to water their horses. The banks of the pool were so steep that one of the clumsier horses could not get down, and the men had to bring water to the horse in a hat. Most of the pools they found were scarcely fit for human consumption. Roosevelt: "There is very little water, and what there is, is so bitter as to be almost a poison, and nearly undrinkable; it is so alkaline that the very cow's milk tastes of it."[125]

Remounting, they rode on, scanning the tawny country from one divide to the next but finding no game. The sun beat down, the air hung hot and still. Once they encountered a canyon so steep that they had to ride along it for a mile before they found a spot where they could get the horses down, and even then they had to back in the animals. They followed the canyon floor for a hundred yards before finding a place on the other side where they could get the horses out. But the effort led them, in late afternoon, to a large plain in the middle of which grazed three bull bison.

The horses, though, were too worn by riding, heat, and lack of water to run, so the hunters dismounted, left the horses in a hollow half a mile from the buffalo, and stalked on hands and knees, crawling from one sage bush to another. Eventually they had to lie flat and wiggle along like snakes to get within shooting range. Only a few years earlier bison had been easy to approach and shoot and often did not flee at the sound of a rifle even as their cohorts were falling around them. But heavy hunting had taken its toll. "A time did come when they were alarmed readily enough, but this was not until all the large herds had been broken up and scattered, and the miserable survivors had been so chased and harried that at last they learned to start and run even at their own shadows."[126]

While crawling toward the animals, Roosevelt blundered into a patch of cactus, filling his hands with spines painful and difficult to remove. Finally they crawled within 125 yards of the unsuspecting grazers. One stood broadside to Roosevelt, who took aim and fired. "The bullet told on his body with a loud crack, the dust flying up from his hide; but it did not work him any immediate harm, or in the least hinder him from making off; and away went all three, with their tails up, disappearing over a slight rise in the ground."[127]

Roosevelt, if not Ferris, was disgusted with the shooting. The two men dashed back to the horses and rode after the buffalo as the sun set, following them for eight miles before the animals stopped in a hollow that offered no cover for stalking. And so with quirts and spurs the hunters tortured their exhausted horses into a burst of speed and gained on the wounded bison just as darkness fell and a full moon rose. They came to within seventy yards of the bull, but Roosevelt's horse, Nell, was wearing out. Ferris spurred on, closing in on the buffalo, which then swerved, losing ground and allowing Roosevelt to come up within twenty feet of it. He fired and missed, the bull wheeled and charged, and Nell spun around and tossed her head, striking the rifle barrel with such force that it slammed into Roosevelt's forehead, opening a gash that sent blood pouring into his eyes.

The buffalo, meanwhile, turned to Ferris, who retreated with the bull close behind. Roosevelt, ignoring his wound, tried to move in, but Nell had had enough; she stopped dead, and all of Roosevelt's prompting with spur and quirt could not move her. Ferris jumped off his horse and fired two shots at the bull, but neither struck. The buffalo ran off, and Roosevelt, driven by ineffective anger, tried to follow on foot, giving up only when the animal vanished from sight.

That night they slept out on the prairie beside a pool of water gelatinous with slime. The men had had nothing to drink for twelve hours but could not stomach the water. They ate biscuits and bedded down in a hollow with neither fuel for a fire nor anything to which they could tie the horses. They spread their saddle blankets on the ground for beds and tied the horses to the saddles, which they used for pillows, and went to sleep under the blankets they had carried tied behind them all day.

At around midnight, Roosevelt and Ferris were sound asleep when their pillows were whipped out from beneath their heads. They sat up to see the horses galloping off into the night, saddles dragging behind them. Apparently the mounts had been frightened by a passing wolf or wolves. Certain they would not find the horses that night, the men went in search of them anyway. Luck favored them: They found the horses about a half mile away, standing close together and nervously alert. The men led the ponies to camp and went back to sleep, but at three in the morning came a fine, steady rain. They woke to find themselves lying in four inches of water. Yet Ferris heard Roosevelt muttering to himself, "By Godfrey, but this is fun!"[128] They shivered the night away in their wet blankets and rose at dawn to a breakfast of biscuits.

After hours of riding in pouring rain they found a herd of several buffalo and—thoroughly chilled, teeth chattering—were able to stalk on foot to within a hundred yards of a cow. Roosevelt: "To crown my misfortunes, I now made one of those misses which a man to his dying day always looks back upon with wonder and regret."[129] Rain had beaded on his glasses and on the sights of the rifle, so he drew blurry aim on the cow and, shooting high or jerking the trigger in his excitement, missed completely. The whole herd dashed off before Roosevelt, his fingers cold and stiff, could fire again. In "wet, sullen misery we plodded back to the ponies."[130]

The rain continued all day, and the men spent another miserable night out. "Bad luck followed us like a yellow dog follows a drunkard," Ferris would recall. But the next day was bright and sunny. Not that it helped: A rattlesnake nearly bit Ferris' horse; a bluff along which they were riding crumbled under them and sent men and horses falling in a tangled mass; Nell somersaulted after plunging her front hooves into a hole, and Roosevelt catapulted a good ten feet beyond her; and then, when crossing an apparently dry creek, the ground gave way, and Nell was up to her withers in sticky mud, though Roosevelt was able to scramble free to the bank; with a lariat they dragged the mired horse to solid ground, nearly strangling her in the process. With a gift for understatement, Roosevelt would remark, "So far the trip had certainly not been a success, although sufficiently varied as regards its incidents."[131]

That night they returned to the Langs' and to more late-night talk of ranching. "I have definitely decided to invest, Mr. Lang," Roosevelt announced.[132] He asked Lang to take charge of a herd of cattle for him and share profits, but Lang said he could not do so because of his obligations to Pender. He recommended instead that Roosevelt partner with Sylvane Ferris and Bill Merrifield. Roosevelt made his decision with characteristic speed and approved the idea. The next day Gregor sent Lincoln on horseback to bring the two Canadians upriver for a discussion of the business proposition, a trip that took two days because of gumbo mud and high water. Meanwhile, Roosevelt and Ferris continued to hunt. On the evening of the second day they returned to the Langs' to find Sylvane and Merrifield waiting.

After dinner, Roosevelt and the two Canadians took seats on a log outside the Lang cabin and talked over Roosevelt's proposition.[133] Sylvane told Roosevelt that the capital needed for stocking a cattle ranch would "spoil the looks of forty thousand dollars" and that he would need about a third of that amount to get started. The two men agreed to manage Roosevelt's herd if they could get out of their contract with Wadsworth and Halley. Roosevelt said he would buy the Wadsworth and Halley cattle, and the men said they would need to go to Minnesota to make arrangements. "That will suit me," Roosevelt declared. He hauled out his checkbook, wrote a draft for fourteen thousand dollars, handed it to Sylvane, and told the men to buy a few hundred head of cattle in addition to the 150 from Wadsworth and Halley. Asked if he wanted a receipt, he said no. Sylvane: "He turned a check over to us then. All the security he had for his money was our honesty."[134] Roosevelt explained, "If I didn't trust you men, I wouldn't go into business with you."[135]

Fourteen thousand dollars was a significant chunk of Roosevelt's annual income. He was earning only twelve hundred dollars a year as a member of the New York State Assembly, but earnings from investments in railroads and the Wyoming cattle ranch, as well as the family firm and other businesses, added another fourteen thousand dollars to his annual income.[136] Nevertheless, compared to other expenses, his investment in ranching was gargantuan. His diary for 1880 indicates that his expenses for that year were $7,992.50, including $544.03 for housing expenses; his two largest expenses were for gifts, $3,889.80 (1880 was the year he married Alice Lee), and for "amusement," $1,070.12. Alice's "sundries" came to only $133.18.[137]

Roosevelt's investments and expenditures were overseen by his father's elder brother, James, who was head of the Roosevelt and Son banking firm.[138] After talking earlier in the year with Gorringe about the profits to be made in western cattle, Theodore apparently had asked James whether he should put five thousand dollars into Dakota cattle, and James had answered an unequivocal no. James believed that investing in a ranch was as risky as putting money into gold mines. But Theodore had reason to feel comfortable with the livestock business. The winter of 1882–83 had been mild, followed by an early, moist spring, so cattle had plenty of grass and had done well.[139] Under those conditions, Dakota ranching looked like a sound investment.

On the twentieth the Canadians departed for home and then on to Minnesota, while Roosevelt and Joe Ferris headed into the upper reaches of Little Cannonball Creek, west of the Lang spread, and crossed into Montana.[140] Leaving the creek bottom, they skirted a ridge of buttes riven by gullies; their horses threw up their heads, scenting the air and looking up a ravine. Certain the animals had smelled a buffalo, Roosevelt and Ferris dismounted and moved on foot up the gully for about a hundred yards; there they found bison hoofprints. Moments later they spotted the animal itself. Roosevelt: "The wind was just right, and no ground could have been better for stalking. Hardly needing to bend down, I walked up behind a small sharp-crested hillock, and peeping over, there below me, not fifty yards off, was a great bison bull. He was walking along, grazing as he walked. His glossy fall coat was in fine trim, and shone in the rays of the sun; while his pride of bearing showed him to be in the lusty vigor of his prime."[141] Ferris pointed out a yellow spot just behind the buffalo's shoulder. "If you hit him there, you'll get him right through the heart."[142]

Roosevelt coolly took aim and fired. Though big and heavy, the animal nevertheless burst into a run, bounding up the opposite side of the ravine even as Roosevelt fired two more bullets into his flank. At first Ferris thought Roosevelt had missed again; he was about to despair of ever connecting the easterner with a buffalo. Then he saw blood pouring from the bull's mouth and nostrils as it disappeared over the ridge. The hunters knew they had this one. With no sense of urgency they followed the blood trail. In the next gully the buffalo lay on its back. Ecstatic, Roosevelt went into an impromptu faux Indian war dance around the fallen bull. Ferris: "I never saw anyone so enthused in my life, and by golly, I was pretty enthused myself. . . . I was plumb tired out." Roosevelt, in a burst of excess that became practically a ritual after a major kill, handed a hundred dollars to Ferris as a bonus.[143] They then fell to the hard work of cutting off the trophy head and taking off the skin, as well as packing some meat.[144] A cow bison's meat would appeal more to the palate, Roosevelt knew, but hump meat—the strips from each side of the backbone—were excellent fare even from a bull.

Roosevelt wasted no time in breaking the good news to his wife. In a letter dated Tuesday, September 20, and datelined "Little Missouri (10 miles above the station)," he wrote Alice with glee: "Hurrah! The luck has turned at last. I will bring you home the head of a great buffalo bull, and the antlers of two superb stags."[145]

For Ferris, the hunt marked the end of an era: "I never saw any more buffalo after that. They disappeared from the range."[146] In later years he would recall the speed of that loss with regret: "In eighty-two there were lots of buffalo. An old hunter there used to kill the buffalo just for their tongues. He used to smoke their tongues and sell them for twenty-five cents apiece; the next year, eighty-three, there was none left. That was one of the sad things that happened. It was too bad they were allowed to be killed off in such wanton style."[147]

On the twenty-first Roosevelt brought his eventful hunt to an end and headed north toward town, traveling to the accompaniment of a rattling, creaking wagon loaded with the head and hide of a bull buffalo. Gregor Lang, watching the departure, said to Lincoln, "There goes the most remarkable man I ever met. Unless I am badly mistaken the world is due to hear from him one of these days."[148]

Roosevelt stayed in the area a little longer, apparently bunking at the Maltese Cross Ranch and awaiting word from Ferris and Merrifield. On September 23 he received a parcel of letters from Alice, delivered to him by a cowboy, that he read again and again. He also wrote her a brief summary of his recent activities and his thoughts, datelined "the Ferris ranche." He said he was planning to leave for New York City in a couple of days. "I have three splendid trophies, and the heads of the buffalo and stags will look grandly in our hall; and I am feeling in such health as I have certainly not been in for the past four years."[149] He added, "This has been by all odds the pleasantest and most successful trip I have ever made."

Then he made the major announcement: "During these ten days I have also been making up my mind to go into something more important than hunting. I have taken a great fancy to the three men, Merrifield and two brothers named Ferris, at whose ranche I have been staying several days, and one of whom has been with me all the time. I have also carefully examined the country, with reference to its capacity for stock raising; and the more I have looked into the matter . . . the more convinced I became that there was a chance to make a great deal of money, very safely, in the cattle business."

He then addressed the question of risk, his tone suggesting that he may have been trying to persuade himself as much as anyone about the wisdom of his investment: "Of course it may turn out to be a failure; but even if it does I have made my arrangements so that I do not believe I will lose the money I put in; while, if it comes out a success, as I am inclined to think that on the whole it will, it will go a long way towards solving the problem that has puzzled us both a good deal at times—how I am to make more money as our needs increase, and yet try to keep in a position from which I may be able at some future time to again go into public life, or literary life." He suspected that Uncle James wouldn't be pleased, "but I have long made up my mind that any successful step I take must be taken . . . on my own responsibility."[150]

Within days a telegram came from Merrifield saying the deal was done. Roosevelt, now a cattleman, was soon afterward on his way back to New York City.

4

LOVE AND LOSS

AT THE END OF 1883 THEODORE ROOSEVELT SEEMED SINGULARLY
blessed. Not only was his political career advancing, but he had established a ranch in the Dakota Badlands. Most important, Alice was nearing the end of her term with their first child. On Wednesday, February 6,
1884, he wrote to her from Albany, expressing his regret that he could not
be with her as the time for birth neared: "Darling Wifie, I have just received your dear little note; I look forward so much to seeing you tomorrow; I wish I could be with you to rub you when you get 'crampy.'"[1] These
cramps were not seen as a sign of anything amiss, but as a normal part of
pregnancy. The same day he wrote another letter to her, this one, like the
other, on the letterhead of the New York Assembly: "How I did hate to
leave my bright, sunny little love yesterday afternoon! I love you and long
for you all the time, and oh *so* tenderly; doubly tenderly now, my sweetest
little wife. I just long for Friday evening when I shall be with you again."[2]

When Roosevelt arrived home that weekend—the couple was staying at the Fifty-seventh Street house during the final days of Alice's
pregnancy—the weather was rainy and dank, as it had been for days.

Alice was ill and so was his mother, who had gone to bed with what seemed a severe cold.[3]

Monday morning, the eleventh, Roosevelt returned to Albany and his legislative work. Alice wrote to him that day: "Darling Thee, I hated so to leave you this afternoon, I dont think you need feel worried about my being sick as the Dr told me this afternoon that I would not need my nurse before Thursday—I am feeling well tonight but am very much worried over ~~the baby~~ your little mother, her fever is still very high and the Dr is rather afraid of typhoid, it is not in the least catching. I will write again to-morrow and let you know just how she is—dont say any thing about it till then. I do love my dear Thee *so* much. I wish I could have my little new baby soon. ever Your loving wife Alice."[4]

Alice gave birth to a daughter at around 8:30 p.m. on February 12— the birthday of Theodore's role model, Abraham Lincoln. She held her baby and kissed it. The next day, in Albany, Theodore received a telegram telling him the baby was fine but the mother "only fairly well."[5] Later in the day he received another telegram that Alice had taken a turn for the worse and that he should hasten home, which he did on the night train. One of his colleagues in the Assembly would remark years later, "I shall never forget when the news came, and we congratulated him on the birth of his daughter. He was full of life and happiness—and then news came of a sudden turn and he took his departure."[6]

A deep fog shrouded New York City on Wednesday night as the train from Albany bore an alarmed and worried Theodore Roosevelt into Manhattan at about ten-thirty. The 145-mile ride usually took five hours, but on this night the train had crawled down the Hudson Valley in the clutching fog.

At the train station Roosevelt hired a carriage for the ride to 6 West Fifty-seventh Street. The carriage moved through a fog so murky that elevated trains inched down their rails, the engineers unable to see lighted track signals. Pedestrians felt their way blindly along sidewalks to the sound of hidden horses and carriages clopping and grinding over veiled streets. The skies had been cloud-laden for most of early February. Sunlight had broken through over Manhattan only once in the previous week and a half, and rain had been falling for days as far west as the Ohio Valley. The *New York Times* on the morning of the thirteenth had run an editorial calling the gloom "suicidal weather. Life does not seem worth living to a sensitive person easily influenced by atmospheric conditions. There is something comfortless and unhappy in the raw and chilly air, something suggestive of death and decay in the dampness that fills the world."[7]

Just before midnight Roosevelt reached home. In the mists above glowed the lighted window of the third-floor bedroom where Alice lay. As he stepped inside, his older brother, Elliott, told him, "There is a curse on this house. Mother is dying, and Alice is dying too."[8]

Theodore hurried to his wife's bedside to find her so ill she could barely recognize him. He took her in his arms and held her closely. Church bells tolled midnight, Valentine's Day. On this date four years earlier, Theodore and Alice had publicly announced their engagement.

He held her until, two hours later, he received word that if he wished to see his mother before she died he must go now to her room, the same second-floor bedroom in which his father had died only six years earlier. Roosevelt was at his mother's side when she succumbed at 3:00 a.m. to acute typhoid. She was forty-eight years old. Standing by her, Roosevelt said, "There *is* a curse on this house."[9]

He returned to Alice on the third floor, holding her as her life drained away. The fog deepened at dawn, until a violent midmorning rain swept it away. But the sun shone for only a few minutes before clouds and fog returned. Roosevelt still held his wife, her kidneys failing, her body giving out. The cramps that Alice had experienced had been related to nephritis, not childbirth.[10]

At about two in the afternoon of Valentine's Day 1884, the woman Roosevelt often called his "little pink wife" died of kidney failure as he held her. She was twenty-two years old. In his diary that day Roosevelt drew a large black X at the top of the page and wrote under it, "The light has gone out of my life."[11]

The Roosevelt family was stunned. Theodore's maternal aunt Anna: "The blow was so sudden, and *so* appalling it is very hard to bear it. All was over, and they were both dead in three days. We had so little warning. It is a great mystery. They were so much needed, and were so much beloved! . . . Poor Theodore, our grief is almost lost in his, he has so much to bear. If his little daughter is spared to him I hope she will be a great—comfort—sometime."[12]

The Assembly, after hearing of the deaths, voted on Friday, February 15, to adjourn until 8:00 p.m. the following Monday. In the adjournment resolution, the Assembly expressed condolences: "Though no words nor resolutions can assuage the grief or allay the anguish which, at a moment's warning, has entered his soul, we yet feel that an expression of our sincere and sorrowing sympathy is not only peculiarly appropriate, but that it may serve to strengthen and fortify him in this moment of his agony and weakness."[13]

Some two thousand people attended the double funeral that started at ten in the morning on Saturday. The service took place in the same massive red-brick church that had witnessed the funeral of Theodore's father—the Fifth Avenue Presbyterian on the corner of Fifth Avenue and Fifty-fifth Street, "the largest and finest Presbyterian Church in the city," with a congregation that was "large and enormously wealthy."[14] Joining Theodore in the front pews were his brother, Elliott, his sisters, Corinne and Anna, and Alice's father, George Cabot Lee. Allies and opponents from the New York legislature attended.[15]

The paired rosewood coffins in front of the altar were covered with roses, lilies, and green vines. At the door to the church two hearses stood side by side. The service started with a solo; the Reverend John Hall then offered an invocation, followed by biblical readings on death and resurrection from the Epistle to the Romans.[16] After a quartet sang *Rock of Ages*, Hall began his address: "There is something very peculiar and unusual in the conditions in which we are gathered together to-day and again brought face to face with death. That two members of the same church, two members of the same family, dwelling together in the same house, should on the same day be taken out of this mortal life, and on the same day, with the same services, to their last resting-place—this is surely something very peculiar, very solemnizing, deeply affecting. I do not remember any thing quite like it in all the years of the ministry in which I have served."[17]

People cried as Hall said he could understand that God had called home the older woman, because her family was raised and her work done, but the younger woman was at the start of life, and it seemed strange that she should be taken away. Tears flowed down his cheeks as he prayed for Theodore Roosevelt and his newborn: "And we beseech thee, O Lord! for the parents and the other kindred of her who in her early youth has been snatched away. . . . But especially do we beseech thee for him of whose life she has been so great a part, that thou wilt strengthen him, that thou wilt comfort him, that thou wilt enable him to address himself afresh to the duties that thou givest him to do, manifesting his true submission of soul to thee by the zeal, fervor, and activity with which he tries to serve thee while his life is continued on the earth. And the little child that is mother-less, O Lord Jesus! we bring and with our hearts place it in the hands of that dear Redeemer who said: 'Suffer the little children to come unto me, and forbid them not, for of such is the kingdom of heaven!' "[18]

As the funeral cortege left the church, the choir sang "Angels of Jesus, Angels of Light." The immediate family followed the coffins to Brooklyn's Green-Wood Cemetery for burial.[19]

The day after the funeral Roosevelt held his daughter, Alice Lee, as she was baptized. His aunt Anna thought the baby "a very sweet pretty little girl, so much like her beautiful young Mother in appearance, I hope she will be like her in character, for then she will go about shedding sun-shine upon all around her."[20] During the ceremony, the baby wore a silver locket that held a clip of her mother's hair.[21]

Around the time of the funeral Theodore wrote in his diary of himself and his wife: "We spent three years of happiness greater and more unalloyed than I have ever known fall to the lot of others. . . . For joy or for sorrow my life has now been lived out."[22] He shortly came to a resolution about his twin tragedies: "There is nothing left for me except to try to so live as not to dishonor the memory of those I loved who have gone before me."[23]

Theodore was "in a dazed, stunned state" in the days following the funeral, wrote Arthur Cutler, the tutor and companion who had prepared Roosevelt for his entrance exams to Harvard. "He does not know what he does or says."[24] At home he paced his room ceaselessly, seemed bewildered by condolences, ignored his baby, and led his family to fear that he would lose his mind.

He had three key problems with which to deal: the disposal of his mother's property, the care of his new baby, and his career. For the first two he turned to his sister Anna. Both of Theodore's sisters—Corinne, three years younger then he, and Anna, almost four years older and nicknamed "Bye," "Bysie," and "Bamie"—were very close to him; in later years, family members thought the sisters loved him more than they did their husbands.[25] Like their brother, both had suffered through illness—Corinne was asthmatic throughout her life, though not as seriously as he, and Anna had a severe deformity of the spine, the product of an unidentified childhood disease that required the wearing of a brace and caused her much pain. Nevertheless, both "had charm and keen minds and were extraordinarily well read. Their conversation was vivid and their sense of fun almost as great as their brother's. They loved people and people loved them, and they lived joyously."[26]

Corinne "had much of her brother Theodore's gaiety and joy in life. More volatile than he, she was also more mercurial."[27] She could be laughing one moment, in tears the next. Her sense of humor and outgoing personality usually put her at the center of attention. She loved to entertain, hosting dinners and lunches. Meals at her house "were loud with laughter and, as she was adept at drawing out people, often rich in good talk."[28] Nevertheless, she lacked the "granite stability" that the family found so demonstrative in Anna.[29]

Anna "exerted a greater influence on Theodore than did Corinne, if for no other reason than that she was nearly four years his senior and that her mother had left much of the care of the younger children in Bamie's competent hands."[30] When, as children, the Roosevelt siblings stayed in Europe, Anna not only watched over the others but monitored Theodore's education; when he went to Harvard in 1876, she furnished his rooms and introduced him to her Boston friends; when he and Alice married, Anna made arrangements for their honeymoon; and when Alice died, Anna kept house for Theodore. When the four young Roosevelts were children, Theodore, Corinne, and Elliott thought of themselves as "we three," while Anna was considered one of the adults.[31] Theodore called Anna "the Driving Wheel of Destiny and Superintendent-in-Chief of the Workings of Providence" as well as "the sweetest sister who ever lived."[32]

Given Anna's dependable, "granite" nature, Theodore's decision the day after the funeral to put Baby Lee, as she was called, in her care seems natural. Anna also took over responding to condolence letters and assumed responsibility for putting her mother's possessions in order.[33]

Almost immediately after the funerals, the Roosevelts put up for sale the house at 6 West Fifty-seventh Street; it sold in less than a week, but the family had until May to move out.[34] Theodore also sold the house on West Forty-fifth Street that he and Alice had shared, casting from him one of the most meaningful memories of his married life. A letter he had sent to Alice from the Kenmore Hotel in Albany on New Year's Eve 1882 hinted at what the house symbolized for him: "I can not say how I feel when I think of the cosy little room, with its pretty furniture and well stocked book shelves, a bright fire of soft coal in the grate, and above all my bewitching little mistress, with some soft, dainty dress on, to sit and play backgammon with."[35] Unable to make himself go back there after Alice died, he asked Anna to close it. On March 1 he contracted John H. Wood & Son, carpenters in the Long Island town of Lawrence, to build his Oyster Bay house, Leeholm.[36] Predictably, Anna took over management of that process, too.[37]

As for his responsibilities in the state Assembly, he fled to them as to a sanctuary, taking a train to Albany the evening of Tuesday the nineteenth, only three days after the funeral.[38] In a letter to William Sewall, his hunting guide in Maine, he wrote that although the deaths were a grim and evil fate, "I have never believed it did any good to flinch or yield for any blow, nor does it lighten the pain to cease from working."[39] He wrote more pointedly to political ally Carl Schurz, "I think I should go mad if I were not employed."[40]

He went back to Albany "a changed man," remembered a colleague. "From that time on there was a sadness about his face that he never had before. He had that same indomitable spirit, however, he never manifested it. He did not want anybody to talk to him about it, he did not want anybody to sympathize with him. It was a grief that he had in his own soul."[41] In his legislative agenda he found merciful relief, manufacturing a hectic schedule that kept him traveling frequently between Albany and New York City, sleeping in snatched moments on the train.[42] He introduced dozens of bills in the Assembly and produced huge reports on political corruption in New York City as part of his responsibilities on the City Investigating Committee, including two documents that incorporated a million words of testimony.[43]

In April he went to Utica for the Republican state convention, where the party would select its delegates for the national convention, to be held in Chicago later that spring. Going into the presidential campaign season, the Republican Party, in Roosevelt's thinking, was divided into three parts.[44] The one to which he belonged—the Independents, also derogatorily called Mugwumps—were "generally men of wealth, culture, and honesty of character, men who had read much, and were in advance of the rest of the party."[45] Hailing mostly from the coastal regions of the Northeast, they wanted to sweep out the party's machine men, or Stalwarts, who were seen as part of a corrupt and corrupting political system. One of Roosevelt's allies, William Roscoe Thayer, put the Independents' opinion of the Stalwarts in a nutshell: "The Republican Party was grown fat with four and twenty years of power, and the fat had overlain and smothered its noble aims. The party was arrogant, it was corrupt, it was unashamed. After the War, immense projects involving huge sums of money had to be managed, and the Republicans spent like spendthrifts when they did not spend like embezzlers. . . . But now a new generation was springing up, with its leaven of hope and idealism and its intuitive faith in honesty."[46]

A third group, Roosevelt believed, composed the "great bulk of the party," those "whom Lincoln called the plain people, who were perfectly honest, according to their own light, but who were rather narrowminded, slow to receive ideas and slow to give them up. It was they who gave the main strength to the party in times past."[47] This group strongly favored the senator from Maine, James G. Blaine, as the 1884 Republican presidential candidate, but the Independents saw him as a corrupt politician who had engaged in illegal business deals with railroads. Another leading contender was the current president, Chester Alan Arthur, whom the Independents believed was politically too weak, after battles with political power brokers, to survive.[48] In Utica—where he was widely seen as "the glorious promise" of the Independents—Roosevelt scored a major victory by engineering the election of independent delegates to the national convention.[49] He returned to Albany in triumph as head of the New York delegation. His efforts to quash Arthur and Blaine became key parts of the Independents' efforts to purge their party of corruption.

Thayer's feelings about Blaine were typical of those who sided with Roosevelt: "During the days of suspense before the Chicago Convention met, the proposed nomination of Blaine weighed upon me like a nightmare. I would not admit to myself that so great a crime against American ideals could be committed by delegates who represented the standard of any political party, and were drawn from all over the country. I cherished, what seems to me now the sadly foolish dream, that with Roosevelt in the convention the abomination could not be done. I thought of him as of a paladin against whom the forces of evil would dash themselves to pieces. I thought of him as the young and dauntless spokesman of righteousness whose words would silence the special pleaders of iniquity. I wrote him and besought him to stand firm."[50]

Despite his win in Utica, upon returning to Albany Roosevelt wanted a break from the routine of the past two years. Believing that "black care rarely sits behind a rider whose pace is fast enough; at any rate, not when he first feels the horse move under him," he came up with a plan that he outlined in a letter to the editor of the *Utica Morning Herald*, an ally during the convention: "My work this winter has been very harassing, and I feel both tired and restless; for the next few months I shall probably be in Dakota, and I think I shall spend the next two or three years in making shooting trips, either in the far West or in the Northern Woods—and there will be plenty of work to do writing."[51]

A greater impetus than he revealed in his letter may have stood behind Roosevelt's intention to drop a burgeoning political career. William Roscoe Thayer concluded that the twenty-five-year-old politico had "felt the emptiness of life's prizes when the dearest who should have shared them with him were dead."[52] Roosevelt also may have been subject to outside influence. Arthur Cutler recalled that after the deaths, the family had been "really alarmed for his reason, he appeared to be utterly stunned by the sudden blow. A family council was held and it was decided to get him to go out to the Far West."[53] Roosevelt himself reportedly said that he went west to battle for his health.[54] The cleaner air in Dakota Territory made it a good choice for an asthma sufferer: In the 1880s, the use of soft coal for fuel flooded New York City air with fine ash; fashionable women found soot outlines of their veil patterns on their faces.[55]

★ ★ ★

Roosevelt began his exit in May, when he left New York for Chicago to help lead the Independents in their fight to nominate Vermont senator George F. Edmunds as the Republican presidential candidate.[56] Edmunds, who had grown up in a village in the Green Mountains, had been elected to the Senate in 1866 and had built his career on his "poor-but-honest" background and on his support of issues such as civil-service reform.[57] His personality was somewhat drab, however, compared to the flamboyant Blaine—a notably strong orator—and Blaine had vast support. Although Roosevelt was "a human fighting machine" at the convention, when Blaine's name was placed in nomination the audience of some ten thousand people "became worked up to a condition of absolutely uncontrollable excitement and enthusiasm. For a quarter of an hour at a time they cheered and shouted so that the brass bands could not be heard at all, and we were nearly deafened by the noise."[58] When the convention ended, Blaine had won. Roosevelt: "Well, the fight has been fought and lost, and moreover our defeat is an overwhelming rout. . . . That such should be the fact speaks badly for the intelligence of the mass of my party, as well as for their sensitiveness to the honesty and uprightness of a public official, and bodes no good for the future of the nation."[59]

Thayer and other Independents waited to see if the delegates who opposed Blaine would bolt the party and support a Democratic nominee. Roosevelt declined to say what he would do and left Chicago for the Dakota Badlands. Downcast but stoic, he pondered how to deal with "the two evils to which our choice is now limited viz:—a democratic administration or four years of Blaine in the White House."[60] Concluding that in forty-nine out of a hundred cases the voice of the people was likely to be "the voice of the devil, or, what is still worse, the voice of a fool," he considered backing the Republican Party and its platform without publicly endorsing Blaine.

Backing Blaine implied compromising his political ideals, a matter that held great import for Roosevelt, as he had suggested in his pre-convention letter to the editor of the *Utica Morning Herald*: "Although not a very old man, I have yet lived a great deal in my life, and I have known sorrow too bitter and joy too keen to allow me to become either cast down or elated for more than a very brief period over success or defeat. I have very little expectation of being able to keep on in politics; my success so far has only been won by absolute indifference to my future career. . . . I will not stay in public life unless I can do so on my own terms; and my ideal, whether lived up to or not, is rather a high one."[61]

On the way west he participated in newspaper interviews in Chicago and in St. Paul, Minnesota, suggesting in the latter that he would not bolt the party but would support Blaine. With the interviews behind him, he seemed to want only to put politics on hold and to lose himself in the vast reaches of the Badlands.[62] He wrote his sister Anna from St. Paul, "I am now on my way to the Little Missouri; I shall probably be back about July 10th, but will write or telegraph to you before; perhaps I shall be back much earlier, as I intend to take quite a long hunting trip this fall, there being now no necessity of my taking part in the political campaign."[63]

5

UNDER WESTERN SKIES

When Roosevelt set his sights on the Badlands he was joining a historic trend that had begun after the Civil War—the expansion of the United States into the remote reaches of the West.[1] The three decades from 1870 to 1900 marked the most rapid period of colonization in U.S. history, with 430 million acres settled and 225 million put under cultivation, compared to 409 million settled and 189 million cultivated between 1607—when the British founded their first permanent colony in North America—and 1870.[2]

The result was that the West transformed quickly before the disbelieving eyes of the pioneers themselves. Granville Stuart, who had come into Montana in the late 1850s searching for gold and had evolved into a rancher by the 1880s, wrote:

> It would be impossible to make persons not present on the Montana cattle ranges realize the rapid change that took place on those ranges in two years. In 1880 the country was practically uninhabited. One could travel for miles without seeing so much as a trapper's bivouac.

Thousands of buffalo darkened the rolling plains. There were deer, antelope, elk, wolves and coyotes on every hill and in every ravine and thicket. In the whole territory of Montana there were but two hundred and fifty thousand head of cattle, including dairy cattle and work oxen.

In the fall of 1883 there was not one buffalo remaining on the range and the antelope, elk, and deer were indeed scarce. . . . but in the fall of 1883 there were six hundred thousand head of cattle on the range. . . . Small ranches were being taken by squatters along all the streams and there were neat and comfortable log school houses in all the settlements.[3]

People went west for a variety of reasons: "Many a young man, on his own initiative and for love of adventure, on medical advice and for hope of recovery, or on parental compulsion and for chance of reform, exchanged a metropolis for the bunch-grass and mesquite. . . . Liquor and undesirable affairs of the heart accounted for the presence of many, and here and there was one who in England had been socially sentenced to a disappearance until his people should succeed in paying his debts, and so wipe out a stain on a title."[4] Some were criminals escaping the law, finding refuge in a region where no one questioned a man's name, even it if were nothing more than "Texas Ike." Theodore Roosevelt came for his health, to escape his grief, and to profit, he hoped, from the open range—the vast stretches of land virtually unclaimed except by railroads and the federal government. The belief by the early 1880s was that "cattle could be raised and fattened on the open range, seeking their own food, water, and shelter without any aid from man, from the time they were dropped until they were in condition to be driven to a railroad station for shipment to market."[5]

Open-range ranching began in Texas, where Mexican cattle and horses, first imported from Spain in the 1500s, strayed and ran wild. The feral cattle gave rise to the animal that would be called the Texas longhorn—a rangy creature, long-legged, sinewy, armed with distinctive horns and a wicked temper. Local cattle tenders, called vaqueros, developed the gear and the techniques for working with these animals, including the broad-brimmed hat, the chaps for protection against the arid region's thorn-bearing plants, the saddle, the lariat, the spurs, and other accoutrements. In the early 1800s,

Americans began moving out of Alabama, Mississippi, and Louisiana into Texas. They encountered the ranchers of Spanish origin and adopted their habits.[6] By 1830, perhaps 100,000 cattle roamed Texas.

Texas became a state in 1845 without ceding its range lands to the federal government. The state sold grazing grounds to ranchers for fifty cents an acre.[7] For livestock, a rancher could capture wild horses and longhorns.[8] Texans developed a reputation for being the consummate cowboys. Teddy Blue Abbott, who hailed from Nebraska before drifting west at age eighteen and finally settling into ranching on the border of Montana and Dakota Territory, said Texans "used to brag that they could go any place a cow could and stand anything a horse could. It was their life."[9]

During the Civil War, Texas cattle multiplied while the men were away fighting for the Confederacy.[10] "By the time the war was over they [cattle] was down to four dollars a head—when you could find a buyer. Here was all these cheap long-horned steers overrunning Texas; here was the rest of the country crying for beef—and no railroads to get them out."[11]

Change came after the war, when railroads spread west, moving across Nebraska in 1867 and establishing the first transcontinental line in 1869.[12] In 1867, Texas ranchers started moving cattle to northern railheads for shipment to eastern markets, giving rise to a western adage: "To the grass on the hoof, to the butcher in the train."[13]

Another factor that brought Texans and their cattle north was the discovery, in the mid-1860s, that cattle fattened better on the less arid northern plains and prairies.[14] This revelation was "greater in its importance than the discovery of gold in California, or silver in Nevada, or petroleum in Pennsylvania."[15] The open northern grasslands were doubly attractive to Texans because in the mid-1800s Texas was becoming crowded with settlers.[16] The move north proved lucrative—a calf bought in Texas for five or ten dollars might sell at market for twenty-five after fattening on free grass; the cost of trailing them to market was about a penny per mile per head.[17] Texas cattlemen began moving herds to northern grazing lands in 1866, and from that year until 1885, in no twelve-month period did fewer than three hundred thousand cattle trail north; in top years, the number could be twice that.[18] The open-range cattle industry peaked in 1885, with 7.5 million head on the Great Plains north of Texas and New Mexico.[19] The northern plains, from Nebraska and Colorado to Canada, became known as the cattle range, or cattle country.[20] In 1884, the market value of the surplus cattle on the northern plains was about forty million dollars.[21]

In the 1880s, investing in a western ranch was practically a fad among wealthy Easterners with a yen for outdoor sport. Abbott: "Rich men's sons from the East were nothing new as far as I was concerned. The range in the eighties was as full of them as a dog's hair of fleas, and some of them were good fellows and some were damn fools."[22]

Ranching also had become a popular investment for Europeans, particularly for the English, many of whom had visited the West to hunt bison, already had had some experience raising cattle, and were enchanted by the idea of free grazing lands.[23] A ranch might not only earn money but also offer a chance for riding and hunting, while "herdsmen," in the guise of cowboys, did the real work.[24] Between spring and fall 1884, English investors put five million dollars into Montana ranching.[25] During the Panic of 1873, a depression that lasted six years, many English investors in the Northern Pacific Railroad exchanged their stock for rights to land along the rail line in Dakota Territory; consequently, Englishmen owned tens of thousands of acres there.[26] Abbott: "In the seventies and eighties there were a lot of Englishmen over here playing the part of amateur cowpunchers. There were remittance men mostly, younger sons living on money that was sent them by their families, and some of them got to be real cowpunchers after awhile."[27]

Rumors were rife that ranchers were making annual returns of 35 to 40 percent in parts of the West.[28] Or even better: Cattle were rumored to improve in value by five to eight dollars yearly per head, with the cost of keeping them only a dollar per head.[29] The *Bad Lands Cow Boy* newspaper, published in Medora, contended, "It seems to be an undisputed fact that the cattle business yields larger and surer returns than any other business in the world." The writer calculated that an investment of twenty thousand dollars would buy a thousand head of cattle. With overhead, including forty dollars a month each for nine cowboys and one hundred dollars a month for a foreman, he calculated a net profit of $161,210 in seven years.

How realistic these figures, and the expectations they engendered, really were is impossible to tell. Even official reports promoted settlement more than they provided accurate information. The Dakota Territorial Governor's Report for 1885 extolled the virtues of the Badlands without mentioning winter temperatures that sank to fifty degrees below zero, snow that piled into towering drifts along windbreaks, and summer temperatures in excess of one hundred degrees. "Bunch and buffalo-grass cover almost every inch of the ground," the report declared.[30] "Generally no hay need be cut, as the grass cures standing, and keeps the cattle in as good a condition all winter as if they were stall-fed. The only reason for putting up hay is to avoid a scarcity of feed in case of heavy snows. This very seldom happens, however, as very little snow falls in the Bad Lands. . . . Even in the dead of winter a meadow has a very perceptible tinge of green."

Such hyperbole could lead to disaster for those inclined to believe it. Frank Wilkeson ranched in Kansas in the early 1870s. Local boosters told him that winters would be so mild he would not need a coat and that grass would grow tall by the first of March.[31] He found instead that "November came in with a blizzard, and, with slight interruptions, kindly allowed by Nature for the purpose of affording us opportunities to skin dead cattle, the blizzard lasted until March, and the cold, stormy weather for two months longer. There was no new grass until the middle of May."[32] Cattle losses were as high as 80 percent, rarely less than 50 percent. "The next summer, bankruptcy stalked over the Kansas plains and struck men down."[33]

Another threat to the livestock industry was overstocking. In the Badlands, a rancher needed about thirty-five to forty acres per head for cattle.[34] Roosevelt said twenty-five acres per animal would do, a much more liberal figure.[35] Exceeding such limits damaged grazing lands. "In 1873 the Arkansas Valley in Colorado was carpeted with nutritious grass; in 1881 it was a desert where dust clouds coursed," Wilkeson recalled.[36] He saw the same thing happen in Montana's Dearborn Valley—which follows a seventy-mile-long tributary of the Missouri River—between 1871 and the early 1880s. Consequently, by the mid-1880s local ranchers were trying to limit the number of cattle released on the northern range.[37]

The men who worked the cattle range could be divided into two classes, the cattlemen or ranchers, who owned livestock, and the cowboys, who worked for the cattlemen. Historian David Courtwright of the University of North Florida: "A cattle*man* was a capitalist and employer, generally married, who lived in a ranch house built on his own land. A cow*boy* was an employee, unmarried, who tended cattle marked with another man's brand and who lived in a bunkhouse ('doghouse,' 'shack,' 'dump,' or 'ram pasture') built on another man's land."[38] He adds, "Cowboys, in short, were lower-class bachelor laborers in a risky and unhealthful line of work."[39] Novelist and western essayist Wallace Stegner held a similar view: "The real-life cattle baron was and is about as democratic as a feudal baron. The cowboy in practice was and is an overworked, underpaid hireling, almost as homeless and dispossessed as a modern crop worker, and his fabled independence was and is chiefly the privilege of quitting his job in order to go looking for another just as bad."[40]

Contemporaries of the 1880s cowboys also took a dim view of the men on horseback. The *Cheyenne Daily Leader* in 1882 called them "foulmouthed, blasphemous, drunken, lecherous, utterly corrupt."[41] The hardworking, often lonesome cowboy, "when led to the trough of 'civilization,' drank deeply of its offerings." Although cowboys when sober were dependable, drinking turned them into vicious menaces, riding down main street with guns blazing. "Cowboys on sprees shot up towns, terrorized tenderfeet, squandered their wages on gambling and whores. 'Nobody then thought of them as romantic,' recalled a Montana rancher's wife. 'They were regarded as a wild and undesirable lot of citizens.'"[42] And yet, some witnesses found the gunplay and wild times seductive. After watching a cowboy riding through town shooting off his gun while a young woman wearing only a chemise rode beside him on another horse, an English visitor "born and raised in the sleepiest, most conservative little country town in Wessex" thought, "This was Life with a capital L."[43]

The frontiers were male-dominated—women stayed in cities or settled areas—and the men who went to the frontier were, all in all, a rough lot.[44] "Male migrants were typically losers in a natal lottery. They had poor parents or were crowded out of a comfortable inheritance by too many siblings."[45] A farmer's son, with limited prospects for inheriting land, was left with four choices: learn a trade, enlist in the military, go to sea, or move to the frontier.[46]

Male dominance was the main factor in making the West wild. The problem was not just a matter of gender but also of age. With the exception of some of the bosses and cattle owners, the average age of cowboys in the 1880s was twenty-three or twenty-four. Young men then, as now, accounted for most of the violent crime in American society.[47] Frontiersmen, in particular, were prone to violence because they were "contemptuous of other races and touchy about personal honor, which they were inclined to defend by violent means . . . The guns and knives they carried increased the likelihood that such conflicts would have fatal results."[48] Ranging from their late teens to their twenties, these men composed the social group most likely to kill or be killed, to abuse alcohol, to steal, rob, and vandalize.[49] Consequently, "the frontier was the principal arena of single male brutality in American history. Tens of thousands of drunken and disorderly white frontiersmen perished prematurely, as did countless native and animal inhabitants whose territory they despoiled."[50]

Teddy Blue Abbott, who shot and wounded a local lawman while still in his teens, made the same point: "A kid is more dangerous than a man because he's so sensitive about his personal courage. He's just itching to shoot somebody in order to prove himself."[51] The itch was often scratched. One Medora resident remembered years later, "Yes, I ran into lots of shooting scrapes. Pretty nearly all of the quarrels took this course before they ended."[52] Roosevelt encountered intimations of this bloodlust in the most amiable of contexts one night at his ranch. After reading to his men from a book on British history, he described the magnificent garb and superb horses of a regiment of English hussars he once had seen; one of his hired men, listening while gazing into a flaming fireplace, rubbed his hands together and said "with regretful emphasis, 'Oh, how I *would* like to kill one of them!'"[53]

Frontier towns offered a variety of vices, from drinking to gambling. One Englishman who visited Cheyenne, Wyoming, around 1869 found that "Professor MacDowell's Museum" featured machines with crank handles that flipped over stereoscopic views of half-dressed dancing women and even hardcore pornography "absolutely impossible to describe."[54] Saloons, populated by armed young men, were hotbeds of violence: "Saloons multiplied occasions of conflict, both because of the imperative of guarding one's honor before other men and because of the presence of gambling, prostitution, prizefighting, and other activities which inspired drunken competition and arguments. The opportunity to extract patrons' wages drew gamblers, pimps, and their ilk to saloons, usually with the knowledge and connivance of the proprietor. Vice added armed and hardened criminals to the already dangerous mix of inebriated men, ensuring that the saloon would be the historical epicenter of American violence and disorder."[55]

Much of the shooting in frontier towns was playful, as when making a newcomer dance. "It was a common thing around Medora in those early days for the cowboys to get a tenderfoot and commence shooting around his feet. It was their pastime."[56] Often, the man who was made to dance was expected to buy drinks afterward. Nevertheless, a resident or visitor of some cow towns was ten to forty times more likely to be murdered than was a visitor or resident of an eastern city. Communities sometimes tried to control the local hazards, for example by outlawing "furious riding," but westerners tolerated at least some violence because cowboys brought business to town.[57] "Cowboys would not come to town if they could not have a good time. To deny business to local saloons and brothels was to deny it to the dry-goods stores and banks as well."[58]

The key to taming the West was not cavalry or gun-toting lawmen, it was women. "Nineteenth-century American men, especially frontiersmen, were notorious for their anti-intellectualism and indifference to the arts, which, like religion, they took to be the domain of women. . . . Given the prevailing masculine lack of interest, no community could regularly support sophisticated artistic and humanistic enterprises without a critical mass of women, who were indispensable as audiences, critics, performers, and instructors. . . . The history of the maturation of frontier towns is the history of women turning them into places actually worth living in."[59]

Cowboys were afraid of only two things, according to Abbott: "a decent woman and being set afoot." They didn't consider themselves proper company for "respectable ladies." "We didn't know how to talk to 'em anyhow. That was what I meant by saying that the cowpunchers was afraid of a decent woman. We were so damned scared for fear that we would do or say something wrong—mention a leg or something like that that would send them up in the air."[60]

The scarcity of women in the West made social encounters with them rare. Richard Townshend, an Englishman who ranched in Colorado in the 1870s, wrote that "among the pioneer cattle-men out on the Great

Plains in the early seventies I do not remember a single one who had a wife."[61] But rarity granted women a certain authority. One English traveler in the West observed, "A lady is a power in this country. From the day when a silk dress and a lace shawl were seen in Main Street, that thoroughfare became passably clean and quiet; oaths were less frequently heard; knives were less frequently drawn; pistols were less frequently fired."[62]

One realm in which women played a key role in the West was religion. Cowboys were highly irreligious and irreverent; one of the popular sources of humor in the West, widely passed around, was a parody of the Bible.[63] Westerners said then that "Sunday stopped at the Missouri River."[64] A Medora cowboy recalled that "anything or any one associated with religion or spiritual living was shunned."[65] He added that religion was looked on as "an institution for old women and weaklings . . . Such early congregations as clustered about the pioneer churches were the newly arrived 'nesters' or homesteaders of the towns; the cowboys, never. There could be no possible community of interests between book-learned men of sedentary profession and a half-tamed, open range horseman."

The arrival of women into a community could abruptly change the religious quotient, as Lincoln Lang recalled of the arrival of his mother and sisters. "Like a bolt out of the blue, the feminine hand had descended upon us, ruthlessly sweeping us from the perch of our fancied supremacy and making us toe the mark. Civilization was upon us, alas, and God only knew where we would bring up. . . . For one thing, we were promptly given to understand that working on Sunday didn't 'go' any more. Prior to that we seldom knew when it came around. . . . Then again, there was less cussing and more dressing going on around the place."[66]

During its earliest days, Medora offered residents little in the way of entertainment aside from drinking, gambling, and races between favorite local horses.[67] The arrival of a train was a major social event, usually attended by "the most intoxicated cowboys who happened to be in town."[68] The cowboys would shoot over the top of every passenger train that stopped; sometimes they fired *through* the windows.[69] Train crews warned passengers in advance so as not to scare them. Some passengers felt disappointed if there were no shooting.

Medora cowboys reserved a special vindictiveness for dress or "hard" hats, which came in two varieties, "plug" or top hats and "pot hats" or derbies. In the mid-1880s it was a rule that no hard hats would survive in Medora.[70] After paying a boy fifty cents to knock off a visitor's hat with a rock, the cowboys would shoot the hat to pieces. Some exceptions were allowed. Roosevelt said he would wear any hat he wanted in town. "Nobody ever meddled with his hat. They had an idea that they might as well let his hat alone."[71] Despite such lapses, the town soon built "a reputation for iniquity with overland tourists which the cowboys felt in duty bound to live up to."[72]

A favorite prank was to gather in Bob Roberts' saloon, located near the station, when a train with passengers was waiting and to fire off guns inside, then carry out one of the local men as if he had been shot and killed. They would carry him around to the back of the saloon, go inside through a back door, and start over again, alternately shooting and carrying, shooting and carrying, to impress travelers with the town's body count.[73]

Medora nights were generally punctuated with shooting sprees. Cowboys would ride in and start blasting away at nine or ten o'clock and keep it up until two in the morning, "making the night hideous with their shooting and yelling."[74] The next night, they would do it again.

If gunplay were not celebratory enough, the cowboys could resort to more refined pursuits, one of which was to turn loose two bears, owned by saloonkeeper Bob Roberts, when a train came in.[75] The bears would pull people off the train and nearly killed one man. Sometimes the cowboys eschewed torturing tourists and just released the bears to practice roping them.[76]

By summer 1884, Medora was growing. The Dickinson paper took note: "This town, situated in Pyramid Park on the banks of the Little Missouri River and surrounded by the Bad Lands with their fine scenery, is, at the present time, one of the most prosperous and rapidly growing towns along the line of the Northern Pacific. New buildings of every description are going up as fast as a large force of carpenters can do the work and an air of business and enterprise is apparent that would do honor to many an older town."[77] Locals were already saying, or fantasizing, that someday it would be the state capital.[78] The Marquis de Morès had brought in a young college graduate to edit a newspaper, the *Bad Lands Cow Boy* (one-year subscription, two dollars).[79] A Chinese laundry was on hand "to keep the more aspiring citizens in boiled collars with a shine to them."[80]

Since Roosevelt's bison hunt, Joe Ferris had opened a general store.[81] In late February 1884, Jerry Paddock—now a partner with Frank Moore in running the Pyramid Park Hotel—was planning to help divide the hotel's second floor into rooms, counting on summer tourists to "repay the outlay abundantly."[82] Paddock also partnered with Bob Roberts to haul up to seventy-five wagonloads of scoria to pave Medora's streets, "forming a good road-bed even in the muddiest times."[83]

Spring brought new distractions. In late March "a number of the boys" were beginning to practice baseball daily after dinner; "[a] nine will be organized soon, which will result in considerable sport, if not glory."[84] Serious events, in which so dynamic a politician as Theodore Roosevelt could not fail to take an active interest, also were afoot. In March and April, ranchers held at least three meetings in Little Missouri to establish a Badlands stockmen's association for dealing with such matters as organizing the periodic cattle roundups.[85] A primary concern was putting limits on the number of cattle that could be released on the range; the prevailing sense was that the Badlands would be overstocked within three years.[86]

The driving force behind much of this activity was the Marquis de Morès, without whom the town of Medora would not have existed. Nevertheless, his reputation in the Badlands was not helped by his heavy-handed business tactics. The "Roosevelt outfit," as locals sometimes called the Ferris and Merrifield spread, came face-to-face with the Marquis in spring 1884, while Roosevelt was still sorting out life on the Albany–New York City axis.[87] De Morès ordered his ranch foreman to drive fifteen hundred head of beeves onto a rich grassland across the river from the Maltese Cross Ranch and to lay permanent claim to the grazing site. This land lay within the four miles of river frontage that the Roosevelt outfit claimed. Under the common law of the range, the tract was Roosevelt's, because ranchers "claimed" the grazing rights to land within a certain radius of their ranch houses depending upon how many cattle they owned.[88] Although in practice all cattle mingled on the range, this system helped to ensure that the region was not stocked with more cattle than it could feed without damage.

Merrifield promptly told de Morès' foreman to move the cattle by dawn, to which the foreman replied, "I've got my orders from the Marquis to keep the cattle here. That's all there is to it."[89] Although it was by then late at night, Merrifield and Sylvane Ferris saddled up and rode to town for a visit with the Marquis, taking with them a neighboring cowboy as a witness on the assumption that "the Marquis is a hard man to deal with."[90]

They reached town at midnight and found de Morès still in his office. He asked what Merrifield and Ferris could possibly want at that late hour, and one of them said they wanted a written order telling the ranch foreman to move the cattle at daylight. De Morès asked what they planned to do if he refused. "I guess there's nothing to it but what we'll have to move them ourselves," Merrifield said. In fact, he and Ferris had already decided that they would stampede the cattle—a throwing down of the gauntlet almost certain to lead to gunfire.

The Marquis may have understood this threat implicitly. In any event, he tried to work out a compromise, offering fifteen hundred dollars to use the grazing land for three weeks. No dice. Ferris and Merrifield were convinced that the three weeks would gradually extend into forever and that making any deal would lead to trouble. Merrifield: "We knew there'd be no living with a man like the Marquis if you made statements and then backed down at any price."[91] Merrifield told de Morès that the time for talk was over; issue the order or the two men would move the cattle themselves. The Marquis, saying he was sorry they would not do him this favor, wrote out the order. Merrifield and Ferris delivered the note to the ranch foreman, and at dawn he moved the cattle.

6

THE RANCHMAN

THEODORE ROOSEVELT DEBARKED FROM A NORTHERN PACIFIC RAIL-road car on the chill Medora evening of Monday, June 9, 1884, his breath clouding in the cold, dry air, the temperature barely above freezing. The station now stood in Medora, across the river from the town of Little Missouri, one of many changes from the previous September.[1] Although Billings County could boast a permanent population of only 122 men and 27 women, transients aplenty had swelled Medora from a sprawling tent city to eighty-four buildings and still growing, while the town of Little Missouri was ebbing away.[2] Joe Ferris was planning to expand his store and to start selling groceries, a man named John O'Sullivan was building a barber shop, and Bob Roberts was preparing to move his saloon into Medora.[3]

The Badlands was a far cry from the cravetted and derbied world of teas, carriage rides, and parties at the Astors that Roosevelt knew in New York. The open range was the Wild West, the Far West, "a land of vast silent spaces, of lonely rivers, and of plains where the wild game stared at the passing horseman. It was a land of scattered ranches, of herds of long-horned cattle, and of reckless riders who unmoved looked in the eyes of life or of death." In that land Roosevelt would lead "a free and hardy life, with horse and with rifle."[4]

Medora and its environs offered a cornucopia of frontier types more original than any that Roosevelt had encountered as a child in the Mayne Reid novels. Prairie denizens accumulated on the wooden sidewalks that flanked the alternately dusty and muddy streets of Medora, coming in on business or "to frequent the flaunting saloons and gaudy hells of all kinds in search of the coarse, vicious excitement that in the minds of many of them does duty as pleasure."[5] There were hunters in buckskin and fur hats, "with resolute faces and sullen, watchful eyes"; teamsters "surly and self-contained," in slouch hats and high boots; stage drivers, "their faces seamed by the hardship and exposure of their long drives with every kind of team, through every kind of country, and in every kind of weather, proud of their really wonderful skill as reinsmen and conscious of their high standing in any frontier community"; trappers and wolvers, "whose business is to poison wolves, with shaggy, knock-kneed ponies to carry their small bales and bundles of furs"; sheepherders, "with cast-down faces, never able to forget the absolute solitude and monotony of their dreary lives, nor to rid their minds of the thought of the woolly idiots they pass all their days in tending"; Indians draped in blankets "with stolid, emotionless faces" stalking silently among the whites, or joining in gambling and horse races; as well as "sinewy lumbermen, rough-looking miners, and packers, whose business it is to guide the long mule and pony trains that go where wagons can not."[6] Mingled with them were the various classes of "desperadoes," ranking from "the gambler up through the horse-thief to the murderous professional bully, or, as he is locally called, 'bad man.'"

In Roosevelt's view, most important among the plainsmen were the cowboys, who rode sitting loosely in their saddles, "smaller and less muscular than the wielders of ax and pick; but they are as hardy and self-reliant as any men who ever breathed—with bronzed, set faces, and keen eyes that look all the world straight in the face without flinching as they flash out from under the broad-brimmed hats. Peril and hardship, and years of long toil broken by weeks of brutal dissipation, draw haggard lines across their eager faces, but never dim their reckless eyes nor break their bearing of defiant self-confidence." However prone they might be to shooting up towns during sprees, they were usually quiet, self-contained men hospitable to strangers. Roosevelt: "They are much better fellows and pleasanter companions than small farmers or agricultural laborers; nor are the mechanics and workmen of a great city to be mentioned in the same breath."

Despite their differences and diversity, Badlands residents shared an overriding trait, in the view of frontier doctor V. K. Stickey: "Every man was a law unto himself and accountable only to the will of his fellows for his conduct. All that was asked of any man was that he live in the open, that he show the essential qualities of manhood while he dwelt among us, and that he live up to the old code of the range which demanded that every one be able to look any man in the world straight in the eye, and tell him to go to hell."[7] Winning over the inhabitants of the Badlands would prove a test of Roosevelt's ability to partner with "the plain people." Medorans soon found that, unlike the standoffish de Morès, Roosevelt "got right in with everyone," and he became "very popular with everyone for that reason."[8] Ben Bird, who rode with Roosevelt during one of the roundups, recalled decades later, "Roosevelt was a man that was a friend to everyone that was right with him."[9]

Initial impressions were another matter. A few Medorans had heard that Roosevelt was in the Badlands in part to avoid taking sides in regard to Blaine.[10] One resident saw him as too thin and sickly and believed he had come out for his health.[11] Roosevelt himself recognized his deteriorated condition and was determined to overcome it by becoming a "great hunter," even though he believed he had "fewer qualifications for being a hunter than any man I know" and understood that success would require "a lot of grit and courage."[12] His hunting plans involved extensive hikes over prairie and mountain in clean country air, a good regimen for overall fitness.

Local residents also came to know that he was mourning the loss of his wife and was in the Badlands "to kinda drown his sorrows."[13] Recalled one ranch woman, "When he first came out, he was sad and quiet, for his wife had just died."[14] Word about his sorrow could have spread rapidly on the prairie gossip circuit because Roosevelt, though reticent in talking about Alice in the East, did talk about her in the West, lamenting his loss to his ranch hands.[15] Although he was seeking to conquer his physical ailments while in the Badlands, he told some of his western associates that he did not expect to overcome his sorrows. His happiness was finished.

One cowboy remembered him as "a slim, anaemic-looking young fellow dressed in the exaggerated style which new-comers on the frontier affected, and which was considered indisputable evidence of the rank tenderfoot."[16] Yet getting into full regalia mode in the Badlands and stocking up on new garments and accoutrements was well within character for Roosevelt, who had been a dandy at Harvard and in the state assembly. His "exaggerated style" was less a matter of being a rank tenderfoot than it was a manifestation of his personality. Accordingly, in the West he was decked out in all the cowboy splendor that New York City haberdashers could conceive. He carried ivory-handled six-shooters, his initials carved on one side of the handle and the head of a bison on the other, to commemorate his 1883 kill; so ornate a gun was rare then.[17] He wore silver spurs also emblazoned with his initials, and he strapped them to alligator boots; his belt flashed with a silver buckle engraved with the head of a grizzly, his gun belt and holster were tooled, his Colt revolver was engraved with rich scrollwork and plated in silver and gold; he carried a bowie knife, a species of weapon with a good western pedigree and related historically to the battle at the Alamo, but his was custom-made at Tiffany's.[18]

Most of his garb was, nevertheless, practical, and the styles he wore generally appropriate for the region. His wide-brimmed hat was worn in proper northern plains style, the crown flat on top, indented in a way that reduced its height to about two and a half inches.[19] Had he been ranching in the Southwest, he would have been expected to wear his hat with the seven- or eight-inch crown at full height, with three or four vertical, evenly spaced dents above his head. Cowboys spent as much as six months' wages to buy a good hat with an ornamental belt of leather or horsehair around the crown that could be tightened to adjust the fit and to keep the hat from blowing off in high wind.[20] The belts often were decorated with conches, gold nuggets, rattlesnake rattles, and other western objects. The hat's wide brim provided protection from sun and rain; the hat also could be used to carry water and to fan a kindling fire, as a pillow or for signaling a distant rider.

Roosevelt wore his hair short, a good choice in the West. Vigilantes usually hung horse thieves but sometimes showed mercy and merely ordered a culprit to get out of the region. To ensure that he did, they would notch his ears like those of a cow, marking him for a violent end if he showed up again.[21] Earmarked rowdies would sometimes grow their hair long to hide the notch; consequently, a man with "a load of hay on his skull" was distrusted.[22]

Some photographs show Roosevelt in the straight-legged "shotgun" chaps popular then in the Badlands and sometimes adorned with fringe.[23] Chaps were not worn as much in the north as in Texas, where riders needed extra protection. Roosevelt's boots peek out at the end of the chaps. The upper part of a typical cowboy boot reached almost to the knee, with a forward-sloping heel about two inches high—or higher for cowboys who paid for custom-made boots.[24] Cowboys preferred boots with pull straps sewn into the inside of the tops and rising perhaps an inch high. Long "mule ear" straps that flopped several inches over the top of the boots connoted a dude or a newcomer. Boots cost seven to fifteen dollars; custom boots could cost as much as a cowboy was willing to pay.

Cowboys were almost as particular about slacks as they were about boots.[25] They favored close-fitting wool trousers and brown jeans of duck or twill. The pockets slanted across the front rather than running along the seam, to keep objects from falling out while riding horseback. Cowboys also favored army slacks and shirts and would trade for them with soldiers.[26] The most distinctive cowboy slacks were "California pants," cut to fit almost skintight and usually striped, but sometimes buckskin colored against a darker plaid design. They generally cost about seven and a half dollars a pair and, according to one old Badlands cowpoke, were "the best pants ever made to ride in."[27] They were much preferred over Levi's, which were considered poor-man's wear or farmer slacks. Because shirts had only one pocket, and trousers were generally too tight for using the pockets, cowboys wore vests with pockets for extra storage.[28]

Like all plains cowboys, Roosevelt wore a kerchief around his neck. The kerchief was both decorative and vitally useful: When herding cattle, cowboys put the bandannas over their faces, bandit style, to keep from breathing dust.[29] Neckwear was often brightly colored, dressing up the generally brown, black, and gray clothing. Spurs, too, were partly ornamental, so Roosevelt was not far astray in embossing his with initials. Called "grappling irons" and used to control unruly horses and to dig in for added traction when a horse bucked, they were sometimes inlaid with gold or worn with straps decorated with conchas. They usually made a jingling sound, often enhanced by wearing "danglers"—pear-shaped, inch-long pendants hung from the rowel's axle.[30]

Roosevelt's Colt revolver would have been the pièce de résistance. The single-action Colt Model 1873 revolver was the most popular among cowboys, and on the range would be carried in a holster on a cartridge belt that held one full box of bullets—fifty shells; in town, handguns were concealed under coats.[31] The guns usually had handles of wood or, after 1882, of hard black rubber, so Roosevelt's ivories were a bit much. At the Golden Gun Armory in Dickinson, locals could buy Colt .45s for fourteen dollars and a hundred cartridges for two dollars and seventy-five cents.[32] Rifles were not popular in the Badlands once the Indians ceased to be a threat, because they added weight to a horse's load and could interfere with roping.[33] Some ranchmen would not permit their cowboys to carry rifles.

Badlands cowboys were not particularly skilled at shooting. One 1880s resident guesstimated that about a third of the cowboys in the Medora area could be called really good shots.[34] A few were superior and a mortal danger to all who challenged them. Just carrying a firearm openly could invite trouble. The English rancher Richard Townshend, who arrived in Colorado in 1869, was warned early on that carrying a gun "is all right riding out on the range. But if you go around these yer' frontier towns with it slung to your tail, it's kind of a challenge, and some feller's liable to take you on sudden and make you look a fool. . . . You put that gun away in your blankets; it's right enough for the road; but in a place like this, if you want to pack a gun around, put it somewheres where folks can't see it. 'Nuff said."[35] A. T. Packard—the editor of the Medora newspaper and an opponent of carrying sidearms—urged Roosevelt to leave his six-shooters at the newspaper office when in town, to avoid run-ins with skilled gunman.[36] To make his point, Packard had a local adept put on an exhibition in which he shot simultaneously with two revolvers at two tin cans thrown in the air, hitting each one with five shots before they hit the ground. Roosevelt came away persuaded of the wisdom of Packard's perspective.

Roosevelt probably first met Packard on the chill June day of his arrival, after Bill Merrifield and Sylvane Ferris picked him up at the train station in a wagon.[37] On the way out of town they stopped at the office of the weekly *Bad Lands Cow Boy*, another de Morès venture.[38] The twenty-by-thirty-foot building of perpendicular twelve-inch planks stood under a gnarled cottonwood tree just north of the Marquis' general store and had first seen service as his blacksmith shop.[39] Marked by a sign painted in Gothic letters legible from twenty-five yards away, it was the gathering place for those who "loved conversation more than whiskey" and "who liked to smell printers' ink and feel civilized."[40] A corner of its single room, with a new wooden floor, was partitioned as living quarters for Packard, the dark-bearded, twenty-two-year-old graduate of the University of Michigan who had already worked as an editor and writer at the *Bismarck Tribune* and the *Mandan Pioneer*.[41]

Packard ran articles from the merely sordid, such as a description of how some cowboys tried to get a drunk to wrestle with Bob Roberts' bears, to the locally significant, such as the news that Howard Eaton, of the Custer Trail Ranch, had started putting up a prefabricated barn in March that threatened to become the biggest in the county.[42] Packard also ran articles of wider and more serious interest. In the issue just prior to Roosevelt's arrival, he reprinted a piece from the *Texas Lone Star Journal* that described how, at the 1882 annual meeting of leading Texas stockgrower associations, a measure was taken to "banish the deadly six-shooter from the cattlemen's belt."[43] Resolutions, unanimously passed, pledged ranchers not to employ hands who carried deadly weapons. "That spring, there was an absence of deadly encounters and shooting sprees observable throughout the range country." In 1883, no action was taken by stockmen in regard to the six-shooter and "since that time serious and deadly shots have been fired. In almost every section of the West murders are on the increase, and cowmen are too often the principal in the encounters. The six-shooter loaded with deadly cartridges is a dangerous companion for any man, especially if he should unfortunately be primed with whisky. Cattlemen should unite in aiding the enforcement of the law against the carrying of deadly weapons."

When Roosevelt entered the office, the editor and a handful of locals were gathered around the sole source of heat, a cannon stove that burned lignite coal. After introductions and greetings, Roosevelt learned that a downed telegraph wire had blocked news from the Republican convention. The members of Packard's salon were eager to know the outcome. Roosevelt held forth with a vivid report. At the end of the discussion, his demeanor—the "snap of his jaw and the expression on his face"—gave

Packard the instant impression that here was a man who could not "be driven, and the man who goes after him rough-shod will always get up against a stone wall of determination and obstinacy."[44]

On the tenth, Roosevelt was at the Maltese Cross Ranch. Ferris and Merrifield were now using the old ranch house as a stable and were living in a new, one-and-a-half-story cabin that featured such extravagances as a shingle roof and a cellar.[45] The two ranch hands slept in the room on the second floor, at least when Roosevelt was there—he took over a smaller chamber that opened off the large main room of the first floor. East of the house a vegetable garden grew near a round horse corral with a snubbing post in the center for tying reluctant mounts during saddling or breaking. Beyond the garden was a larger corral for branding cattle. Hayricks and sheds lay between the cow corral and the house. Roosevelt also had a new cowhand, a former Ohioan named George Myers.[46] Eventually Myers would start his own horse ranch, but for now he was busy digging post-holes for a four-mile barbed-wire fence the men were putting up near the river.[47] Sylvane, who had feared that Roosevelt would need to be tended to, found that he wanted "to carry his own pack."[48] Roosevelt asked Ferris to show him how to saddle his horse, and after that always equipped his horses himself, garnering points with the cowboys.

While Roosevelt was learning to saddle up, his *St. Paul Pioneer Press* interview reached the New York papers. It quoted him saying that the Republican platform was a good one, that he was a Republican, not a reformer, and that he would not leave the party to support another candidate.[49] Various independent newspapers doubted the veracity of the interview, and the *New York Evening Post* telegraphed him in Medora for confirmation as to whether he was supporting Blaine. Roosevelt's reply was published in the *Post* on June 12: "To my knowledge have had no interview for publication. Never said anything like what you report." He may have been making a cagey distinction when he said "no interview for publication."

Regardless of political developments back home, Roosevelt was pleased to find that he was doing well in the West. He had lost only about two dozen head of cattle to cold and other conditions over the winter and his herd had produced 155 calves.[50] Ruminating over this evidence of impending success, he decided to buy another thousand head and began to plan for a second ranch, to be managed by his two hunting guides from Maine, Bill Sewall and Sewall's nephew Wilmot Dow. He had written to Sewall in March, less than four weeks after Alice died, proposing that the woodsmen join him in the cattle business: "I have thought often of you. I hope my western venture turns out well; if it does, and I feel sure that you will do well for yourself by coming out with me, I shall take you and Will Dow out next August."[51] The following April, Sewall stopped in New York on his way to Maine after accompanying the remains of a deceased aunt to Illinois. He and Roosevelt talked about the cattle business, and Roosevelt repeated that he would bring Sewall to the ranch if he decided to invest further.[52]

The cost of expanding his operation began with a twenty-six-thousand-dollar check he gave Merrifield and Ferris for buying cattle.[53] The men would purchase eastern or "states" cattle, domestic animals with shorter horns and meatier bodies than a rancher could expect from the rangy, half-wild Texas longhorns.[54] Eastern cattle did not withstand the winters as well as the Texas stock, but, also unlike a longhorn, an eastern animal would not try to kill a cowboy who pulled one out of mud or quicksand and would never attack a wagon with battering, six-foot-long horns.[55] The more expensive eastern animals also were easier to ship, because with their short horns they did not need as much room in corrals and rail cars. Some ranchers were trying to cross them with longhorns to "improve" the Texas stock. Roosevelt's order for eastern stock put him on the path to creating a grade-A herd.

In addition to cattle, Roosevelt incurred other expenses. The ranch ledger for 1884 shows that of his original $14,000 investment, $13,023 went for 78 steers and 362 heifers as well as $266 for three ponies, $40 for two saddles, $50 for a buckboard, $38 for a harness, $17 for two lariats, and $216.15 for barbed wire.[56] Building the house and other expenses came to $300. His new investment would bring his total cash overhead to $40,000, about 20 percent of his total inheritance of $187,500 from his father's estate and his mother's trust.[57]

To square the new deal, Roosevelt rode on June 11 with Merrifield and

Ferris to the Langs' to have Gregor draw up a contract that, in the end, used mostly the language of the first.[58] They signed the paper on the twelfth. That day, Roosevelt mentioned to Lincoln Lang that he wanted to shoot a pronghorn and to get a buckskin suit; the boy came up with a plan to achieve both. He told Roosevelt that a woman named Maddox, who lived "at a desolate little mud road ranch on the Deadwood trail" about twenty-five miles from the Lang place, sewed first-class buckskin garments "of great durability." Between her ranch and the Langs' lay good pronghorn country.[59] He and Roosevelt could ride to her place and shoot along the way.

The sun shone brightly as the duo rode up the river valley, flanked by sheer bluffs.[60] The greening grass was dappled with spring blossoms, the river valley thick with fodder, the air scented with the fragrance of silvery purple sagebrush. Cattle fed peacefully, stopping to watch the riders pass by. Birds called from all sides. Overhead, western kingbirds, about the size of robins, with gray backs and yellow breasts, dive-bombed hawks that ducked and swooped to avoid the attacks.

The ride would cover fifty miles round trip, but Roosevelt found time to take a shot at a coyote and to inspect plants and birds new to him. The men also saved a half-grown jackrabbit they found suffocating in the coils of a bull snake. After they beat the snake to death with their quirts, Roosevelt held the rabbit in the crook of his arm until it was recovered enough to limp off. "There goes a sore but wiser rabbit," Roosevelt remarked.

They soon came to a gulch that allowed them to ride out of the river valley and on to the broken plains above, where travel was easier. There they began to see pronghorn antelope—tan and white animals with black markings that are not really antelope; their closest living relatives are goats, and they themselves are the lone species in a family all their own. They are unique among horned animals in that their forked horns, usually found only on the males, or bucks, shed the black outer layer each year. Pronghorn are the fastest mammals on the continent and one of the fastest in the world, capable of hitting sixty miles per hour. Prior to European settlement in the West, pronghorn mingled with bison and elk on western grasslands and may have numbered forty million as late as the 1870s.[61] By 1908, the U.S. Biological Survey estimated that only about seventeen thousand remained after years of uncontrolled hunting. At the time Roosevelt came to the Badlands, pronghorn had become wary; on that first morning he decided not to stalk them, because the wind was to his back, making it easier for the animals to scent him.

Roosevelt and Lang came that afternoon to the house of Old Lady Maddox, as she was locally called, though she was probably not yet forty. She was, however, one of the first women to come into the Badlands, "a true pioneer and always a grand woman to those who took her right."[62] Lang: "Heavy set, muscular, rather short of stature, with strong regular features, her direct, honest-looking eyes always held a warm twinkle for her friends and a suggestion of cold steel for her enemies. Strong, active, altogether fearless, a dead shot with a rifle, familiar with every aspect of frontier life, she was well qualified to hold her own under the strenuous conditions pertaining to that period." She had been married to a man who "was a worthless devil."[63] Once, drunk on whisky he had obtained from a group of Missouri bullwhackers, he had tried to beat her, and she had knocked him senseless with an iron stove-lid handle. The bullwhackers had taken him away, leaving her the sole owner of the ranch, along with a pet pronghorn fawn that hopped up on a chair to stare at Roosevelt but never let him touch it.[64]

Maddox seemed to take an instant liking to Roosevelt, chatting volubly, something she rarely did. She took his measurements and promised him a suit in two weeks or so; it actually would be made by Mrs. Maddox's niece, though under the older woman's direction.[65]

For Theodore Roosevelt this buckskin suit, with its "fringed tunic or hunting-shirt . . . belted in at the waist," was more than just hide and thread; it was a symbol of the American frontier and "the most picturesque and distinctively national dress ever worn in America. It was the dress in which Daniel Boone was clad when he first passed through the trackless forests of the Alleghanies and penetrated into the heart of Kentucky, to enjoy such hunting as no man of his race had ever had before; it was the dress worn by grim old Davy Crockett when he fell at the Alamo."[66] A buckskin suit imbued Theodore Roosevelt with the aura of backwoodsmen and allowed him to take on the living guise of Basil, the lead character in Mayne Reid's *The Boy Hunters*. Basil "was all buckskin—except the cap, which was made from the skin of a raccoon, with the ringed tail hanging over his shoulders like a drooping plume. He wore a hunting shirt with fringed cape, handsomely ornamented with beads. A belt fastened it around his waist, from which was suspended his hunting knife and sheath, with a small holster, out of which peeped the shining but[t] of a pistol. He wore deerskin leggings, fringed down the seams, and moccasins upon his feet. His dress was just that of a backwoods hunter."[67]

In the Badlands, some frontiersmen harbored a jaundiced view of buckskin garb. Howard Eaton protested that the shirt was impractical: "Buckskin shirts were all right as long as they didn't get wet, but when they got wet they'd shrunk up. I never did like that buckskin hunting shirt he had but he wouldn't have anything else."[68] One of de Morès' managers, J. C. Fisher, would say almost forty years later that his first impression of Theodore Roosevelt "was not exactly favorable; he was dressed in a fringed buckskin shirt and wore glasses. A fringe buckskin shirt, in that country at that time was indisputable evidence of the rank tenderfoot and backed up by the glasses made it a dead certainty; he was a slim, rather anemic looking young fellow then."[69]

With his buckskin suit now in progress, Roosevelt could turn back down the trail for home with a sense of accomplishment.[70] But he still had the matter of a pronghorn to settle. Along the way he and Lincoln spotted two pronghorn that apparently had not spotted them. The hunters left their horses and started to stalk. Moving in a crouch up a hill, they reached the top and looked down to see the quarry feeding peacefully unaware about a hundred yards off. With cool self-control, Roosevelt shouldered his rifle, drew a bead, and killed one of the pronghorn almost instantly. Roosevelt erupted into the sort of faux war dance that had marked his killing of the bison, brandishing his rifle in one hand and waving his hat in the other as he shouted, "I got him, I got him, I got him."

The other pronghorn, apparently confused, began running in circles, at one point coming within twenty-five yards of the two hunters. "Get him too," Lincoln shouted, but Roosevelt was too excited. The pronghorn got away, and Roosevelt told Lang that he could not have shot at the animal to save his own life. As he often did in the moments after a successful hunt, he offered Lincoln an expensive gift—his new shotgun. The teenager turned it down, thinking that once Roosevelt came to his full senses, he would regret giving it away. The two then went to the dead animal, and Roosevelt dressed it under Lang's supervision.

Roosevelt stayed with the Langs another day, shooting in the vicinity, and rode back to the Maltese Cross on the seventeenth.[71] He promptly sent his sister Anna an epistolary outpouring of good cheer over his ranching experience: "Well, I have been having a glorious time here, and am well hardened now (I have just come in from spending *thirteen* hours in the saddle). For every day I have been here I have had my hands full. First and foremost, the cattle have done well, and I regard the outlook for making the business a success as being *very* hopeful."[72] He was pleased with his personal progress. "I have never been in better health than on this trip," he told Anna. "How sound I do sleep at night now!" He added, "I am really attached to my two 'factors,' Ferris and Merrifield; they are very fine men."[73]

He was pleased, too, with the Badlands. "The country is growing on me, more and more; it has a curious, fantastic beauty of its own. . . . There is not much game however; the cattle men have crowded it out and only a few antelope and deer remain. I have shot a few jackrabbits and curlews, with the rifle; and I also killed eight rattlesnakes."[74] He added, "Tomorrow my two men go east for the cattle; and I will start out alone to try my hand at finding my way over the prairie by myself. I intend to take a two months trip in the Fall, for hunting." He wanted to stay away from the presidential campaign and even from election day; he would return to New York City soon, he told Anna, and would visit his wife's parents at Chestnut Hill, though in none of his letters home did he ask about or even mention his daughter.

The day he arrived at the Maltese Cross, he found a telegram from Henry Cabot Lodge, an ardent anti-Blaine Bostonian who had been one of Roosevelt's closest allies at the Chicago convention. Having read no newspaper since arriving in the Badlands, Roosevelt did not know until he received Lodge's wire that a political tempest had followed the Blaine nomination, with leading Republicans and Republican papers switching to the Democrats.[75] Moreover, the *New York Evening Post* had accepted

Roosevelt's telegraphed denial of the St. Paul interview and was editorializing that he intended to desert the Republican Party in opposition to Blaine.[76] Roosevelt, however, had not yet made up his mind.

Meanwhile, Lodge, running for the House of Representatives from Massachusetts, had refused to bolt the Republican Party and so had drawn the disdain of his upper-crust Boston friends. He was snubbed on the street; one former friend said of Lodge's decision to support Blaine, "I call it not a change of mind but a change of soul."[77] Lodge: "It was the bitterest thing I ever had to do in my life. All my friends (social) with few exceptions went into the bolt. . . . it was mere truism that I had sold my conscience for a Congressional nomination."[78] Roosevelt wrote from the Maltese Cross that he was ignorant of what had transpired in the East and ended, "I hope soon to be back when I will see you and decide with you as to what we can do."[79]

He soon received from Lodge a longer letter about the Blaine situation and the Minnesota interview. Roosevelt again denied the interview and added, in regard to Lodge's decision to stay in the Republican Party, "You are pursuing precisely the proper course; do not answer any assaults unless it is imperatively necessary; keep on good terms with the machine, and put in every ounce, to win. . . . I am very anxious you should take no steps hastily."[80] It would appear, then, that Roosevelt was denying his support for Blaine and the party in public but urging cooperation with Blaine and the Stalwarts in private.

On the eighteenth, Merrifield and Ferris left for Minnesota to buy cattle, and Roosevelt—leaving politics behind—took off alone across the prairie "in the very earliest morning, when the intense brilliancy of the stars had just begun to pale before the first streak of dawn."[81] He was living a childhood ambition of "playing at frontier hunter," which involved riding the plains alone with horse and rifle to see if he "could not do perfectly well without a guide."[82] He also was inaugurating the physical testing of himself, the building of health and strength, in the mode of the pioneer—a man against the wild.

By the time the sun was rising into a rosy glow, he was riding up a winding creek valley that would lead him out of the Badlands. "The air was fresh and sweet, and odorous with the sweet scents of the spring-time that was barely passed; the dew lay heavy, in glittering drops, on the leaves and the blades of grass, whose vivid green, at this season, for a short time brightens the desolate and sterile-looking wastes of the lonely western plains. The rose-bushes were all in bloom, and their pink blossoms clustered in every point and bend of the stream; and the sweet, sad songs of the hermit thrushes rose from the thickets, while the meadow larks perched boldly in sight as they uttered their louder and more cheerful music."[83] The coo of the mourning dove may have struck a personal chord, as he wrote that its voice "always seems far away and expresses more than any other sound in nature the sadness of gentle, hopeless, never-ending grief."[84] The curlews, with their long, drooping bills, seemed to annoy him: "Whenever they discover a wagon or a man on horseback, they fly toward him, though usually taking good care to keep out of gunshot. They then fly over and round the object, calling all the time, and sometimes going off to one side, where they will light and run rapidly through the grass; in this manner they will sometimes accompany a hunter or traveller for miles, scaring off all game."[85]

He rode up red scoria buttes, passed magpies perched on a buffalo skull, and finally came out on "the great, seemingly endless stretches of rolling or nearly level prairie, over which I had planned to travel and hunt for the next two or three days."[86] The sun was by then high and beat down from a cloudless sky. On his saddle hung a telescope, and he periodically scanned the country for wildlife. The immense and empty reach of the country sank in on him: "Nowhere, not even at sea, does a man feel more lonely than when riding over the far-reaching, seemingly never-ending plains . . . their very vastness and loneliness and their melancholy monotony have a strong fascination for him. The landscape seems always the same, and after the traveller has plodded for miles and miles he gets to feel as if the distance was indeed boundless. . . . Nowhere else does one seem so far off from all mankind; the plains stretch out in death-like and measure-less expanse, and as he journeys over them they will for many miles be lacking in all signs of life."[87] Objects shimmered and danced in the heat of the sun, and distances became hard to judge: "A mile off one can see, through the strange shimmering haze, the shadowy white outlines of something which looms vaguely up till it looks as large as the canvas-top of a prairie wagon; but as the horseman comes nearer it shrinks and dwindles and takes clearer form, until at last it changes into the ghastly staring skull of some mighty buffalo, long dead and gone to join the rest of his vanished race."[88]

He tried to stalk pronghorn twice in the morning heat, spending an hour each time wriggling through the bush, his hat off, only to have the animals flee before he got within range. He fired half a dozen times into one retreating herd, on the premise that he had to "expend a good deal of powder and lead before bagging" pronghorn, but in the end he expended much and bagged none.

For lunch he stopped at a small pool along an otherwise dry creek, watering himself and his horse before setting down for a biscuit. He dozed for a couple hours, giving the horse time to eat, then mounted up. Almost immediately he mired in quicksand, but he was able to flounder out. Sometime in the afternoon he rode over a hill and found a band of six to eight pronghorn about a quarter mile to his right. The wind blew to the game from him; the animals looked up to see him, then broke into a run that would take them straight across the direction Roosevelt was traveling. He clapped his monogrammed spurs to the side of his horse and took out at a flat run. Horse and herd converged, and as the two leading pronghorn crossed in front of him, Roosevelt pulled up short, leaped from his horse, fired at a fine buck about forty yards away, "and as the smoke blew off I saw the buck roll over like a rabbit, with both shoulders broken. I then emptied the Winchester at the rest of the band, breaking one hind leg of a young buck."[89] But the injured animal got away—the day was hot, and Roosevelt did not want to tire his horse at the start of the trip by pursing a still fleet, though lame, quarry.

Roosevelt cut out the pronghorn's hams—the lightweight animals, designed for speed, carry little other meat—and took its head for a trophy. He next found a good-sized creek and stopped for the night in a bend with shade trees for firewood and with good grass for the horse. He was traveling light, with a blanket for bedding, an oilskin coat for rain, a large metal cup for boiling water, some tea and salt and biscuits, and a waterproof bag containing half a dozen personal items, including a book.[90] He soon had water boiling for tea and a pronghorn steak roasting on a forked stick. Roosevelt: "It was wonderful how cosy a camp, in clear weather, becomes if there is a good fire and enough to eat, and how sound the sleep is afterwards in the cool air, with the brilliant stars glimmering through the branches overhead."[91]

He resumed hunting the next day, succeeding in shooting a pronghorn at three hundred yards—"It was a very good shot; the best I ever made at antelope." And so the trip continued. One night it rained, but he learned that he could cope with such hardship, that "a man becomes able to roll up in a wet blanket and sleep all night in a pelting rain without hurting himself—though he will shiver a good deal, and feel pretty numb and stiff in those chill and dreary hours just before dawn."[92]

After four days he turned back toward the ranch. "In the dusk the brown level land stretched out in formless expanse ahead of me, unrelieved, except by the bleached white of a buffalo's skull, whose outlines glimmered indistinctly to one side of the course I was riding. On my left the sun had set behind a row of jagged buttes, that loomed up in sharp relief against the western sky; above them it had left a bar of yellow light, which only made more intense the darkness of the surrounding heavens. In the quarter toward which I was heading there had gathered a lowering mass of black storm-clouds, lit up by the incessant play of the lightning. The wind had totally died away, and the death-like stillness was only broken by the continuous, measured beat of the horse's hoofs as he galloped over the plain, and at times by the muttered roll of the distant thunder."[93]

A storm burst over him, torrents of rain drenching him within minutes, and he had to guide himself by flashes of lightning that illuminated the landscape. "I was right glad, half an hour afterward, to stop and take shelter in the log hut of a couple of cowboys, where I could get dry and warm."

He reached the Maltese Cross that night but the next day headed north toward town, planning to seek out a place where he could establish a second ranch site. He wanted more isolated living quarters than the Maltese Cross, which could be reached from Medora on horseback in as little as twenty-seven minutes and stood adjacent to a frequently traveled trail.[94] As he rode north he met Howard Eaton of the Custer Trail Ranch heading south; Eaton told him to take a look at a bottomland about thirty miles upriver from town, near where Eaton himself had established another ranch.

Along the way, Roosevelt stopped at the Medora newspaper office, and Packard told him that messages on the wire indicated the St. Paul interview had trigged virulent reactions back east. Roosevelt responded that the ado was caused by the stupidity of the press. Packard duly reported in the next issue of the paper, "Theodore Roosevelt, the young New York reformer, made us a very pleasant call Monday, in full cow-boy regalia. New York will certainly lose him for a time at least, as he is perfectly charmed with our free western life and is now figuring on a trip into the Big Horn country. He is perfectly non-committal on politics and the alleged interview with him, published in the St. Paul Pioneer-Press, speaks more for the reporter's assininity than for his perspicacity."[95]

After visiting with Packard, Roosevelt moved down river and found the spot Eaton had recommended. A curve in the river was flanked by tall buttes, with a stand of cottonwoods and a grassy meadow to the west. A trapper, reportedly named Henry Bennett, already had a cabin nearby; to remove his tenuous claim, Roosevelt paid him four hundred or five hundred dollars.[96]

Roosevelt had accomplished a lot during little more than two weeks in the Badlands and was planning to leave for home at the end of June. Meanwhile, he had made the acquaintance of the Marquis de Morès. A couple of months before Roosevelt arrived in Medora, the Montana Stockgrowers' Association, under the presidency of rancher Granville Stuart, had met and decided to take private rather than official action against thieves who had accounted for hundreds of stolen horses, including two hundred from the Medora area.[97] On June 24, de Morès attended a meeting of select ranchers and cowboys at which Stuart explained that he wanted to organize a vigilante committee to take care of the marauders. De Morès wanted to sign up, but Stuart told him the group had to avoid the sort of attention the Marquis' presence would draw. De Morès complained to Roosevelt about this situation at some point, and on June 26 the two went to Miles City, Montana, to plead for a role in the vigilantes. However, Stuart made clear that their eminent social positions made their participation impossible. Roosevelt, who did not protest too much over the refusal, later seemed glad that he did not take part. In his *Autobiography*, he alleged, "The vigilantes, or stranglers, as they were locally known, did their work thoroughly; but, as always happens with bodies of this kind, toward the end they grew reckless in their actions, and paid off private grudges, and hung men on slight provocation."[98]

7

THE POLITICIAN

ROOSEVELT LEFT MEDORA AT THE END OF JUNE 1884 FOR NEW YORK City, where he stayed with his sister Anna at 422 Madison Avenue. Soon after his arrival he wrote to his friend and former Maine hunting guide, Bill Sewall, laying the groundwork for bringing Sewall and his nephew Wilmot Dow out west. "I enclose you the check of three thousand, for yourself and Will Dow, to pay off the mortgage, etc., etc. I have arranged matters in the west, have found a good place for a ranche, and have purchased a ~~thousand~~ hundred head of cattle, for you to start with."[1] He explained that the work would be hard and that during the first two years the men would not be likely to earn "much more" than they were at present, but he predicted that they would make "about a thousand dollars for the third year, with an unlimited rise ahead of you and a future as bright as you yourself choose to make it."

The promise of a thousand dollars was better than most cowboys received. The maximum monthly wage in the 1880s for a top hand was forty dollars, while a marginal hand might start at twenty-five dollars; a foreman might make fifty to eighty dollars, though on a big ranch as much as two hundred.[2] Roosevelt was cutting in his men for a share of the profits.

Roosevelt added, "Now, I take it for granted that you will not hesitate at this time. So fix up your affairs *at once*, and be ready to start before the end of this week." Roosevelt was in haste: "We must be on the ranche by August 1st, as I can not hold it longer. So write me as soon as you receive this letter, telling me the earliest possible day at which you can be ready— and make it as early as possible." He concluded: "And write *at once*."

He then turned to family matters. His daughter Alice was living in Anna's house, of course, and he planned to take her to see her maternal grandparents at Chestnut Hill, but almost immediately upon arriving at Madison Avenue he left to visit his sister Corinne in New Jersey, leaving Alice behind. His hasty departure after reuniting with his daughter, combined with the absence of any mention of her in his recent letters to his family, suggests he was trying to shut her out of his mind.

His diaries offer no comment on his feelings about his daughter, but his relationship with another woman indicates how memories of his wife affected him. A frequent overnight guest at Anna's house was Edith Carow, who was also his sister Corinne's closest friend.[3] Roosevelt asked Anna to warn him if Edith was going to visit the house, so he could make sure he was not there.

During Roosevelt's childhood, Edith and her family had lived with her father's older sister in a large house that backed to the Fourteenth Street mansion of Cornelius Van Schaack Roosevelt. Theodore's parents socialized with Edith's parents, and the children of both broods became "pledged friends from the time of their birth."[4] When the Roosevelts traveled, letters from Edith seemed always to make little Theodore homesick.[5] In the early 1870s, Edith was a member of a group Corinne formed to meet weekly for lemonade, donuts, and the reading of one another's poetry and other wordcraft.[6] Initially they called themselves the Paradise of Ravenous Eaters, later the Party of Renowned Eligibles.

Edith Carow's paternal grandfather was not unlike Theodore's. He headed one of New York City's richest shipping families.[7] Her father, Charles, married Gertrude Elizabeth Tyler of Connecticut, whose family was connected with Jonathan Edwards, a prominent New England revivalist preacher of five generations earlier.[8] Edith received an excellent education in New York and Paris and became an avid reader who "loved music, was appreciative of the arts, and spoke and read French fluently."[9]

She was bookish as a child and came from a bookish family. At Miss Comstock's private school on West Fortieth Street, Edith's schoolmates thought her pretty, elegant in fine dress, but distant, more inclined to slip off alone to read than to engage in girlish chatter. "I believe you could live in the same house with Edith for fifty years and never really know her," one schoolmate said.[10] Perhaps a critical factor in Edith's background made her uneasy with others or made her shun intimacy: From her sixth year onward, her family had no home of its own, and her father had no job.[11] Income from Charles' shipping business had dropped at the same time that prices rose after the Civil War. The Carows were forced to live with relatives, moving from house to house with the seasons. In later years Charles suffered a breakdown—likely a euphemism for drinking—and lost much of his money.

Nevertheless, Edith and Theodore were close. They attended dance school together in the early 1870s, and at social events during that time his name appeared on her dance cards more often than the names of other boys.[12] They were so close that friends "in the days of their youth took for granted that these two would marry."[13] Edith in later life said that Theodore had proposed to her several times in 1877 and 1878, and family members of both sides corroborated her statement.[14] Something went awry between them, however, in August 1878, when she visited the Roosevelts at Tranquillity. Theodore occupied much of her time, taking her sailing on the nineteenth, rowing the next day, and for a drive to Cold Spring to pick water lilies the day after that. On the twenty-second they sailed, attended an evening party, and then went to the summer house, where a dispute, the details of which they never publicly divulged, caused a break in their relationship.[15]

Theodore's subsequent behavior seems a casebook example of redirected anger: Two days after the rupture he shot a neighbor's dog when it barked at him as he rode by on his horse; shortly after that incident he sailed out into Long Island Sound with some cousins and shot at anything in the water, including bottles, buoys, sharks, and dolphins.[16] He mentioned the breakup cryptically to his sister Anna in an 1886 letter: "Eight years ago she and I had very intimate relations; one day there came a break, for we both of us had, and I suppose have, tempers that were far from being of the best. To no soul now living have either of us ever since spoken of this."[17] "Now living" implies that one or both of them discussed the matter with his or her parents.

Whatever had happened, they remained friends. She hosted a party for him on October 13, 1880, two weeks before his wedding.[18] She also attended the wedding, saying later that she had "danced the soles off her shoes" at the reception.[19] She was one of eight bridesmaids when Corinne married Douglas Robinson on April 29, 1882.[20] When Theodore won his seat in the Assembly in November that year, Edith honored him with a celebratory party in the townhouse at 114 East Thirty-sixth Street, where she and her family lived.[21]

In November 1882 Edith's maternal grandfather died, leaving forty-seven thousand dollars to Edith's mother, with the will requiring that the money be left invested and that the mother take only the interest, about five thousand dollars yearly, for the remainder of her life.[22] Though not wealthy, the family seems to have preserved its status. In 1883, Edith was selected to dance the star quadrille at Alva Vanderbilt's Easter Monday "Ball of the Century," a costume party that featured Mrs. Cornelius Vanderbilt dressed as an electric lightbulb, resplendent in white satin trimmed with diamonds. However, Edith's father died from the effects of alcohol abuse on March 17, 1883, at age fifty-eight, and the proprieties of mourning forced Edith to miss the party.[23]

Edith clearly was of Roosevelt's social class and a friend from his earliest years; after Alice's death he sought to avoid her because, with their history, he might find himself still attracted to her.[24] Such an attraction would threaten his assurance that, as a widower, life was over for him, a conviction based on "that awful sentimentality about the concept that you loved only once and you never loved again."[25] So there it stood: If Edith was at the house, Anna must forewarn him.

In addition to being the guardian of Theodore's fidelity, Anna had become a surrogate mother for little Alice, who would say in later years that Anna "quickly became cherished. She was the only one I really cared about when I was a child. . . . She was the single most important influence on my childhood."[26] Alice would remember Anna's house as fragrant with the scent of baking bread, a place where the food was always good, where

for afternoon tea she enjoyed steaming Earl Grey with generously but-
tered bread cut paper thin.[27] In later years Anna, whom Alice called Auntie Bye, would provide the girl with the few tenuous links she would ever
have with her mother. Initially, Theodore dubbed his child "Baby Lee" to
avoid even the name she shared with her mother. "[He] never ever mentioned my mother to me," Alice said years later.[28] "And my maternal
grandparents, with whom I stayed every year in Boston, never mentioned
her either. Nor my aunts. Finally, Auntie Bye did tell me something very
revealing, such as that she had been very pretty or attractive. . . . The
whole thing was really handled very badly."[29]

Roosevelt's silence about his wife extended well beyond his daughter.
In his *Autobiography*, published after his terms in the White House, he
never mentioned her. He took for himself advice he would give some
twenty-five years later to his sister Corinne when her daughter's fiancé
died: "The one and only thing for her to do now is to treat the past as past,
the event as finished and out of her life; to dwell on it . . . would be both
weak and morbid. Let her try not to think of it; this she cannot wholly
avoid; but she can wholly avoid speaking of it . . . let her never speak a
word of the matter, henceforth, to you or to anyone else. In the long future, when the memory is too dead to throb, she may if she wishes again
speak of it; but if she is wise and brave she will not speak of it now."[30] Roosevelt biographer Carleton Putnam commented on Roosevelt's advice for
Corinne—and indirectly on Roosevelt's reaction to Alice's death—when
he wrote, "To order a young woman never to speak to her mother of her
dead fiancé is Spartan beyond reason. It contains more than a trace of the
abnormal."[31]

After returning from New Jersey, Roosevelt took Alice to Massachusetts
to visit her grandparents' home for the first time. Seeing his daughter in
the setting in which he had first met her mother must have compounded
his melancholy. For Alice, though, the visit was the beginning of a beautiful relationship with her forebears. "I loved it there because I had much
more freedom and could do exactly as I pleased," Alice wrote in her 1933
autobiography. "I ran wild there and really hated to go back to Sagamore

[Theodore Roosevelt's later home] and the dreary round of tea in the play-room with crustless brown bread instead of the delicious French rolls I had become accustomed to at the Lees'.... and the moment I got home I would start crying and sniffling. For at least three days I was desperately homesick for my grandparents."[32]

After only a few days at Chestnut Hill, Roosevelt left Alice to visit Henry Cabot Lodge at his summer home in Nahant, Massachusetts. Lodge had experienced heavy fire from reformers who thought he had abandoned the cause by endorsing Blaine.[33] When Roosevelt returned to Chestnut Hill on Saturday, July 19, he immediately set up an interview with a reporter from the *Boston Herald* and announced that he too would not bolt the party but would support Blaine and fight corruption from within. In taking this position, Roosevelt was bucking such powerful anti-Blaine forces as Harvard president Charles W. Eliot, most of the Harvard faculty, and the Lee family itself. Roosevelt was convinced that his deci-sion would cost him his political career, but he was already acting in ac-cord with a belief he would formulate in later years, that when a politician "begins to consider the possible effect of his actions upon his own political future, he loses his public usefulness."[34] He told the *Boston Herald* re-porter, "I intend to vote the Republican presidential ticket.... I am going back in a day or two to my Western ranches, as I do not expect to take any part in the campaign this fall."[35]

That he intended to avoid campaigning should have been a clue to re-formers that he was still on their side, but instead they dunned him with letters, leading him to remark, "Most of my friends seem surprised to find that I have not developed hoofs and horns."[36] He declared that those who bolted the party "were suffering just at present from a species of moral myopia, complicated with intellectual strabismus."[37]

Editors at independent newspapers, such as the *Evening Post,* may have felt betrayed after accepting Roosevelt's refutation of the St. Paul inter-view.[38] It seemed now that Roosevelt had been in the Blaine camp all along. At least some of the Lee family felt put out. Henry Lee said to his cousin, Roosevelt's father-in-law, George Lee, "You can tell that young whipper-snapper in New York from me that his independence was the only thing in him we cared for, and if he has gone back on that, we don't care to hear anything more about him."[39]

How Roosevelt's former allies at the Chicago convention felt might be gleaned from William Roscoe Thayer's response: "I was dum[b]founded. . . . My old acquaintance, our trusted leader, whose career in the New York Assembly we had watched with an almost holy satisfaction, seemed to have strangely abandoned the fundamental principles which we and he had believed in, and he had so nobly upheld. . . . We assumed that because he was with us in the crusade for pure politics, he agreed with us in the estimate that we put on party loyalty. . . . There was nothing sacred in a political party."[40] Roosevelt, however, believed that "party transcended persons, and that only in the gravest case imaginable was one justified in bolting his party because one disapproved of its candidate." Thayer understood Roosevelt's thinking but still at the time rejected it: "If the rule, 'My man, or nobody,' were to prevail, there would be no use in holding conventions at all. . . . Nevertheless, Roosevelt's decision, in 1884, to cleave to the Republican Party disappointed many of us. We thought of him as a lost leader."

For the moment, Roosevelt gave up politics. Too stricken after Alice's death to seek reelection to the New York Assembly, he also refused two separate offers to run for Congress and, after the 1884 convention, retired from public life.[41] By the end of July, he had arranged for Bill Sewall and Wilmot Dow to meet him in New York City for the train ride to the Badlands.

What credentials of his two former Maine guides would account for this plan are hard to imagine, since neither had ranching experience, though he did believe "they were tough, hardy, resolute fellows, quick as cats, strong as bears, and able to travel like bull moose."[42] While at Harvard, Roosevelt had spent a total of sixty-nine days on three trips to Maine, during which he had covered more than a thousand miles, shooting mostly ducks and grouse but also a deer, a lynx, a fox, and a raccoon.[43] He also unsuccessfully pursued woodland caribou, a species now extinct in the state. He was nineteen when he first met Sewall and Dow in September 1878.[44]

Fifteen years older than Roosevelt, Sewall was a robust outdoorsman with a massive full beard and a lifetime of wood lore—he could turn an axe and a copse of trees into a complete house. He provided Roosevelt with his first, and favorable, experience with men outside his own class. Roosevelt found that he was comfortable with this physically imposing outdoorsman who shared his own strong views about right and wrong, morality and principle. Sewall: "We hitched well, somehow or other, from the start. He was different from anybody that I had ever met; especially, he was fair-minded. He and I agreed in our ideas of fair play and right and wrong. Besides, he was always good-natured and full of fun. I do not think I ever remember him being 'out of sorts.' He did not feel well sometimes, but he never would admit it."[45] Perhaps most significantly, Sewall shared Roosevelt's infatuation with the pioneer past: "I have always been glad that I was destined to live at this time, although I feel that I should have enjoyed living a hundred years sooner. All the tales of the pioneers are dear to me, and I have always believed I could have gotten along peacefully with the Indians of old."[46]

Sewall was in fact the pioneer type Roosevelt admired. His parents had been the first settlers in Island Falls, Maine, where Sewall was born on April 13, 1845, in a sixteen-by-twenty-six-foot log house.[47] He made an early commitment to learning the lore of the woodlands: When twelve years old, he watched an Indian build a birch-bark canoe "in order that I might know how to do it myself if the time should ever come when I myself had need of such a craft. I wished to make note of every detail in the process."[48]

Like Theodore Roosevelt, Sewall was sickly as a baby. He had suffered fever and an earache as a small child after falling into a snowbank and could not play in snow or rain without becoming ill. He envied strong, healthy children. But he had to take on the challenges of a hard life. His father suffered a serious illness that forced the children to work at logging in winter, at moving logs down streams in spring, at clearing land for farming in summer, and at harvesting grain in fall. In the summer of his sixteenth year, Sewall recalled, "Brother Sam and I took four acres of trees to cut. We got twelve dollars for the job and were much pleased to earn that much real money. We had to go five or six miles to reach our work." The three thousand dollars Roosevelt had sent him in June must have seemed a fortune.

By his late teens, Sewall had emerged from this life empowered. "I had now reached the time of life to which I had always looked forward hopefully. I was satisfied with what the Lord had given me. They tell us that 'prayer is the desire of the heart,' and I had desired above all things to be well and strong. I was *both* now. I was six feet tall, weighed 180 pounds and could endure more hardship than most men of equal or greater size. I felt I was at the head of my class."

While still in Massachusetts, Roosevelt wrote to Sewall with urgency: "We will leave New York early on the morning of the 28th; so be there, with all your outfit, some time on Sunday the 27th, *without fail*; come to my house, 422 Madison Avenue; I will have your tickets bought."[49] He closed, "Be sure you allow enough time to get to New York by the evening of the 27th (Sunday)."

Sewall arrived as planned, his sister's son, Will Dow, ten years Sewall's junior, in tow. Sewall: "We all started for Dakota together on July 28th. We reached Chimney Butte Ranch . . . on the 1st of August."[50] Sewall's initial impression of the cattle country was that "the man who first called that part of the world the 'Bad Lands' had hit it about right."

8

A TIME OF PREPARATION

When Sewall and Dow arrived in Dakota Territory, the Badlands region was enjoying unusually good grass growth. Someone reputed to be the area's oldest inhabitant said he could not recall "a more prolonged season of verdure in the northwest than at present."[1] Nevertheless, when Roosevelt asked Sewall, at the end of his first day on the Maltese Cross Ranch, what he thought of the Badlands, Sewall responded that he "liked the country well enough, but . . . didn't believe that it was much of a cattle country."[2]

Roosevelt, sounding a touch put out, said, "Well, Bill, you don't know anything about it. Everybody here says that it is."

Sewall replied that while it was true he did not know anything about it, it was also true that to him it did not look like very good cattle country—ironic, given that he was soon to take charge of the new ranch, a process that would begin the next day.[3]

About a week before Roosevelt's return, Bill Merrifield and Sylvane Ferris had driven a thousand head of yearlings and two-year-olds—"said to be the best lot of cattle shipped west this year"—from the Medora train stop to the Maltese Cross.[4] Wishing to break in Sewall and Dow slowly, Roosevelt had a hundred head of his original herd cut out for the new hands to "practice on this winter." On the easterners' second day in the Badlands, he sent them downriver to the new ranch under the guidance of a local herder remembered only as Captain Robins. Small, dark-complexioned, his face almost obscured by a beard half an inch long, Robins had been a sailor and a trapper and had learned to work cattle in South America.[5] He had served for a time as the Langs' cook.[6] The three men started out with the cattle early on August 2. Once in the saddle, the woodsmen looked discomforted and unhappy; Sewall remarked that his only previous equestrian experience was riding logs.[7] His horse was equally inexperienced with riders: When Sewall spurred, the horse began kicking and rolled over with him into a washout.[8]

The ride to the new ranch took two days, in part because cattle move slowly, about twenty miles per day, but also because the river was high, forcing the neophyte cowboys to take the herd out of the Badlands and across the higher prairie, then back to the river.[9] It was not a task calcu-lated to please the Maine men, especially Sewall; his roughly trained mare was hard to control and problem enough, but he also took a dislike to Robins, who he soon concluded was "a man of many orders."[10] Sewall made slow progress with his recalcitrant horse and could not help with the herding to the extent that Robins wanted. Finally Robins vehemently commanded him to hurry up. Sewall replied with equal vehemence that he was doing as well as he could and "wasn't going to be found fault with."[11] He also told Robins never to speak to him "in such a manner as that again as long as you live."[12]

Robins later said to Dow, "That Sewall is a kind of quick-tempered fellow."[13]

"I don't think he is," Dow replied.

"He snapped me up."

"You must have said something to him, for he ain't in the habit of doing such things."

Robins did not pursue the subject, but a few days later, when he knew the woodsmen better, he told Roosevelt, "You've got two good men here, Mr. Roosevelt. That Sewall don't calculate to bear anything. I spoke to him the other day, and he snapped me up so short I did not know what to make of it. But I don't blame him. I did not speak to him as I ought." Roosevelt diplomatically passed on this comment to Sewall, and Sewall and Robins worked well together afterward.

While Sewall and Dow were in training, Roosevelt was at loose ends. He was planning to hunt in Wyoming's Bighorn Mountains and was waiting for his men to put together supplies for the trip.[14] Meanwhile, he killed time in almost aimless wandering. First he rode from the Maltese Cross Ranch to visit the Langs, delivering to them their good friend Massiter, a globe-trotting big-game hunter from England whom Roosevelt had met on the train trip to Medora.[15]

During the visit, Roosevelt and Massiter hunted waterfowl on foot— fully fledged mallard ducks that could not yet fly. The men frightened them into stands of pond reeds, "there to enjoy a vast amount of fun in chasing them, since they proved to be about as illusive as so many blue-racers."[16] Roosevelt also may have caught up on local gossip with the Langs. They could hardly have avoided discussing Granville Stuart and his vigilantes, the Stranglers, who had been working the region just across the border in Montana, with occasional forays into the Badlands.[17] Although the Stranglers were an extralegal group, the Montana legislature supported them, and the territorial governor, in his 1884 annual report to the secretary of the federal Department of the Interior, contended that "some application of hemp and lead" was necessary to stop rampant live-stock thieves; he added, "It is useless to complain of these violations of the forms of law, as our people feel that self-protection is the older and stronger law."[18]

After two days with the Langs, Roosevelt rode to the new ranch. He found Robins, Sewall, and Dow working well together, and he pitched in to help. Because the hundred Minnesota shorthorns the three men had brought in were new to the ranch, they were not yet at home there. To keep them from wandering off, Robins put them on "close herd," keeping them near the house on a bottomland about a mile square and walled in with cliffs.[19] Each day at dusk the men drove the cattle out of nearby valleys where they had been grazing and bedded them by the river. Then the men took turns riding in circles around the animals through the night in two-hour shifts, or "tricks."[20] This activity probably marked Roosevelt's first real work on either of his ranches.

It may have been during this time that Roosevelt, exploring with Sewall, found two elk skulls with locked antlers.[21] Looking at the two skulls, Roosevelt remarked to Sewall, "Theirs had been a duel to the death."[22] He named his ranch the Elkhorn.

Sewall was learning quickly about Badlands life and was not as enamored of it as Roosevelt was. Writing to his brother Sam, at home in Maine, he declared, "It is not hard work to look after [the cattle] and it is not the plan to work very hard here the workers are a lazy set I think. . . . It is a dirty country and very dirty people on an average but I think it is healthy. . . . The river is the meanest apology for a frog pond that I ever saw. . . . It is a queer country. You would like to see it but you would not want to live here long."[23] He added, "If I had enough money to start here I never would come. Think the country ought to have been left to the animals that have laid their bones here."[24]

Sewall, Dow, and Robins were sleeping outdoors while cleaning up the hunter's shack that Roosevelt had purchased with the new ranch site, but the shack would be a temporary dwelling at most.[25] Sewall: "The first thing we had to do was to build a ranch-house of hewn cottonwood logs, the only timber in the country. It was thirty feet wide and sixty feet long. . . . Walls seven feet high, flat roof. We had to send to Minneapolis for lumber for the roof."[26] Also in the plans was a branding corral to go up about two or three miles from the house, for use during the seasonal roundups.[27] The two Maine woodsmen were soon back in their own element, felling trees, hewing off branches, trimming up logs.

In the evenings at either ranch, Roosevelt would read books by the hour.[28] He had advised his men that he did not want to discuss politics— he had come west, he said, to "forget all about that."[29] Sylvane Ferris recalled that they were happy to avoid the topic. "We were all on the reservation, anyhow, we did not have any vote, and had no interest in national affairs. We were in the Dakota Territory at that time."[30]

Roosevelt, on the other hand, was in the Badlands in part *because* of politics; he told Howard Eaton, "For the present I am out here because I cannot get up any enthusiasm for the Republican candidate, and it seems to me that punching cattle is the best way to avoid campaigning."[31] Roosevelt's political thinking was self-contradictory, however. He told Henry Cabot Lodge in an August 12 letter that he was planning to campaign for the Blaine ticket in the fall.[32] The same day he wrote Anna, "I think it will be a good many years before I get back into politics."[33]

While at the Elkhorn, Roosevelt received a curt letter from the Marquis de Morès saying that the New Yorker had no right to graze cattle at the new ranch site because, in summer 1883, the Marquis had put twelve thousand sheep there, giving him a claim.[34] Roosevelt responded in a letter that all the sheep had died over the winter, leaving the Marquis no right to the land. Roosevelt warned Sewall and Dow to be wary of the Frenchman, especially because Roosevelt had hired Jack "Dutch Wannegan" Reuter as a hand at the Maltese Cross. Reuter was one of the three men who had shot it out with de Morès in June 1883. By hiring him, Roosevelt may have contributed to de Morès' antagonism toward the Elkhorn.[35] The Marquis' recent bid to squeeze Merrifield and Ferris off the Maltese Cross gave Roosevelt even better reason for alerting his new men. De Morès' letter was the sort of declaration that could be a harbinger of gunfire.

On Monday, August 11, Roosevelt was back at the Maltese Cross, where he wrote Anna that "everything so far has gone along beautifully. I had great fun in bringing my two backwoods babies out here. Their absolute astonishment and delight at every thing they saw, and their really very shrewd, and yet wonderfully simple remarks were a perfect delight to me."[36] He advised his sister that he might be out of touch for awhile: "In two or three days I start across country for the Bighorn Mountains, and then you will probably not hear from me for a couple of months. I take a wagon and six ponies, riding one of the latter."[37]

The ponies caused a delay. He had not yet acquired a large number of horses for his ranch and had to locate animals specifically for the trip. Selecting the proper mounts was key to a successful hunt. Roosevelt: "A hunting-horse is of no use whatever unless he will permit a man to jump from his back and fire with the greatest rapidity."[38] Roosevelt certainly did not want a skittish animal that would abandon him on the plains. "I can imagine few forms of exercise so soul-harrowing as that of spending an hour or two in running, in shaps, top boots, and spurs over a broken prairie, with the thermometer at 90°, after an escaped horse."[39]

Roosevelt's favorite hunting horse was one he called Manitou, which he bought from a Medora cowboy known as Hell-Roaring Bill Jones for seventy-five dollars in June 1884.[40] "[Manitou] is perfectly surefooted and as fast as any horse on the river. Though both willing and spirited, he is very gentle, with an easy mouth, and will stay grazing in one spot when left, and will permit himself to be caught without difficulty. Add to these virtues the fact that he will let any dead beast or thing be packed on him, and will allow a man to shoot off his back or right by him without moving, and it is evident that he is nearly as perfect as can be the case with hunting-horseflesh."[41]

While his men tracked down suitable ponies, Roosevelt went off on another of his nomadic rides. Probably during this time one of the signature episodes of his Badlands career occurred.[42] He had been riding the range all day when he stopped in Mingusville, Montana, about thirty-five miles west of Medora. As he approached Nolan's Hotel, where he hoped to find a bed for the night, he heard shots from the saloon on the hotel's first floor. He was reluctant to enter, but he had nowhere else to go on a cold night.[43]

Almost as soon as he stepped inside he was confronted by a bully with a six-gun in each hand who had just put two or three bullet holes in the face of a wall clock. He called Roosevelt "Four Eyes" and ordered him to buy drinks for everyone in the bar. Roosevelt tried to laugh it off and found a seat behind a stove, hoping to avoid further notice.

The armed man followed and again ordered Roosevelt to buy drinks. "My assailant was neither a cowboy nor a *bona fide* 'bad man,' but a broad-hatted ruffian of cheap and commonplace type who had for the moment terrorized the other men in the bar-room, these being mostly sheep-herders and small grangers. The fact that I wore glasses, together with my evident desire to avoid a fight, apparently gave him the impression—a mistaken one—that I would not resent an injury." Concluding that he had been pushed as far as he could reasonably allow, Roosevelt said, "Well, if I've got to, I've got to," stood up, and delivered his fists right, left, right to the man's jaw.[44] The guns went off, and the man fell, hitting his head on the bar and sprawling senseless on the floor. Roosevelt collected the guns, and the other patrons dumped the unconscious man in a shed outside. The following morning, Roosevelt was pleased to hear that the bully had fled town on a freight train.

The dust-up in Mingusville established Theodore Roosevelt's reputation in the Badlands. According to one Medora resident, Roosevelt "was regarded by the cowboys as a good deal of a joke until after the saloon incident. After that it was altogether different."[45] Ironically, within a week or so of the fight, an excerpt from an interview Roosevelt had done earlier with the *New York Tribune*, dealing with the subject of western violence, appeared in the *Bad Lands Cow Boy*: "The cowboys are a much misrepresented set of people. It is a popular impression that when one goes among them he must be prepared to shoot. . . . But if a man minds his own business and at the same time shows that he is fully prepared to assert his rights—if he is neither a bully or a coward and keeps out of places in which he has no business to be, he will get along as well as in Fifth avenue."[46]

Roosevelt found in his wide wanderings through the Badlands that "I grow very fond of this place. . . . at evening I love to sit out in front of the hut and see [the buttes'] hard, gray outlines gradually grow soft and purple as the flaming sunset by degrees softens and dies away; while my days I spend generally alone, riding through the lonely rolling prairie and broken lands."[47] Much of the appeal came, of course, from Badlands hunting opportunities. "Ranch life undoubtedly offers more chance to a man to get sport than is now the case with any other occupation in America, and those who follow it are apt to be men of game spirit, fond of excitement and adventure, . . . and who naturally take kindly to that noblest of weapons, the rifle."[48]

He conceded that he was not the best man behind a gun. A fellow outdoorsman once asked Roosevelt if he considered himself a good shot, and Roosevelt said, "No, but I shoot often."[49] He could back this statement with data, because in the West he kept a meticulous record of the number of cartridges he fired for every game animal killed and the distance at which it was shot.[50] He fired an average of three cartridges for every bison, bear, moose, elk, caribou, bighorn sheep, and mountain goat he killed, taking them down on average at eighty yards. With wolves and coyotes his luck, or his aim, was not quite so sure: He managed to kill one of each, but at a cost of fifty cartridges. Mule deer he took down generally at about ninety yards, with an average of four shots per kill. Pronghorn were among the toughest to bag: Shooting them on average at about 150 yards, he fired off nine bullets for each one he collected.

For big game in the Badlands, Roosevelt could choose among white-tailed deer, mule deer (which Roosevelt, along with most residents of the area, called black-tailed deer), pronghorn, bighorn sheep, elk, and—if lucky—bison and bear.[51] All of these were beleaguered species. The *Bad Lands Cow Boy* reported that "Professor E. D. Cope, of Philadelphia, recently returned from the west, writes that the bison, the elk, and other of the larger game animals of this country, are approaching extermination. The elk, has been eliminated from the confines of civilization, and exists only in the forests; and the bison, unable to hide his giant frame upon the open prairie, is nearer to extinction than any of his smaller co-sufferers."[52] Bison were so uncommon in the Medora area in 1884 that any appearance was news fit to print in the *Bad Lands Cow Boy*, though the stories usually ended with the bison shot dead.[53]

Roosevelt developed a contradictory approach to vanishing animals. On the one hand, he suggested that he practiced self-imposed limits. "I have never sought to make large bags, for a hunter should not be a game butcher. It is always lawful to kill dangerous or noxious animals, like the bear, cougar, and wolf; but other game should only be shot when there is need of the meat, or for the sake of an unusually fine trophy. Killing a reasonable number of bulls, bucks, or rams does no harm whatever to the species; to slay half the males of any kind of game would not stop the natural increase, and they yield the best sport, and are the legitimate objects of the chase. Cows, does, and ewes, on the contrary, should only be killed (unless barren) in case of necessity; during my last five years' hunting I have killed but five—one by a mischance, and the other four for the table."[54]

Yet he shot animals that he was convinced were being hunted to extinction, and he justified killing off bison. "While the slaughter of the buffalo has been in places needless and brutal, and while it is to be greatly regretted that the species is likely to become extinct . . . it must be remembered that its continued existence in any numbers was absolutely incompatible with any thing but a very sparse settlement of the country; and that its destruction was the condition precedent upon the advance of white civilization in the West. . . . Above all, the extermination of the buffalo was the only way of solving the Indian question. As long as this large animal of the chase existed, the Indians simply could not be kept on reservations, and always had an ample supply of meat on hand to support them in the event of a war; and its disappearance was the only method of forcing them to at least partially abandon their savage mode of life. From the standpoint of humanity at large, the extermination of the buffalo has been a blessing."[55]

He avidly shot mule deer—"I have myself shot as many of them as of all other kinds of plains game put together"—with no evident remorse that because of such killing mule deer were disappearing.[56] "It is the favorite game of the skin hunters and meat hunters," he wrote, "and has, in consequence, already disappeared from many places, while in others its extermination is going on at a frightfully rapid rate, owing to its being followed in season and out of season without mercy. . . . [I]n a few years it will have ceased entirely to be one of the common game animals of the plains."[57] He shot one deer just for its antlers: "On one occasion, while hunting in the mountains, I saw an old buck with remarkably large horns, of curious and beautiful shape, more symmetrical than in most instances where the normal form is departed from. . . . We were in no need of meat, but the antlers were so fine that I felt they justified the death of their bearer."[58] He fired at the buck at least five times before bringing it down. "The antlers are the finest pair I ever got, and form a magnificent ornament for the hall."

Elk, too, had been common in the Badlands until 1881, after which they survived only in scattered bunches or individuals. But Roosevelt did not hesitate to kill an elk near his ranch, "probably the last of his race that will ever be found in our neighborhood."[59] By then, every elk killed along the Little Missouri River was labeled "the last of its race," only to have another appear. "For several years in succession I myself kept killing one or two such 'last survivors,'" Roosevelt recalled.[60] That he repeatedly drew a bead on what he thought might be the last elk in the Badlands suggests that wiping out the local population never concerned him. He also pursued declining small prey. "We have trapped (or occasionally shot) on the ranch during the past three years several score beaver," even though he was convinced that "the extinction of the beaver throughout the plains country is a question of but a short time."[61] He was once pleased to kill thirteen ducks with two blasts of his shotgun.[62]

The profligacy of Victorian hunters is hard to understand, but their blasé cruelty is incomprehensible. Roosevelt wrote of the pleasure of coursing, or chasing, pronghorn with dogs. But as pronghorn are among the fastest animals on the planet, the odds were greatly against the dogs, so Roosevelt and his fellow hunters would shoot a pronghorn in the leg to give the dogs a better chance of closing in and savaging the quarry to death. "It was astonishing to see how fast an antelope with a broken leg could run," was Roosevelt's comment.[63]

Roosevelt often hunted for meat and found that doing so heightened his pleasure in the sport. "Hunting in the wilderness is of all pastimes the most attractive, and it is doubly so when not carried on merely as a pastime. . . . Among the hunts which I have most enjoyed were those made when I was engaged in getting in the winter's stock of meat, or was keeping some party of cowboys supplied with game from day to day."[64]

Ranchers generally did not kill cattle for the larder.[65] Roosevelt and his men in spring and summer ate mostly pronghorn, because the meat was the best available and the bucks were easily distinguished from does.[66] Sharp-tailed grouse were the most plentiful of feathered game.[67] As a rule, ranchmen and cowboys did not hunt birds, because cowpunchers preferred revolvers and rifles to the shotguns used for wing shooting, but Roosevelt suffered no such prejudice. He also collected curlew and prairie chicken eggs for food. Each autumn, he tried to kill enough deer to get his men through winter.[68] Smoked venison lasted into the first weeks of spring. Sewall concluded, however, that deer were wasted, with only the choice "saddle" removed, and the rest left to rot.[69]

Shooting animals was not always the main pleasure of hunting. On some days there was "sunny weather, not cold enough to bring discomfort, and yet so cool that the blood leaps briskly through a man's veins and makes him feel that to be out and walking over the hills is a pleasure in itself, even were he not in hopes of any moment seeing the sun glint on the horns and hide of some mighty buck, as it rises to face the intruder. On days such as these, mere life is enjoyment; and on days such as these, the life of a hunter is at its pleasantest and best."[70]

But for Theodore Roosevelt hunting was never just an unalloyed pleasure. It also took on the trappings of the cult of masculinity, teaching a hunter the skills needed to function as a warrior and to keep the nation strong. He put a heavy social burden on what would seem a simple sport: "It is a mere truism to say that the qualities developed by the hunter are the qualities needed by the soldier. . . . No training in the barracks or on the parade-ground is as good as the training given by a hard hunting trip in which a man really does the work for himself, learns to face emergencies, to study country, to perform feats of hardihood, to face exposure and undergo severe labor. It is an excellent thing for any man to be a good horseman and a good marksman, to be bold and hardy, and wonted to feats of strength and endurance, to be able to live in the open, and to feel a self-reliant readiness in any crisis. Big game hunting tends to produce or develop exactly these physical and moral traits."[71]

Despite the hunting, the ranch work, and the wandering, Roosevelt fell prey to memories of Alice. Sewall: "Roosevelt was very melancholy at times, and, the first year we were in Dakota, very much down in spirits. He told me one day that he felt as if it did not make any difference what became of him—he had nothing to live for, he said."[72]

While waiting to depart for his Wyoming hunt, Roosevelt penned a memorial to Alice.[73] On its opening page appeared his last public expression about her: "She was beautiful in face and form, and lovelier still in spirit; as a flower she grew, and as a fair young flower she died. Her life had been always in the sunshine; there had never come to her a single great sorrow; and none ever knew her who did not love and revere her for her bright, sunny temper and her saintly unselfishness. Fair, pure, and joyous as a maiden; loving, tender, and happy as a young wife; when she had just become a mother, when her life seemed to be but just begun, and when the years seemed so bright before her—then, by a strange and terrible fate, death came for her. And when my heart's dearest died, the light went from my life for ever."[74]

After that declaration came the impenetrable silence, rarely broken, and even then with only a few friends.

Finally, on August 17, all was ready for the hunt. On stationery bordered in black, he wrote to Anna that he and Merrifield would leave the next day, along with a light "prairie schooner" drawn by two horses and piloted by "an old French halfbreed."[75] He reported with apparent satisfaction: "I wear a sombrero, silk neckerchief, fringed buckskin shirt, sealskin chaparajos or riding trowsers; alligator hide boots; and with my pearl hilted revolver and beautifully finished Winchester rifle, I shall feel able to face anything." He thought he would stay out at least six weeks, though he would "try to be back to vote." Always conscious of appearances, he added, "Yesterday I rode 72 miles between dawn and darkness; I have a superb roan pony, or rather horse; he looks well, with his beautifully carved saddle, plaited bridle, and silver inlaid bit, and seems to be absolutely tireless."[76]

9

GRIZZLY HUNT

THEODORE ROOSEVELT LEFT FOR WYOMING'S BIGHORN MOUNTAINS ON the morning of August 18, 1884. His party consisted of himself, Bill Merrifield, and a teamster named Norman Lebo, who drove the supply wagon and cooked.[1] Short, stocky, and bearded, Lebo had trapped beaver in the Badlands region and had tried gold mining as far west as Oregon.[2] Truly the wandering kind, he reportedly said, "If I had the money, no two nights would ever see me in the same bed."[3] He once left his family for a week-long hunting trip and disappeared for three years, finally showing up to spend only a week at home before leaving again.[4] According to a rumor circulating at the time of the Bighorn Mountains hunt, Mrs. Lebo did not let her spouse join the expedition until Roosevelt promised to pay her three years' support if Norman did not return as planned.

Bill Merrifield was an experienced hunter. During his first two years in the Badlands he had made a living by selling deer and bison meat to hotels and railroad dining cars for a nickel a pound.[5] Roosevelt called him daring, self-reliant, a good rider, and a first-class shot, adding, "I can kill more game with him than I can alone."[6]

Despite the broad frontier experience that Merrifield and Lebo embodied, neither had ever been to the Bighorn Mountains. Knowing only that the mountains lay somewhere to the southwest, the trio set a general course toward the southeast corner of Montana Territory.[7] The trip would take them 235 miles from Medora and eight thousand feet up forested mountains; with various side trips, they would cover nearly a thousand miles in less than two months.[8] Given the distance and the time, supplies, and manpower needed, such a hunting trip could be undertaken only by wealthy sportsmen; it illustrates the nature of wilderness travel in the 1880s and typifies Theodore Roosevelt's many western hunting trips.

Roosevelt did not believe a hunter should "refrain from comfort of a wholesome sort when it is obtainable."[9] Consequently, this trip allowed the luxuries of the covered wagon and the cook. "By taking the wagon we could carry a tent to put up if there was foul weather. I had a change of clothes to put on if I was wet, two or three books to read—and nothing adds more to the enjoyment of a hunting trip—as well as plenty of food; while having two men made me entirely foot-loose as regards camp, so that I could hunt whenever I pleased, and, if I came in tired, I simply rested, instead of spending two or three hours in pitching camp, cooking, tethering horses, and doing the innumerable other little things which in the aggregate amount to so much."[10] Roosevelt did not travel in the wagon. He and Merrifield rode horseback; to keep from wearing out their mounts, they brought along two extra riding horses.

While on the trail, Roosevelt favored his buckskin suit, with light alligator-hide shoes for rocky ground and heavy moccasins for the woods.[11] He admitted that buckskin was not as good as flannel when wet and was hotter than flannel in warm weather, but he felt it offered the necessary concealing coloration. In the wagon he also packed a raccoon-skin coat, an otter-fur robe that he buttoned up to use as a sleeping bag, an oil slicker, overalls, a jersey, two flannel shirts, three light and three heavy sets of underwear, heavy socks, many handkerchiefs, soap, towels, washing and shaving items, and rubber blankets.[12]

For food, in addition to wild game, he carried flour, bacon, beans, sugar, salt, and coffee as well as brandy and "cholera mixture."[13] He also packed the firearms and ammunition that he called his "battery." It consisted of a 10-gauge shotgun, a .45-caliber Winchester repeating rifle, a

Colt .45 revolver, a .40-caliber Sharps, and a .50-caliber Webley Express.[14] To ensure that the weapons never had a dull moment, he brought along 300 shotgun shells, 150 cartridges for the Colt .45, 1,000 for the Winchester, 150 for the Sharps, and 100 for the Webley. He was ready, literally, for bear—the Webley bullets measured a half inch in diameter.

Initially they followed the Little Missouri River south. Roosevelt and Merrifield rode ahead of the slowly moving wagon, climbing atop a divide that separated the watersheds of two large creeks; consequently, early in the afternoon they were far from shelter when towering clouds blackened the northwest sky, rolling down on them "at furious speed . . . Against the dark background of the mass could be seen pillars and clouds of gray mist, whirled hither and thither by the wind, and sheets of level rain driven before it. . . . the wind shrieked and moaned as it swept over the prairie."[15]

The riders spurred their horses hard and let the reins go slack in a race to find cover in a ravine along a creek. "The first gust caught us a few hundred yards from the creek, almost taking us from the saddle, and driving the rain and hail in stinging level sheets against us. We galloped to the edge of a deep wash-out, scrambled into it at the risk of our necks, and huddled up with our horses beneath the windward bank. Here we remained pretty well sheltered until the storm was over. Although it was August, the air became very cold."[16]

Meanwhile, in the river valley the wind slammed into the wagon and would have overturned it if the canvas top had been up. Lebo and the horses hid on the lee side of the wagon, the wind coming with such force that hail the size of pigeon eggs blew over horizontally with the rain.[17] As rain poured through the night, Lebo camped out, while Roosevelt and Merrifield stayed at the Langs'.[18]

In the morning, heavy mist shrouded the river bottom. The mounted men and the teamster headed separately for the Fort Keogh Trail.[19] If the two riders separated, they could find the road easily and could tell by tracks if the wagon had passed; then it was just a matter of riding along the trail to camp.

Showers burst over Roosevelt and Merrifield throughout the day as they slogged along; at dusk they found Lebo camped at Lake Station, about ten miles inside Montana Territory. With no stream or pond nearby, Roosevelt and Merrifield stood in their slickers in the rain, an old rubber blanket stretched between them, to collect enough water for drinking and coffee.[20]

As they started a fire with logs from the old station house, a pronghorn came up to within two hundred yards, but they missed the only shot they took.[21] For dinner Lebo fried some of the five ducks Roosevelt had killed that day—"a good supper," Roosevelt called it.[22] And thus the day ended. "Our shaps and oilskins had kept us perfectly dry, and as soon as our frugal supper was over, we coiled up among the boxes and bundles inside the wagon and slept soundly till daybreak."[23] At least Roosevelt and Merrifield did. Lebo slept under the wagon.[24]

On the twentieth they watered the horses at noon, then traveled until nightfall.[25] The waterlogged earth slowed the wagon to a crawl, and they covered only a dozen miles.[26] Again the riders did not stick with the wagon. They loped into a wide stretch of broken ground "with chains upon chains of steep hills, separated by deep valleys, winding and branching in every direction, their bottoms filled with trees and brushwood."[27] Looking across a broad ravine into a copse of trees about 125 yards away, Merrifield thought he saw a deer. Instantly Roosevelt leaped from his horse, throwing the reins over its head, and looked "long and eagerly toward the spot indicated."[28] But he could not find the deer. The problem was his eyesight. Unless a game animal was out in the open with a contrasting background, he had a hard time spotting it if it remained motionless.[29] This handicap might explain how, on one occasion, Roosevelt crawled a hundred yards to creep up on a pronghorn buck, only to find that he had been stalking a dead sunflower.[30]

Merrifield told him to look for a patch of red—the color of a deer in summer. Roosevelt now spotted the patch, "glimmering through the bushes, but should certainly never have dreamed it was a deer if left to myself." He watched it until it moved, then killed it with one shot. He also killed two sage grouse that day.[31]

They went into camp early, around three in the afternoon, so they could dry their gear. Roosevelt and Merrifield had had no lunch, but they could choose between grouse and venison for dinner.[32] After eating, the hunters rode across the plains to visit a group of men camped two or three miles away. The visit was a safety measure: "You were liable to meet horse thieves in those days. It was customary to go and find out who your neighbors were."[33] In fact, western etiquette governed travel on the plains as surely as it governed visits to ranch houses.[34] If you rode within view of another man on the plains, for example, you were expected to come over and say hello; to do otherwise was almost an admission that you were up to no good. If you approached someone from the rear, you should say hello before you got within pistol range. When entering another person's camp, you were supposed to signal in advance and enter along a route that gave a distant view.

The strangers turned out to be a cattle outfit bringing stock to Mingusville. The foreman, "an awfully nice fellow," told the hunters, who were still unsure of the route to the Bighorns, that if they backtracked his trail it would lead them to the mountains.[35]

The hunters woke the next day to frost, but the skies were clear. The wheeling proved much easier, and they covered twenty-five miles through broken prairie and came to what Roosevelt believed were the headwaters of O'Fallon Creek. They saw no game that day, only hundreds of buffalo skulls and old carcasses.[36] "No sight is more common on the plains than that of a bleached buffalo skull. . . . Bad Lands, plateaus, and prairies alike, are cut up in all directions by the deep ruts which were formerly buffalo trails. . . . many of the ruts are worn so deeply into the ground that a horseman riding along one strikes his stirrups on the earth."[37] Because buffalo preferred to travel over the easiest terrain, their trails often provided the best routes for both cattle and horsemen.

Six days into the hunt they camped on Montana's upper Powder River, and Roosevelt wrote to his sister and to Lodge, making sure to tell both, "I am writing this on an upturned water keg, by our canvas covered wagon, while the men are making tea."[38] They had met a cowboy on the trail, and he had agreed to post the letters.

Roosevelt told Anna, "I enjoy the life greatly. One night we camped in a most beautiful natural park; it was a large, grassy hill, studded thickly with small, pine crowned chalk buttes, with very steep sides, worn into the most outlandish and fantastic shapes. All that night the wolves kept up a weird concert round our camp; they are most harmless beasts."[39]

To Lodge he lamented not being involved in politics but also indicated that he was so heated over recent developments that he was not in a frame of mind suitable for campaigning.[40] He had received, he said, fifty invitations to speak at political events, including requests to kick off the campaign in Vermont and Minnesota, but he was glad he was not at home where he could accept them. "I get so angry with the 'mugwumps,' and get to have such scorn and contempt for them, that I know I would soon be betrayed into taking some step against them, and in favor of Blaine, much more decided than I really ought to take."

The next day Roosevelt noted in his diary that Merrifield "missed a snap shot at a cougar in a thicket." Merrifield told a different version of the story in later years. According to him, as Roosevelt stalked a flock of prairie chickens, Merrifield spotted a mountain lion. He told Roosevelt not to shoot and to stop walking, but Roosevelt persisted. The lion got away. Merrifield: "I told him then, now whenever I hold up my hand, stop still where you are. He learned on this trip to do what he was told. He learned his lesson in absolutely obeying that stayed with him all during our trips after that."[41]

Merrifield's version and tone offer some evidence of the ego that made him widely disliked in the Badlands.[42] Nevertheless, Merrifield was valuable both for his expertise as a hunter and—perhaps even more important—for backup in an emergency.[43] One potential risk was being left on foot by a runaway horse.[44] "Moreover, in galloping at full speed after the game it is impossible now and then to avoid a tumble, as the horse may put his leg into a prairie-dog hole or badger burrow; and on such occasions a companion may come in very handily."[45] On Monday, August 25, an incident occurred that underscored the value of a riding partner. Merrifield was leading his horse up the almost vertical wall of a washout about thirty feet deep when the animal lost its balance and toppled over backward, nearly bowling over Roosevelt and his horse, which were following behind. Merrifield's pony turned two complete somersaults before landing on its back at the bottom of the wash.[46] The horse soon struggled to its feet, but the incident could have left Merrifield without a mount.

Each day at nightfall the travelers would seek a campsite with wood, grass, and water.[47] The men cleared the ground of stones and cactus before putting out blankets and robes. Lebo gathered wood, started a fire for coffee, and fried bacon with game meat. One evening in every three or four Lebo baked bread or biscuits in a Dutch oven. Roosevelt: "On such a trip one soon gets to feel that the wagon is home; and after a tiresome day it is pleasant just to lie still in the twilight by the side of a smouldering fire and watch the men as they busy themselves cooking or arranging the beds, while the solemn old ponies graze around or stand quietly by the great white-topped prairie schooner."[48] Roosevelt would read at the camp-fire, often far into the night, slapping his leg at favored passages and sometimes adding, "By golly, that's great."[49]

Traveling with a wagon had its drawbacks.[50] They had to cross the Powder River nine times on the twenty-eighth, once coming close to sinking in quicksand.[51] On Friday the twenty-ninth the wagon stuck three times crossing deep washouts and had to be pulled out with the help of the riding horses.[52]

That day the two hunters stirred up three mule deer bucks from a stand of sagebrush about two hundred yards away and below them. It was a long shot; Roosevelt missed, and the deer disappeared into a valley below.[53] Waiting for them to reappear, he elevated the sights of his rifle to four hundred yards. Soon, calmer now, one of the deer walked into view and stood broadside, but so far off that Roosevelt could not see its antlers. He raised his rifle to his shoulder, and just then a second deer walked toward the first. Reasoning that two deer would offer a bigger target than one, Roosevelt waited until the animals stood side by side. He aimed and fired; both bucks fell, the bullet breaking their backs. Roosevelt paced off the shot while Merrifield did the hard work of dressing out the animals: more than four hundred yards. In his diary that night he wrote tersely, "Best shot I ever made. Kept bullet."[54]

The next day they crossed into Wyoming, and he had another adventure at a Cheyenne Indian camp. The Cheyennes were among the Indians who had finished off Custer only eight years earlier. Merrifield decided to ride into their camp to assess any possible risks, though by 1884 the Indians of the northern plains were thoroughly subdued. During the visit, Roosevelt and Merrifield challenged the Cheyennes to a shooting match. Merrifield: "You go among Indians and they find out you are superior to them in anything, especially shooting, and they at once have a great deal of respect for you. . . . I would ask them who was their best shot. They'd point him out, then I would sign-language them to put up a mark, then I'd always beat them. The Indians would look you up and down, walk up and down looking you all over. Roosevelt beat them also."[55] The interaction was not quite what Roosevelt might have experienced had he ridden across the same range ten years earlier, but it was the sort of quasi-pioneer experience he relished.

The country through which they passed was not pristine wilderness. Roosevelt mentions seeing several cattle herds along Little Beaver Creek and the Powder River.[56] On Tuesday, the twenty-sixth, he met a cowboy with a good-looking horse and bought the animal for a hundred dollars. That evening he stayed at the N-Bar-N cattle outfit on the Little Powder River. It was owned by an Englishman named Wallop, who noticed the monogram on the handle of Roosevelt's six-shooter and recognized the eastern politician. "He had read considerable about Mr. Roosevelt. He at once introduced himself and told the outfit who Mr. Roosevelt was."[57] He entertained the hunters until ten or eleven that night and even had their horses shod.[58]

On the twenty-eighth, the expedition first spotted the Bighorn Mountains rising blue and snow-streaked above the plain. The men arrived at Buffalo, Wyoming, at the foot of the mountains on Monday, September 1, Roosevelt limiting his comments cryptically to "Quite a frontier town."[59] A doctor at Fort McKinney, a nearby army post, had hunted in the Bighorns and gave them advice on where to shoot as well as on the best route to take.[60] A government agent with seventeen years' experience asked them to kill two grizzlies along Crazy Woman Creek, the site of a sawmill to which they were headed. He wanted to hunt deer along the creek but was afraid of two bears roaming there. "I'm telling you," Merrifield said years later, "that those bears were fierce, and you had to watch out for them and be a good shot or else you'd get into trouble sure."[61]

They spent the night in Buffalo and the next day moved on to a sawmill on Crazy Woman Creek. There they loaded supplies onto three of their seven horses, taking along the wagon cover for a tent but leaving the wagon.[62] They had the other three horses for riding and one for a spare. On Wednesday, the third of September, the ponies "proved fractious," stalling departure until ten in the morning. Following a steep pony trail left along a creek by soldiers who had hunted there, they endured seven and a half hours of slow progress in part because none of the three men knew how to secure cargo on a horse.[63] The packs constantly slipped; sometimes the horses stampeded with loads only half tied on, and other times balked.[64] The party camped that evening on Willow Creek, listening to the rush of its water during a night so cold that ice formed. For dinner they could choose from two blue grouse Roosevelt shot on the way up and venison left from the double kill.

The following day, Thursday September 4, they led the horses along a trail that wound through tall, slender, closely packed pines. The horses struggled through openings strewn with fallen trees. In one of a series of small glades punctuated with bogs, Roosevelt spotted a band of cow elk just as the animals vanished into woods on the opposite side. Instantly he tried to leap from his horse to shoot, but the horse reared and turned before Roosevelt could free his left foot of the stirrup; by the time he finished dancing with the pony, Roosevelt could see only one elk, and it was disappearing behind a dead tree. He fired hastily anyway, and missed. Roosevelt: "I was a good deal annoyed with this, feeling that it was an omen of misfortune."[65]

They covered only six miles that day and camped early by a rushing torrent of icy water in steep and broken country, the dense timber broken by open meadows and clear lakes.[66] Out of meat, they split up, each hunting on foot, Lebo upstream, Merrifield down, and Roosevelt, moving silently on moccasined feet, following the track of the elk that got away.[67]

The elk trail led across a series of wooded hills that paralleled the stream in the direction Merrifield had taken. Roosevelt followed the animals for a mile or two through stands of pine and spruce and came upon them bedded down in brush atop the crest of the hills.[68] Accidentally slamming his rifle barrel against a tree, he sent the elk running away, but he was able to cut them off and get within twenty yards of them. Although in the dense timber he could see only fleeting glimpses of the animals, he fired four rounds, breaking the neck of an adult cow and killing her in her tracks. He also broke the hind leg of a bull calf.[69]

He followed the herd and in a glade killed the wounded calf. The rest of the herd crossed paths with Merrifield, who killed two. Roosevelt left Merrifield to butcher the animals and returned to camp to find Lebo with the hams and tongues of two deer he had shot. Roosevelt told Lebo to go to Merrifield with a horse to pack in the elk. With so much meat, they decided to shoot no more cows and calves.[70]

That night in camp they heard the bugle-like mating calls of bull elk, "a most singular and beautiful sound . . . very much the most musical cry uttered by any four-footed beast. When heard for the first time it is almost impossible to believe that it is the call of an animal; it sounds far more as if made by an Aeolian harp or some strange wind instrument. . . . Heard in the clear, frosty moonlight from the depths of rugged and forest-clad mountains the effect is most beautiful; for its charm is heightened by the wild and desolate surroundings."[71]

The following day, with the horses "nearly done up," they did not ride out but stretched the elk hides and started drying meat. Roosevelt went off alone in pursuit of the bull elk he had heard the night before, but despite spending the whole of the rainy day in the woods he shot only a rabbit and a grouse.[72] That night snow fell, and they woke to find the ground covered. Willow bushes bowed under the snow that lined their branches, and the pines were frosted with white. Rain and sleet came throughout the day, so the men stayed in camp under the shelter of the wagon cover, a log fire cracking and roaring in front of it. In the afternoon Roosevelt rode off into mist and rain, a brisk ride that lasted three hours.[73]

On the seventh, Roosevelt went out with Merrifield in the early morning and stayed out until dusk. Roosevelt: "We rode through awful ground. While hunting through a great burnt slash on foot we struck elk tracks; following them up, we found three bulls; we wounded all three (I two and M. one) and went after them helter-skelter, running, tumbling, jumping, falling and shooting. One got away; while following it, I ran across and killed a blacktail doe."[74] Roosevelt's diary indicates that he killed two of the wounded elk. He had shot the deer by mistake, thinking it was one of the wounded elk when it broke cover.[75]

The two bulls proved disappointing as trophies, their ten-point antlers small, twisted, and poorly shaped, "in fact hardly worth preserving, except to call to mind a chase in which during a few minutes I did as much downright hard work as it has often fallen to my lot to do."[76] The third of the three wounded elk was never found, though Roosevelt was convinced it had been fatally wounded.[77]

After that burst of activity the hunting fell into a lull. The following day, Monday the eighth, the hunters split up. Roosevelt killed a dozen blue grouse that proved good eating, while Merrifield treed and shot a black bear, leaving Roosevelt envious.[78] Merrifield had been hunting about ten miles away when he killed the bear, and in that area he also had found signs of grizzlies. Roosevelt decided that they would shift camp into that region the following morning.

That night brought more snowfall that continued on Tuesday as they moved camp six miles to a branch of the Ten Sleep. Moonlight poured brightly over the snow-shrouded woodlands, the men fed on the rich meat from Merrifield's bear, and Roosevelt felt better than ever.[79] But the big-game hunting did not improve, and Roosevelt and Merrifield spent Thursday the eleventh at a lake catching about fifty trout.

While they were alone on the trail, Roosevelt's talks with Merrifield shed light on his state of mind and his plans. Merrifield: "Yes, he had political ambitions. He had his ambitions to be President. Absolutely, he attached his kite to the skies. He talked about it; what he would do and just talked right on about everything."[80]

One night he told Merrifield, a widower, about Alice's death and said he was "beyond any healing."[81] Merrifield: "The loss of his wife shot him to pieces. He was tremendously fond of her. . . . I can remember so distinctly his saying, 'Now don't talk to me about time will make a difference—time can never change me in that respect.'"[82]

Roosevelt also touched on his health, saying that his doctors had told him "he could not possibly live more than four years. That man would eat heart medicine when we were out together. He always had some in his pocket."[83]

The day after the fishing expedition they moved camp again, shifting down about six miles toward the foothills and camping in a narrow valley with steep, wooded sides. At three in the afternoon the two hunters went into a pine wood that ran up the edge of a broad valley with sheer rock walls.[84] There they found fresh elk tracks. Shortly they found a bull elk about eighty yards away, thrashing his antlers against a sapling. "He stopped and faced us for a second, his mighty antlers thrown in the air, as he held his head aloft. . . . As the bull turned to run I struck him just behind the shoulder; he reeled to the death-blow, but staggered gamely on a few rods into the forest before sinking to the ground, with my second bullet through his lungs."[85] The bull proved to be the finest Roosevelt had killed; three days later he shot another nearly as big. This shooting introduced him to a new thrill: "No sportsman can ever feel much keener pleasure and self-satisfaction than when, after a successful stalk and good shot, he walks up to a grand elk lying dead in the cool shade of the great evergreens, and looks at the massive and yet finely moulded form, and at the mighty antlers which are to serve in the future as the trophy and proof of his successful skill."[86] It also yielded to him two themes that would run throughout his writings—the nobility and manliness of hunting and hunter: "Still-hunting the elk on the mountains is as noble a kind of sport as can well be imagined; there is nothing more pleasant and enjoyable, and at the same time it demands that the hunter shall bring into play many manly qualities."[87]

On the day he killed his first good bull, Roosevelt immediately said to Merrifield, "Now we'll go out tonight and get a bear."[88] Leaving the elk with Merrifield, Roosevelt walked back to camp alone toward nightfall and found the tracks of a grizzly. "It gave me rather an eerie feeling in the silent, lonely woods, to see for the first time the unmistakable proofs that I was in the home of the mighty lord of the wilderness."[89] Eerie or not, as daylight failed he followed the track until he could no longer see in the darkness, and only then went back to camp.

The following day, Saturday the thirteenth, he and Merrifield visited the elk carcass late in the afternoon and saw signs that a grizzly had fed on it the previous night. The large footprints of the bear pocked the area around the carcass, which the bear had partially covered with leaves and dirt. The grizzly was likely to be nearby. The men climbed up the trunk of a fallen tree that had come to rest at an angle among the branches of a standing tree, and there they sat until evening obscured the sights of their rifles and forced them to climb down.

They were positioned on the wooded side of a ravine. On the opposite side grew only sagebrush, so daylight was still bright there, though the sun had set. Crossing to the sunny side and hiding under brush, they waited again, until "the pine trees in our front blended in one dark, frowning mass. We saw nothing; but the wild creatures of the forest had begun to stir abroad. The owls hooted dismally from the tops of the tall trees, and two or three times a harsh wailing cry, probably the voice of some lynx or wolverine, arose from the depths of the woods. At last, as we were rising to leave, we heard the sound of the breaking of a dead stick, from the spot where we knew the carcass lay."[90] Soon they heard the bear, but the darkness was too great, and they had to give up.

Back at the elk carcass the following morning they found that the bear had fed again, leaving immense, fresh footprints. They followed the track easily over soft moss and pine needles. All his senses alert, Roosevelt felt a thrill course through him at every sudden sound.[91] Ravens cawed overhead, wind sighed through the pines.

The bear turned off down an elk trail, its tracks still clear in the dirt. In the middle of a thicket the two hunters crossed a tangle of fallen logs. Merrifield, in the lead, passed a great pine tree and knelt suddenly on one knee, half turning to Roosevelt; the excitement that burned in Merrifield's face signaled that the grizzly was near.

Roosevelt eased past his companion, rifle ready; only ten strides away the vast bear rose slowly from its bed among young spruce trees—the first grizzly Roosevelt had ever seen. "Then he saw us and dropped down again on all fours, the shaggy hair on his neck and shoulders seeming to bristle as he turned toward us. As he sank down on his forefeet I raised the rifle; his head was bent slightly down, and when I saw the top of the white bead fairly between his small, glittering, evil eyes, I pulled trigger. Half-rising up, the huge beast fell over on his side in the death throes, the ball having gone into his brain, striking as fairly between the eyes as if the distance had been measured by a carpenter's rule."[92]

Roosevelt filled with pride as he stood over the huge dead creature in the cool shadows of the pines.[93] He grabbed Merrifield with both arms and would not let go. "He was as tickled as a boy over that bear."[94] They estimated that it weighed twelve hundred pounds, which Roosevelt admitted would be unusually large; in any event he believed it outweighed any of their horses. An old bear, its teeth and claws worn and blunt, it had been healthy, the fat on its back a finger's length thick.

They skinned the grizzly the following morning. Later that day Roosevelt fired six times at a mule deer before killing it.[95] As he and Merrifield collected its head for a trophy—they certainly did not need more meat with the literally tons of animal flesh they had killed—a female grizzly and her nearly grown cub appeared in a valley below. The country was open, and the men threw off their hats and gave chase, running downhill as fast as they could.

When the mother bear spotted the hunters she continued to walk along, stopping intermittently to sit down and look at them; consequently, the men were able to run ahead of her. Roosevelt was soon out of breath; Merrifield went on ahead, disappearing over a bank as Roosevelt pitched full-length over a bush. Knowing he could not catch up, Roosevelt sat down and started blasting away at the grizzly, a good three hundred yards away on a hill opposite him. His fourth shot hit her flank, but she was able to run off into nearby forest, Merrifield coming up not far behind her.

In the woods the bear turned on Merrifield, who dispatched her with a single shot to the chest. He wounded the cub with a stomach shot.[96] When Roosevelt finally came up to join him, Merrifield was walking toward the cub to shoot it with his revolver. The bear bolted, and Roosevelt killed it with his rifle. "There, my good man, we came mighty near losing that bear with your fooling, only for me," Roosevelt said.[97]

They had killed three grizzlies but were not done yet. On Monday the fifteenth they found another big male grizzly on an elk carcass, and Roosevelt let Merrifield shoot it on his own—so far, the grizzlies Merrifield had shot had already carried Roosevelt bullets.[98] "Rather a reckless fellow, and very confident in his own skill with the rifle," Merrifield had regretted that none of the bears they had shot had charged, so he proposed shooting the bear in the leg to see how it would react. "Having no ambition to be a participator in the antics of a three-legged bear," Roosevelt wrote later, "I hastily interposed a most emphatic veto; and with a rather injured air he fired, the bullet going through the neck just back of the head."[99] The bear collapsed and, unable to rise, attacked its own paws, biting its left wrist so hard that it separated the bones of the paw and arm.

Merrifield recalled the incident much differently thirty-five years later. He said *Roosevelt* shot the bear in the neck and then kept missing. "The bear was roaring and making a terrible fuss. Well, I saw there was no time to be lost, and I fired the last shot that killed him. The bear's roaring and charging was too much for Mr. Roosevelt. [The bear] would put his own paw in his mouth and just set there and you could hear him crunch the bones in his own paws."[100] However, Roosevelt described the kill in his journal that night, his memory fresher than Merrifield's would be decades later, recording that "M. has not yet got one solely to his own gun; so I made him shoot it."[101]

On the sixteenth the three men set off through the woods in search of more grizzlies. They found none, but Roosevelt did bag his second large elk that day. At about this point Roosevelt concluded, "We have got all we have come for and there is no use of slaughtering game for the sake of killing it."[102] The next day they broke camp and headed out of the mountains; on Thursday, September 18—a month to the day after leaving the ranch—they reached the wagon.

They wheeled to Fort McKinney, near Buffalo, on the nineteenth; the officers invited Roosevelt to dinner.[103] Merrifield had only his hunting clothes and so could not go, but Roosevelt had "some good clothes with him" and dined with the brass. At the fort the next day, he wrote to Anna on his black-bordered stationery, giving Merrifield credit for finding most of the game but adding, "I really shot well this time."[104] He tallied up the animals he had killed: "three grizzly bears, six elk (three of them have magnificent heads and will look well in the 'house on the hill') and as many deer, grouse and trout as we needed for the table. . . . I now have a dozen good heads for the hall."

Although his published accounts of the trip give readers the impression that in the mountains he and his men were alone in a wilderness, he told Anna, "We met or heard of a dozen parties either of English or Eastern amateurs, or of professional hunters, who were on the mountain at the same time we were; but not one of them had half the success I had. This was mainly because they hunted on horseback, much the easiest and least laborious way, while Merrifield and I, in our moccasins and buckskin suits hunted almost every day on foot, following the game into the deepest and most inaccessible ravines." He warned her that as a result of his meetings, she might receive visitors. "If any Englishmen named Farquahr, Lee or Grenfell call, get Douglas or Elliott to do anything they can for them; I met them hunting."[105]

He also turned his mind to politics, if only to deny that he was doing so: "I suppose all of our friends, the unco' good, are as angry as ever with me; they had best not express their discontent to my face unless they wish to hear very plain English. I am sorry my political career should be over; but after all it makes very little difference."[106] He also suggested for the first time that he missed Baby Lee. "I hope Mousiekins will be very cunning," he wrote, meaning cute. "I shall dearly love her."

The trio headed east later that day.[107] The trip home suffered from ups and downs and small crises. On the twenty-second Roosevelt wrote in his diary that the horses were "not in good condition"; the men also noticed that the bear skins were spoiling and so stopped for two days to flesh and dry them. Prolonged rain fell during the last few days of September. By the twenty-ninth the wagon team was "nearly done out." The next day, with the road wet and slow, an exhausted team horse had to be replaced with a saddle horse.[108] Rain and gale winds struck the next day, stalling their progress. On Thursday, October 2, the rain continued.[109] The men wanted to move on, but the horses had strayed. The hunters did not find all of them until noon, and one of the team horses was sunk in a mud hole; the men lost two hours getting her out, after which she was so tired she could barely stand—and so another night in camp with wet beds.

Finally, on the third, they pushed off across the prairie. The wind was still strong, but rain was scant. Saturday, October 4, waxed clear and cold. Roosevelt shot a jackrabbit and two sharp-tailed grouse, the last prey of the long hunt. All day he and Merrifield plodded along beside the wagon, following a trail left by Montana cattle on the way to market.[110] When they stopped for dinner they studied the draft horses. The tired animals would need three more days to get to the Maltese Cross Ranch. Merrifield and Roosevelt concluded that they would leave the wagon and team with Lebo and ride straight through the night, getting back to the Maltese Cross in time to "wake the boys up for breakfast."[111] They saddled up at nine that night, mounting the same horses they had ridden all day, and squeezed another nine hours out of them, moving mostly at a lope. Roosevelt: "The hoof-beats of our horses rang out in steady rhythm through the silence of the night, otherwise unbroken save now and then by the wailing cry of a coyote. . . . We could see clearly enough to keep our general course over the trackless plain, steering by the stars where the prairie was perfectly level and without landmarks; and our ride was timed well, for as we galloped down into the valley of the Little Missouri the sky above the line of level bluffs in our front was crimson with the glow of the unrisen sun."[112]

He had spent seven weeks away, but only fifteen days in the mountains. He had killed 125 animals.[113] In memory of the experience, he gave Merrifield a watch inscribed, "If it's a black bear I can tree him. If it's a grizzly, I can bay him."[114]

★ ★ ★

Theodore Roosevelt's bloodletting in the Bighorn Mountains, and the number of gunmen he met there doing the same, illustrates how uncontrolled hunting chipped away at wildlife. Riflemen eager to take down whatever game was left were flocking to the last strongholds of native wildlife. In Medora, the Pyramid Park Hotel, under new management, was doing "a rushing business."[115] Hunters killed large numbers of deer near the town that autumn.[116] In mid-November a Russian nobleman, Count Rembielinski, spent ten days along the Little Missouri River, killing sixty-five deer and antelope.[117] On Christmas Day, the *Bad Lands Cow Boy* remarked that a local market hunter "came in Sunday, and reports killing eighty-nine deer and antelope. Sixty-nine of them he killed in five days." Although the near extinction of the bison had reduced the robe trade at St. Paul, Minnesota, from ten thousand hides in 1883 to a total of only four in 1884, when someone reported a herd of buffalo about twenty-five miles southwest of Medora in late October, several local hunters hurried after them.[118]

This level of slaughter makes Roosevelt's serial killing of elk in the Bighorn Mountains seem moderate and offers a measure of his restraint. It also backs naturalist William T. Hornaday's notion that "the idea of the frontiersman (the average, at least) has always been to kill as much game as possible before some other fellow gets a chance at it, *and before it is all killed off!*"[119]

Because each wildlife species is an important link in a natural web of life, destruction of bison, elk, deer, and other prey species brought unanticipated difficulties for ranchers. Badlands wolves, for example, turned to preying on cattle. Having contributed to elimination of the wolf's food base, ranchers now complained that livestock losses to wolves were constantly increasing. "It has not reached any alarming proportions as yet, but it is enough to show that unless active measures are immediately taken, the loss is liable to be considerable. Some of the cattlemen and hunters are poisoning carcasses, and have good success in killing wolves, but the movement is not universal enough to produce the desired result.... every man should pledge himself to do his utmost toward exterminating the growing pest. It would be a good plan to pay a bounty for all pelts brought in."[120]

Someone soon did: In January, the *Bad Lands Cow Boy* announced, one ranching operation was putting a bounty on wolves. "This move cannot be commended too highly, and should be followed by every outfit in the country. By making it worthwhile, men can easily be found who will exterminate the wolves in a short time."[121] Inducements to join this effort included provisions, poisons, and payment of a dollar per coyote pelt and five dollars per wolf, along with the right to keep the pelts, which could be sold for fur. Slaughter of hoofed animals begat slaughter of predators.[122]

Whatever its impact on local wildlife populations, the Bighorn Mountains hunt left a strong impression on Theodore Roosevelt. He had discovered the thrill of facing death: "While danger ought never to be needlessly incurred, it is yet true that the keenest zest in sport comes from its presence, and from the consequent exercise of the qualities necessary to overcome it. The most thrilling moments in an American hunter's life are those in which, with every sense on the alert, and with nerves strung to the highest point, he is following alone into the heart of its forest fastness the fresh and bloody footprints of an angered grisly; and no other triumph of American hunting can compare with the victory thus to be gained."[123]

But the thrill had not been only about killing. Roosevelt had noticed that "going noiselessly through [the mountain forests] in our dull-colored buckskin and noiseless moccasins, we kept getting glimpses, as it were, of the inner life of the mountains. . . . I by degrees grew to feel as if I had a personal interest in the different traits and habits of the wild creatures. . . . [T]he characters of the animals differed widely, and the differences were typified by their actions; and it was pleasant to watch them in their own homes, myself unseen, when after stealthy, silent progress through the sombre and soundless depths of the woods I came upon them going about the ordinary business of their lives. . . . The true still-hunter should be a lover of nature as well as of sport, or he will miss half the pleasure of being in the woods."[124]

Roosevelt also benefited physically. Merrifield believed that he "gained in health . . . He was very strong after the Big Horn trip."[125] In his letter to Anna, Roosevelt himself signaled that the hunt helped him find peace of mind: "So I have had good sport; and enough excitement and fatigue to prevent over much thought; and moreover I have at last been able to sleep well at night."[126]

10

GUNFIGHTERS AND BLAINE

BILL SEWALL SAID HE HAD NEVER WANTED TO GO ON A HUNT AS MUCH
as he had wanted to go on the expedition to the Bighorns. Roosevelt had
invited him, but in the end Sewall had stayed behind because he did not
want to leave Wilmot Dow alone to cut the logs for the Elkhorn house.[1]
In addition to hand-hewn logs, the house would require some sixteen
thousand board-feet of rafters, joists, floors, partition boards, and roof
boards shipped in via Medora; the house included a cellar for a dark-
room.[2]

After moving cattle and logging cottonwoods, Sewall still did not like
the Badlands; on that basis alone, he might be expected to have enjoyed
getting away to forested mountains more reminiscent of his home in
Maine. He wrote his brother that if he had the money for train fare he
would send it to him so he could come west too, "but then if I was as able
as that I would not stay here myself."[3] He thought he would like winter
better than summer, which was too hot. "The sun when it shines clear
strikes the bare sides of the Buttes and comes down on the treeless bottoms[.] hot enough to make a Rattlesnake pant[.] if you can get in the

shade thare is most always a breeze[.] the grand trouble is you cant get in the shade[.] thares no shade to get into and the great sandy Desert is cool compared with some of the gulches."[4] He already was saying he would stay no longer than he felt obliged to do.[5]

On Sunday, October 5, Roosevelt—his face a bright terra-cotta red from his days on the hunt—rode up to the Elkhorn Ranch dugout that served as temporary quarters for Sewall and Dow while they built the new house.[6] No doubt Roosevelt, in his infectiously manic way, spilled out his story of the Bighorn Mountains hunt. But Sewall had important news for him as well. In Roosevelt's absence, de Morès seemed to have been reasserting his claim to the Elkhorn Ranch land. A few weeks earlier, while Dow was helping at a round-up, he had overheard two cowboys say that Paddock was threatening to shoot him and Sewall and that some day "there would be dead men" around the Elkhorn Ranch. Sewall: "Of course, Dow told me of this and right there we decided that if there were any dead men there, it would not be us."[7] They kept their rifles and Colt revolvers close by while cutting trees. "We were working at the edge of a piece of timber and there was quite a thicket behind us. We knew that if anybody came, he would come by the trail and we intended to make for the timber, and if he wanted to hunt us there, why, we would see who was best at the business." Paddock, Sewall said, had been threatening to shoot Roosevelt, too.

Roosevelt replied, "Is that so?"[8] Then he turned back down the trail and rode alone directly to Medora, where Paddock still lived in a shack on the west side of the river. Roosevelt knocked on Paddock's door, and Paddock answered. "I understand that you have threatened to kill me on sight," Roosevelt said. "I have come over to see when you want to begin the killing and to let you know that, if you have anything to say against me, now is the time for you to say it."[9]

Paddock reportedly was disconcerted—"flabbergasted," said Sewall, who heard about it secondhand—by the sudden appearance at his door.[10] In any event, he denied the threat and said he had been misquoted. Whatever other words were exchanged between the two men is lost, but after this incident, Sewall recalled, the two potential adversaries became friends.

Roosevelt left for New York on October 7, apparently convinced that the situation with Paddock was resolved. But on a Sunday morning at the Elkhorn, while Roosevelt was away, an incident occurred that suggested otherwise. Dow had gone out for a walk, and Sewall sat in the dugout writing his weekly letter home. "Suddenly," Sewall recalled, "I heard a great fusillade; something over twenty guns were fired as fast as I could count. Very soon afterward a half dozen men rode up to the shack. They were cowboys. I knew one of them as the right-hand man of the Marquis de Morès, and decided that they had come down to look us over."[11]

Sewall chose beans over bullets: "I asked them in a friendly manner to dismount and come in, which they did. As it was getting near noon, I asked them if they wouldn't like to have something to eat. They said they would. I told them the cook was out, but that I would do my best. We had a good pot of beans that we had baked in the ground, woods fashion. I dug them out and got what bread we had on hand. We had plenty of hard bread. I made them some coffee and got out all the best things we had in the shack. I had decided to treat them just as nicely as I knew how. Then if they started any trouble I intended to make sure of the leader [Paddock] first thing. I think he had had a little whisky, as he certainly had a very sharp appetite."[12]

Paddock was quite taken with the baked beans. "He said he never saw such good baked beans and he didn't know when he had had anything as good as they were. I had plenty of beans and kept urging him to have more. I knew that that was a good way to make a man feel good-natured."[13] Apparently the ploy worked. After dinner, Sewall showed the men around; they complimented the temporary house and general layout, then rode off without further shooting.

The purpose of the visit, presuming it was anything more than a spontaneous drop-in by cowboys who happened to be riding past, remains unknown. If the Marquis had sent them, the men presumably would have had a message from him. Or perhaps the threat was merely implied. Whatever the visit meant, nothing seemed to spring from it. Paddock was always friendly to Sewall afterward and seemed to bear out what one observer said of western rustlers, robbers, and hold-up men: "Though most of these persons in these callings might kill when 'on duty' and performing the functions of their crafts, many of them when 'off-duty' were very human, warm-hearted and companionable beings, normal in everything except moral attitude toward horses, cattle, public vehicles, and bank safes."[14]

Roosevelt, back in New York City, was fighting battles of his own.[15] Once home, he immediately launched into the political activities he had said for months he wanted to avoid. Between his arrival home and the election on November 4, he engaged in a series of speeches and newspaper interviews promoting the election of Maine senator James G. Blaine, whose nomination had been anathema to Roosevelt and other reformers during the Republican National Convention. Although Blaine was widely believed to have used his office to enrich himself, and he symbolized the corruption that reformers were trying to purge from the party, Roosevelt supported him in seven speeches, including three in Massachusetts in which he also backed Henry Cabot Lodge's candidacy for the House of Representatives.

Grover Cleveland, the governor of New York and Blaine's Democratic opponent, had to deal with corruption issues of his own. On July 21, 1884, newspapers revealed that he had fathered an illegitimate child eight years earlier with a woman in Buffalo, New York.[16] However, his reaction to the exposure seemed to defuse a potentially explosive threat to his candidacy. He never denied that the child was his, and he explained that he had supported the child over the years. Although Cleveland was a bachelor, the Republican Party tried to tar him as an adulterer, but the issue gained little traction with voters.[17]

The campaign became furiously partisan. "You could rob a man of his good name or his fortune or indulge in any other similar playful antic with impugnity but to criticize his political faith was a serious matter. Families were disrupted, old friendships destroyed and a disagreeable atmosphere persisted throughout the entire campaign. It was a great relief when it ended."[18]

In such an atmosphere Roosevelt labored to explain his Blaine endorsement. In a *New York Sun* interview, given only two days after he returned home, he said that while on the ranch he had thought over the campaign and had concluded that he must support Blaine. "It is altogether contrary to my character to occupy a neutral position in so important and exciting a struggle, and besides my natural desire to occupy a position of some kind, I made up my mind that it was clearly my duty to support the ticket."[19] He knew that this statement would incense former allies, but he had long since resolved himself to their animosity. "A number of independents were dissatisfied with my course in declaring for Blaine, but this is not creditable to their intelligence," he had told a St. Paul reporter in July. "It has always been my luck in politics, and I suppose always will be, to offend some wing of the party—generally the machine, but sometimes the independents. I should think little of myself should I permit the independents to dictate to me any more than the machine."[20]

As the election lurched toward a conclusion, Blaine seemed likely to win. Then, on Wednesday, October 29, just back from a successful campaign swing through the West, Blaine attended a meeting of a thousand ministers in the hall of the Fifth Avenue Hotel. At the podium, the Reverend Dr. Burchard, of the Murray Hill Presbyterian Church, referred to the Democrats scathingly as the party of "rum, Romanism, and rebellion." This seemingly simple statement was packed with potential damage for the Blaine campaign, because it attacked three major voting blocs—anti-prohibitionists, Catholics, and southerners. Blaine, sitting nearby but engrossed in thoughts of his own upcoming remarks, failed to absorb the alliterative accusation.[21]

In the evening, Blaine attended a fund-raising dinner at Delmonico's, a poor choice for a candidate who was promoting himself as a man of the people. Housed in a massive brick building on Fifth Avenue at Twenty-sixth Street, Delmonico's was "the scene of the Patriarch's balls, of innumerable brilliant social events, and of nearly all the grand banquets that have been given for a generation. Many of the belles of the 'Four Hundred' have made their *débuts* at Delmonico's. The place is the social centre of the wealth and exclusive portion of New York."[22] The restaurant's status-conscious management was so concerned about maintaining a proper address that the restaurant had moved six times in fifty years.[23] "A public banquet or private dinner at Delmonicos . . . was a solemn rite that would put a Roman Emperor on his mettle. Viands and wines that have gone out of epicurean parlance were served. Terrapin, Canvas-back, Venison, Pheasants, Mallard, Quail, Rooster's Combs, and other now almost obsolete comestibles, were in profusion. Every course had its appropriate wine.

Amontillado with soup, Burgundy with fish, Mumm's Extra Dry with the entrée and roast, Port and Madeira with the dessert and Cognac with coffee was *de rigeuer*."[24] To make matters worse for the oblivious Blaine, he was feted there as the guest of some of the city's most elite businessmen, including Jay Gould, whose name had become a metaphor for dirty deals and corruption both political and commercial.

That Blaine had been the victim of a double whammy—only six days before the election—soon became clear. With stunning speed, the Reverend Dr. Burchard's rolling rhetoric alienated Irish Catholic voters, even though Blaine's mother was Catholic and his sister the mother superior of a convent. The phrase also sent anti-prohibitionists fleeing, along with potential southern voters who resented aspersions on the rebellion. Those desertions alone probably were enough to sink him—Whitelaw Reid, a liberal Republican leader and longtime editor of the *New York Tribune*, thought the comment cost Blaine ten thousand votes in Manhattan and Brooklyn alone. But the reversal of fortune was not over. Democratic newspapers zeroed in on the fund-raising dinner; the *New York World*, for example, asked, "Is there a workingman now who believes that James G. Blaine is sincere when he pretends to be the friend of labor? While Blaine and his millionaire admirers were feasting at Delmonico's last night, thousands of children in this great city, whose fathers labor twelve hours a day, went to bed hungry and many of them supperless."[25]

The election was close, with the New York vote the deciding factor. Cleveland won the state by 1,149 out of 1,167,169 votes (nationwide he won by 23,005 out of 10,052,706).[26] Conventional wisdom suggested that the comment about rum, Romanism, and rebellion killed Blaine's election. Blaine himself put the onus on an editorial cartoon in the *New York World* that drew attention to the Delmonico's dinner.[27] In any event, the Republicans had lost the presidency for the first time since Lincoln was elected in 1860. Roosevelt's disappointment in the outcome focused less on Blaine than on Henry Cabot Lodge, who had lost his bid for a seat in the House of Representatives at least partly due to Blaine backlash. Three days after the election he wrote Lodge, "I just did not have the heart to write you before. It is simply cruel; and I do not dare trust myself at present to speak to an Independent on the subject."[28]

Roosevelt had succeeded in alienating progressive politicians—his natural political bedfellows—by choosing his party over his reform goals. "Blaine's nomination meant to me pretty sure political death if I supported him," he wrote Lodge on the eleventh.[29] "That I realized entirely, and went in with my eyes open. . . . I have not believed and do not believe that I shall ever be likely to come back into political life; we fought a good winning fight when our friends the Independents were backing us; and we have both of us, when circumstances turned them against us, fought the losing fight grimly out to the end. What we have been cannot be taken from us; what we are is due to the folly of others and to no fault of ours."

Roosevelt's allegation that the Republican defeat heralded the end of his political career may have been a touch melodramatic; he had, after all, turned down nominations for the federal House of Representatives and the New York Assembly, which hardly seem the opportunities offered a man on his political deathbed.[30] He also was still in demand as a speaker. On the evening of the eleventh he addressed the Nineteenth Century Club, a city reform organization, telling members, "The Republican Party had been most successful when it was in accord with the independents. Yet sometimes the independents ran a little mad."[31] In the past election they "fell into the error of calling those names who refused to leave the Republican Party. Many called Blaine a machine man. That was not so, for the independents had to fight him with the aid of the machine men." He blamed the Republican loss on urban independents but also on the lack of support from rural prohibitionists. "Had Blaine received the Prohibition vote, he would have been elected in spite of the independents and of the machine, and had the machine men pulled straight, the Republicans would have been successful in spite of both the others."

With that off his chest, Roosevelt was ready to return to Medora and would "in all probability be unable to get back from the west until Xmas."[32]

11

WINTER, 1884–85

On the cold Monday morning of November 17, 1884—not twenty-four hours after his return to the Badlands—Theodore Roosevelt and his Maltese Cross men drove a herd of cattle into Medora for shipment to market.[1] At one-thirty in the afternoon he rode out of town alone, following the trail north along the Little Missouri River. His destination was the hunter's shack he had purchased the previous summer, upstream from where Sewall and Dow were building the new house. He was hoping to cover the twenty-some miles before nightfall and expected Captain Robins to be at the shack, overseeing a small herd of cattle.

With the temperature near zero, Roosevelt loped along at a quick pace, fearing that otherwise he might not reach the shack before dark.[2] The trail left the river bottom, snaking up and down ravines and across a plateau where a punishing wind swept the brown grasses clean of snow. After curving a dozen miles out, the trail led back into the bottomland, where it was sheltered from the wind but required Roosevelt to cross the frozen river multiple times. His horse frequently broke through the ice and "would then have to plunge and paw his way through to the opposite shore."[3]

The sun set while Roosevelt was still miles from the hut, laboring along a trail barely visible in the starlight. He spurred on, pushing as hard as he could, certain he would be unable to find the way as night deepened, especially as clouds began to veil the stars. Coming finally to the last river crossing before the shack, he watered his horse and then splashed over to a half-mile-square cottonwood grove on the other side. He passed completely through the grove without finding the shack, lost in darkness among the trees, but blundered upon the cow corral, where he groped on foot for the pathway to the hut.

It was a low, windowless structure, not quite twelve feet square—and empty: Captain Robins had run out of food and left.[4] Roosevelt had with him only a packet of tea and some salt. He turned the pony loose to forage, built a fire in the fireplace, and made tea after axing through river ice to collect a pail of water. Roosevelt: "I should have liked something to eat, but as I did not have it, the tea did not prove such a bad substitute for a cold and tired man."[5]

At sunrise, hundreds of sharp-tailed grouse flew down from surrounding trees to feed on chokecherries and wild plums, the woods alive with their ceaseless clucking. Those still in the trees made perfect targets, silhouetted against the brightening sky; Roosevelt shot five, "and it was not long before two of the birds, plucked and cleaned, were split open and roasted before the fire. And to me they seemed most delicious food, although even in November the sharptails, while keeping their game flavor, had begun to be dry and tough."[6]

Later that day he rode to the Elkhorn Ranch and was pleased to find that Bill Sewall and Wilmot Dow were within days of finishing all the logs for the house.[7] On Wednesday, November 19, he chose the exact site for the ranch house—a wooded flat beside the river, backed in the near distance by high buttes. The next day he and Captain Robins rode the range checking cattle, and Roosevelt shot seven more grouse.[8] On Friday he rode with Sewall and Dow back to the Maltese Cross Ranch, snow falling and the thermometer sinking to twenty degrees below zero. "As you may imagine," he wrote his sister Anna, "my fur coat and buffalo bag have come in very handily."[9] In this letter he did not neglect Alice: "Give many kisses to the wee baby."

The "buffalo bag" Roosevelt mentioned was a sleeping bag made from a buffalo robe sewn closed on three sides, which, though very warm, still had to be supplemented with beaver robes and bearskins when temperatures bottomed at sixty-five below zero.[10] Roosevelt and his men "wore the heaviest kind of all-wool underclothing, with flannels, lined boots, and great fur coats, caps, and gauntlets or mittens, but yet after each ride one or the other of us would be almost sure to come in with a touch of the frost somewhere on him." On one trip Roosevelt froze his nose and cheek.[11] His fifty-dollar raccoon coat was beyond the means of the average cowboy, who might wear a "sourdough" coat of canvas or duck, lined with heavy flannel or blanketing and sometimes painted to make it windproof and waterproof.[12]

Roosevelt did not so much stay at his more southern ranch as pause there. On Saturday, with the temperature still below zero, he and Sewall rode into Medora for unknown purposes.[13] A new sign of impending civilization stood tall in the town: a red-brick church, built under the patronage of the Marquise de Morès, whose name was engraved on the cornerstone.[14] But frontier amusements still prevailed. "The boys" had been amusing themselves by giving beer to Bob Roberts' pet bear, Nellie, "which seemed to please her very much. It made her tipsy, and her efforts to draw beer from the bottle were very ludicrous. She finally stood on her head and held the bottle between her paws and sucked it dry. It got the best of her, and she was compelled to lie down and sober up."[15]

On the twenty-fifth, Roosevelt and Sewall rode to the Langs' ranch, urging ranchers along the way to participate in Roosevelt's newest enthusiasm, an upcoming meeting to organize a regional cattlemen's association.[16] He also announced in the Bad Lands Cow Boy that the organizational meeting would be held at eleven in the morning on Friday, December 19.[17] The idea of a local association was very much in the air. The previous February, Howard Eaton had called a meeting that included A. T. Packard, Bill Merrifield, and E. G. Paddock, but another scheduled in April must have failed, as the Bad Lands Cow Boy ran a story indicating that further planning would be delayed until fall.[18]

In making his pitch, Roosevelt stressed the need to stop thieves.[19] Another critical issue was the uncontrolled number of cattle being put in the Badlands. In the roughly twenty years during which the cattle business had spread throughout the West, repeated overstocking had led to ruinous losses for cattlemen, especially when added to the challenges of weather and other natural conditions.[20] Even in good years losses were heavy among weaker animals in regions where grass was overgrazed; in a severe winter, losses became "simply appalling."[21] A stockmen's association could block unwanted newcomers. "In the cow country," Roosevelt observed, "a man is peculiarly dependent upon his neighbors, and a small outfit is wholly unable to work without their assistance when once the cattle have mingled completely with those of other brands."[22] And so, when an area had as many cattle as it could hold, ranchers refused to work with anyone who put out another herd.

After drumming up interest in the livestock association, Roosevelt waited at the Maltese Cross Ranch for Sylvane Ferris to return from the town of Spearfish with a herd of new horses.[23] On Saturday, November 29, Roosevelt rode into Medora and had lunch with de Morès, any tensions that existed between them apparently at rest. The Marquis had been doing well—less than a month before, he had received an order from Chicago for five hundred cattle.[24] His myriad plans for the livestock industry and for cutting meat prices were turning him into a local hero: "The man who lowers the prices of every mouthful of food for humanity does the world infinitely more good than the hero of Austerlitz, who conquers armies and overturns empires. The Marquis de Morès may be called the pioneer in a business which promises to revolutionize the food supply of the civilized world."[25] Roosevelt's scantly written diary offers no description of his lunch with de Morès.

On November 30, still waiting for the horses, Roosevelt sent Sewall and Dow back to the Elkhorn Ranch and then hunted for several days with Merrifield. On December 2 they searched all day for bighorn sheep without seeing any; the following day Roosevelt stayed at the house with a fever. On the fourth and fifth he hunted on foot near the house, bagging four grouse, three mule deer, and one white-tailed deer.[26] He tried again for bighorn sheep on the fifth and again failed to see any. The following day, Sylvane arrived with fifty-two horses. Now would begin the serious work of breaking the mostly untamed stock.[27]

The two and a half score horses Roosevelt had bought were not an excessive number for a ranch; eventually he would have eighty.[28] Large ranches might have several hundred horses, called ponies in this region—"small, wiry beasts, not very speedy, but with good bottom, and able to pick up a living under the most adverse circumstances."[29] Such numbers were needed because almost all ranch work was done on horseback, and although cowboys supplied their own saddles, bridles, and lariats, they rarely had their own mounts.[30] Each hand was assigned his own string of nine or ten horses, including one for morning work and one for afternoon, with each horse released onto the range for three days' rest after it was ridden.[31] Other horses were held at the ranch house, ready to be saddled at any time of day as needed, for which reason they were called "night horses" or "kept-up ponies."[32] Cowboys preferred to work only in the saddle and would mount up to ride even short distances around a ranch house.[33]

Riding broncos was a new experience for Roosevelt and not one he liked: "I am no horseman, and I can not ride an unbroken horse with any comfort."[34] Few could. A. T. Packard recalled that the first time he rode a wild horse, "my legs were practically paralyzed for ten minutes after I dismounted. It seemed to me a compound of a parachute leap, a shoot-the-chute and an earthquake."[35] He remembered at least one horse that "specialized in seizing the foot or leg of the rider in his teeth and jerking forward with his head. Lucky indeed was the rider if he escaped being jumped on by the horse after he had been pulled from the saddle. Nine times in ten the rider, when thrown, is momentarily shocked. For a few seconds at least he is motionless on the ground. That is the danger point if the horse is 'spoiled' and of the vicious type. He may attack the fallen man with teeth and hoofs. He is as ferocious as a grizzly. He can break bone or tear off a bunch of flesh with his teeth. He can kill a man by striking with either front foot or by a kick with his hind feet."[36]

Roosevelt preferred to break horses gently and gradually, "spending much time over it, and choosing the horses that seemed gentle to begin with."[37] Cowboys rarely took the time for this approach, which they considered a farm method. Packard: "Roosevelt was a firm believer in really 'gentling' and not 'breaking' a horse. . . . He argued that the farm colt, by birth and training, developed an affection for mankind, while the range horse as naturally considered every man his enemy. The farm colt was handled daily and was halter-broke in early infancy. The range colt might readily live to full growth without a man's hand ever touching him. His idea of man was that of an enemy of superior powers and from whom he tried to flee at sight."[38]

The day after the horses arrived, Roosevelt sent for Sewall and Dow so they could help with the breaking before herding about twenty of the ponies to the Elkhorn. Although Dow rode broncs, Sewall refused; "I didn't come out here to make a fool of myself trying to do what I know I can't do," he said.[39] A cowboy told him that if he didn't ride, he would "have the contempt of everybody." Sewall replied, "That won't affect me very much. If I were younger, it might, but it won't now." He finally told the others to stop harassing him. "I suppose you fellows can ride broncos, but you cannot ride me, and if you get on, your feet will drag." His frustration was compounded because he knew that breaking the horses delayed putting up walls for the Elkhorn house by two weeks even as temperatures were falling to twenty-six below zero at night.[40]

The men from the Elkhorn arrived on the tenth, and Roosevelt helped break horses on the eleventh. Meanwhile, he had given up on day hunts for bighorn sheep and had concocted a more elaborate plan. He had heard that a small band of the animals was roaming a steep and broken region about twenty-five miles upriver and had concluded that he needed to set up a base camp there from which he could hunt until he shot one.[41] His plan was to have one of his hired men, George Myers, drive a buckboard loaded with bedding and food to a hut near where he wanted to hunt, while he and Merrifield rode horses.[42] He would launch this plan as soon as the new ponies were broken. But then, "owing to a funny mistake made by one of the cowboys," the trip started earlier than he had anticipated.

Friday, December 2, 1884, started as usual, with the men eating breakfast at five in the morning even though the sun did not appear until almost eight. After breakfast, they rode out on night horses to collect the new broncos, riding under the stars into a world so cold that the frozen river "lay fixed like a huge bent bar of blue steel"; trees cracked in the night, and cattle huddled forlornly in thickets, their backs hoary with frost, heads held low, icicles hanging from their lips.[43]

After rounding up the horses and putting them in a corral near the house, the cowboys came inside, stamping their feet and trying to warm numbed hands at the fire. One of them had something to report that was of paramount interest to Roosevelt: While looking for the broncos he had seen two bears go into a washout, and he was sure he could locate them.

Roosevelt decided that he would go after the bears and then leave directly for the bighorn hunt. After giving George Myers instructions about the wagon, he donned a long fur coat and a fur hat that could be pulled down over his ears, "mounted in hot haste" on Manitou, and rode off before sunrise with Merrifield and the cowboy. Galloping around cattle too cold to move, they went up a long valley that brought them out on the rolling highlands. Warmed up now from riding, they came shortly to a washout that cut for two or three miles along a valley bottom. Into this washout, the cowboy reported, the bears had vanished.

The two hunters moved upwind. Finally, a half mile away, a pair of dark animals emerged from the washout onto the plain. For a brief moment Roosevelt thought he had spotted the bears, but then he realized that no, these animals—the animals the cowboy had seen—were not bears. They were horses. "The cowboy's chap-fallen face was a study; he had seen, in the dim light, the two ponies going down with their heads held near the ground, and had mistaken them for bears. . . . He knew only too well the merciless chaff to which he would be henceforth exposed, and a foretaste of which he at once received from my companion."[44] Roosevelt had the cowboy drive the ponies to the corral, while he and Merrifield departed for the sheep hunt.

Only twenty miles separated them from the rendezvous site with George Myers, so they did not need to ride hard. They took time for excursions into the rugged high country favored by bighorn sheep, sure-footed creatures that weighed up to three hundred pounds and could climb nearly vertical slopes. The men dismounted and led their horses over steep, icy terrain that the animals could barely manage. Sometimes they left the horses behind, along with their coats and chaps, while they checked out particularly rugged areas. Roosevelt: "Up the slippery, ice-covered buttes we clambered, clinging to the rocks, and slowly working our way across the faces of the cliffs, or cautiously creeping along the narrow ledges, peering over every crest long and carefully, and from the peaks scanning the ground all about with the field-glasses."[45] The cold seeped into them, hands and feet numb and ears tingling. But they saw no sheep that day, only tracks.

As night fell they rode hard for the hut, racing the setting sun. They hoofed into a grove of leafless cottonwood trees along the river just after daylight faded behind a line of hills in front of them. There they found the hut and a fire Myers had stoked. In the deepening night, wind whistled through the chinks of the log walls. They could not keep the hut "anywhere near freezing-point," and so, after a sparse supper, were "glad to cower down with our great fur coats still on, under the pile of buffalo-robes and bear-skins."[46]

On Saturday, with temperatures ranging from a high of twenty-five degrees to a low of minus ten, Roosevelt and Merrifield hunted again, leaving the horses in camp because they had been a hindrance in the high country. Again the men came up empty-handed, though Roosevelt found even this experience instructive: "Hunting for a day or two without finding game where the work is severe and toilsome, is a good test of the sportsman's staying qualities; the man who at the end of the time is proceeding with as much caution and determination as at the beginning, has got the right stuff in him."[47]

However, Roosevelt's staying qualities could not survive a day without gunfire; he finally shot at a prairie chicken, which he missed. At the rifle's blast the head of a large animal appeared over a ridge about six hundred yards away—too far to identify it. Hurrying to where the animal had stood, the hunters found the tracks of a deer.

The next day they rode the horses, intending to work a chain of tall buttes where they had seen fresh tracks. As they set off, they saw towering, grayish white clouds massing in the northwest—an approaching storm. The hunt took on new urgency.

In high, rough country where knife-edged ridges fell off into steep gorges, they tethered the horses and walked up a coulee only a couple of feet wide at the bottom. There they found sign that mountain sheep, perhaps only moments before, had come down the ravine wall, jumped across to the opposite side, and climbed up.

Pressing ahead, the hunters moved up the ravine wall. At the top, Roosevelt ran along a ridge, hiding behind masses of sandstone, until he saw two bighorn rams about ninety yards away, the larger of them standing broadside. Dropping to one knee and shouldering his rifle, Roosevelt put his bead just behind the ram's shoulder and fired. The ram staggered, pitched forward, recovered, and disappeared over the ridge. Roosevelt and Merrifield hastened to where they had last seen the animal; they found it lying dead about two hundred yards away, at a spot to which they could easily pull up the horses.

After loading the sheep onto Manitou, Roosevelt tracked the other bighorn for half a mile before giving up. With storm clouds darkening the sky, the men were eager to get back to the ranch. They took an hour to return to George Myers at the cabin, where they loaded the sheep into the wagon. Then they rode on ahead, reaching the Maltese Cross just as the storm struck. Soon they sat before the fire; what happened to Myers, out in the blizzard with his wagon, Roosevelt does not say.[48]

The evening of the fourteenth he wrote to Anna about his successful hunt—"I have now killed every kind of plains game"—and about the arrival of his many horses.[49] He added that he planned to attend the Little Missouri stockmen's association on Friday the nineteenth and would start home on Saturday the twentieth.

Roosevelt opened the stockmen's meeting at the appointed hour in Roberts Hall. Those present included a roster of familiar names: Gregor Lang, E. G. Paddock, the Marquis de Morès, Howard Eaton.[50] Having taken the bit between his teeth in starting the Little Missouri River Stockmen's Association, Roosevelt was elected chairman, even though he was one of the least experienced ranchers in the area: "He was direct, he was fearless; he was a good talker, sure of his ground, and, in the language of the Bad Lands, 'he didn't take backwater from anyone.' He was self-reliant and he minded his own business; he was honest and he had no axe to grind. The ranchmen no doubt felt that in view of these qualities you might forget a man's youth and forgive his spectacles."[51]

The meeting included routine business. De Morès was named a committee of one to liaison with a Montana-association committee that lobbied the territorial legislatures.[52] The group passed a resolution calling for a possible legal test case against the Northern Pacific Railroad should any member's livestock be run over by a train without compensation, as well as seven other resolutions to govern future actions until bylaws were drafted.

The control that the members wanted the association to exert over ranchers is clear in three of these resolutions. One required that each member put out on the range no fewer than ten bulls for every hundred head of cattle, another demanded that no member gather or brand calves between December 1 and the spring roundup without giving "reasonable notice beforehand to the other ranchmen in the neighborhood," and the third declared that the association and its members would refuse to help or would bar from the seasonal roundups any ranching operation that failed to follow the association's rules and bylaws.[53]

The association launch received a good review on the front page of the *Bad Lands Cow Boy*: "The stockmen's meeting last Friday morning bids fair to be the beginning of a very efficient organization. The utmost harmony and unanimity prevailed, and under the able chairmanship of Theodore Roosevelt, a large amount of business was transacted in a short time."[54]

The day after the meeting Roosevelt, as he had promised his sister, boarded a train for New York City. Before he left, Sewall expressed reservations about cattle survival in the harsh Badlands winter. Having raised cattle in Maine, Sewall believed that when a cow produced one calf after another without supplemental feeding in winter, she was likely to die after the third calf.[55] He also was certain that cows that calved in cold weather were likely to freeze their udders and lose their calves. "Those cows will either have to be fed or they'll die," Sewall told Roosevelt.

"No one hereabouts seems to think there's any danger of that sort," Roosevelt responded. "I think, Bill, that you're wrong."

"I hope I am." The cows were not given special feed.

In Roosevelt's absence, life in the Badlands settled into its winter routine. "For the ranchman the winter is occasionally a pleasant holiday, but more often an irksome period of enforced rest and gloomy foreboding."[56] Many ranch hands were laid off, because winter was cattle country's most inactive season.[57] Some stayed on through the season, though, doing perhaps the most difficult and hazardous work of the year—riding the line. The line was an artificial boundary along the east side of the river composed of small camps about twenty miles apart. The line riders stayed in cabins if they were lucky, or in tents in a coulee if they were not. Usually two men were stationed in each camp. In the morning they would ride in opposite directions, turning back when they met the men from the next camps. They were looking for cattle wandering from the Badlands toward the eastern prairies, where they might drift endlessly before a storm or become trapped against a barrier and die in a blizzard. The cowboys also looked out for early calves, getting them to shelter, and might corral and feed animals that looked too weak to survive on their own. "Line-riding is very cold work, and dangerous too, when the men have to be out in a blinding snowstorm, or in a savage blizzard that takes the spirit in the thermometer far down below zero."[58]

Other less routine but no less important work also had to be tended. The men at the Maltese Cross Ranch periodically drove a wagon three or four miles south of the house to a coal vein in the side of a clay bluff, where they loaded coal into the wagon and drove home over the frozen river.[59] Part of each day, at least one man had to check cattle.[60] To pass the cold winter nights, the cowboys played old sledge, casino, checkers, and chess and read books—Roosevelt was surprised to find them reading and "in large part comprehending" Henry Cabot Lodge's book *Studies in Literature*.[61] Medora was quiet in winter, the abattoir closed, the butchers gone east for winter, the carpenters no longer at work.[62] There was nothing to do in town but drink or attend the occasional dance, such as those held at Thanksgiving and Christmas. Roosevelt opened one such "cowboy ball" by dancing the lancers with Paddock's wife, acknowledging that Paddock "knew all the steps far better than I did. He could have danced a minuet very well with a little practice."[63]

Other entertainments cropped up. The Medora Gun Club—later called the Bad Lands Gun Club—started in February 1885 to hold the first of five contests, with competitors given five shots at each of several targets set up at one hundred to three hundred yards.[64] Paddock and Packard vied for first place, and in the end the newspaper editor won by hitting five straight bull's-eyes at seventy-five feet and averaging 53 3/20 out of a possible score of 60 points. The skating rink—now charging men twenty-five cents for admission and ten cents for skates (women enjoyed free admission but had to pay a quarter for skates)—held a masquerade contest, with a prize for the best costume; masks cost a quarter at the local confectioner's and at the news depot.[65]

The winter of 1884 and 1885 was "another ideal one for range stock."[66] Even so, it was sometimes ominous. Roosevelt: "When the days have dwindled to their shortest, and the nights seem never-ending, then all the great northern plains are changed into an abode of iron desolation. Sometimes furious gales blow down from the north, driving before them the clouds of blinding snow-dust, wrapping the mantle of death round every unsheltered being that faces their unshackled anger. They roar in a thunderous bass as they sweep across the prairie or whirl through the naked canyons; they shiver the great brittle cottonwoods, and beneath their rough touch the icy limbs of the pines that cluster in the gorges sing like the chords of an Aeolian harp. Again, in the coldest midwinter weather, not a breath of wind may stir; and then the still, merciless, terrible cold that broods over the earth like the shadow of silent death seems even more dreadful in its gloomy rigor than is the lawless madness of the storms."[67]

Sewall continued to bemoan Badlands life in letters to his brother. "As to our coming back [to Maine], you need not worry about that," he wrote. "As soon as I serve out my time and my sentence expires I shall return. Am having a good time and enjoy myself[; I] should anywhere if I knew I could not do any better and was obliged to but this is just about like being transported to Siberia—just about as cold, barren, desolate and most as far out of the way. . . . as soon as I get straightened out you will hear the patter of my little feet, also my musical voice. . . . There is nothing here for me to like."[68]

In February a man named James Watts stopped by the Elkhorn Ranch on his way to trade at an Indian village sixty or seventy miles downriver. Sewall thought Watts was "a genuine specimen of a frontier man—just like you have read of and seen pictures of."[69] His father had been killed by Indians; Watts had lived with the Lakota for five years and had been a mail carrier, a scout, and a hunter. He claimed to have been shot with bullets seven times and with arrows five times as well as having had his head split and a shinbone broken during encounters with tomahawks. He owned "scalps he had taken himself; said he always scalped all he could." He had lived with an Indian woman "but soon got enough of that. Has a wife now somewhere east." He urged the Elkhorn men to join him on the trip to the village, which they did.

Watts helped the ranch hands trade with the Indians. Sewall: "We bought a lot of moccasins, buckskins and buckskin clothes; also the best buffalo robe in the tribe of Gos ventre pronounced Grovon. It was owned by the renowned Mr. Sitting Owl and is flowered with quills and paint on the inside. He had been offered $25.00 but sold it to us for 15.00 being hard up. We were offered 20.00 for it before we got home. We got suits of Buckskin for 12.00. They ask from 30.00 to 50.00 for them here. We need them for the Rose bushes will wear out a pair of good stout duck pants in two days if you are walking and when we hunt Deer we have to go into them on foot."

The shopping spree continued: "We also bought a lot of war plumes and a mountain lion skin, some other curiosities. Saw a regular Indian camp; went to a feast, also a council. Saw the pipe of peace smoked. Will took a whiff. I passed. We also heard them sing and saw them dance."

The Indians seemed fascinated by Sewall's long red whiskers, and one "old fellow" braided them. Sewall: "I let him work. They were all laughing and talking. In the lodge the old Squaw was making a jacket for us and I went in to see how she was getting along. She was Mrs. Sitting Owl. Well, after the fellow got them braided he picked up a big knife as if he was going to cut them off. I had been watching him closely and when he reached for the knife I grabbed him by the topy of the head quick and motioned as if I was going to strike. I think it really scared him and all laughed. I saw scalps; might have bought one for $5.00 but thought it would be cheaper to take one myself if I wanted it very badly. The ones I saw were not more than three inches in diameter and was taken by Mr. Bobtailed Bull. There were some Sioux and Mandans but mostly Gos Ventres. It was really worth seeing but was a desperate cold ride."

Roosevelt had arrived in New York City a day or two before Christmas.[70] While in the East he drafted the bylaws for the new cattlemen's association and, in Albany in January, helped one friend from his legislative years campaign unsuccessfully for the Assembly speakership and another successfully for the U.S. Senate. He tended to Alice at least briefly, when Anna took a trip to Washington, D.C., during which Theodore sent her a postcard saying, "The baby is in a condition of rampant and vocal good health; very happy and prepared to greet its Aunt Bye with inarticulate affection."[71]

His spirit remained in the Badlands, crowding his thoughts with gun-men and cattle, frozen rivers and wild animals, the charge of a grizzly and the howling of wolves—images that flowed from his pen onto paper: At a desk in Anna's home he was writing his first book about western life, *Hunting Trips of a Ranchman*. As he wrote, he sometimes scowled, some-times grinned, in keeping with the mood of the story he was writing.[72] He took liberal literary license, describing winter nights by the fireplace in the Elkhorn Ranch house even though it was not finished until spring 1885, *after* he had sent the manuscript to his publisher.[73] He also fobbed off his few months in the West as the experiences of a seasoned cowboy. Of his bison hunt, he wrote, "One September I determined to take a short trip after bison. At that time I was staying in a cow-camp a good many miles up river from my ranch," neglecting to mention that he had never been in the Badlands before, nor had he yet established a ranch.[74] He even left out Joe Ferris when narrating how he shot his first bison, even though Ferris had been with him and had told him where to place the bullet.

He also exhibited his judgmental nature. He wrote that mule deer, which he called black-tailed deer, are "nobler looking" than pronghorn, that hunting mule deer is "beyond all comparison the nobler sport" com-pared to hunting white-tailed deer, because hunting the mule deer "calls into play, and either develops or implies the presence of, much more manly qualities than does the other."[75] The elk was "as noble and lordly game as is to be found in the Western world."[76] He declared there was "no manlier form of sport" than hunting on horseback with hounds.[77] In his mind there was even a hierarchy in firearms, implying that the rifle is nobler than the shotgun: "The rifle is the freeman's weapon."[78]

Roosevelt finished the nearly one-hundred-thousand-word manuscript for his book by early March and sent it to his publisher.[79] He wrote Henry Cabot Lodge on March 8, "In a fortnight I shall go out West; my book will be out before I return. The pictures will be excellent—as for the read-ing matter, I am a little doubtful."[80] In the same letter he returned to what may have been a festering wound, the 1884 election, stating that he and Lodge knew that politically they had been "pretty effectually killed as soon as Blaine was nominated. If our consciences would have permitted it I have not the slightest doubt that by bolting we could have done an immense amount for ourselves, and would have won a commanding position—at the cost . . . of black treachery to all our warmest and truest supporters and also at the cost of stultifying ourselves as regards all our previous declarations in respect to the Democracy [the Democratic Party]."[81]

At about the time of the letter, in a discouraging resurgence of the illnesses that had plagued him since childhood, he suffered an enteritis attack, probably from the strain of his marathon writing blitz. The illness forced him to delay his departure, scheduled originally for March 22.[82] He was not so ill that he could not take part in a March 29 fox hunt.[83] Not until April 14 did he board a westbound train; as a result, he missed not only the second official meeting of the Little Missouri River Stockmen's Association, slated for April 1, but a sighting of four bison at the headwaters of the Little Missouri by one Bill Huggins, who killed one and brought its head and hams to town.[84]

12

ROUNDUP

THEODORE ROOSEVELT WAS BACK AT THE MEDORA TRAIN STATION ON a Friday in mid-April 1885 dressed in city garb—"store clothes" in the local parlance—including a derby, the bullet magnet much disdained by cowboys.[1] But no one molested the pot hat on this particular head, and he left almost immediately for the Elkhorn Ranch.[2]

Cowboys meeting Roosevelt at this time thought he looked sickly, bone thin, weak. "You could have spanned his waist with your two thumbs and fingers," one herder recalled.[3] He was gaunt enough to worry his family: His sisters arranged for regular reports on his health from Bill Sewall. When Roosevelt learned of this surveillance, he was indignant. "They had no business to write you," he told Sewall. "They should have written to me."[4] Sewall suggested that they did not take that avenue because "they knew you wouldn't write about how you were getting on. You'd just say you were all right."

Roosevelt also chided Sewall about his comment the previous year that the Badlands looked like poor cattle country. "Bill, you were mistaken about those cows. Cows and calves are all looking fine."[5]

"You wait until next spring, and see how they look," Sewall replied, with the reservations of a man who had lived most of his life subject to the vagaries of nature. Roosevelt, however, had already made up his mind about the future of the Badlands cattle industry—he had sent Merrifield to Minnesota in early March to buy another fifteen hundred head.[6] On April 23 he had Sewall, Dow, and Sylvane Ferris leave by train to meet Merrifield, brand the cattle, and ship them to Medora.

The spring thaw had begun in the Badlands. Down the country's thousands of coulees and washouts, water ran high and fast, the Little Missouri a rushing torrent.[7] Sodden ground around water holes and along the river turned into bottomless sinks in which horses and cattle mired hopelessly unless pulled out by rope. Riders never knew when the earth might collapse and swallow them.

During his spring stay, Roosevelt tried to cross the Little Missouri River near Medora, where he had the option of using the railroad bridge.[8] Instead, he chose to ride across a dam that the Marquis de Morès had built to create an ice pond for his refrigerating plant. An ice-cutting crew warned Roosevelt away, but he trusted his horse. "If Manitou once gets his feet on that dam, he'll keep them there and we can make it finely," he said, even though the river had overtopped the dam, and he needed help from the ice cutters just to find where the dam met the bank.

Manitou stepped calmly into the flow but walked only a few paces before he lost his footing. Rider and mount tumbled into the river, disappearing underwater. Moments later, Roosevelt surfaced. He was swimming for shore on the downstream side of his horse, one hand on the saddle horn and the other pushing ice floes out of the way. Joe Ferris watched the whole event from the front of his store and later suggested that Roosevelt was reckless, to which Roosevelt replied, "I suppose it might be considered reckless, but it was lots of fun."

The Maltese Cross Ranch was Roosevelt's cattle headquarters; there he employed half a dozen hands, including Sylvane Ferris, Bill Merrifield, George Myers, and Jack Reuter.[9] The Elkhorn Ranch served mostly as Roosevelt's hunting lodge, managed by Sewall, Dow, and Captain Robins.[10] He rode back and forth between the two ranches and seemed to have a rapport with his cowboys. Bill Merrifield and the Ferrises even tried to take ownership of him; they were "intensely jealous of their connection with Mr. Roosevelt, and secretly resented his showing interest in anybody else."[11] Others were more measured in their dealings with Roosevelt. Jack Reuter: "He struck me like a sort of rough-an'-ready, all-around frontiersman. Wasn't a bit stuck up—just the same as one of the rest of us."[12] Sewall, who had known Roosevelt longer than anyone in the Badlands, said, "Roosevelt out in Dakota was full of life and spirit, always pleasant. He was hot tempered and quick, but he kept his temper in good control."[13] During a conversation with visitors at his store, Joe Ferris boiled down his opinion to: "I wouldn't be surprised if Roosevelt would be president."[14]

In late April, Roosevelt moved into his new Elkhorn Ranch house. Cottonwoods shaded its long, low veranda, "a pleasant place in the summer evenings when a cool breeze stirs along the river and blows in the faces of the tired men, who loll back in their rocking-chairs (what true American does not enjoy a rocking-chair?), book in hand—though they do not often read the books, but rock gently to and fro, gazing sleepily out at the weird-looking buttes opposite, until their sharp outlines grow indistinct and purple in the after-glow of the sunset."[15]

The house stood a story high, of hewn logs, with eight rooms divided by a central hall that ran north to south.[16] Roosevelt's bedroom in the southeast corner adjoined a larger room with a massive fireplace, built by an itinerant mason. The large room served as his study during the day and as the gathering place for all residents at night. Wilmot Dow had made andirons for the fireplace out of a steel rail he had found floating down the river attached to a yellow pine.

The Elkhorn outfit settled into something of a routine, within the broad boundaries of western ranch life. In summer they rose before dawn and went to bed about nightfall. By day they rode the range checking for sick cattle and hunting stray ponies. Food had to be hauled from town, firewood chopped, or coal dug and hauled.[17] Sewall: "Roosevelt led the regular life of a Dakota ranchman except that he did a good deal of reading and writing which ranchmen, as a rule, are not such good hands at."[18] When he was too tired to write at night, one of his hands recalled, Roosevelt would say, "How'd you like to talk on ancient history? Well we would say fine, and then he would go ahead and talk on ancient history or any other kind of history for hours and he would repeat it word for word, and it was just the same as it was in the book, and it was good history, too."[19] While expounding, Roosevelt rocked his chair at a speed that matched the intensity of his feelings.[20] He punctuated culminating points "by a sudden cessation of the rocking, together with an equally sudden forward projection of his shoulders and lower jaw, which spelt finality."[21]

On the first Tuesday in May, Merrifield, Sewall, and Dow arrived by train in Medora with the Minnesota cattle, which had arrived in fair condition following a gauntlet of trials.[22] After the stress of being corralled and branded they had gone without food for two or three days before they were crowded into railroad cars for a punishing three-day ride to Medora. Sewall had to move constantly among the train's twenty-two cars, checking the animals and keeping them on their feet to save them from being trampled. Most of the new stock were steers—neutered males—but the herd also included shorthorn bulls and one polled Angus.

That Tuesday, after passing time during lunch with de Morès by talking about fox hunting on Long Island, Roosevelt met his men and helped unload the cattle in a cold rain.[23] Weaker animals began dying, and Roosevelt lost about a dozen yearlings. The Maltese Cross crew took five hundred head. Roosevelt had five men to help him drive the other thousand to the Elkhorn, and he put in charge of the operation the only one of the five with experience as a cowhand.[24] However, he proved an incompetent manager, and Roosevelt took over.

The drive north took six days, about twice as long as it should have, in part because the weather veered wildly.[25] Snow fell throughout the second day, and strong winds forced the drovers to move the cattle into a sheltered valley as the temperature fell below freezing; two days later the men were sweltering in heat. The river was flooded, so on the third day they headed the cattle onto the higher plains, causing further delay; when night fell the herd was miles from water and had not had a drink since morning. As the long Badlands dusk ebbed into darkness, the situation grew dangerous—thirsty animals might stampede at the smell of water.[26] Roosevelt and his crew then would have to head them off and stop them, or at least keep them grouped together, one of a cowboy's most dangerous tasks: "It was riding at a dead run in the dark, with cut banks and prairie dog holes all around you, not knowing if the next jump would land you in a shallow grave."[27] Teddy Blue Abbott recalled a cowboy whose horse went down in a stampede. When he and his horse were discovered the next morning they were "mashed into the ground flat as a pancake. The only thing you could recognize was the handle of his six-shooter."[28]

The Elkhorn crew bedded down the cattle, and Roosevelt and another of the men stood first watch. Shortly after "darkness had become complete, the thirsty brutes of one accord got on their feet and tried to break out," Roosevelt wrote. "The only salvation was to keep them close together, as, if they once got scattered, we knew they could never be gathered; so I kept on one side, and the cowboy on the other, and never in my life did I ride so hard. In the darkness I could but dimly see the shadowy outlines of the herd, as with whip and spurs I ran the pony along its edge, turning back the beasts at one point barely in time to wheel and keep them in at another. The ground was cut up by numerous little gullies, and each of us got several falls, horses and riders turning complete somersaults. We were dripping with sweat, and our ponies quivering and trembling like quaking aspens, when, after more than an hour of the most violent exertion, we finally got the herd quieted again."[29]

Despite this dangerous episode, or perhaps because of it, Roosevelt was able to write Henry Cabot Lodge a few days after his return to the Elkhorn, "I have had hard work, and a good deal of fun since I came out here. . . . I had my hands full, working night and day, and being able to take off my clothes but once during the week I was out."[30] He added, "Tomorrow I start for the roundup."

The spring roundup ranked as one of the biggest annual events in cattle country, slated to start that year in late May at Box Elder Creek.[31] A cowboy commented in the Medora newspaper that the roundup was a stockman's "fourth of July, and generally lasts a month and a half."[32] The spring-to-early-summer roundups were held primarily to brand cattle, especially new calves; the fall "beef roundups" gathered steers for shipment to market.[33] During the roundup, cowboys became highly competitive; when orders were given, cowboys jumped to beat each other at getting work done. "To get kicked out of a roundup, indeed, constituted about the biggest disgrace that could attach itself to the cowboy of the period, so it but rarely happened. When it did, the ignominy clung like gumbo mud, obliging him to seek new and distant fields for his future activities."[34]

Each roundup covered a district of neighboring ranches. Roosevelt's district ran along the Little Missouri from the mouth of Beaver Creek to the mouth of Little Beaver Creek, about two hundred miles away.[35] Each rancher sent up to four men, totaling perhaps forty or fifty cowboys. The men and the roundup were put under the direction of a "captain"— generally a first-class foreman. He determined which areas were to be covered each day and assigned the men various tasks, such as herding un-used saddle horses, roping calves and adult cattle, and driving the day herd—cattle selected for holding in camp in order, for example, to be shipped to market.

At each participating ranch, preparation for the roundup began with the gathering of horses for the riders. Some of these animals had not been ridden in months and were likely to buck.[36] Because horses quickly wore out under the strains of the roundup, each rider chose a string of about ten ponies. In divvying up horses for the 1885 spring roundup, Roosevelt drew straws with his men rather than take first choice, as was his right as the boss.[37] Consequently, he ended up with one or two rough horses in his string.

The ranchers also had to set up chuck wagons for carrying food and goods.[38] Small ranches might share a chuck wagon, which was an ordi-nary wagon body with a tall box on the back with a door that dropped down to form a table, with two legs hinged on one end.[39] The box held shelves for storing food, including flour, cornmeal, sugar, coffee beans, bacon, and lard, as well as cooking utensils and other items. The chuck wagon also carried a barrel of water, with a faucet that went through the side of the box.[40] Hung horizontally beneath the rear axle might be a cooney—a dried cowhide used for storing fuel for cooking fires. The "jewelry chest" outside the front of the wagon contained various items such as ammunition and materials needed for wagon repair, including rawhide, which was the duct tape of its day. In the wagon box the men loaded enough provisions, bedding, and clothing to get them through the roundup.

Food was the chuck wagon's most important cargo. In Texas, and on the Texas trail drives, food was Spartan—cornbread, bacon, and beans.

In the northern range, the food was better in part because wealthy easterners could afford better food, wanted a bit of comfort, and had to eat the same food as the men. The result was that cowboys on northern roundups ate canned fruit, white-flour biscuits and pancakes, dried apples, canned tomatoes, and other delectables. Some outfits even had tents for sleeping.[41]

The driver-cook was usually elderly and might be called the "pot wrangler" or the "gut robber," although he was respected and valued.[42] Breakfast might be served as early as two in the morning and usually included bread and butter, beefsteak, coffee, and perhaps donuts and canned tomatoes.[43] Roosevelt advocated feeding roundup crews wild game rather than beef both to avoid the hands getting too free with whose cattle they killed and also to "save more grass for cattle."[44]

As the start of a roundup approached, participants headed for the rendezvous site. Getting there might take three or four days.[45] Another two days might be spent waiting for all participants to show up. Meanwhile, the cattlemen or their foremen met with the captain to plan the operation, and the cowboys held horse and foot races, wrestling matches, and other competitive games.[46] During the roundup, Roosevelt boxed with Eric North, an Englishman later to be Lord North.[47] "Though outweighed, Roosevelt gave an excellent account of himself, being so active on his feet that North succeeded in landing but rarely." North then boxed with Alden Eaton, who "saw to it that the flies had no chance to light on his opponent while the bout was in progress." After that, the event turned into a free for all.

Although the hardest work of the year occurred during the roundup, Roosevelt believed that it was the pleasantest part of cowboy life.[48] "His food is good, though coarse, and his sleep is sound indeed; while the work is very exciting, and is done in company, under the stress of an intense rivalry between all the men, both as to their own skill, and as to the speed and training of their horses. . . . When the work is over for the day the men gather round the fire for an hour or two to sing songs, talk, smoke, and tell stories; and he who has a good voice, or, better still, can play a fiddle or banjo, is sure to receive his meed of most sincere homage."[49] Teddy Blue Abbot agreed: "The roundup was something everybody looked forward to, on the range. You got to see a lot of people that way and hear all the news. Cowpunchers was alone so much, that was why they appreciated company."[50]

The roundup put together many male strangers, increasing the likelihood of violence. "Men who congregate with other men tend to be more sensitive about status and reputation. Even if they are not intoxicated with drink or enraged by insult, they instinctively test one another, probing for signs of weakness."[51] At stake was a man's honor, "defined as a system of beliefs in which a man has exactly as much worth as others confer upon him. Good opinion is won or lost by the way he handles himself in conflicts. To fail to respond to a challenge or insult is to lose face and therefore to surrender self-esteem."[52]

In this environment, Roosevelt again had to establish himself as a man among men; it did not help that he was the only rider in the outfit to carry an inflatable rubber pillow, a toothbrush, and a razor and that he kept his blankets and tarp singularly clean.[53] Roosevelt: "When I went among strangers I always had to spend twenty-four hours in living down the fact that I wore spectacles, remaining as long as I could judiciously deaf to any side remarks about 'four eyes,' unless it became evident that my being quiet was misconstrued and that it was better to bring matters to a head at once."[54] He told one harassing Texan who called him "Storm Windows" to "put up or shut up," to fight or be friends.[55] The Texan chose "friends," and they shook hands. One witness said that, after they shook, "nobody said anything, but we was all thinking the same thing, I guess. We wanted to get up and shake his hand too. We were proud of him."[56] The foreman of the Berry-Boice Company, who was captain of a roundup in 1885, concluded of Roosevelt, "His glasses made him look kind of unusual, and I says to myself, 'Here's one of them dudes from Carroll's dude ranch come from the East to get over the taste for strong drink.' But he wasn't no dude. I remember the other boys feeling that his glasses was against him, but I remember we all forgot about his glasses when we saw that he meant to play the game with no favors."[57]

And so Roosevelt, as one rider put it, took his place as a common cowboy. "He had his own string of ten horses, and stood trick at night guard with the others. The work was hard, the hours long, and little time was given for sleep. Saddle scalded and half dead from exhaustion, I could have cried from sheer distress, but the ethics of cowboy life called for grim, dogged silence;—'make good' or pass out."[58] Roosevelt explained years later, "As with all other forms of work, so on the round-up, a man of ordinary power, who nevertheless does not shirk things merely because they are disagreeable or irksome, soon earns his place."[59]

Once everyone had arrived and understood the rules and the area to be covered, the roundup began.[60] Each morning, the chuck wagons moved along the river valley and stopped to camp at midday, along with scores of unridden horses driven by herders. Meanwhile, the cowboys, riding big, sturdy horses, scattered into the surrounding country in early morning darkness, going out ten or fifteen miles from the river valley and turning back toward it, combing through every coulee, valley, and wash and driving all the cattle they found to the campsite, usually arriving by noon.[61] This was called circle riding.

At the campsite, the men exchanged their muscular circle-riding horses for smaller, more agile ponies and then cut out—separated—the cattle belonging to individual ranches.[62] "A young heifer or steer is very loath to leave the herd, always tries to break back into it, and can run like a deer, and can dodge like a rabbit; but a thorough cattle pony enjoys the work as much as its rider, and follows a beast like a four-footed fate through every double and turn."[63] Roosevelt's favorite cutting horse on the 1885 roundup was Muley, who "never seemed to tire or lose his dash."[64]

Cattle with which the cowboys had no work to do were released back into the rangelands that already had been covered. Other animals, such as bulls being collected for winter, cattle that had strayed far from their home range, and cows with unbranded calves, were surrounded by mounted cowboys or put into a nearby corral, built round to avoid corners in which livestock could find refuge.[65] The men then roped or grabbed calves to be branded.

Horses that could stop or turn on a dime were called "peg whittles" and were highly valued by ropers.[66] Aside from Texans, cowboys rarely tried to rope an animal more than twenty-five feet away.[67] The object was to rope the cow or steer, tie the other end of the rope around the saddle horn (though in some parts of the country the rope was always kept tied to the horn), and have the horse fall back almost on its haunches, digging in its hooves. The horse had to face the roped quarry at the moment the rope went taut, a powerful jerk called "the bust."[68] If the horse was sideways to the bovine, the horse would be pulled over, rider and all.

Once a calf was in hand, it was dragged to a wood fire where branding irons glowed orange in the flames. Calves were branded with the same mark their mothers wore. Mavericks—calves whose mothers could not be determined—were branded with the sign of the largest nearby cow herd. Bull calves were "cut"—castrated—during branding. The cowboys usually put the freshly removed testicles into the fire and then ate them "with great gusto."[69] One Roosevelt hand, Bill Rowe, opposed branding. At the roundup, with the smell of burning hair and skin acrid in the air and the calves bawling, he told other cowboys, "Branding cattle is rotten, and you who do the branding are all going to hell."[70]

"Mavericking" was the term used for the practice of claiming stray livestock that might or might not belong to the claimant. For example, a steer that strayed from a Texas herd moving north and turned up on a rancher's land might be claimed and branded by a mavericking rancher. The practice was a form of stealing, wrote one livestock grower, "but stealing is an ugly word, and people preferred to talk about 'mavericking.' Under the peculiar conditions of life in the Far West it naturally behooved any man who went in for 'mavericking' to be an extra good shot."[71]

Roosevelt threw himself into branding. He "used to take his trick at anything he could do. He would grab a calf or cow and help drag them right into the fire to be branded. He could wrassel a calf just as good as anybody. He used to be all over dirt from head to foot."[72] But he faced limitations. His eyesight alone made it impossible for him to rope well, and his lack of experience was another critical issue.[73] Merrifield: "You see to cut the cows and calves out it took someone who was perfectly familiar with the different brands and we never sent a man in to do the cutting out unless he had had at least three years experience. There was too much of a chance to get things all mixed up. Roosevelt never did any cutting out because as I have explained before, his eye-sight was against him."[74]

Frank Roberts, a trapper and cowboy in the Medora area, said of Roosevelt, "No, he never shirked his duty. He was always there ready to do everything he possibly could. He wanted to do it. Tried to do it."[75] But he didn't always, or even often, succeed. Roberts: "It just wasn't in him to learn to be a cowboy. Wasn't natural for him, you know. Cowboy's gotta have a lot of experience to be a roper and a rider and all such things as that. You ain't born that way."[76] The result was that Roosevelt "was kinda in the way more than anything else . . . But he wanted to do everything himself. He wanted to do it for the experience, you know. He got bucked off his horse and a rider would say, 'Mr. Roosevelt, I'll ride that horse for you.' He'd say, 'Cowboy, I know *you* can ride him, I've seen you ride, but I want to find out if *I* can ride it. If I can't ride him, I'll let you ride him.'"[77]

The work of the roundup did not cease at nightfall.[78] All night long, cowboys had to ride in a circle around the sleeping day herd and any other animals held in camp. On a clear night this process required little more than a capacity for monotony and a good sense of direction, though in the depths of a prairie night even a herd of cattle might be swallowed in darkness. Roosevelt once set off in the wrong direction for night riding and did not find the herd until sunrise, "when I was greeted with withering scorn by the injured cowpuncher, who had been obliged to stand double guard because I failed to relieve him."[79]

Trouble for night riders came on stormy nights, or even toward sunrise, when the cattle became restless. Cattle spooked easily during a night storm, even if it was far off, just thunder rolling across the prairie, lightning on the horizon. The threat of a stampede might build slowly as electricity in the air flashed on the horns of the cattle and on horses' ears as well as on the moustaches of the cowboys.[80] Such conditions could be harbingers of danger. In one storm in 1882, Montana cowboy Teddy Blue Abbott saw fourteen cattle killed, as well as six or seven horses and two men.[81]

At night, especially if the cattle were jumpy, circling cowboys calmed the animals with song. They used old melodies and whatever words came to mind, including nonsense verse or even the ingredients memorized from the labels of canned foods.[82] A favorite night song of the period went:

> The days that I was hard up,
> I never shall forget.
> The days that I was hard up—
> I may be well off yet.
> In days when I was hard up,
> And wanted wood and fire,

I used to tie my shoes up
With little bits of wire.

A song might speak of the strains of cowboy work, as one called "The Kansas Line" did, with stanzas such as:[83]

The cowboy's life is a dreadful life,
He's driven through heat and cold;
I'm almost froze with the water on my clothes,
A-ridin' through heat and cold.

I've been where the lightnin', the lightnin' tangled in my eyes,
The cattle I could scarcely hold;
Think I heard my boss man say:
"I want all brave-hearted men who ain't afraid to die
To whoop up the cattle from morning till night,
Way up on the Kansas Line."

Or a song might take a melancholy tone, as in "The Cowboy's Dream," sung to the tune of "My Bonnie Lies over the Ocean," which in part went:

Last night as I lay on the prairie,
And looked at the stars in the sky,
I wondered if ever a cowboy
Would drift to that sweet by-and-by.

Roll on, roll on;
Roll on little dogies, roll on, roll on,
Roll on, roll on;
Roll on little dogies, roll on.

The road to that bright, happy region
Is a dim, narrow trail, so they say;
But the broad one that leads to perdition
Is posted and blazed all the way.

They say there will be a great roundup,
And cowboys, like dogies, will stand,
To be marked by the Riders of Judgment
Who are posted and know every brand.

There was even a song about singing songs on a roundup:

When threatening clouds do gather and herded lightnings flash,
And heavy rain drops splatter, and rolling thunders crash;
What keeps the herds from running, stampeding far and wide?
The cowboy's long, low whistle and singing by their side.

Roosevelt was pulled from his blankets the night of Tuesday, June 2, near Chimney Butte to help control a herd in a storm.[84] He rode out to find the animals stirring. "After a while there was a terrific peal of thunder, the lightning struck right by the herd, and away all the beasts went, heads and horns and tails in the air. For a minute or two I could make out nothing except the dark forms of the beasts running on every side of me, and I should have been very sorry if my horse had stumbled, for those behind would have trodden me down."[85] At that moment the herd split into two, part of it veering to one side and the other going straight. Roosevelt stayed beside the latter, galloping at top speed to try to get ahead of the lead cattle and turn them, "when suddenly there was a tremendous splashing in front. I could dimly make out that the cattle immediately ahead and to one side of me were disappearing, and the next moment the horse and I went off a cut bank into the Little Missouri."[86] The horse stayed upright despite its plunge into the river and made it to the other side. There Roosevelt met another cowboy, from whom he was immediately separated. Galloping hard, he stopped the part of the herd with which he was riding, but it stampeded again; he had to stop it two more times.

In the morning the few cattle he still held came to a halt. Roosevelt dismounted and leaned against a tree to rest, but the herd started off again, and he had to pursue them. At dawn he was finally able to determine where he was and turned the cattle back toward camp. As he proceeded, he found more cattle and herded them along too. Then he met the cowboy he had encountered the night before, now on foot and carrying his saddle. The cowboy explained that his horse had galloped into a tree and fallen dead.

When Roosevelt reached camp he found that only about half the night herd had been recovered. He changed horses and set out again after a quick breakfast. He did not return for ten hours. He then changed horses and rode with the cattle until after dark before coming back to camp. He had spent nearly forty hours in the saddle—his longest stint on horseback—changing mounts five times. His clothes, soaked in the rain, had dried, and he rolled into his blankets and fell instantly asleep. Abbott thought lack of sleep was the worst problem when driving cattle.[87] The cowboys had tricks for helping them stay awake, such as rubbing tobacco juice in their eyes: "It was rubbing them with fire."[88] They might also take catnaps in the saddle.

In addition to fatigue, floods, and stampedes, Roosevelt battled horses, including an infamous bronco named Ben Butler—"He'd throw you so high that eagles could build nests on you"—that reared up and fell over, landing on Roosevelt and breaking the point of his shoulder.[89] With the nearest medical help perhaps two hundred miles away, Roosevelt's only remedy was to endure the pain for the rest of the roundup.[90] "I'd rather have ridden a red-hot stove than one of those horses," Roosevelt told Merrifield.[91]

By June 20 Roosevelt was finished with the roundup. On that date he signed a contract with Sewall and Dow, turning over to them eleven hundred head of cattle costing twenty-five thousand dollars, which they were to take charge of for three years, after which they were to return to Roosevelt the equivalent in value; anything over that twenty-five thousand dollars would be divided, with Roosevelt getting two-thirds and Sewall and Dow a third.[92] Meanwhile, they could sell cattle as they saw fit, provided that no sale reduced the value of the herd to less than twenty-five thousand dollars, unless Roosevelt gave them orders to do so.

The day after he signed the contract, Roosevelt left for New York in the company of Wilmot Dow, who was visiting Maine long enough to marry and to bring back, along with his new bride, Sewall's wife and sixteen-month-old daughter.[93] On the way to New York, Roosevelt suffered a few interviews with reporters, who seemed ever fascinated with him. They discovered a new, post-roundup Roosevelt who, it was immediately apparent, was no longer the wan, sickly man of only two months before. Their repetitious heralding of his profound physical change suggests a turning point in his long quest for good health. He was now, according to a reporter for the *Pioneer Press*, "rugged, bronzed and in the prime of health" as he "passed through St. Paul yesterday, returning from his Dakota ranch to New York and civilization. There was very little of the whilom dude in his rough and easy costume, with a large handkerchief tied loosely about his neck; but the eye glasses and the flashing eyes behind them, the pleasant smile and the hearty grasp of the hand remained. . . . The slow exasperating drawl and the unique accent the New Yorker feels he must use when visiting a less blessed portion of civilization have disappeared, and in their place is a nervous, energetic manner of talking with the flat accent of the West."[94]

A *Pittsburgh Dispatch* reporter agreed, telling readers, "What a change! Last March he was a pale, slim young man, with a thin, piping voice and a general look of dyspepsia. . . . He is now brown as a berry and has increased 30 lbs in weight. The voice which failed to make an echo in the seven million dollar capitol [in Albany] when he climbed upon his desk and shook his little pocket handkerchief and piped 'Mistah Speakah,' is now hearty and strong enough to drive oxen."[95]

Roosevelt had a newly "sturdy walk and firm bearing," wrote a reporter who met him in New York City.[96] The *St. Paul Dispatch* on June 22, 1885, reported an interview in which Roosevelt's words, even on the printed page, seemed to crackle with energy:

"Yes, I am a regular cowboy, dress and all"—and his garb went far to prove his assertion, woolen shirt, big handkerchief tied loosely around his neck, etc. "I am as much of a cowboy as any of them and can hold my own with the best of them. I can shoot, ride and drive in the round up with the best of them. Oh, they are a jolly set of fellows, those cowboys; tip-top good fellows, too, when you know them, but they don't want any plug hat or pointed-toe shoes foolishness around them. I get along the best way with them." Also, "Do I like ranch life? Honestly I would not go back to New York if I had no interests there. Yes, I enjoy ranch life far more than city life. I like the hunt, the drive of cattle and everything that is comprehended in the frontier life. Make no mistake; on the frontier you find the noblest of fellows. How many cattle have I? Let's see well not less than 3,500 at present. I will have more another year." Also, "I am out of politics. I know that is often said by men in public life, but in this case it is true. I really am. There is more excitement in the round up than in politics, and it is far more respectable. I can't presume to speak of politics. I shall go direct to New York and attend to business there, but I shall not be content to remain long. I prefer my ranch and the excitement it brings to New York life, though I always make it a point to enjoy myself wherever I am."[97]

13

AT HOME IN EAST
AND WEST

DURING SUMMER 1885 IN NEW YORK, ROOSEVELT WAS CONCERNED primarily with two issues. One was the publication of his book. Reviews of his Badlands memoir began rolling in by early July. Because he had organized it into chapters on ranching and on individual species he had hunted, the book was episodic and lacked a narrative and a chronology. But the content was interesting, informative, and often lyric. The *New York Times* reviewer wrote that *Hunting Trips of a Ranchman* would "take a leading position in the literature of the American sportsman."[1]

The book exemplified, however, a comment about the West made by Austrian sport hunter and writer William A. Baille-Grohman: "There is, I suppose, no country in the world on which so much has been written, based on less personal experience."[2] This matter of personal experience— Roosevelt had spent a total of barely six months in the West—led to a review less enthusiastic than that of the *Times*, though generally laudatory. In the July 2, 1885, issue of *Forest and Stream*, a biweekly magazine on outdoor sport and wildlife conservation, editor George Bird Grinnell pointed out that "Mr. Roosevelt is not well known as a sportsman, and his experience of the Western country is quite limited." He added, "We are sorry to see that a number of hunting myths are given as fact, but it was after all scarcely to be expected that with the author's limited experience he could sift the wheat from the chaff and distinguish the true from the false."[3]

Thirty-five years old when he wrote the review, Grinnell was a more authentic western denizen than was Theodore Roosevelt. Grinnell was born in Brooklyn, New York, on September 20, 1849, in a family as distinguished as Roosevelt's.[4] His father was the "principal agent in Wall Street of Commodore Cornelius Vanderbilt, who controlled the New York Central system of railroads."[5] His ancestors included five colonial governors and Betty Alden, credited as being the first European woman born in New England. Taking advantage of a rail line completed in 1849 that ran up the west side of Manhattan, his family in 1857 moved to Audubon Park, which overlooked the Hudson above what is now Columbia University. Their house was built on land purchased from Lucy Audubon, the widow of the famed wildlife artist John James Audubon, who had died six years earlier.[6] Lucy still lived in the Audubon home and ran a small school in which Grinnell enrolled, linking him firmly to birds and nature.

Grinnell later attended a military school in the town today called Ossining and entered Yale in 1866, where he was an indifferent student but received a bachelor of arts degree in 1870.[7] In summer 1870 he accompanied paleontologist O. C. Marsh on a six-month fossil-hunting expedition across Kansas, Nebraska, Wyoming, and Utah. He made annual trips west after that one—more time in the West than Roosevelt ever spent—and in 1874 served as naturalist on a Black Hills expedition led by George Armstrong Custer. Also in the mid-1870s, Grinnell explored the area then recently set aside as Yellowstone National Park and hunted bison when the herds were still vast.[8] Custer invited him to join a military foray in pursuit of Indians in eastern Montana Territory in 1876, but Grinnell's work as the assistant in osteology at Yale's Peabody Museum kept him from going; he might otherwise have sown the earth of the Little Bighorn with his own bones.[9] In 1880 he received a doctorate in osteology and vertebrate paleontology.[10]

Grinnell took a leading role in a movement then in its infancy—wildlife conservation. In the mid-1880s he founded the National Audubon Society to lobby for bird protection laws, but as early as 1873 he sought protection for bison even though they were "still often sufficiently numerous to blacken the plains."[11] Grinnell could see that "their days are numbered, and unless some action on this subject is speedily taken not only by the States and Territories, but by the National Government, these shaggy brown beasts, these cattle upon a thousand hills, will ere long be among the things of the past."[12]

In response to Grinnell's book review, Roosevelt visited the office of *Forest and Stream*, where he and Grinnell "talked freely about the book, and took up at length some of its statements."[13] Roosevelt proved open to criticism. Grinnell recognized that Roosevelt had reported on the West and its wildlife "faithfully and accurately" but had suffered "the youthful— and common—tendency to generalize from his own observations and to conclude that certain aspects of nature were always and in all places as he had found them in one place. Moreover, he was inclined to accept as fact some statements made in books, and others by men with whom he had talked, who were either bad observers or careless talkers."[14]

While discussing the book, the two wildlife enthusiasts segued into talk of hunting in the West. Grinnell: "I told him something about game destruction in Montana for the hides, which, so far as small game was concerned, had begun in the West only a few years before that, though the slaughter of the buffalo for their skins was going on much longer and by this time their extermination had been substantially completed."[15] Grinnell did not record Roosevelt's response. They continued their discussions when Roosevelt made repeat visits to see Grinnell, giving Roosevelt "his first direct and detailed information about this slaughter of elk, deer, antelope, and mountain-sheep. No doubt it had some influence in making him the ardent game protector that he later became."[16]

The second major preoccupation for Roosevelt that summer was the house he had been building—under sister Anna's management—at Oyster Bay. He went to see the new domain on June 25, the day after his return to New York from the Badlands.[17]

His massive, squat house took a commanding, hilltop view of his ninety-five acres of meadows and trees, of rolling, wooded hills above the gleaming waters of Oyster Bay and Long Island Sound. The mansion's mustard-colored wood siding, red brickwork, and dark green trim, its gables, dormers, and verandas, encompassed twenty-two rooms and eight fireplaces.[18] Despite its size, it was smaller than the average Oyster Bay vacation home and, at $16,975, cost significantly less than the area's median home price of about $25,000.[19] Anna's gardeners had seeded a new lawn and had put in shrubs, trees, and vines; Theodore had had the family motto, *Qui plantavit curabit* (whosoever has planted, will preserve) engraved in gold over the west door.[20] From the house he could see Tranquillity, the summer rental where he had spent his youth and his honeymoon. He still called the new house Leeholm, after Alice, but he would change the name to Sagamore Hill the following autumn, a sagamore being a chief of the Indian tribes that had once inhabited the area.[21]

He entered a period of relaxation, his first in two years. He had friends stay at Sagamore Hill, led vigorous hikes, and swam in the sea. With him was Alice—Baby Lee—who was just learning to walk and with whom he played on the newly grown lawn.[22] His brother's ten-month-old daughter Eleanor, who one day would marry Franklin Delano Roosevelt, was visiting the nearby home of Roosevelt's aunt Anna. On August 8 he traveled to New York City for Ulysses S. Grant's funeral and interment in a temporary crypt on upper Riverside Drive while the soon-to-be-famous tomb was being completed.[23] As a captain in the National Guard, Roosevelt marched in the funeral parade, staring tensely ahead.

While Roosevelt remained in the East, preparing to populate his new house with the heads of western game animals, Sewall's reservations about the Badlands as cattle country were being reinforced as the sun parched the land, turning grass into little more than hay with roots. Moreover, fires were ravaging the prairie, set, ranchers suspected, by Indians trying to starve out the cattlemen who had stolen their land.

Despite his opinions, Sewall was beginning to see that living in the West took a special kind of person, or at least folk different from those he knew in Maine. He wrote his brother, "If people would live at home as they do here they could lay up money[.] but people at home wont live in a Outdoor cellar without any floor and onely one room perhaps 12 × 20 ft and not burn more than two or three cords of wood in a year and go ragged and as dirty as they can be[.] [Nor will they] eat ransid Bacon and bread when they cant get Deer meat and Potatoes [or] have no Schools and no social advantages not know when Sunday comes half of the time and when they do [it] never make[s] any difference[.] now if people would live that way at home perhaps they could lay up money but what would their lives be worth [?] more than an Indians [?] . . . the Cattle men have money behind them and of course have things in better shape[.] I was speaking of the poor settler such as the country at home is mostly made up of."[24]

For the Fourth of July, Sewall rode into Medora after hearing that "a great celebration" was in the works.[25] Medora seemed to be thriving. "In two years," observed the *Mandan Pioneer*, "it has grown from absolutely nothing to be a town which possesses a number of fine buildings, and represents a great many dollars of capital. The Black Hills freight depot is a well-built, substantial building. A number of brick houses have been built during the last year, including a very neat and attractive Catholic church, and a large hotel."[26]

Most of the buildings were the work of the Marquis de Morès, which suggests that Medora's prosperity was only a heartbeat, or a few misguided business decisions, away from collapse. De Morès was launching other enterprises, such as a stagecoach and cargo line to Deadwood. The hotel that bore his name and the church his wife had built attracted other businesses, including a barber shop, drugstore, hardware store, and clothing store.[27] Saloons were a major feature, including Bob Roberts' new two-story establishment, paid for by the Marquis after Roberts' first barroom had burned down the previous January.[28] The second floor was a large room, called Roberts Hall and used for meetings, such as those of the cattlemen's association, and for dances, some of which Roosevelt and the Marquis attended. Competition was tough in the Medora saloon business; Roberts sometimes stood in front of his barroom, shot off a few rounds, and waited for cowboys to come rushing in to see what the fuss was all about, whereupon they soon converted to paying customers.[29]

On the Fourth, Sewall found "lots of cowboys" engaging in footraces and horse races, which he thought "exciting to watch."[30] By nightfall, many of the men had been drinking, and "bad whisky had begun to show its effects." The cowboys were becoming "pretty noisy and hilarious." One group came into the hotel where Sewall was staying, drank, then moved up the street. Within a minute "all hands began to shoot. The bullets went whistling by the front door of the hotel, striking the railroad buildings or the embankments. The hotelkeeper peered out cautiously and said, 'It's pretty noisy out there.' Then he pulled down his blinds and locked his doors."[31] Sewall decided to go to bed, but during the night he was awakened "a good many times by a fusillade, which sounded a good deal like firing India crackers by the bunch, only a good deal louder. After the shooting there was generally a chorus of yells. As I was in a brick house, perfectly safe, I didn't allow it to disturb me very much."

The next day he left the hotel for the ranch. The town was silent. "The greater part of the crowd had been paralyzed and were lying around like poisoned flies, wherever the paralysis had taken them. . . . The dead-shot whisky had been worse than the pistol-shooting. Nobody had been hurt by that."[32]

At home Sewall prepared for a trip that he would later describe as a search for stolen horses and cattle.[33] In fact, he was part of a vigilante committee. The cattlemen's association had determined that it needed to send a team of riders into the region north of the railroad line between the Missouri and Little Missouri rivers to eliminate livestock rustlers, and Roosevelt had been one of half a dozen ranchers who sent a representative.[34]

Sewall joined five other men at the Eaton ranch ten miles north of the Elkhorn, including two other men from Maine; the group took along about thirty horses, so the riders would always have fresh mounts. Sewall immediately announced to the others that "I was entirely new, but if they could find anything for me to do, where they thought I would be of any use, to tell me and show me how. I would do the best I could and would be a good fellow if I wasn't good for anything else. That amused them and they were very nice to me during the whole trip."[35] He soon found that he was better at early rising than were the other men, so he took on the task of making fires for morning coffee and of cooking bacon while the boss—a Texan named W. P. Osterhaut, who had fought as a rebel in the Civil War—baked bread in a frying pan held over an open fire.[36]

During the day, Osterhaut and a man named Armstrong scouted in the vanguard as the vigilantes moved through dangerous country near the Canadian border and the Gros Ventre reservation, a region that was "a great resort for Horse Thieves and cattle thieves and all kinds of Thieves and Cut throats."[37] The men spent eighteen days on the trail, covered an estimated five hundred miles, and survived a hailstorm, but they found no missing livestock and nothing in the area "worse than ourselves," other than the graves of soldiers killed by Indians and the fresh corpse of an Indian left, inexplicably, in a tent.[38] Sewall enjoyed the trip "very much," recalling in later years that the "country at that time was at its best. Acres of wild roses were in bloom, and here and there were plums, wild morning-glories, and cactuses, which really made the country, in places, look beautiful."[39]

Nevertheless, his feeling about the Badlands had not changed. He wrote his brother, "I would not live all my life here for the whole Terrytory but I had a good time an injoyed the trip for I got a better idear of the country and the people that live in it than I have had before. . . . most of them are pretty well informed and have seen better days but I think they have gone back about 200 years and a man that could come from New England and like [it] better than at home must have a depraved idear of life or hate himself or both."[40]

On August 8, Dow arrived with his new wife and with Sewall's wife and daughter.[41] Even having his family did not improve Sewall's outlook: "It makes a great difference haveing them but I never shall like this country for a home."[42]

The Chicago Limited brought Roosevelt to the Badlands the night of Tuesday, August 25, 1885. Apparently he stopped at the newspaper office and talked with A. T. Packard, because two days later the editor ran an article marking Roosevelt's arrival and reporting that he planned to stay until the fall roundup ended in early October. Packard had been editorializing of late on the need for a stockmen's association meeting; Roosevelt—perhaps taking the hint—put a notice in the *Bad Lands Cow Boy* for a meeting on September 5.[43]

During his train ride, Roosevelt talked, as usual, with newspaper reporters. This time, journalists in St. Paul and Bismarck asked persistently if Roosevelt and the Marquis de Morès had had a falling-out. The questions left Roosevelt perplexed. As far as he knew, he and the Marquis were on good terms.[44] They shared an interest in organizing the local cattle industry, the Marquis had proposed Roosevelt for membership in the Montana Stockgrowers' Association, and Roosevelt often had lunched at the de Morès chateau.[45] On the other hand, Roosevelt was close friends with people the Marquis considered enemies, including the Langs. The dispute over land rights at the Maltese Cross Ranch had flared briefly, and Roosevelt had hired as a night rider one of the men de Morès had shot at during the June 1883 gunfight, Dutch Wannegan. Nevertheless, Roosevelt could think of no basis for a dispute other than an incident that had happened months earlier. He had agreed the previous spring to sell about a hundred head of cattle to the Marquis for six cents a pound, only to find when he delivered the livestock that de Morès would pay only five and a half cents, because prices in Chicago had dropped.[46] Insisting that a deal was a deal, Roosevelt took back his cattle and declared he would never do business with the Marquis again.

Roosevelt soon learned why interest in the Marquis was building, though he still did not see the connection to himself and any dispute. During the summer, a grand jury in Mandan had been investigating potential murder charges against de Morès for the 1883 Luffsey shooting.[47] He had been deemed innocent twice by justices of the peace, but Luffsey's friends pressed for a jury trial. The grand jury indicted the Marquis for murder on August 19, 1885.[48] De Morès had been expecting this result. He had even been told that if he doled out fifteen hundred dollars to the appropriate people, the indictment would be quashed. His response: "I have plenty of money for defense, but not a dollar for blackmail."[49] Paddock and two other de Morès men also were indicted and jailed in Mandan without bail. In addition, Paddock was charged with forcibly entering the home of Frank Moore's mother and taking away furniture while armed.[50] Local gossip suggested that all the charges against Paddock had been brought to discredit him as a key witness in de Morès' defense.[51] The Marquis, who had been traveling in the East, returned to Medora at the end of August for his appointment with the Mandan jail, where a lynch mob gathered, but without tangible effect.[52]

Roosevelt, meanwhile, embarked upon his usual western avocations. Summer heat did not diminish the charm of the Badlands as he rode to the Elkhorn Ranch: "Even in the hot weather the ride toward the plains over the hills was very lovely. It was beautiful to see the red dawn quicken from the first glimmering gray in the east, and then to watch the crimson bars glint on the tops of the fantastically shaped barren hills when the sun flamed, burning and splendid, above the horizon. In the early morning the level beams threw into sharp relief the strangely carved and channelled cliff walls of the buttes. There was rarely a cloud to dim the serene blue of the sky."[53]

The Elkhorn Ranch was more posh than most. Many ranchers filled their larders with nothing more than salt pork, canned goods, and bread.[54] But Roosevelt had a supply of chickens, which provided eggs as well as meat, and the two or three tame cows his men milked also provided butter when there was time for churning.[55] Sewall and Dow's wives had introduced window curtains and more rounded meals. Dow's wife made excellent bread and cake, Sewall grew plenty of potatoes, and the group had jellies and jams made from wild plums and buffalo berries. However, for meat they ate mostly venison interrupted occasionally with duck or prairie chicken.[56]

Despite these intimations of domesticity, Roosevelt was soon off on another escapade. At some point he had spoken with an old hunter who had shot a cow elk no more than twenty-five miles from the ranch and who had seen the tracks of at least two others.[57] The species was almost extinct in the Badlands, so Roosevelt, despite his discussions with George Bird Grinnell, immediately concluded, "Such a chance was not to be neglected." He and Dow mounted up—Roosevelt on Manitou, his favorite hunting horse—and, accompanied by a ranch wagon, started off "in the direction of the probable haunts of the doomed deer."[58]

At nightfall they camped by a deep pool along a spring that ran near an old Indian encampment, probably below the mouth of Beaver Creek.[59] Soon their ponies were grazing by the light of a flickering fire as venison steaks sizzled on hot coals. Later, in the cool September darkness, Roosevelt lay awake long after going to bed, gazing up at the countless stars of a brilliant prairie sky.

They rose with the sun. The air was still, and haze hung over the country as they looked out from a tableland onto "a great stretch of broken country, the brown of whose hills and valleys was varied everywhere by patches of dull red and vivid yellow, tokens that the trees were already putting on the dress with which they greet the mortal ripening of the year." They soon found traces of a lone bull elk—first old tracks, then fresh. "With painstaking and noiseless care" they hunted for many hours before Roosevelt, riding up over the edge of a narrow ravine, heard crashing among the woods and glimpsed a bull elk trotting up a steep hill through a stand of young trees. Once out of the woods the elk stopped and turned half around to look back at the hunter, who fired a single round that struck the animal farther back than intended; the elk galloped a quarter mile before collapsing in death. The bull was big, his antlers disappointingly small, but for Roosevelt the hunt was a success. He had shot an animal that was "probably the last of his race that will ever be found in our neighborhood."

Two days later Roosevelt chaired the Badlands livestock association meeting. The members set the date and place for the fall roundup and unanimously reelected Roosevelt chairman, over his objection that they should install someone who lived locally year-round. The real drama occurred behind the scenes. Either the evening of September 4 or the following morning, Roosevelt received a terse letter from de Morès, then cooling his heels in a Bismarck jail after a change of venue from Mandan.[60] Dated September 3 and written on the Marquis' Northern Pacific Refrigerator Car Company letterhead, the note read:

My Dear Roosevelt

> *My principle is to take the bull by the horns. Joe Ferris is very active against me and has been instrumental in getting me indicted by furnishing money to witnesses and hunting them up. The papers also publish very stupid accounts of our quarrelling—I sent you the paper to N.Y. Is this done by your orders? I thought you my friend. If you are my enemy I want to know it. I am always on hand as you know, and between gentlemen it is easy to settle matters of that sort directly.*
>
> > *Yours very truly,*
> > *Mores*

> *I hear the people want to organize the county. I am opposed to it for one year more at least.*[61]

Apparently de Morès had misinterpreted, or been misinformed about, certain activities in Medora. Sixteen witnesses had been subpoenaed for his trial, probably all Medora men. They had needed money for train fare and other expenses, and they got the money from Joe Ferris, who acted as an unofficial banker among cowboys who trusted him.[62] Two key prosecution witnesses, Dutch Wannegan himself and "Dynamite Jimmie" McShane, were among those who withdrew money from Ferris before the trial. The Marquis had concluded that Ferris was paying these men to testify against him, perhaps on behalf of Theodore Roosevelt, who had invested in Ferris' store and had a room on the store's second floor.[63]

With his penchant for melodrama, Roosevelt concluded that the Marquis was challenging him to a duel—though de Morès' postscript hardly seems the kind of amendment a duelist would add to a challenge. Roosevelt told Sewall that he was opposed to dueling, but if challenged he would accept.[64] As the challenged party, he would have the choice of weapons, and, in deference to his poor shooting ability, he thought he would choose Winchester rifles at twelve paces—near enough that he might be able to hit a Frenchman renowned for shooting birds on the wing with a rifle. They would fire and advance until one of them was satisfied. He asked Sewall to be his second, and Sewall agreed skeptically, saying that a man "who would lay in ambush and shoot at unsuspecting men would not fight such a duel as that."[65] Sewall apparently did not know that the Marquis had already killed at least two men in duels in France.

Roosevelt drafted a response to the Marquis on the back of the note de Morès had sent him:

> *Most emphatically I am not your enemy; if I were you would know it, for I would be an open one, and would not have asked you to my house nor gone to yours. As your final words, however, seem to imply a threat it is due to myself to say that the statement is not made through any fear of possible consequences to me; I, too, as you know, am always on hand, and ever ready to hold myself accountable in any way for anything I have said or done.*
>
> *Yours very truly,*
> *Theodore Roosevelt*[66]

A few days later a letter arrived from de Morès, and Roosevelt was able to tell Sewall, "You were right, Bill." The marquis in his letter explained that he had implied no threat, that he had only meant that "there is always a way to settle misunderstandings between gentlemen—without trouble."[67] Roosevelt took this as an apology.

Others were not so sure. Lincoln Lang believed that Roosevelt had misinterpreted the marquis's first letter, that the marquis never intended to initiate a duel and that he certainly would not have turned tail in response to Roosevelt's reply: "Whatever else is to be said for or against de Morès, even his worst enemy could not accuse him of cowardice."[68] Another rancher agreed: "The Marquis was a fine man and game as a pebble; when they tell the story of Roosevelt backing him down, they are sure guessing wrong."[69] Joe Ferris said that de Morès sent a man to ask about Ferris' distribution of funds, which was "about all there was to it. The Marquis was a peculiar sort of man, but I don't remember his ever challenging Roosevelt to a duel."[70] The manager of de Morès' ranch, John Goodall, also did not think there was any truth to the rumor of a feud between the two men.[71]

The existing notes concerning the affair indicate a basis in fact, however. Perhaps Roosevelt read more between the lines than was warranted. Or perhaps few Badlands residents knew of the incident because Roosevelt kept the story close to his vest. Aside from a letter to Sewall in 1893, Roosevelt is known to have mentioned the duel only once. During dinner at Howard Eaton's, Roosevelt said that after accepting what he thought was de Morès' challenge, "the Marquis de Morès sent me an apology quick as he could get it to me and said that I was entirely mistaken about his letter—he never thought of such a thing as a duel and wouldn't I come up to the Chateau and have dinner with him? So I accepted his apology and went to the Chateau and had dinner with him and we talked about hunting and books and such as that, had a nice visit with him, and when the Marquis went east he came to my place at Oyster Bay and had dinner with me. We visited there, so the Marquis and I have been just as good friends as we've ever been."[72]

After the cattlemen's association meeting, Roosevelt went back to the Elkhorn for more hunting. He also fought prairie fires, which the ranchers blamed on Indians.[73] The fires actually may have been started by sparks from trains, as the fires typically occurred along a strip about eighteen miles on either side of the Northern Pacific rail line, which was at least twenty-five miles from most ranches.[74] However, grass along the line was a vital need when cattle were driven to railheads, because livestock lost weight on drives even under the best conditions.[75]

One of the means for fighting a fire was to kill a steer, cut the body in half lengthwise with an axe, and then drag the body over the flames bloody side down.[76] This procedure required two men on horses, with ropes tied to the front and hind legs of the carcass and each rope tied to a horse's saddle horn. As the riders dragged the body over the leading edge of the fire, other men followed on foot, beating the fire with wet saddle blankets. Roosevelt: "It was exciting work, for the fire and the twitching and plucking of the ox carcass over the uneven ground maddened the fierce little horses so that it was necessary to do some riding in order to keep them to their work. After a while it also became very exhausting, the thirst and fatigue being great, as, with parched lips and blackened from head to foot, we toiled at our task."[77]

Blaming Indians for the fires suggests residual animosity, though the Indian wars had ended five or six years before.[78] Cowboys even had a song about their fear of Indians:[79]

I'd rather hear a rattler rattle,
I'd rather buck stampeding cattle,
I'd rather go to a greaser battle,
Than—
Than to—
Than to fight—
Than to fight the bloody In-ji-ans.

I'd rather eat a pan of dope,
I'd rather ride without a rope,
I'd rather from this country lope,
Than—
Than to—
Than to fight—
Thank to fight the bloody In-ji-ans.

In September 1885, Roosevelt had an encounter with Indians while alone in a remote region northeast of his ranch in the direction of the

Killdeer Mountains. He was riding Manitou across a plateau on the edge of the prairie when five mounted Indians suddenly came up over the horizon. Their appearance signaled a potentially ticklish situation: "You never can tell what an Indian will do, especially when there are several of them and only one of you."[80]

When they saw Roosevelt, they whipped out their rifles and charged at full speed, whooping. Roosevelt jumped off Manitou and held his rifle ready to fire. He suspected the Indians were only bluffing and had no intention of killing him, but he also suspected that if he did not stand them off they would rough him up and take his horse and rifle. In any event, he felt confident of his position: "The level plain where we were was of all places the one on which such an onslaught could best be met. . . . The fury of an Indian charge, and the whoops by which it is accompanied, often scare horses so as to stampede them; but in Manitou I had perfect trust, and the old fellow stood as steady as a rock, merely cocking his ears and looking round at the noise. I waited until the Indians were a hundred yards off, and then threw up my rifle and drew a bead on the foremost."[81]

The Indians split up, reminding Roosevelt of birds scattering under fire. "Indians—and for the matter of that, white men—do not like to ride in on a man who is cool and means shooting, and in a twinkling every man was lying over the side of his horse, and all five had turned and were galloping backwards, having altered their course as quickly as so many teal ducks."[82]

The Indians gathered and parlayed, then one of them rode up alone, waving a blanket over his head and making a show of dropping his rifle. When he was within fifty yards, Roosevelt told him to stop, and the Indian held up a document to show that he had permission to leave the reservation. "How, me good Indian," he said.

Roosevelt said he was glad to hear that he was a good Indian, but kept him at a distance. The Indian asked for sugar and tobacco, and Roosevelt said he had none.[83] The Indian's companions began to move in, and Roosevelt aimed his rifle at the man in front and made him back away. The Indians "slipped to their side of their horses and galloped off, with oaths that did credit to at least one side of their acquaintance with English."[84]

Roosevelt had handled himself bravely in a situation in which he had thought his life might be in danger, but evaluating the accuracy of his perception is difficult. Schuyler Lebo, son of the wagon driver who had accompanied Roosevelt into the Bighorn Mountains, had been shot in the leg by an Indian while hunting in the Badlands in winter 1884, but arguably the shooting was not an unreasonable reaction on the Indian's part given that ranchers and cowboys murdered Indians with impunity. "Many white men shot whatever Indians they came upon like coyotes, on sight; others captured them, when they could, and, stripping them of their clothes, whipped them till they bled."[85]

In contrast, Lincoln Lang recalled, "We often had Indian hunting parties around the ranch, but they never gave us any trouble."[86] He thought it was "one of these parties" that Roosevelt "mistook for hostile Indians." Lang believed the Indians were being unfairly blamed for the troubles ranchers endured. He had been told that the Indians were "natural thieves. That they were stealing cattle and horses, setting prairie-fires and so on, all of which, as far as we ever knew, had no foundation in fact."[87] He added, "And so it always appeared to me that [the ranchers] were down on the race more from hearsay, or because it was the fashion of the period, rather than for justifiable reasons of their own."[88] He thought Roosevelt had been led by Badlands cowboys to see Indians in a negative light.[89]

The Lang range bordered the west side of the Standing Rock Sioux Reservation, so, Lang thought, "we must have found out something about [Indian depredations] during the twenty-odd years of our residence there." What the Langs found was that "from '85 on, we saw a good deal of them at the ranch. And they were *always hungry*. Hungry, because they had no food with them, that we ever saw; because game was steadily growing scarcer, and because such rifles as they were permitted to carry were more or less antiquated and inadequate."[90] When Indians showed up at the Lang ranch waving travel permits, as they had with Roosevelt, the Langs fed them and made friends of them.[91] Lang called the permits "a passport of the invading White Man—symbol of Reservation slavery—beneficently entitling them to hunt for a couple of weeks in their own country. In their beloved Bad Lands—their stolen hunting grounds—where for aeons the race had hunted before he came; title to that which they held from God Almighty Himself."[92]

Roosevelt had little sympathy for the Indians, saying that the land had not been stolen from them because they had had no title to it. "During the past century a good deal of sentimental nonsense has been talked about our taking the Indians' land. Now, I do not mean to say for a moment that gross wrong has not been done the Indians, both by government and individuals, again and again. The government makes promises impossible to perform, and then fails to do even what it might toward their fulfillment; and where brutal and reckless frontiersmen are brought into contact with a set of treacherous, revengeful, and fiendishly cruel savages a long series of outrages by both sides is sure to follow. But as regards taking the land, at least from the western Indians, the simple truth is that the latter never had a real ownership in it at all."[93]

Indians, he argued, merely followed the animals they hunted. He compared them to white market hunters: "When my cattle came to the Little Missouri the region was only inhabited by a score or so of white hunters; their title to it was quite as good as that of most Indian tribes to the lands they claim; yet nobody dreamed of saying that these hunters owned the country. Each could eventually have kept his own claim of 160 acres, and no more. The Indians should be treated in just the same way that we treat the white settlers. Give each his little claim; if, as would generally happen, he declined this, why then let him share the fate of the thousands of white hunters and trappers who have lived on the game that the settlement of the country has exterminated, and let him, like these whites, who will not work, perish from the face of the earth which he cumbers."[94]

He could sense a shortcoming in this approach, but it did not bother him. "The doctrine seems merciless, and so it is; but it is just and rational for all that. It does not do to be merciful to a few, at the cost of justice to the many."[95] Roosevelt's view of Indians could be boiled down to this: "I don't go so far as to think that the only good Indians are the dead Indians, but I believe nine out of every ten are, and I shouldn't like to inquire too closely into the case of the tenth."[96]

But Roosevelt was complex and self-contradictory. In later years, he declared that Indians should receive the same protections as white citizens and that whites who murdered Indians should be punished in accordance with the law.[97] As president, he told a woman of Indian descent to whom he was introduced that he had "but one regret in the matter of genealogy . . . That I have none of the true American blood in my veins."[98] His intention in making this point, however, is ambiguous. Roosevelt encouraged the intermarriage of Indians and Euro-Americans because he believed that through interbreeding the latter would absorb and wipe out the former.[99]

And yet Roosevelt often led the cutting edge in redressing racial iniquities. During his tenure on the Civil Service Commission from 1889 to 1895, he advocated that federal appointments should not discriminate on the basis of color, and as governor of New York State in 1899 and 1900, he sought to appoint African Americans to state posts and encouraged hiring them as police officers.[100] During his presidency, he drew harsh criticism from southern elected officials when he invited Booker T. Washington to dinner at the White House.[101] Even so, only a few years later, when he formed the Progressive Party in 1912 in opposition to Republican presidential candidate William Howard Taft, he excluded blacks from the party; four years later he wrote to Henry Cabot Lodge that the "great majority of the negroes in the South are wholly unfit for the suffrage."[102]

In view of his racial attitudes, irony is palpable in at least one of Roosevelt's actions in autumn 1885. In mid-September he left the Badlands, despite his original intention to remain there until after the fall roundup, and went east to work at the state Republican convention in Saratoga, New York. There he supported a plank in the platform calling for greater protections and support for the black vote in southern states, where Jim Crow laws were disenfranchising tens of thousands of black voters.[103] His interest was clearly political—in that era, the Republican Party was still the party of Lincoln, and the black vote could be expected to swing to the Republicans; suppression of the black vote in the South was seen by many Republicans as the underlying reason that Blaine had lost the presidential election to Cleveland.[104]

At the convention, Roosevelt unsuccessfully supported a reform candidate as the Republican nominee for governor. Roosevelt also helped shape the party platform, but overall his impact on the convention is hard to calculate, because he did not take as active a role as he had in the previous presidential campaign. He told one reporter that he was serving as a private rather than as a commander.[105]

★   ★   ★

A development far more momentous for Roosevelt than mere political maneuvering occurred at this time: The young widower who had vowed never to love again, who had written that with Alice's death the light had gone out of his life forever, fell in love.

Probably in early October 1885, Roosevelt entered his sister Anna's home at Sixty-second Street and Madison Avenue to find coming down the stairs toward him a slim, sensually rounded woman with peach complexion, wide mouth, and pale blue eyes. She was the one woman he wanted most to avoid: Edith Carow. Here was the childhood friend to whom he may have proposed before meeting Alice. Here was the woman he had banished from his life since Alice's death.[106] The two may not have so much as seen each other in almost two years. During that time, both had changed. Roosevelt was fitter, sturdier, darkened by sun and worn by wind, tempered by sorrow and restored by the slow recovery of his emotional bearings. She was now twenty-four; her family fortune had declined so rapidly after her father's death that Edith and her mother and sister were preparing to move to Europe, where they could stretch their income.[107] Rumors had circulated in her social set that she had almost married for money.[108] Why she remained single at an age that all but branded her an old maid is unknown.

Roosevelt's encounter with Edith Carow must have struck both with profound shock. No record remains of that meeting, but the results are clear. Roosevelt began to see her again, presumably stopping at her home on East Thirty-sixth Street.[109] He invited her to Sagamore Hill for the Meadowbrook Hunt Ball on October 26, the day before his twenty-seventh birthday and probably her first visit to the house, certainly the first during which Roosevelt was present.

It was a memorable day not just for Roosevelt and Carow but also for little Alice, now nearing two years old. Roosevelt had been riding with the Meadowbrook Hunt Club off and on since college and had developed into what he termed "a respectable rider."[110] He held a high opinion of fox hunting, justifying it as he did other outdoor sports: "All kinds of hunting on horseback . . . tend to bring out the best and manliest qualities in the men who follow them, and they should be encouraged in every way."[111]

The day of the hunt ball he was riding a horse named Frank, not a top-notch mount but one whose price had been within the limits of Roosevelt's purse. Frank had been a buggy horse, but a poor one: The animal now and then had "insisted on thoughtfully lying down when in harness."[112] It never lay down when saddled, however, and it had shown itself to be a natural jumper during its buggy days by leaping fences on its own when out to pasture. On the day of the ball at Sagamore Hill, Roosevelt was fox hunting with Frank for the eighth time. About forty riders left Sagamore Hill at one o'clock in pursuit of the hounds. Roosevelt and Frank led the field for about a third of the trip before Frank seemed to go lame. Nevertheless, Roosevelt spurred him on, with the result that the horse tripped as Roosevelt forced it over a five-foot-high stone wall; horse and rider crashed into a rock pile.

Roosevelt remounted as the horse recovered its feet. They took off in pursuit of the retreating field, jumping over fences up to four feet high, many of the taller ones missing their upper rails thanks to previous horses that had not quite cleared them.[113] On about the fourth jump Roosevelt felt pain in his left arm as bones he had unknowingly broken in the fall slipped past one another.[114] He ignored the injury and, with his lame and bruised horse, regained the hounds; two miles further the hunt ended, and Roosevelt became the center of interest, his face covered with blood and his left arm hanging lifelessly.[115] Roosevelt said the injuries were "a mere trifle."[116]

The sight of Theodore Roosevelt and his injuries were more than a trifle for Alice Lee: "One of my earliest memories of my father was his coming back from hunting with a broken arm and a bloody nose. I started screaming at this apparition and he started shaking me to shut me up, which only made me scream more. So he shook more. It was a theme which was to be repeated, with variations, in later years."[117]

For Roosevelt, it was all in a day's play. He attended the ball that evening with a bandage on his nose and his arm in a sling and danced with Edith. He wrote afterward to Henry Cabot Lodge, "I don't grudge the broken arm a bit. . . . I'm always ready to pay the piper when I've had a good dance; and every now and then I like to drink the wine of life with brandy in it."[118]

Theodore and Edith's relationship blossomed secretly; even close friends, even Corinne and Anna, knew nothing about it.[119] Nor were they aware when Roosevelt proposed to Edith on November 17, and she accepted. The couple sealed the relationship with a ring, a watch, and a pearl necklace.

Now they had critical issues to settle: Where would they live, given that Edith was not fashioned for a log cabin overlooking the Little Missouri River? What would they do with Alice Lee? How would they deal with Edith's responsibilities in helping her mother and sister settle in Europe?

Moreover, for this marriage to happen, Roosevelt not only had to let go of his ideas about fidelity to Alice—which his daughter later referred to as "that awful sentimentality about the concept that you loved only once and you never loved again"—but he and Edith together had to face society's disapproval if their social set learned that Roosevelt had, in less than two years, found succor in the arms of another woman—particularly a woman with whom he had been linked before his marriage.[120] "He obviously felt tremendously guilty about remarrying," his daughter Alice said, adding, "He was obviously horrified by himself. The awful fidelity to the memory of the one who died!"[121] She concluded, "It was pathetic, yet very tough at the same time." She also believed that his guilt over remarrying informed his effort to shut his first wife out of his memory. "I think my father tried to forget he had ever been married to my mother. To blot the whole episode out of his mind. He didn't just never mention her to me, he never mentioned her to *anyone*. Never referred to her again."

The couple continued to keep their relationship and engagement secret. Most of the surviving letters that Edith wrote to Theodore during this period end with the admonition "Burn this." In his diaries, he denotes joining her for some event or activity with only a cryptic "E."[122] They were secretive not only with their peers but with posterity.

Meanwhile, they plunged into the social season—Roosevelt's diary indicates he attended twenty-four dinner parties in January and February—which gave them the perfect cover for appearing together in public.[123] Whatever plans Roosevelt may have had for returning to the Badlands that winter evaporated; for the rest of autumn and through the winter he attended parties, operas, plays, and other social events with Edith, but so decorously that no one suspected their relationship.[124] In his diary for Valentine's Day 1886—the second anniversary of Alice's death—he drew a heart with an arrow through it, a sharp contrast with the deep, dark cross he had etched into the page for February 14, 1884.[125]

Despite the going concerns of his ranch, the impending marriage, and the vortex of New York City social life, he agreed in February 1886 to write a biography of Thomas Hart Benton as part of the prestigious American Statesman Series.[126] Lodge, who was writing a series book on George Washington, helped land the assignment for Roosevelt, who wrote to Lodge, "I feel a little appalled over the Benton; I have not the least idea whether I shall make a flat failure of it or not. However I will do my best and trust to luck for the result."[127]

During this period he engaged in his usual potpourri of activity. He gave political speeches, including a key address to the Young Republican Club of Brooklyn on October 17, 1885, in which he again outlined concerns about ensuring blacks the right to vote in the South; he started research on a four-volume history of colonial America, *The Winning of the West*; he gave at least five lectures on life in the West, which by late January netted him about a hundred applicants for ranch jobs.[128]

In January 1886, *Harper's Weekly* published an article that Roosevelt had written as a guide for the would-be westerner. In passages that seemed to imply more than a little self-praise, he declared in so many words that the West demanded men to match its mountains. "In reality a wild, new country calls for the existence of all the robuster and more virile virtues on the part of those who would try to live therein. The far West is the place of all others where the weak will most surely and quickly be pushed to the wall."[129] The refinements sought in the East—artistic talent, higher education—won little or no praise in cow country. "The man most apt to succeed in the West is he who knows a trade well or who is a skillful craftsman with his hands."

By the end of the winter Roosevelt had tired of eastern social life. He wrote Lodge, "Not even the charm of Mrs. Z. would make me content to pass another purely 'society' winter. To be a man of the world is *not* my strong point."[130] But he and Edith had come to an arrangement that would set him free: In April she would go to Europe with her family as planned, while he would go west and sort out his career—would he be writer, politician, or rancher?[131] He set March 15 for his departure date. His diary entries for the ten days preceding that Monday almost all bear but one repetitive entry, the intial "E."[132]

14

ON THE TRAIL
OF OUTLAWS

THEODORE ROOSEVELT'S LONGEST UNBROKEN VISIT TO DAKOTA TERRI-
tory ran from mid-March to early July 1886, yet an observer of that period
senses uneasy change in the Badlands and in Roosevelt's experience of the
West—a feeling almost of gloom.

When he arrived on Thursday, March 18, Sewall and Dow met him at
the train station, but Roosevelt spent the night with Joe Ferris, the guide
for the 1883 bison hunt that started Roosevelt's sojourn in the West.[1] Ferris had married in New Brunswick over the winter; his bride met Roosevelt for the first time when he was fresh from the train and dressed in his
"city get-up," such flawlessly tailored and impeccably stylish clothes that
Mrs. Ferris found him daunting.[2] "I was scairt to death," she said in later
years.[3] He was a wealthy easterner of some fame, a society man accustomed to dining at the home of the Astors of New York, and Mrs. Ferris
was uneasy about what kind of guest he would make and what she could
offer at her home and table. He told her to treat him like "one of the
boys."[4] She soon found that there was not "much of the New York money-
bag about him; he is more like a big boy let loose from school."[5]

The next day, decked out in well-worn western garb, he headed for the Elkhorn with Sewall and Dow in a wagon pulled by four horses. Snow blanketed the Badlands, the Little Missouri was iced in places, and progress was slow because the wagon had to cross the river eleven times. They reached the house long after sunset, the cold light of a full moon showering the bleached landscape. The river, edged with shattered ice floes, looked like a miniature mountain range. February sometimes had been cold enough to freeze the river solid, other times as warm as May.[6] Alternate thawing and freezing had created a wreckage of ice that moved slowly downstream, periodically jamming the river. Only days before Roosevelt returned, the ice jam had creaked and groaned past the house and dammed the river downstream.[7] As the Elkhorn men and women were about to eat dinner, Sewall had bellowed, "Ice gorge, ice gorge," and all had dashed outside to find the Little Missouri rising rapidly. The men rushed for the blue mackinaw boat they kept near the bank, dragged it to a fence that encircled the house, and tied it there.[8] The river lapped behind them, rising nine feet in three minutes. It washed up against the relocated boat and came within five feet of flooding the house. Since then the river had broken through the jam, leaving ice piled along both banks for miles.[9]

Little wonder that the group from Maine talked constantly of the time when they could go back home.[10] The wives, who missed having neighbors, were particularly eager to leave.[11] One late winter day, Sewall's wife, Mary, wrote to Nancy Sewall that she and Lizzie Dow were contented but that she guessed "we all will be glad when the time comes for us to start back home[.] we think of it most every day."[12] To pass the time she was reading Roosevelt's *Hunting Trips of a Ranchman*. She found the book "very interesting" and added, "they are fifteen dollars so you may know they are a nice book."

Her spirits probably were not helped by the severe colds that almost everyone in the household was suffering at about that time.[13] Moreover, Sewall was becoming convinced that they would not make any money at the ranch.[14] Although he knew by late February that Roosevelt would not lose many cattle that year, he thought spring 1887 would see a heavy loss. More Elkhorn cows would have calves in 1886 than in previous years, and the calves would drain the cows' energy and health, making them particularly vulnerable in the winter of 1886–87. Sewall wrote his brother, "it is too cold here to raise cattle that way I think[.] [I] dont believe thare is any money in she cattle here and [I] am afraid thare is not much in any unless it is the largest heards[.] and they are crowding in cattle all the time and I think they will eat us out in a few years[.] I don't like so free a country[.] one man has as good a right as another[.] nobody really has any right so when feed gets scarce in one place they drive their cattle whare it is good without regard to whos[e] range they eat out[.] I am satisfied that by the time we are ready to leave grass will be pretty scarce here and I don't think thare will ever be very much maid out of what cattle we have[.] of course we are all right but I am afraid Mr. Roosevelt was led to believe thare was more money in it than he will ever see[.] I cant find any body yet that has made anything out of a small lot of cattle[.]"[15]

Roosevelt looked at the same livestock as Sewall and came to a more optimistic conclusion, writing to one of *his* siblings, "Things are looking better than I expected; the loss by death has been wholly trifling. Unless we have a big accident I shall get through this all right; if not I can get started square with no debt."[16]

Roosevelt intended to stay in the Badlands for five months and work on his book about Thomas Hart Benton—a task he found slow going and "intensely irksome."[17] When not writing he tramped around the country, now all slippery ice and deep, sticky mud. He shot prairie chickens and a deer.[18] He made plans to travel down river with Dow in the blue boat, hunting waterfowl, bears, and mountain lions and visiting the Gros Ventre Indian village where Dow and Sewall had bought buckskin clothing.[19]

Perhaps Roosevelt had this trip in mind when he, Sewall, and Dow rowed across the river on Monday, March 22, to retrieve four deer that the two woodsmen had killed and left tied in a cedar tree before Roosevelt's return.[20] The tree proved no protection against mountain lions, which had devoured the carcasses. The men followed a trail of fresh lion tracks, clear in the snow, but lost them in a tangle of rocky hills and cedar-cloaked gorges.[21] On the way home, they visited a hunter who had traveled much of the continent, from his birthplace in New York to California—fifty-six-year-old W. J. Tompkins, whom Roosevelt had given permission to live in the cabin Captain Robins had formerly used, a few miles south of the Elkhorn house.[22] Roosevelt arranged with Tompkins to go after the mountain lions the next day, intending to camp out for several nights.[23] The Elkhorn men then poled along the river and hauled out the boat at the only place where the ice allowed them to reach shore. There they tied the mackinaw firmly to a tree.

That night strong winds shook the house. Nevertheless, three men were on the river fighting wind and ice. The leader was Mike "Redhead" Finnegan, a stocky local desperado with a brick-red complexion and long red hair. Ranchers suspected that he was a horse thief and cattle rustler and lately had talked about hanging him.[24] He was facing the dangers of the river that night because he was in a "die dog or eat the hatchet" dilemma and "was bound two get out of that country cost what it might, when People talk Lynch law and threaten a Persons life, I think that it is about time two leave."[25]

He had a long history of bad behavior in Medora. One story of his exploits tells as much about the local culture as it does about Redhead Finnegan. He had been the victim of a practical joke one night the previous March, when he passed out in Bob Roberts' saloon. John Goodall, de Morès' foreman, had the idea to lay out Finnegan on the billiard table and clip off his beard on one side of his face, his long red curls on the other side of his head, and the fringe off half his buckskin shirt.[26] When Finnegan came to the next day "he went berserk," took a position in brush near the Marquis' store, and fired randomly into buildings with a heavy-caliber rifle. He nearly killed at least one person before A. T. Packard rushed up on horseback and knocked him out. He woke locked in a boxcar, but a friend let him out, and he fled downriver to his cabin.

The following December, after he had filled himself with "valley tan," he shot up Medora again. The new marshal, Fred Willard, arrested him and took him to Dickinson, where the court fined him five dollars and costs and put him in jail for about three weeks.[27]

Finnegan's companions on the river were a stout, muscular man who was half Indian, named Burnsted, and a shiftless old German named Chris Pfaffenbach whose mind had been corroded by bad whisky.[28] The boat in which they were traveling was laden with stolen goods from ranch houses along the way; they planned either to use or to sell the loot, including deer and bighorn sheep heads and three sacks of books and magazines, among them a Jesse James biography popular with border ruffians as well as an unlikely collection of high-society novels.[29]

As they fled north, they encountered Theodore Roosevelt's blue boat. While Roosevelt was "in his dreams," they cut the rope tying it to shore and stole off with it.[30] Boats were rare in the Badlands, and the ice along the banks prevented travel by horse, so the thieves felt certain no one would pursue them.[31]

The next morning Sewall, thinking of the heavy winds the night before, went to check the boat. He found the severed rope; nearby, Dow found a red wool glove with a leather palm.[32] Sewall then engaged in a brief subterfuge that a modern observer might interpret as a bit of repressed hostility or a touch of passive-aggressive behavior. At breakfast he listened as Roosevelt talked "all about his plans for crossing the stream, and I let him talk along, thinking, 'Little you know about what's been happening.' When he was nearly through I spoke up quietly, telling him I did not think he would get across that day.

"He spoke up kind of sharply, wanting to know why.

"I told him that we had no boat and explained how the boat had been stolen in the night after the wind went down."[33]

Roosevelt found the theft "very annoying" not only because it meant he had to cancel his hunt but also because he kept his saddle horses on the other side of the river and needed the boat to cross over and look after them. And then there was the issue of male honor. Roosevelt: "In any wild country where the power of the law is little felt or heeded, and where every one has to rely upon himself for protection, men soon get to feel that it is in the highest degree unwise to submit to any wrong without making an immediate and resolute effort to avenge it upon the wrong-doers, at no matter what risk or trouble. To submit tamely or meekly to theft, or to any other injury, is to invite almost certain repetition of the offense, in a place where self-reliant hardihood and the ability to hold one's own under all circumstances rank as the first of virtues."[34] The boat, bought in St. Paul for thirty dollars, assumed an importance beyond its monetary worth, the more so because, at some point in his Badlands career, Roosevelt had been made a deputy sheriff.[35]

Roosevelt suspected that the thieves were the "three hard characters who lived in a shack, or hut, some twenty miles above us, and whom we had shrewdly suspected for some time of wishing to get out of the country, as certain of the cattlemen had begun openly to threaten to lynch them."[36]

His initial reaction was to mount horses and ride after them, but Sewall pointed out that the river valley was a rubble of ice, so a horse would do no good, especially as the low ground was so wet that in places they could not get within a mile of the channel. They agreed that the thieves would be in no hurry, believing they had the only boats available. Sewall suggested that he build a new boat.[37] Roosevelt agreed and sent Bill Rowe into Medora for supplies and to telegraph to Bismarck and other communities that the three men should be arrested if they appeared.[38]

While Sewall built the new boat, Roosevelt hacked away at the Benton book. "Writing is horribly hard work to me; and I make slow progress," he wrote Lodge. "I have got some good ideas in the first chapter, but I am not sure they are worked up rightly; my style is very rough and I do not like a certain lack of sequitur that I do not seem able to get rid of."[39]

By Saturday, March 27, Roosevelt had written the first chapter of his book, and Sewall had finished the boat. The Elkhorn crew was prepared to leave on Monday, but the weather turned so cold, and river ice ran so heavily, that they did not shove off until Tuesday. Sewall sat in the rear of the flat-bottomed boat, Dow in front, and Roosevelt in the middle. They had with them two weeks' worth of flour, coffee, and bacon, plenty of warm bedding, and layers of heavy clothes, including long fur coats. "Altogether we felt as if we were off on a holiday trip, and set to work to have as good a time as possible."[40]

Pursuit of the boat thieves must have been the ultimate hunt, the quarry not some unarmed animal but dangerous men who would shoot at the first sign of a threat. The thieves had almost a week's lead, but Roosevelt had on his side two Maine woodsmen who knew how to pole and paddle a boat through ice floes with all haste. Sewall: "The cowboys and hunters were mostly bow-legged and past-masters at riding, but they were not web-footed and used to riding logs and handling boats in rough waters the way Dow and I were."[41]

They pursued the thieves through "a strange, wild, desolate country of rough and barren bad lands."[42] Sometimes the riverbanks were bare; sometimes the boat passed ice walls ten feet high, where falling chunks threatened to swamp it. The first evening they landed and shot three prairie chickens for dinner. The night grew colder, the morning colder still. Ice ran thick in the river. They hunted for deer but found none, and so headed downstream. Not until midday was the sun warm enough to ward off the chill, and a constant wind blew into their faces. They passed the Gros Ventre camp, deserted now; what lay downriver beyond it was largely unknown to the boatmen.

For lunch they stopped on a sandbar, drinking tea and eating fried bacon and fresh bread cooked over a driftwood fire. The afternoon wind waxed harsher, and ice formed on the poles. The men were glad to get off the water and shoot prairie chickens for dinner. The next morning, April 1, the thermometer stood at zero, and the river congealed into slush. Finding plentiful signs of deer, the men delayed their departure long enough to shoot a buck and a yearling doe, which cheered them.

Meanwhile, the three thieves, after stealing Roosevelt's boat, had moved downstream into the teeth of a blizzard—the worst storm Finnegan had ever seen, he would later claim. Seeking refuge, they arrived at the mouth of Cherry Creek, about a hundred miles from the Elkhorn Ranch. Snow fell, wind howled. Burnsted said, "We're all right here, Bully Boy," to which Finnegan gave silent assent.[43] They camped there. They soon found that the ice jam that had nearly flooded Roosevelt's house was now only a little below their camp, blocking progress downriver. They were not worried, however. Finnegan believed that Roosevelt was "an ordinary eastern tenderfoot" who would not give chase even if he had a boat. They could camp there until a thaw cleared the ice. On April Fool's Day, Burnsted and Finnegan went hunting, leaving Pfaffenbach in camp.

By early afternoon, Roosevelt, Sewall, and Dow were just above the mouth of Cherry Creek. As they rounded a bend, Sewall spotted something. "There's your boat," he said. "Get your guns ready."[44] He headed toward a stretch of ice-free bank. On shore a column of smoke rose from a stand of small cottonwoods.

Roosevelt and Dow armed themselves. As soon as the hull touched land they jumped out and moved toward the smoke. Sewall tied up the boat.

The posse's main concern was Redhead Finnegan. They knew he was a "shooting man"; if he spied them before they saw him, "he was liable to make it very unhealthy for us."[45] They knew Pfaffenbach was harmless. Burnsted was an unknown quantity.

Luck was on their side. When Roosevelt and Dow burst into the camp,

Pfaffenbach was still alone, his weapons on the ground. He put up no resistance. They took his guns and knives and assured him they would not hurt him. He said he had come down the river with the other men because they had told him they would have a good time and catch a lot of fish. Sewall suspected they had taken him along because he had a little money, while Burnsted and Finnegan were broke.

Keeping Pfaffenbach by the fire, the Elkhorn men hid behind the riverbank looking across level land that stretched for about a hundred yards, covered with grass and shrubs only about waist high. About half an hour later Burnsted came in. When he was within about twenty yards, the three cowmen rose and told him to put up his hands, which he did instantly. "We took his gun and gave him a seat under the bank with the cheerful information that if he made any noise or tried to get away we would shoot him."[46]

Another half hour passed before Finnegan showed up, carrying his rifle. The Elkhorn men knew it was his only weapon—they had found his Smith and Wesson revolver in camp.[47] They repeated the process used in netting Burnsted. Finnegan, however, hesitated when ordered to put up his hands. Roosevelt walked to him, centered his rifle on the outlaw's chest, and again commanded him to put his hands up.[48] Dow said, "Damn you, drop that gun."[49] As a man who prided himself on knowing when the game was over, Finnegan surrendered. Later he recalled, "Surprised? You might say so. Wasn't we though, when that damned New Yorker covered us with his guns for a hands up. What could we do with our flukes wet and full of mud, our clothes wringing wet and minds preoccupied? What would you have done? The New Yorker got the best of us."[50] Sewall, watching Finnegan, was sure that the outlaw was not frightened, just angry: "if he had had any chance [I] think he would have tried us[.] but few men would try to fight when they saw three men with cocked guns aimed at them and not more than twenty feet off."[51]

Roosevelt and his men wrapped the outlaws' weapons in bedding. Finnegan asked Roosevelt not to take him back to Medora, as he feared he would be hung there; he was relieved when Roosevelt said he was going to take him to Mandan.[52]

The Elkhorn men ordered Finnegan and his partners to collect firewood. The cold was so intense that Roosevelt could not tie up the outlaws for fear of cutting off blood circulation and causing the men's hands and feet to freeze. Instead, he put the three thieves on the side of the fire opposite him and his crew and took away their boots. Roosevelt and his men guarded the prisoners in turns, dividing the watch into half nights so that each of the Elkhorn men got a full night's sleep every third night.

The next morning they again took to the river, now with three boats. Roosevelt, feeling that Finnegan was the greatest threat, kept him by his side in the boat Sewall had made. The other two men he put in their original, leaky craft filled with booty so they would have little or no chance of escape. Roosevelt need not have worried—the flotilla soon came up against the massive ice jam. Unable to pass, they would have to wait for a thaw, which they expected soon.

Now the drudgery set in. Roosevelt: "The next eight days were as irksome and monotonous as any I ever spent: there is very little amusement in combining the functions of a sheriff with those of an arctic explorer. The weather kept as cold as ever. During the night the water in the pail would freeze solid. Ice formed all over the river, thickly along the banks; and the clear, frosty sun gave us so little warmth that the melting hardly began before noon. Each day the great jam would settle down-stream a few miles, only to wedge again, leaving behind it several smaller jams, through which we would work our way until we were as close to the tail of the large one as we dared to go. Once we came around a bend and got so near that we were in a good deal of danger of being sucked under."[53]

They passed the time reading and talking. Roosevelt had brought with him a volume of Matthew Arnold and a copy of Tolstoy's *Anna Karenina*.[54] Finnegan initially was sullen but eventually loosened up. He said of their initial encounter, "If I'd had any show at all, you'd have sure had to fight, Mr. Roosevelt; but there wasn't any use making a break when I'd only have got shot myself, with no chance of harming any one else."[55]

And so the days passed. In short time they had nothing to eat but flour, which they mixed with muddy river water for unleavened bread. They hunted but found nothing. Roosevelt feared he would have to let the thieves go, they were so nearly out of provisions. Sewall spent a day searching for a ranch on the other side of the river but found only a bunch of cattle. That evening the Elkhorn men concluded that Roosevelt and Dow should go down the camp side of the river the next day and, if they did not find a ranch, should kill one of the cattle Sewall had found. "It was rather risky business to kill other folks's cattle," so in the morning they took with them an empty tomato can so that if they did shoot livestock, they could leave a note explaining who they were and why they had done it.[56]

Sewall watched the prisoners while Dow and Roosevelt were away. At sunset he spotted his partners a long way off, trudging toward camp. Dow was loaded with provisions he and Roosevelt had collected at a ranch—flour, baking powder, bacon, sugar, and coffee. That night they had a good supper, and "even the thieves felt quite happy."[57]

Roosevelt had arranged for a wagon team so he could take the prisoners overland to Dickinson, about forty-five miles south, rather than down-river to more distant Mandan. The next morning the whole party started on foot for the ranch, arriving at noon. They stayed until the following morning, when they walked another fifteen miles to the outfit of the old frontiersman who had agreed to provide the wagon. He was "a large, power-fully built man with a deeply wrinkled, sunburnt, tough old face that looked about like the instep of an old boot that had lain out in the weather for years."[58] When they arrived at his camp, he stepped up to Finnegan and shook hands, saying, "Finnegan, you damned thief, what have you been doing now?"[59] The old-timer told Sewall that he knew Finnegan. "I had him in my care once for nine months with a ball and chain hitched to his foot."

Finnegan said he had been acting the fool again. Sewall: "He seemed to be disgusted with himself a good deal of the time. At one time I saw him kick an old tin can and, asking him what he did it for, he told me that he did it because he couldn't kick himself."[60]

Roosevelt sent Sewall and Dow back to the river to take the boats downstream. He took charge of the prisoners, putting them in the wagon to get them to Dickinson and the county jail. "It was a most desolate drive. The prairie had been burned the fall before, and was a mere bleak waste of blackened earth, and a cold, rainy mist lasted throughout the two days. The only variety was where the road crossed the shallow headwaters of Knife and Green rivers. Here the ice was high along the banks, and the wagon had to be taken to pieces to get it over."[61]

Alone with his three captives and the teamster, whom Roosevelt did not know well enough to trust, he kept his distance, walking behind the wagon the entire time, mostly through ankle-deep mud. They spent the night in a granger's hut, Roosevelt staying awake to guard his prisoners. After thirty-six hours without sleep he slogged into Dickinson on April 11 and turned the men over to the sheriff. As a deputy sheriff he would later, under territorial law, collect fifty dollars in fees and mileage for his work.

Once shed of the prisoners he went in search of a doctor to treat his feet, which had been badly used during the long trip. He stopped a man on the street to ask directions, and the man introduced himself as Dr. Victor Stickney, the only physician within 150 miles. He washed and bandaged Roosevelt's badly blistered feet. "He . . . had had no sleep for forty-eight hours, and he was all teeth and eyes; but even so he seemed a man unusually wide awake," the physician remembered. "You could see he was thrilled by the adventures he had been through . . . he was, in his own phrase, 'pleased as Punch' at the idea of having participated in a real adventure. He was just like a boy."[62]

Roosevelt spent the night in a Dickinson hotel. Before leaving town the next day, he appeared in court to press charges against the three boat thieves. The justice of the peace bore the unlikely name Western Starr and, in an even more unlikely coincidence, had been a classmate of Roosevelt at Columbia Law School. Later that day, Roosevelt took the train to Medora.

Meanwhile, Sewall and Dow were still on the river.[63] After taking leave of Roosevelt they had spent the night at the ranch near their former campsite. When they found next morning that the ice had broken up, they gave the rancher Finnegan's boat and set off downriver, still in possession of the stolen goods. Sewall: "We now had a long stretch of river before us and an uninhabited country, with only a ranch here and there. We had gotten rid of the thieves and, although we had lost Theodore and were sorry that he had to go alone, we felt greatly relieved ourselves. We now planned to have some sport."[64]

Ducks and geese appeared in the sky and on the river, giving the men hope of seeing larger game. The current was strong, promising a swift journey, but the river was so crooked that they frequently found themselves facing into a stiff wind that slowed them down. One day Dow shot two geese. Shortly afterward they rounded a bend in the river and saw a large party of Indians on shore, apparently attracted by the gun-fire. Their reaction to the Indians—probably on or near the Gros Ventre reservation—contrasts with Roosevelt's response to the three he encountered on the plains. Sewall: "We didn't want them to think we were afraid of them, so we landed and tried to talk with them. We didn't succeed in talking very much. . . . About the only thing the Indians could say was 'Shug.' They all wanted sugar. We had a great plenty, so I took a dipper and dipped out a pint, while an old fellow came with his old black hat, which looked as though it might be about as old as the Indian. I dumped sugar into it."[65]

In another day or so they reached the Missouri River, about 125 miles upstream from Mandan. On the big river they saw thousands of geese resting on sandbars, the birds rising in honking clouds when the boats spooked them, their wings sounding like a great wind. That night the men camped near a village eighty miles by road from Mandan and bought provisions. The next day they started out with a swift current and high wind that speeded them along. They coursed through rapids and waves, sometimes taking on water and sometimes rushing along at a speed that intimidated them, the water foaming so badly that they were unable to look out for dangerous rocks or submerged trees. Sewall in later years wrote that this stretch of the river yielded the swiftest run for the longest distance that he ever traveled. They reached Mandan at four o'clock that afternoon. There they turned in the stolen goods and gave the boat Sewall had made to a man with whom they spent the night and who carted Roosevelt's blue boat to the train station.

In the dining car of the train a waiter offered Sewall and Dow a lunch menu; Sewall told him that they had not eaten for three weeks and to bring them everything he had. The waiter recognized them as Roosevelt hands and set them up with a good meal. That night Sewall and Dow were back in Medora, and the following day they boated to the Elkhorn, arriving at eleven that night. Sewall concluded, "This had been a trip that we had all enjoyed. There had been a good deal of hard work connected with it; some parts had been very pleasant and some very unpleasant. It had been a very cold, barren time, for one thing. . . . Still, we were all foolish enough to enjoy most of it, after all, and looked back to it with pleasure and satisfaction."[66]

Local response to Roosevelt's escapade was almost unanimous. The cattlemen told him "he was a damn fool for bothering so much with those fellows. They said the thieves would have killed him if they had got the chance, and wanted to know why he didn't kill them. No doubt they would have killed him, too. Theodore said that he hadn't gone out there to kill anybody, but all he intended to do was to defend himself. If there wasn't anybody else to defend him, he intended to protect himself."[67]

On April 13, the day following his return to Medora after capturing the thieves, Roosevelt chaired the spring meeting of the local stockmen's association and was elected a delegate to the Montana association's annual meeting in Miles City.[68] During the four days between the Medora meeting and the annual event, Roosevelt drifted between his two ranches. He sent a letter to Corinne on April 15, enclosing a card to send with flowers to Edith upon her departure for Europe.[69] He ended the letter with a request that might have perplexed his rowdy cowboy colleagues: "Will it bother you awfully to have an apothecary send me three or four cakes of that nice transparent soap? I have nothing but castile soap here. Express it to me."

At about this time Billings County residents voted to organize the county, electing the officials needed for a government.[70] Joe Ferris was elected county clerk and Sylvane clerk of the circuit court.[71] Merrifield became the first deputy of the Old Court House. Accustomed to informality, residents continued to settle disputes out of court, so no legal business arose for the first four years after the county was organized. Roosevelt believed that organization brought an end to lawlessness, observing that residents "elected some good officers, built a log jail, prohibited all shooting in the streets, and enforced the prohibition, etc., etc."[72]

On the eighteenth, Roosevelt left for Miles City with Sylvane Ferris to join the hundreds of cowboys streaming into town for the three-day annual meeting.[73] It began as a sort of carnival, with a parade led by the Fifth Infantry band from Fort Keogh, followed by carriages full of officials and their ladies.[74] Behind them came "a cavalcade of wild cowboys just brought in from the adjacent ranges, followed by about 150 cattlemen marching four abreast."[75] The procession was almost two and a half blocks long and snaked through the main streets, ending at the skating rink, where the livestock association would meet. As the parade neared the rink, the

The fair-haired child of a leading New York City family: Theodore Roosevelt in autumn 1863, about the time of his fifth birthday. His childhood was plagued with illness, particularly asthma, an ailment that followed him into adulthood.
Theodore Roosevelt Collection, Harvard College Library (520.11-003)

The hallway of the ornate house that Theodore Roosevelt Sr. built for his wife, Mittie, at 6 West Fifty-seventh Street in Manhattan. Theodore Jr.'s mother and his wife Alice died in this house on the same day shortly after Alice gave birth to his first child.
Theodore Roosevelt Collection, Harvard College Library (560.11-016)

Alice Lee, left, and Theodore Roosevelt pose with Alice's friend Rose Saltonstall during a December 7, 1878, photo session that Roosevelt dubbed "a tintype spree." He arranged the date, with Rose functioning as chaperon, less than two months into his ardent courtship of Alice, who would succumb to his entreaties of marriage after more than a year of relentless pursuit. *Theodore Roosevelt Collection, Harvard College Library (bMS Am 1541.9 [135])*

The Marquis de Morès equipped for a ride on the range. He founded the town of Medora, the focal point of life in Roosevelt's Badlands, and had grandiose plans for a ranching and farming empire in the region. Roosevelt and the Marquis were sometimes rivals but usually friends. *State Historical Society of North Dakota (0042–078)*

The Maltese Cross Ranch house, located about seven miles north of Medora, was the headquarters for Roosevelt's first Badlands cattle operation. Roosevelt's ranch manager Sylvane Ferris sits in the carriage; the other man is unidentified. The house is presently displayed at Theodore Roosevelt National Park, outside Medora, North Dakota, and is open to visitors. *Theodore Roosevelt Collection, Harvard College Library (560.14-062)*

This picture of Alice Lee at age fourteen was Theodore's favorite image of his first wife, who died in her early twenties. He once wrote that until he met this effervescent young woman with golden hair and dove-gray eyes, he had never cared "a snap of my finger for any girl."
Theodore Roosevelt Collection, Harvard College Library (bMS Am 1541.9 [122])

Bob Roberts' saloon, a popular den of iniquity and the site of many frontier practical jokes designed to reinforce among visitors the reputation for violence that Medora had earned. The second floor was used for meetings, including some of the periodic gatherings of the local cattlemen's association, headed by Theodore Roosevelt.
Theodore Roosevelt Collection, Harvard College Library (560.14-082)

Theodore Roosevelt, about twenty-six years old, in full cowboy regalia. His clothing was practical and appropriate for the time and place, but a bit more upscale than most cattlemen and cowboys could afford. His hunting knife, for example, had been made for him by Tiffany. *Theodore Roosevelt Collection, Harvard College Library (R500.P6qa-012)*

Roosevelt in the Badlands with his
favorite hunting horse, Manitou.
He wrote of this horse, "He is nearly
as perfect as can be the case with
hunting-horseflesh," being "perfectly
surefooted and as fast as any horse
on the river" yet very gentle and
calm. Roosevelt is wearing the type
of fringed buckskin hunting suit
that he believed was "the most
picturesque and distinctively national
dress ever worn in America."
*Theodore Roosevelt Collection, Harvard
College Library (520.14-007)*

Roosevelt, far right, with his hunting
guides in Island Falls, Maine,
March 1879. The bearded man at left
is William Sewall, and in the center
is Wilmot Dow. Both men won
Roosevelt's respect on rugged hunts,
and he took them with him to
manage his second Badlands ranch,
the Elkhorn.
*Theodore Roosevelt Collection, Harvard
College Library (520.12-015)*

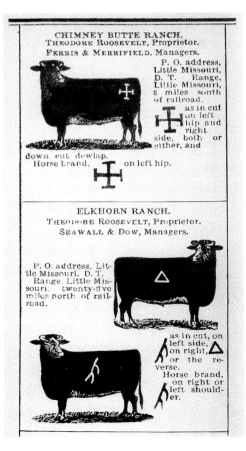

The Elkhorn Ranch house, built by Sewall and Dow mostly from timber they cut themselves, was shaded by trees and faced the Little Missouri River. Roosevelt sometimes shot deer from the porch, where his favorite activity was reading in a rocking chair as he watched evening sunlight fade from the buttes. *Theodore Roosevelt Collection, Harvard College Library (560.14-001c)*

Roosevelt registered three brands in the local newspaper—the Maltese Cross, the triangle, and the Elkhorn. Ranchers used brands to determine livestock ownership. *Theodore Roosevelt Collection, Harvard College Library (560.14-102)*

Preparing for the summer roundup. This photograph by Roosevelt shows a typical chuck wagon at left, which held food, ammunition, and other supplies. The man on horseback is John Goodall, the Marquis de Morès' foreman and a cowboy with such a good reputation for reliability that he was made roundup captain one year, putting him in charge of the entire operation.
Theodore Roosevelt Collection, Harvard College Library (560.14-095)

During the roundup, each cowboy might have as many as ten horses assigned to him. Those not being ridden were herded along and held during stops in a corral that was little more than a rope. Roosevelt took this photo, which features his Maltese Cross Ranch manager Sylvane Ferris in the foreground. *Theodore Roosevelt Collection, Harvard College Library (560.14-096)*

Bill Sewall's wife (far right) holds her daughter, Kitty. Next to her, in the sunbonnet, is Wilmot Dow's wife. The other two women are neighbors. Scarce in the open-range West, women were widely viewed as a civilizing influence. One English traveler observed, "From the day when a silk dress and a lace shawl were seen in Main Street, that thoroughfare became passably clean and quiet; oaths were less frequently heard; knives were less frequently drawn; pistols were less frequently fired." *Theodore Roosevelt Collection, Harvard College Library (560.14-095a)*

Roosevelt, center, with Bill Sewall (bearded) and Wilmot Dow attired for chasing down three men who stole Roosevelt's boat. Roosevelt caught and jailed the men; local ranchers were perplexed that he didn't just hang them. *Theodore Roosevelt Collection, Harvard College Library (520.14-005)*

Dow (by the wagon wheel), Sewall (in black hat), and local hunter W. J. Tompkins pose with a cow elk Roosevelt just shot. Elk were growing rare in the Badlands by Roosevelt's time, and on more than one occasion he shot one that he thought might be the last of its kind in the region. *Theodore Roosevelt Collection, Harvard College Library (560.14-054)*

Edith Kermit Carow about the time of her 1887 marriage to Theodore Roosevelt. She and
Roosevelt had been childhood friends, and he reportedly proposed to her several times before
he met Alice Lee. Nevertheless, he felt tremendous guilt when he became engaged to
Edith less than two years after Alice's death. *Theodore Roosevelt Collection, Harvard College Library*

Alice, three years old, and her aunt Anna, who raised her almost from birth. This 1887 photograph was taken the year that Alice went to live with her father and his new wife, Edith. She would later complain that her father never told her anything about her mother, after whom she was named. *Theodore Roosevelt Collection, Harvard College Library (bMS Am1541.9 [142])*

horses in the lead carriage bolted, charging through the marching band. One horse jumped the wagon tongue and became entangled with the horse on the other side, allowing the men in the carriage to vacate speedily. This antic triggered a "wild charge of cowboys, accompanied with such yells as would strike terror to the heart of the tenderfooted."[76]

Like the Medora confab, this meeting was fairly routine, with one exception. Among the most absorbing issues was overstocking of the range, which led to a dispute between two ranchers so vehement that Roosevelt feared it would degenerate into gunfire.[77] He suggested that the two men fight it out hand to hand, and he helped set up an improvised boxing ring. The two men fought, but the outcome is no longer remembered.

Roosevelt left Miles City pleased with his performance: "I took my position very well in the convention, and indeed these westerners have now pretty well accepted me as one of themselves, and as a representative stockman."[78] He recognized a pragmatic advantage to this acceptance: "I am on the Executive Committee of the Association, am President of the Dakota Branch etc.—all of which directly helps me in my business relations here."

After returning to the Badlands, Roosevelt went pronghorn hunting with Merrifield for a week, then settled down at the Elkhorn for three weeks—the longest stint he would ever spend there.[79] On May 12 he wrote Corinne, "If I was not afraid of being put down as cold blooded I should say that, though I honestly miss greatly and all the time think longingly of all you dear ones, yet I really enjoy this life. I have managed to combine an outdoors life, possessing much variety and excitement and now and then a little adventure, with a literary life also."[80] As for politics: "I am really pretty philosophical about success and failure now. It often amuses me when I accidentally hear that I am supposed to be harboring secret and biting regret for my political career; when as a matter of fact I have hardly ever when alone given it two thoughts since it closed, and have been quite as much wrapped up in hunting, ranching and bookmaking as I ever was in politics." He closed by thanking her for sending the soap he had requested in April.

On May 15 he wrote to Anna, who apparently was planning a trip to the ranch. With a delicacy his eastern friends may have appreciated but his western cohorts may have thought a bit stuffy, he assured her that

"Mrs. Seawall and Mrs. Dow are very nice; they will do all they can to make you comfortable next summer if we can arrange a visit; though I rather dread seeing you at table, for we have of course no social distinctions, and the cowboys sit down in their shirt sleeves."[81]

He may have been aware of social distinctions, but he was not without heart. In the same paragraph he asked Anna for a favor. "The poor little mite of a Seawall girl, just baby Lee's age, has neither playmates nor play toys. I don't appreciate it as a table companion, especially when fed on, or rather feeding itself on, a mixture of syrup and strawberry jam (giving it the look of a dirty little yellow haired gnome in war paint); but I wish the poor forlorn little morsel some playtoys." Sewall's daughter, Lucretia—whom Roosevelt called Kitty—stood about three feet tall and was a perpetual-motion machine, up at dawn and active until nine at night.[82] She often toddled up and down the porch with Roosevelt.[83] The nearest children about her age lived six miles away—she needed on-premises distraction. Roosevelt asked for a big colored ball, picture blocks, letter blocks, a little horse and wagon, and a rag doll.

He closed by writing, "I miss both you and darling Baby Lee dreadfully; kiss her many times for me; I am really hungry to see her. She must be just too cunning for anything. Yet I enjoy my life at present. I have my time fully occupied with work of which I am fond; and so have none of my usual restless, caged wolf feeling."

From late May into June he was on the roundup, which started with sixty men; they put in fourteen- to-sixteen-hour days, and Roosevelt was tired the whole time.[84] During a cold snap he took a break to hunt with Sewall and Tompkins in the divide between the Little Missouri and Yellowstone rivers, as he had heard that elk had appeared there.[85] During the hunt, Sewall spotted a cow elk lying in a clump of thick bushes. "Roosevelt was very near her but could not see her[.] Tompkins was between him and I showed her to the old man and by telling him whare to look I had to holler to him[.] then he calld to R[oosevelt] who was very fierce to do the shooting[.] Tompkins showed her to him and he shot her [and] also the calf[.] she was about the bigges[t] fool I ever saw or she would have cleared out."[86] Sewall was eager to go on an elk hunt with only Dow so that "we can do the shooting ourselves."

When the roundup was near Medora, Roosevelt dined with the Marquis de Morès at the chateau, eating cherries—the only fruit he had had since leaving New York.[87] He also borrowed a copy of Tolstoy's *War and Peace* from the Marquise, in French, as he referred to it as *La Guerre et La Paix* in a letter home. He complained that he had little time to read it, though he was "very fond of Tolstoi"; less than two weeks later he had finished the tome and had concluded that "La Guerre et La Paix, like all Tolsoi's work, is very strong and interesting. The descriptions of the battles are excellent, but though with one or two good ideas underneath them, the criticisms of the commanders, especially Napoleon, and of wars in general, are absurd. . . . [W]hen he again and again spends pages in descanting on the wickedness and folly of war, and passes over other vices without a word of reproach he certainly in so far acts as an apologist for the latter, and the general tone of the book does not seem to me to be in the least conducive to morality."[88]

Eventually the roundup reached the Elkhorn Ranch, where the New England wives made breakfast and lunch for about twenty men. The Sewalls gave the cowboys all the milk, cream, bread, and butter they wanted, along with cake, cookies, and coffee. Mary Sewall: "They seemed to be well pleased and each man thanked us and went out[.] the Cow Boys are all very Polite fellows appearantly but some times they act pretty ruff."[89] William took Mary and Lizzie Dow to see the roundup when it stopped about six miles from the house—some three or four thousand cattle and five hundred horses. Mary did not want to watch much of the branding.

Roosevelt was enough of a Dakota celebrity to be chosen keynote speaker—at Dr. Victor Stickney's urging—for the 1886 Dickinson Independence Day celebration, the town's first, held on Monday, July 5.[90] The temperature reportedly hit 136 degrees, but still the largest crowd ever seen in Stark County gathered in Dickinson for a parade starting at ten in the morning, followed by a reading of the Declaration of Independence in the public square and a community singing of "My Country 'Tis of Thee."[91]

Roosevelt spoke at two in the afternoon, introduced by Dr. Stickney, who served as master of ceremonies. Roosevelt spoke in simple language, though he "was plainly embarrassed and the delivery was in a high key between a squeak and a shriek."[92] He lectured: "The duties of American citizenship are very solemn as well as very precious; and each one of us here today owes it to himself, to his children, and to all his fellow Americans, to show that he is capable of performing them in the right spirit. You have been told that in the end we are to fall heir to most of this continent. Well, I think so myself. I hope to see the day when not a foot of American soil will be held by European power. But we must meantime remember that we can only prove our fitness to hold sway over our neighbor's possessions by the way in which we rule ourselves. It is not what we have that will make us a great nation; it is the way in which we use it."[93]

He warned: "We must remember that the republic can only be kept pure by the individual purity of its members, and that if it become once thoroughly corrupt it will surely cease to exist. . . . If you fail to work in public life as well as in private, for honesty, and uprightness and virtue—if you condone vice because the vicious man is smart, or if you in any other way cast your weight into the scales in favor of evil, you are just so far corrupting and making less valuable the birthright of your children."[94]

He preached: "It is peculiarly incumbent on us here today to so act throughout our lives as to leave our children a heritage for which we will receive their blessings and not their curses."[95] And he urged his audience to "keep steadily in mind that no people were ever yet benefited by riches if their prosperity corrupted their virtue."[96]

After the speech he stayed to see horse races between cowboys and Indians.[97]

Packard, who was among those who took the train that day to see what was billed in the Dickinson newspaper as "An Epoch in the History of Our Town that Will Long be Remembered," said later of Roosevelt's speech, "I am sure it was built upon if not an actual oration he had written as a sophomore in college. . . . But the impression left on his audience was one Wendell Phillips might have envied.[98] Every point was thoroughly understood and the plain truths were so thoroughly absorbed that every person who heard the address advanced measurably in good citizenship."[99] After the speech, Packard told Roosevelt that if he continued in public work he could be president someday. "One would suppose that I could remember the actual words he used in reply, but I cannot," Packard said years later. "I remember distinctly that he was not in the least surprised by my statement. He gave me the impression of having thoroughly considered the matter and to have arrived at the same conclusion as mine. Part of his answer was: 'If your prophecy comes true, I will do my part to make a good one.'"[100] On the train ride home that evening, Roosevelt bought champagne for thirty-five or forty people from Medora.[101]

Later on the fifth Roosevelt wrote Corinne to congratulate her on her new baby, a girl. He had received news of the event in two telegrams from her husband, Douglas Robinson, the first announcing the birth, the second assuring Roosevelt that Corinne was fine. Roosevelt's letter betrays a particular anxiety, however, that suggests how Alice's death hung over him. After expressing his joy at receiving the first telegram he added, "But I had not the heart to write you until I received the second the good old boy sent me and knew you were all right too."[102]

In his letter he says nothing of visiting New York, yet three days later, as if he had made a sudden decision, he boarded an eastbound train. He had two issues to settle in the city. First, he had completed a draft of his book on Thomas Hart Benton and wanted to fact-check it at the Astor Library; second, he wanted to investigate the offer he had received from New York City's Mayor Grace for the presidency of the city board of health—an offer that had left him "in a good deal of a quandary" for some time.[103] The position was then held by Alexander Shaler, a former Civil War general who had been indicted the previous December for accepting a bribe.[104] However, Shaler had not been ousted and was fighting the case in court.[105] Lodge had been counseling Roosevelt against taking the job on the grounds that it was beneath his dignity, but Roosevelt thought he was wrong.[106] Perhaps now that he was engaged to Edith, he felt he should find work in the city. Whatever his interest in the offer, he was reluctant to leave the Badlands: "It will fairly break my heart to have to give up this life, and especially my Rocky Mountain Hunting trip this fall. However if I continued to make long stays here I should very soon get to practically give up the east entirely."[107]

While on his way to New York City, Roosevelt passed through a prairie sere and brown. Summer 1886 was reducing cow country to cinders. During the first sixteen days in July, the average daytime temperature in the shade hovered at 102 degrees, that in the sun at 114, with no rain.[108] Medora's oldest resident said he had never experienced a summer like it in Dakota Territory. Ranchers were struggling to find supplies of hay, with little or no success.[109] Outsiders drove cattle from the parched ranges in Texas, Kansas, and Nebraska into the northern range, overcrowding the area.[110] Some Badlands cattlemen worried that if they had a hard winter, thousands of cattle would die.[111] While the land was being undermined, ranchers flooded meat markets with beef, driving down prices. Roosevelt, whom one newspaper called a conversational Gatling gun, told a reporter from the *Mandan Pioneer* that the era of excessive profits in ranching was over because too many people were getting into the business.[112] Drought and overstocking, he said, were causing enormous losses. The *Bismarck Daily Tribune* nevertheless quoted him as saying that his cattle were prospering as well as could be expected.[113]

Lincoln Lang believed that Roosevelt, sensing that grazing in the Badlands was declining, had begun to lose his enthusiasm for ranching.[114] With his "power of close observation," Roosevelt could see that the prairies and river bottoms were buckling under the weight of too many cattle. "Nature, in fact, was beginning to protest forcefully against misusage. Against commercial misdirection of the Bad Lands to uses other than those for which she had destined it. With the changing conditions, the wild romantic charm of the region was, alas, on the wane and no longer was what it had been."[115]

Lang noticed that hunters had killed off most of the beaver native to the Badlands, the largest rodent in North America and a builder of dams on streams.[116] These dams created pools of water that lasted year-round. As beaver vanished, so did their dams, and by 1886 streams were beginning to run dry part of the year. The myriad cattle crowding the Badlands had to search farther for water, cutting a spiderweb of trails across the fragile prairie, trails that eroded in the heavy rains and evolved into washouts. Lang: "Everywhere, now, were to be found filthy trampled mud holes where once had been clear running springs. Everywhere, low level defiled water-holes replacing the sylvan ponds where the wild-fowl had luxuriated but a little while before! Rank and even poisonous weed growths, heretofore unknown, were becoming increasingly in evidence all over the country, more particularly so in the quarters where sheep were ranging. The glorious buttes were becoming more and more scarred and defoliated."[117]

Despite the changes, some ranchers, the Langs among them, continued to be optimistic, presuming that if they could control overstocking "it would work out all right."[118] Others were less confident. As early as April of that year Sewall wrote his family, "as for hard times they are howling out here and lots are leaving the country."[119]

Roosevelt returned to Medora after only three weeks in New York, wrapping up his book and coming to no resolution about the job offer—the incumbent held on.[120] But now, even in the West, he felt the tug of the East. Shortly after arriving in Medora on August 5, he wrote Anna, "I felt more melancholy than you would give your cold blooded brother credit for feeling when I said goodbye to my dearest sister and cunning little yellow headed baby Lee. Do kiss the darling for me and tell her her father thinks of her and of you very often."[121] He added that he was "busily planning" his hunting trip to the Rockies.

15

LOVE, GUILT, AND CITY POLITICS

WHILE PLANNING HIS FORAY TO THE MONTANA ROCKIES, ROOSEVELT stayed at the Maltese Cross Ranch, where life was less domestic than at the Elkhorn. By then, Roosevelt was no longer the sorrowful young man of 1884. He was full of fun, "lively as a cricket," and would "laugh and joke with the men to beat them all."[1] He and Sylvane discussed love, Sylvane contending that it did not exist, and Roosevelt speaking in favor of it. "Sylvane was going with a school teacher. Roosevelt became perfectly wild and had lots of fun with Sylvane. He called Sylvane's room the Cupid room. He used to get under Sylvane's window and call up to him and ask him what was the matter with Cupid."[2]

Affairs of the heart had pursued Roosevelt to the Badlands. Shortly after arriving in the first week of August, he had received a letter from Edith telling him that they could marry that December in England.[3] He had been receiving transatlantic letters from her all year but had managed to keep the engagement secret from his family. In the West he was more open: He readily showed his gun-toting friends photographs of his betrothed.[4]

The settling of his marriage plans coincided with the end of other projects. On August 9 he sent his editor the manuscript of his Thomas Hart Benton biography; he then left Medora for Mandan, to put the final touches on the episode of the boat thieves.[5] At the indictment hearing he dropped charges against Chris Pfaffenbach, saying that the old German "did not have enough sense to do anything good or bad."[6] Pfaffenbach expressed his gratitude to Roosevelt, who later remarked that never before had he been thanked for calling a man a fool.

In Mandan, Roosevelt stayed initially at a hotel in a "vile building entered through an underground drinking saloon, and my room contained two beds, and two fellow boarders, one of them my old friend, the horse thief, Calamity Joe, now out on bail."[7] Then, on the street, he encountered Tilden Selmes, who was married to one of "two nice Kentucky girls" Roosevelt had befriended in the past. Selmes invited him to stay at his house on the outskirts of Mandan, which he owned in addition to a ranch.[8]

Roosevelt enjoyed the visit, as the Selmeses offered the sort of recreational accoutrements he liked—driving teams, Kentucky thoroughbred saddle horses, and greyhounds for coursing coyotes, hares, and pronghorn. "We ride, drive and everything, usually after supper as there is a most superb moon."[9] Roosevelt also showed a great enthusiasm for Mrs. Selmes, who, he wrote on Elkhorn Ranch stationery, "is really to my mind a singularly attractive woman. She is, I think, very handsome, though not with regular features; and, as Madame de Morès says, she is very 'séduisante'—like most Kentucky girls. She is very well read, has a delicious sense of humor and is extremely fond of poetry—including that of my new favorite, Browning, as well as my old one Swinburne. Altogether I have enjoyed my three days here; tomorrow I go back to Medora, but return to the trial a week hence, when I will again stay with the Selmes."[10]

The Selmes couple presumably enjoyed his company, too, but were perplexed to hear him pacing his room at night like Banquo's ghost, the floorboards creaking as he chanted drearily, "I have no constancy. I have no constancy."[11] He was haunted by his pledge that he would never do anything to dishonor Alice, his guilt perhaps amplified by Edith's letter outlining their wedding plans. He muttered that he would give anything to remain faithful to Alice's memory. Certain that he would never again fall in love, he had told others that he would never get over his loss. Now he had to explain that he had. He would have been dismayed by an observation offered years later by Sewall: "Within two years he got pretty well over it all."[12]

During the summer of 1886, Roosevelt was beginning to feel pinched by the limitations of Badlands life as well as despairing at ever finding a task that would match his ambitions.[13] Briefly, in August, he thought he had found a perfect outlet when several American citizens were arrested illegally in Mexico, and a U.S. military officer, Captain Emmet Crawford, was killed. Word spread throughout the West that America would go to war.[14] Roosevelt wrote to the secretary of war, William Endicott, offering to put together a cavalry unit of armed cowboys that he would lead into Mexico.[15] He also asked Lodge to telegraph if hostilities became inevitable, and he summed up his amalgam of hope and hopelessness: "I haven't the least idea there will be any trouble; but as any chance of doing anything in the future worth doing seems to grow continually smaller I intend to grasp at every opportunity that turns up."[16]

The cowboys were "all eager for war, they did not much care with whom; they were very patriotic, they were fond of adventure, and, to tell the truth, they were by no means averse to the prospect of plunder."[17] But he soon found that the incident in Mexico was a minor affair and dropped his plans. He wrote Lodge on August 20, "If a war had come off, I would surely have had behind me as utterly reckless a set of desperadoes as ever sat in the saddle. It is no use saying that I would like a chance at something I thought I could really do; at present I see nothing whatever ahead. However, there is the hunting in the fall, at any rate."[18] He wrote of hunting as if it were no longer an enthusiasm but a consolation prize.

During the Mexican conundrum, Roosevelt visited the Elkhorn Ranch. Sewall's wife had given birth to a son on August 5, and Dow's had done the same a week later to the day, with the wife of Tompkins, the old hunter, as a midwife. Sewall's spouse fell gravely ill, and Dow's was not much better. Sewall: "The only reason they did not both die was because their time had not come."[19] When Roosevelt arrived, Sewall was making a cradle large enough to hold both babies.[20] "The population of my ranch is increasing in a rather alarming manner," Roosevelt wrote Anna.[21]

More alarming was the continuing drought. Although dry summers were supposed to be good for cattle, and Roosevelt's twelve hundred head seemed to be doing well, Sewall feared that the end was near. "If we have much snow next winter it looks to me as if they would have short pick-ing[,] the grass being all dried up now."[22] Sewall could see the drought's effect just outside his door. The garden he had nourished was wilting away, the peas and beans gone and most of the potatoes withered.[23]

Despite the potential threat that the drought posed, Roosevelt devoted considerable thought to his Rocky Mountain hunt and, more specifically, to mountain goats—shaggy, white-haired creatures weighing up to three hundred pounds and armed with rapier-like black horns. Mountain goats in the 1880s were perhaps the rarest of hunter trophies. Roosevelt knew of only one or two eastern sportsmen who displayed goat heads, and he believed that not one in ten professional hunters had ever killed one, at least in part because the animals favored rugged, remote mountains at altitudes up to thirteen thousand feet.[24]

Roosevelt had recently seen a mountain goat head in a Medora taxider-mist shop, shot by Jack Willis, a hunting guide in Thompson Falls, Mon-tana. Roosevelt got Willis' address from the taxidermist and wrote to him: "I want to shoot a white antelope goat. I have heard it is the hardest animal in the Rockies to find and the most difficult to kill. I have also heard that you are a great hunter. If I come to Montana, will you act as my guide, and do you think I can kill a white goat?"[25] Willis, who disdained Medora as a "joke town," at first was going to ignore the note. But Roose-velt's penmanship annoyed him. "It was the worst I had ever seen, bar none, and deciphering his letter was a much tougher job than stalking a silver-tip [grizzly bear]."[26] So he jotted off a short answer: "If you can't shoot any better than you write, NO." Characteristically, Roosevelt was undeterred. Two days before leaving Medora for Thompson Falls on Au-gust 21, he sent Jack Willis a telegram saying when he would arrive and declaring that he wanted Willis to lead him to mountain goats and would pay him well for the work.

Willis was an expert teamster, inexhaustibly resourceful, and unfail-ingly prepared for emergencies. "Through hard experience he had become master of plainscraft and woodcraft, skilled in all frontier lore," wrote Roosevelt.[27] After running away from his Missouri home when no more than fifteen years old, Willy had worked as a teamster on the Santa

Fe Trail and had hunted bison throughout the West, from eastern Montana to Texas.[28] In 1876 he took a riverboat to Montana, where he settled down as a hunter and guide in Thompson Falls, "shortly before the serenity of the hills was shocked by the vulgar whistle and blatant bell of the first locomotive."[29] During a checkered career, he had traded whiskey to soldiers for cartridges, which he sold to the Indians for a dollar apiece; the cartridges were then used to shoot the soldiers.[30] He had hunted and trapped all over western Montana.[31]

Although he was not interested in working with Roosevelt, he deigned to meet Roosevelt's train, "curious to see what he looked like."[32] He was not pleased with what he saw. "Two men climbed down from the Pullman. One of them had on the corduroy knickers and coat of a tenderfoot. I knew he was Roosevelt, and he looked too much like a dude to make any hit with me. He had red cheeks, like those of a brewer's son I knew, and that didn't help any. The only thing about him that appealed to me at all was his eyes. They were keen and bright and dancing with animation. . . . His companion, who was properly garbed in buckskin coat and pants, was William Merrifield, his ranch foreman."

Roosevelt offered to pay twenty-five dollars for every shot he got at a mountain goat. Willis, with the bravado that typified his autobiographical accounts, replied, "I won't work for anyone on salary. I go where I like and when I like and do as I darned well please."[33] But Willis soon found that Theodore Roosevelt was growing on him. "There was something of the savor of the West in his manner and his frankness, and, so long as I could keep my eyes away from his foolish pants, I cottoned to the things he said and the way he said them. In about an hour he had made me forget his knickers and had won me over as far as I would ever go for any man. . . . That was the first evidence I had of his great personal magnetism."[34] Willis admitted that he was planning to leave in two or three days on a hunt and that, although he generally did not like company on the trail, he would let them come along as his guests. He would not guide them or "wet nurse" them. Roosevelt unleashed his toothy smile and said, "That's just fine! Now let's hurry." And so they soon set off for Vermillion Creek, in the mountains west of Thompson Falls.

Unlike Merrifield and Roosevelt in the Bighorn Mountains, Willis knew how to tie supplies on pack horses—he was, as Roosevelt put it, "versed in the mysteries of the 'diamond hitch,' the only arrangement of the ropes that will insure a load staying in its place."[35] Roosevelt: "In a day or two we were in the heart of the vast wooded wilderness. A broad, lonely river ran through its midst, cleaving asunder the mountain chains. Range after range, peak upon peak, the mountains towered on every side, the lower timbered to the top, the higher with bare crests of gray crags, or else hooded with fields of shining snow. The deep valleys lay half in darkness, hemmed in by steep, timbered slopes and straight rock walls. . . . Over the whole land lay like a shroud the mighty growth of the unbroken evergreen forest—spruce and hemlock, fir, balsam, tamarack, and lofty pines."[36]

On the first day of hunting, they staked out a salt lick that goats were likely to visit. The hunters took a position above the lick because, Willis said, goats under attack would run uphill.[37]

In half an hour, Roosevelt had a good shot at a billy goat at two hundred yards but missed. He fired again as the goat ran uphill, and Willis saw a tuft of hair fly from the foreleg. The goat disappeared, and the hunters tracked it for seven miles. Eventually they lost the trail and had to give up.

The next day Merrifield, his feet injured by mountain climbing in western boots, stayed in camp when Roosevelt and Willis left at dawn. Soon after daybreak they spotted a goat atop a butte about four hundred yards away. Roosevelt prepared to shoot, but Willis told him the shot was impossible. Not only was the animal almost a quarter of a mile off, but a wind was blowing at about twenty miles an hour. Roosevelt fired anyway. "I could hardly believe my eyes when I saw the goat jump up and fall back, almost too dead to skin," Willis recalled in later years.[38]

Roosevelt responded with his usual outburst, letting go a "yell of delight" that "could have been heard for two miles in any country." He said that if he killed nothing else the whole trip, he would still consider it a great success, and he tried to force a one-hundred-dollar bill on Willis, who turned him down. When they examined the dead animal, they found it was the one Roosevelt had wounded the day before. Then Roosevelt "rubbed his hands together, in the way he had when he was greatly pleased over anything, and fairly danced around with joy. Nothing would do but he must have a picture of the goat, where it fell, so I walked six miles back to camp after the camera and Merrifield, sore feet and all. Merrifield snapped a photograph, with Roosevelt and me beside the body of his victim, and

Roosevelt was full of joy."[39] In camp, Roosevelt had a special small black velvet tent with a ruby lamp in which he developed his photograph. He was pleased with the plate and later put the image in one of his books.[40]

Willis related this account of the hunt in a memoir. Roosevelt's version was less dramatic. He wrote that the men hunted for three or four days before he shot and wounded a goat twice. The next day, he and Willis tracked the goat—fully aware that it was the wounded animal—before Roosevelt killed it with one more shot at only seventy yards.[41] This account must be the more accurate, as Roosevelt would not have failed to mention a kill at four hundred yards under difficult conditions. In other points the two versions of the Rocky Mountain hunt coincide well, including an account of how, while searching for mountain goats, Roosevelt ran along a ledge covered with loose shale, slipped, and fell off a cliff.[42] At first Willis thought his client was a dead man—beyond the cliff was a fall of sixty feet that ended in a hillside covered with jagged rocks.[43] But Roosevelt enjoyed a stroke of luck—he landed in the top of a pine tree, bounced down through it, and ended up in a balsam, unhurt and still clutching his rifle. He immediately climbed back up and continued the hunt.[44]

During slack periods, when no game appeared, the men held contests to see who could shoot off the heads of the most grouse.[45] When they killed deer, they kept watch over the carcasses, hoping to shoot timber wolves, but saw none.[46] They did find the old tracks of bears and elk.[47] Roosevelt: "Yet although we saw no game it was very pleasant to sit out, on the still evenings, among the tall pines or on the edge of a great gorge, until the afterglow of the sunset was dispelled by the beams of the frosty moon. Now and again the hush would be suddenly broken by the long howling of a wolf, that echoed and rang under the hollow woods and through the deep chasms until they resounded again, while it made our hearts bound and the blood leap in our veins. Then there would be silence once more, broken only by the rush of the river and the low moaning and creaking of the pines; or the strange calling of the owls might be answered by the far-off, unearthly laughter of a loon."[48]

The men grew to know one another around the campfire. Willis: "Tramping over the hills by day and sitting around a campfire at night bring out the real man. Under the mystery of the stars and the witchery of the wilds, he opens his soul and reveals every angle of his character with a naturalness that nowhere else is ever known."[49] Willis learned that Roosevelt disapproved of his guide's market hunting. Willis had a freight car in Thompson Falls half filled with deer hides he had collected for sale; he had planned to finish the load while hunting with Roosevelt. But Roosevelt protested the selling of hides and heads. "There is no sportsmanship about that," he told Willis. "It is just plain murder and a good sportsman like you ought to be ashamed of it."[50]

Willis later recalled that, after he showed Roosevelt his load of deer hides in town, Roosevelt orated along these lines: "'Jack, . . . that is wholesale murder and you must stop it. . . . Men like you will wipe out all of the deer and bear and goats, just as you have practically exterminated the buffalo, if you keep at it. It's indefensible. You haven't a leg to stand on. Killing game the way you are doing is not just wrong; it is cowardly and contemptible and wicked.'"[51] He urged Willis to go into another line of work and said he would back him in any way necessary. Roosevelt also showed by his own example that he meant what he said. "Where he could have killed hundreds of goats, he had been satisfied with four. That impressed me, and gave me something to mull over at night."[52] Willis later claimed that by the end of the hunt—when Roosevelt's final count was actually three goats—he had decided to give up market hunting; he eventually opened a general store that prospered.

After the hunt was over, Willis insisted that Roosevelt and Merrifield stay at his house before leaving for Medora.[53] In later years, Willis would look back on the hunt with nostalgia: "I look at my guns some time," he wrote to Roosevelt in 1905, "and I think of the time I first met you, with my guns as my only friends."[54]

At the Thompson Falls train station, as the Medorans were leaving town, Willis agreed to accept $150 for expenses. Roosevelt handed him a roll of bills that Willis put into his pocket unexamined.[55] He later found that Roosevelt had given him twelve hundred-dollar bills.[56]

This hunt marked a turning point: Despite the beauty of the mountains and the successful shooting, Roosevelt wrote Anna that he had "never felt less enthusiastic over a hunting trip."[57] His primary interest lay with Edith and the future. He did not have long to ponder that loss of zeal for shooting, however. He reached Medora on September 18 to find a crisis awaiting him. His subterfuge in regard to his wedding plans had caught up with him, with a maximally embarrassing effect—the *New York Times* had printed a report that he was engaged to Edith Carow.[58] How word had leaked remains a mystery. He had told no one. Not even Anna knew. Consequently, when the *Times* ran the item, Anna informed the editors that they were in error, and the paper printed a retraction, observing, "Nothing is more common in society than to hear positive assertions constantly made regarding the engagement of persons who have been at all in each other's company, and no practice is more reprehensible."[59]

Roosevelt, in a clearly awkward position, immediately wrote an apologetic letter to Anna. "I am engaged to Edith and before Christmas I shall cross the ocean and marry her. You are the first person to whom I have breathed a word on this subject."[60] And then he gave way to a rush of guilt: "I utterly disbelieve in and disapprove of second marriages; I have always considered that they argued weakness in a man's character. You could not reproach me one half as bitterly for my inconstancy and unfaithfulness as I reproach myself." The fervency of his belief in his own infidelity and weakness is summed up in a single line: "Were I sure there was a heaven my one prayer would be I might never go there, lest I should meet those I loved on earth who are dead." He also was protective of Edith, telling Anna, "I do earnestly ask you not to visit my sins upon poor little Edith. It is certainly not her fault; the entire blame rests on my shoulders." He seemed to offer Anna an emotional bribe while revealing, perhaps, his tepidity toward Alice Lee: "I thoroughly understand the change I will have to make in my life. As I have already told you, if you wish to you shall keep Baby Lee, I of course paying the expense."

As word of the engagement leaked, Roosevelt's friends and colleagues—including those who, in earlier years, had expected Theodore and Edith to marry—were surprised. One recalled, "Although during the previous winter I had seen both Theodore and Edith many times, I had not the slightest suspicion of this *denouement*."[61] J. West Roosevelt, a cousin who was almost the same age as Theodore, was "equally surprised" but wrote a supportive letter: "I am really more than pleased. I had hoped that you would marry, and had talked of the possibility of it with Laura [his wife] who shares my view. Now that you are to marry a girl who has been one of my best friends, a girl whose main characteristic is truth, I am very much delighted. I know that you will be happy, and your happiness is much to me. I know that you will be a better man because you will have a fuller life. You are marrying a woman who can enter into your plans and who can appreciate your aims, and you have the best earnest of real happiness in that. You are marrying one who will love you—that is best of all."[62]

In addition to the publicity surrounding his nuptials, Roosevelt was dealing with a matter of crucial interest. While Theodore had been hunting, Wilmot Dow had taken the Elkhorn's marketable cattle to Chicago and sold them.[63] But prices were low, and the cattle brought ten dollars a head less than it cost to raise and transport them.[64] Sewall was dismayed, because, he later explained, "it looked to me as if we were throwing away his money, and I didn't like it."[65]

When Roosevelt returned from the Rockies, Sewall discussed cattle economics with him; Roosevelt tallied up his accounts and called Sewall into his room, where, Sewall wrote later, "he told me the conclusion he had arrived at. I told him Dow and I had figured it up and we had arrived at the same conclusion exactly—the quicker he got out of there the less he would lose."[66] Roosevelt asked how soon the men could be ready to return to Maine; Sewall consulted the women and concluded they would need ten days.

This decision is hard to evaluate, because variations in market prices are an inherent part of the livestock business.[67] Roosevelt must have understood this fluctuation, because he did not pull out of ranching with the departure of Sewall and Dow. He turned over the Elkhorn herd to Bill Merrifield and Sylvane Ferris under a new contract, even though an unidentified easterner offered to buy the animals.[68] Ferris and Merrifield also turned down the same man's offer to buy their shares in Roosevelt's operation. For the families from Maine, leaving the West may have had as much to do with their dislike of ranch life and the needs of their new babies as it did with finance.

On or about September 30, Roosevelt traveled to Mandan, where he stayed with the Selmes couple before departing for New York City on October 3.[69] He left the ranch a day ahead of the New Englanders.[70] They returned to the East with mixed emotions. Sewall: "We were glad to get back home—gladder, I guess, than about anything that had ever happened to us, and yet we were melancholy, for with all of the hardships and work it was a very happy life we had lived all together. I guess we have all thought all our lives since that it was the happiest times that any of us have known."[71]

If the two families had looked around at their surroundings with a knowing eye, they likely would have concluded that they were leaving in the nick of time. Winter was coming, and ominous signs suggested it would be a bad one. Muskrats along the creeks were building their partially submerged houses of twigs twice normal size.[72] Their fur was heavier and longer than any old-timer could recall. Beavers were unusually busy, storing double their usual supply of brush for winter food. White arctic owls were starting to appear, apparitions that heralded brutal winters. Men who had spent their lives in the West started laying in six months of provisions. "The wild geese and ducks and song birds started south early and many that were accustomed to stay with us all winter disappeared; even the range cattle seemed to take on a heavier, shaggier coat of hair. . . . The old Indians pointed to [the arctic owls] and drawing their blankets more closely about them, gave a shrug and 'Ugh! Heap cold!' expressive of some terrible experience in the long past that still lingered in their memory."[73] Said one of the oldest hunters, "Nature was fixin' up her folks for hard times."[74]

In any event, change was coming for Theodore Roosevelt. Wedding bells alone were bound to affect the harmony of his life in the West, but biographer Hermann Hagedorn, who interviewed many of Roosevelt's Badlands contemporaries, concluded that the New York rancher would have drifted away from Dakota Territory toward the end of 1886 regardless of his matrimonial commitments. "Roosevelt was unquestionably restless," Hagedorn wrote, adding, "The frontier had been a challenge to his manhood; now that he had stood every test it had presented to him, its glamour faded and he looked about for a sharper challenge and more exacting labors."[75]

Back in New York in early October, he found more exacting labors when, on the fifteenth, he attended the Republican county convention in Brooklyn.[76] One of the party goals was the nomination of its New York

City mayoral candidate. To Roosevelt's surprise, party stalwarts asked him to run for the office.

Why the old-liners, whom he had challenged in the Assembly with his reformist goals, made the offer remains unclear. They may have hoped he would bring back into the party the independents and reformers who had left during the last presidential election. Or they may have thought he would pump his personal fortune into the campaign, though in fact his investments in the Badlands and Sagamore Hill had left him barely enough to meet expenses. They may simply have been desperate—Elihu Root, who in the near future would serve as secretary of state under President Theodore Roosevelt, had turned down the nomination, and so had Levi P. Morton, who had served in Congress from 1879 to 1881 and as minister of France from 1881 to 1885.[77] Perhaps a combination of these factors was at work. In any event, Roosevelt—acting out of party loyalty—accepted the nomination, and the convention gave him unanimous approval.

The campaign was a three-sided race that historians still consider one of the finest in New York City history.[78] Both Republicans and Democrats were alarmed by the strong showing of Henry George, a small, balding, red-bearded Labor candidate who espoused taxing land so that government could redistribute wealth to laborers.[79] Roosevelt undoubtedly had met him before, as George was one of the speakers at the May 1883 Free Trade Club dinner at which Roosevelt had met Commander Gorringe.[80] George's campaign marked the first time that labor had organized to fight the two established political parties. He was famed as the author of *Progress and Poverty*, a book that outlined his economic views and that had won him widespread support among workers.

Roosevelt's Democratic opponent was Abram Hewitt, a wealthy industrialist who had served in Congress. Despite his apparent entrenchment in the ranks of the rich, he could count on the support of at least a segment of the labor vote, because he was known for his loyalty to his workforce—during the depression of 1873 to 1878 he ran his iron mills at a loss rather than lay off employees.

New York Republicans gathered on October 27—Roosevelt's twenty-eighth birthday—to ratify his nomination at Cooper Union, a six-story brownstone conglomeration of stores, lecture halls, and a fifteen-thousand-volume library at the junction of Bowery, Seventh Street, and

Third and Fourth avenues.[81] Roosevelt's appearance filled every seat; sightseers came by the thousands. According to one old politician, the last time Cooper Union had hosted such a crowd was in 1860, when Abraham Lincoln gave a speech there that launched him into the presidency.[82]

Roosevelt was introduced by banker Thomas C. Acton, who coined a phrase that would follow the candidate, in one form or another, throughout the campaign: "You are called here to ratify the nomination of the youngest man who was ever nominated for Mayor. I knew his father. He was a stanch Republican. Mr. Roosevelt is the law and order candidate. He will enforce law and order. Don't you make a mistake on that. He is young and vigorous, and can do everything that you want. He is young and able to do it. If you elect him, the city of New York will never regret the cowboy of Dakota. Elect the cowboy of Dakota the next Mayor."[83] After this appearance, Roosevelt would be introduced frequently at speaking engagements as the Cowboy Candidate.[84] Newspapers described him in similar terms. The *World* reported that, before one speech, Roosevelt "swept into the Grand Opera-House not unlike a cowboy into a border town."[85] During another at which he was introduced as the Cowboy Candidate, he told the audience, "As the cowboy vote is rather light in this city I will have to appeal to the Republicans."[86] His listeners that night proved more interested in his stories about the West than in his political views.

Roosevelt was not enthusiastic about running for mayor. He accepted the nomination, he told his lifelong friend Frances Theodora Smith Dana, a writer of children's books, only because prominent Republicans had urged it on him.[87] He was convinced that he had no chance of winning and might be overwhelmingly defeated; the best he hoped for was "a decent run."[88] Had the odds for Republican success been better, he suspected, the party would not have picked him, though "it was of course in a certain sense a compliment to be nominated in the way I was."[89]

Although Roosevelt was not pleased, others were. The *Bad Lands Cow Boy* for October 21, 1886, reported Roosevelt's nomination and added optimistically that "it would not be strange if business as New York's mayor would prevent him from being present at our spring round-up. If the Bad Lands 'cow punchers' could help him out with their votes, he would go in with a rush." The *Sioux Falls Press* looked upon him as a home boy: "The nomination of Theodore Roosevelt as the Republican candidate for Mayor of New York City is something in which Dakota people have taken an even greater interest than the desire that the Nation's metropolis should have clean and efficient government. Theodore is a Dakota cowboy—owner of a ranch out in the bad lands region—and has spent a large share of his time in the Territory for a couple of years. He is one of the finest thoroughbreds you ever met—a whole-souled, clear-headed, high-minded gentleman."[90] Anna Roosevelt was thrilled with her brother's run and saw it as a sign that his equilibrium was back. She wrote Edith on October 23, 1886, "It is such happiness to see him at his very best once more; . . . this is the first time since [Assembly] days that he has enough work to keep him exerting all his powers."[91]

On election day, George's votes were surprisingly strong and Roosevelt's weak. Republican Party leaders sensed Roosevelt was going to lose but wanted to be sure George did not win, so they sent out orders for Republicans to vote Democratic. Roosevelt came in third, with 60,435 votes to Hewitt's 90,552 and George's 68,110.[92] He took the loss with equanimity in public, but privately the campaign held a place of special loathing in his memory. He scarcely ever talked about it, dealing with it much as he did Alice's death. He gave the campaign only a single phrase in his 647-page *Autobiography*: "In 1886 [I] had run for Mayor of New York against Abram S. Hewitt, Democrat, and Henry George, Independent, and had been defeated."[93]

On November 6—four days after the election—Theodore and his sister Anna boarded the ocean liner *Etruria*, traveling to England as Mr. and Mrs. Merrifield to elude the press.[94] They were probably tired. They had been up all night preparing announcements for Theodore and Edith's wedding.

The wedding took place in London on Thursday, December 2, 1886, a day of such impenetrable fog that special guides were needed to lead Roosevelt's carriage to St. George's Church in Hanover Square. The fog that seeped into the church was so thick that Anna could not even see the couple at the altar. Afterward, Roosevelt wrote to Sewall, "My wedding was very quiet as the wedding of a defeated mayoralty candidate should be."[95]

Following the wedding came a European honeymoon that lasted until March. In England Roosevelt went fox hunting and was feted by the social elite.[96] While in Florence, Italy, he worried about money and making ends meet: "My financial affairs for the past year make such a bad showing that Edith and I think very seriously of closing Sagamore Hill and going to the ranch for a year or two; but if possible I wish to avoid this."[97] He ordered Douglas Robinson—Corinne's husband and Theodore's financial manager—to sell some of his horses, including his favorite fox-hunting mount, Sagamore, an animal he valued so highly that he would not let friends ride it.[98] "I *must* live within my income and begin paying off my debt this year, at no matter what cost, even to the shutting up or renting of Sagamore Hill, bitterly as I should hate such an alternative."[99]

On January 6, 1887, he wrote Anna from Florence, asking her to check on photos he had taken, including a shot of an elk in a wagon and of mountain goats, and to see if goat heads he had had shipped from the West had arrived.[100] He mentioned that he had heard from Robinson that his horse Sagamore had not been sold. Roosevelt was relieved, telling Corinne in a letter from Venice dated February 8, "I felt like a reprieved criminal when Douglas wrote he had not sold Sagamore, and had not the strength of mind to telegraph him that he must; but I will hardly be able to hunt atall; it is an expensive amusement, and I am down to hard pan, with a vengeance."[101] While in Rome he wrote six stories on ranch life for *Century*, hoping to raise funds, but was not sure the magazine would want them.[102] Edith helped with revisions.

In mid-March the couple set sail for home. By then Edith was pregnant.[103] In addition to that strain, she had "to live in the house that Theodore had designed with and for his first wife [and] she was faced with the problem of bringing up the child of that marriage."[104] However, taking over Alice's parenting was Edith's choice; in fact, it was her demand. Although Roosevelt had promised Anna that she could keep the child, he found that his wife had other ideas, forcing him to write his sister from Rome on January 10 that "Edith feels strongly about taking baby Lee."[105]

The couple returned to New York on Sunday, March 27, and stayed at Anna's house.[106] When Alice met her new mother that day for the first time since the marriage, the three-year-old was decked out in a dress with flounces of Valenciennes lace, her hair was "licked and prodded into place," and she was positioned at the top of a staircase with a large bouquet of pink roses.[107] As Edith came through the door, Alice moved down the stairs and presented her with the flowers. Roses had special family significance: The Roosevelts took their lineage seriously, and as their name meant "field of roses" in Dutch, they adopted roses as a family crest, putting the flowers on book plates and jewelry, such as a ring Theodore wore, and on the christening gowns of Roosevelt babies.[108]

Theodore and Edith insisted that Alice call Edith "Mother." In later years, Alice was philosophical about the new living arrangement: "I was so young when my father remarried that I never had any consciousness of having a stepmother. If any one spoke of my 'stepmother' I did not like it. It seemed faintly indelicate, rude, unfair—not kindly either to her or to me. . . . That I was the child of another marriage was a simple fact and made a situation that had to be coped with, and Mother coped with it with a fairness and charm and intelligence which she has to a greater degree than almost any one else I know."[109]

So she said in her autobiography, *Crowded Hours*, published while Edith was still alive. But in *Mrs. L: Conversations with Alice Roosevelt Longworth*, published long after Edith had died, Alice was more caustic. She suggested that Edith sometimes sought to limit Theodore's contact with his sisters, and she said Edith "could be mean," as when making the point that Theodore had proposed to her before he proposed to Alice Hathaway Lee.[110] The younger Alice also contended that although Edith "was terribly conscientious about me" and "insisted on keeping me with them when they married," she did little to keep Alice from hearing negative comments about her real mother. "My father obviously didn't want the symbol of infidelity around. His *two* infidelities, in fact: infidelity to my stepmother by marrying my mother first, and to my mother by going back to my stepmother after she died. It was all so dreadfully Victorian and mixed up. My stepmother added a typically caustic twist by telling my brother Ted, who naturally repeated it to me, that it was just as well that my mother had died when she did because my father would have been bored to death staying married to her."[111] Alice said of Edith's attitude about Theodore's first marriage, "I think she always resented being the second choice and she never really forgave him his first marriage. In many ways she was a very hard woman."[112]

After returning from Europe, Edith took only a few days to familiarize herself with Alice before departing with Theodore in early April to visit her relatives in Philadelphia.[113] Not until May would the couple settle down with Alice at Sagamore Hill.[114] In the interim, after a day or two in Philadelphia, Theodore left for the Badlands. Letters from Medora had told him about a disastrous winter and a calamitous loss of cattle, and he wanted to assess the damage.[115] He wrote to Sewall before leaving Philadelphia, "You were mighty lucky to leave when you did; this spring I should have had to rustle pretty hard to pay your fare back. By all accounts the loss among the cattle has been terrible. About the only comfort I have out of it is that at any rate you and Wilmot are all right; I would not mind the loss of a few thousands, if it was the only way to benefit you and Will—but it will be much more than that."[116] He concluded philosophically, "We had pretty good fun at the old ranch at any rate."

16

THE BLIZZARDS
OF 1886-87

"THE WORLD HAS HEARD OF IT," WROTE LINCOLN LANG FORTY YEARS after the fact. "The disastrous winter of '86–'87 that closed down upon the northern range country, like great steel nippers, fully six weeks earlier than winter had been known to strike before within the memory of the White Man. It continuously retained its iron grip with the relentlessness of Doom itself for over four months, relaxing at length only to leave ruin in its wake for the cattle ranchers of the region."[1]

The Badlands offered scant feed for cattle as autumn groaned into winter. The previous summer had left the ground parched. A large number of creeks and streams dried up; the river became a series of shallow ponds. Livestock moved constantly in search of water, so the animals could not put on flesh. Grasshoppers swarmed in, eating up grass, and a "continuous chain of prairie fires" burned through the summer.[2] By the end of September the Badlands could not provide enough food for the two hundred thousand cattle ranging along the Little Missouri and its tributaries; but more and more cattle came from the south.[3] Finally, in the autumn of 1886 the Little Missouri River Stock Growers' Association decided that the range was fully stocked and that "in the near future notice would be given that the men here would refuse to work with any new outfits turning in cattle or horses."[4]

Badlands ranchers sensed in autumn that something freakish was coming their way.[5] In October, a permanent haze hung over the Badlands, starving the region of its clear prairie light. The air hung ominously still, and halos often ringed the sun and the moon. The ranchers hoped nothing would come of these signs, and they paid little attention to the snow that began to fall softly one November night. It seemed the typical wet snow of late autumn. Then the temperature began to fall, the wind rose to gale force, and the worst blizzard in history blasted into the Badlands, filling the air with dry, scouring ice that burned the skin of anyone unlucky enough to be caught outside.[6]

During the night, thermometers sank to forty below zero. In ranch houses, virtually anything that could freeze did. Ice a quarter inch thick built up on windows, and dry snow sifted in through cracks and crevices. Snowdrifts piled up to the eaves of houses. And all the next day and night snow fell, the ice dust so thick that it reduced visibility to a few yards. The ice clogged nostrils and stifled lungs; the cold chilled travelers senseless and left them wandering lost until they died.[7]

After that blizzard came more in quick succession. Travel was impossible by mid-December. Snow formed drifts that reached a hundred feet up the faces of bluffs along streams. Lincoln Lang: "Except for an occasional partial let-up, while the northern furies were concentrating for a new drive, it was always snowing, blowing, and intensely cold. When the sun shone at all, it appeared as if viewed through lightly smoked glasses, always attended by the omnipresent halo and sun dogs."[8]

As the snow began, the cattle eked out a living on grass exposed between drifts; when that food was gone or snowed under, they fed on sagebrush protruding above the snow.[9] When the sagebrush, too, was gone, the animals drifted to sheltered areas and bunched up. Snow piled up around them, drifts rolled over them, and they smothered. Others froze, their carcasses buried by drifting snow; atop those animals later victims would fall, and they, too, would be buried. Lincoln Lang called it "Death's cattle roundup."[10] Sylvane Ferris recalled, "In Medora that year the cows would eat the tar paper off the buildings. You could see cattle piled up dead in every ravine in the country. I seen one place where 25 were piled up in one heap. There wasn't much hilarity in those days. Why, those cattle would even eat dry-goods boxes."[11]

The Langs tried to keep up hope. "As the winter advanced, darker and darker became the outlook. There could be no denying that, even if we were not admitting it for we were never easily depressed. Perhaps conditions were not so bad elsewhere on the range, we thought. So, like many another, we lived in the vain hope that the bulk of our stock might pull through."[12] They passed the dismal nights and dreadful days playing the piano and guitar, singing, dealing cards, playing checkers. But not everyone in the Badlands adapted, and some residents were driven to peculiar measures. Pierre Wibaux, who had gone to France for the winter, leaving his wife in charge of the ranch, received a letter in which his friend Henry Jackson observed drily, "No news, except that Dave Brown killed Dick Smith and your wife's hired girl blew her brains out in the kitchen. Everything O.K. here."[13]

Roosevelt had practically predicted the coming of such a winter, writing in autumn 1886, "In our country, which is even now getting crowded, it is merely a question of time as to when a winter will come that will under-stock the ranges by the summary process of killing off about half of all the cattle through-out the North-west."[14]

The thaw came in March. The *Dickinson Press* took note: "Last Sunday the welcome Chinook wind paid us a visit and before noon the little rills were trickling down the hills and the brown herbage began to appear, through the snow, in every direction; the soft, balmy wind fanning the cheek brought memories and hopes of spring to the winter-wearied denizens of our community."[15]

As the snow melted, the river valley filled with roiling water afloat with ice cakes. From the surrounding coulees the flood washed out dead cattle that had sought refuge in ravines. Lang: "Now, their carcasses were being spewed forth in untold thousands by the rushing waters, to be carried away on the crest of the foaming, turgid flood rushing down the valley. With them went our hopes. One had only to stand by the river bank for a few minutes and watch the grim procession ceaselessly going down, to realize in full the depth of the tragedy that had been enacted within the past few months."[16]

Seventy-five percent of the cattle that had wintered in the Badlands were dead. Carcasses hung among the limbs of trees, left behind by melted snowdrifts. Texas and Minnesota stock had died in the Badlands like sheep; as Sewall had predicted, cows with big calves suffered the most. One of Howard Eaton's neighbors lost perhaps four thousand of the fifty-seven hundred cattle he had bought in 1886. "Everybody is blue as a whetstone. . . . One comfort is that it will stop the big herds from Texas to some extent."[17]

The blizzard taught ranchers two lessons—first, that smaller operations of no more than two hundred head of cattle were more likely to survive than were the large operations, because the former could shelter and feed their cattle; and second, that relying on wild grasses to get cattle through winter was a risky proposition.[18] These two conditions yielded the conclusion that the vast open-range operations were insupportable and would come to a close.

Roosevelt arrived in the Badlands in early April, bringing with him the hope that enough of his five thousand cattle had survived to allow him to rebuild the herd for a few years before selling off.[19] He and Merrifield rode for three days through the Badlands without seeing a live cow. Merrifield: "Every draw and ravine was full of dead cattle; sometimes 20 and 25 in a pile together. I don't know how many thousand we roped and branded on the Elkhorn Ranch that fall before that dreadful winter, but after that terrible winter there wasn't a cow left."[20]

Although Roosevelt proved to be one of the luckier cattlemen—he lost only about two-thirds of his herd—his land, he found, was "a mere barren waste; not a green thing could be seen; the dead grass eaten off till the country looked as if it had been shaved with a razor."[21] He wrote to Lodge, "The losses are crippling. For the first time I have been utterly unable to enjoy a visit to my ranch. I shall be glad to get home."[22] To Anna he wrote, "I am bluer than indigo about the cattle; it is even worse than I feared; I wish I was sure I would lose no more than half the money ($80,000) I invested out here. I am planning how to get out of it."[23]

The most successful ranchers immediately after the blizzards were those who raised horses. "Unlike cattle, or, still worse, sheep, [horses] abused nothing, nor did they affect either the land or themselves adversely. Loose on the range, in most ways they behaved more like the wilder animals,

Nature seeming to favor them in consequence. In the fall they grew tremendous coats of hair. When winter struck, it was part of their psychology to keep moving and rustling, to paw away the snow in order to get at the grass beneath, something neither cattle nor sheep would ever do, thus maintaining both circulation and condition. By nature they distributed their grazing widely enough to give the grass a chance. They did not foul or trample the springs and watering places, nor did they cut paths to any appreciable extent, nor drift before storms. Finally, at a pinch, they would seemingly subsist on cottonwood or willow bark, so that they were practically unkillable."[24] A. C. Huidekoper, one of the early ranchers in the Badlands, did well with his horse operation—he lost only nine old mares out of nearly a thousand head—so he went into horse breeding. Howard Eaton branched out in yet another direction in the late 1880s, buying live wild animals, such as bighorn sheep and pronghorn, from neighboring ranchers and shipping them east for zoos and parks.[25]

After the winter of 1886–87 many cattle investors of Roosevelt's ilk sold out, but Roosevelt did not feel he could afford to sell at the low prices the markets then offered. He had to hang on to what was left of his herd in the hope that natural increase would cut the losses on his eighty-five-thousand-dollar investment.[26] He put Merrifield, who married that year, in charge of the Elkhorn Ranch.[27]

The abrupt decline of the cattle industry flattened the local economy. "The halcyon days of Billings County were over," Hagedorn wrote. "What had been a flourishing cattle country was a boneyard where the agents of fertilizer factories bargained for skeletons."[28] Medora was "very dead" by February.[29] Packard had moved his newspaper offices across the river to the old cantonment, where he lived with his new wife, but the building burned, and the Packards left for the East.[30] Joe Ferris' store nearly suffered the same fate, but the fire was put out when the store was no more than charred.[31]

The Marquis de Morès' business interests had created and driven Medora since its inception, but his business was failing. The slaughterhouse had been intermittently closed by lack of business—the Chicago packing houses had squeezed out the Marquis, and anyway the urban market for the meat of unfattened range cattle proved too small to fulfill his fabulous dreams.[32] The abattoir shut down as usual for winter in 1886 but never reopened.[33] John Goodall, de Morès' foreman, worked for the Marquis until spring 1888, selling off the horses and cattle.[34] De Morès' attempt to establish a stage line between Medora and Deadwood, with nine stops along the way, also failed, in part because he could not secure the government freight and mail contracts he needed to finance his operation.

Through spring and summer 1887, Medora eroded. E. G. Paddock loaded the buildings he owned onto flat cars and hauled them to Dickinson, where he had bought lots.[35] Other residents did the same.[36] Nothing quite so succinctly characterizes the decline of Medora as a note in the August 6, 1887, *Dickinson Press* reporting that the Sweet family had moved from Medora to Dickinson because "Mr. Sweet desired to reside where there was some life and prospect of growth."[37] By November, Medora, according to the *Bismarck Tribune*, had become "about the quietest place in western Dakota. The hotel is closed. There is only one general store and its proprietor declared that the middle of December will find him, stock and all, hundreds of miles from here. The proprietor of the drug store will move early in December, as he cannot make his board in the place."[38]

By 1887, settlers were converting vast reaches of western grazing lands into farms with irrigation ditches that drained local streams. Farmers, in political ascendance, got states to enact laws requiring ranchers to fence their livestock. By 1892, "the stirring West-wide open Range, sick for many years theretofore with wire fence, had died as a national factor, as virtually a state."[39] Even the horse-breeding business was sinking in the late 1880s. The invention of the electric streetcar in 1887 quickly made horses obsolete for urban transportation, robbing horse breeders of one of their biggest customers. The price of broken horses fell from twenty-five dollars to less than fifteen, and unbroken horses crashed from fifteen to worthless.[40]

The frontier itself was closing by the late 1880s. The various homestead acts that gave farmers title to land were dividing the open range into patches of small—often unsustainably small—plots of land. In 1890 the U.S. Census Bureau declared the frontier closed, reporting that the unsettled areas were so broken up by isolated bodies of settlement, with populations of at least two people per square mile, that no frontier line existed.[41]

For Roosevelt, the western adventure was all but over. He attended the April 16, 1887, meeting of the Little Missouri River Stockmen's Association, but attendance was sparse and, reported the *Dickinson Press*, because of cattle losses "it was thought not worthwhile to appoint a general round up for the spring but one will take place later in the season."[42] The delayed roundup was designed in part not to gather cattle but to tally losses; it was, in all, a gloomy meeting.[43] One of Roosevelt's main orders of association business involved initiating the removal of a dishonest stock inspector whose job was checking brands among cattle on their way to market.[44] The annual convention in Miles City, held April 19 and 20, was attended by only 100 of 337 members, Roosevelt among them; still, 62 new members were inducted.[45]

By early May Roosevelt was back in New York. On May 11, 1887, he gave a speech at a New York City Federal Club dinner held in his honor at Delmonico's. In a ballroom on an upper floor, he lambasted virtually every U.S. political entity, from the president to charity organizations to violent anarchists, for a full hour. In regard to the last he said, "There is but one answer to be made to the dynamite bomb, and that can best be made by the Winchester rifle."[46] He drew such accolades that the Republican press began talking about him as a potential 1888 presidential nominee. Apparently they did not know that by election day he would be barely thirty years old—five short of the requisite age for holding presidential office. More objective newspapers thought his unfettered attacks on institutions at all levels of society were misguided. An editorial in *Puck* informed him, "You are not the timber of which Presidents are made."[47]

From the podium Roosevelt turned to the pen, working on a biography of Revolutionary War hero Gouverneur Morris.[48] He wrote the book partly from need, as money was tight at Oyster Bay that year. In late summer he turned in his manuscript to the publisher and was able to focus on the pending birth of his first child with Edith. The excitement, or the tension, that arose brought on his worst asthma attack in recent years. He revived when his first son—another Theodore—was born on September 13, 1887, tipping the scales at about eight and a half pounds. By October 1887, Roosevelt was fox hunting again.

But he still had a yen for wider and wilder pastures. Accordingly, early in November 1887 he went with his cousin J. West Roosevelt and a friend,

Frank Underhill, on a hunting trip in the Badlands.[49] Frank and West soon discovered that the rough life of the plains was too much for them—after ten days they retreated to New York City. For three weeks Theodore hunted alone. During this time he discovered that the Badlands no longer offered a larder of game animals. Since 1883, not only bison had nearly vanished but also elk, grizzly, and bighorn sheep; deer and pronghorn were much reduced.[50] Waterfowl were becoming scarce. Moreover, the grasslands themselves had been grazed to the ground. An ecological debacle was unrolling before Roosevelt's eyes. Nonetheless, he bagged eight deer, four antelope, and two sheep.

Back in New York City by December 8, 1887, Roosevelt determined to preserve vanishing wildlife, if not for its own sake then at least to ensure that his son would be able to enjoy the same outdoor pursuits that so absorbed his father. In 1905 he would put into words what he must have felt as early as 1887: "The most striking and melancholy feature in connection with American big game is the rapidity with which it has vanished."[51] He said almost as much in 1888, in his second book on his Dakota rambles, *Ranch Life and the Hunting Trail*: "We who have felt the charm of the life, and have exulted in its abounding vigor and its bold, restless freedom, will not only regret its passing for our own sakes, but must also feel real sorrow that those who come after us are not to see, as we have seen, what is perhaps the pleasantest, healthiest, and most exciting phase of American existence."[52] This statement is palpable with thoughts of his son and the world in which young Theodore would live. The Badlands had served as a crucible for Theodore Roosevelt, and what it had made of him was about to emerge on the national stage.

17

BADLANDS LEGACY: FROM THE WEST TO THE WHITE HOUSE

AFTER 1887, ROOSEVELT VISITED THE BADLANDS PRIMARILY FOR HUNT-
ing trips, with the Elkhorn Ranch house his exclusive sporting lodge. As
a family man, he could no longer disappear into Dakota Territory for
months at a time. "I have a small son now; and am settling down more and
more to country life for all but a couple of months of the year. My literary
work occupies a good deal of my time; and I have on the whole done fairly
well at it; I should like to write some book that would really take rank as
in the very first class, but I suppose this is a mere dream."[1]

Although he would never return to the Badlands as often and for as long
as he had in the past, he would always carry the Badlands with him in the
form of physical and emotional health. His recovery allowed him to begin
merging his experiences in the West with his political activities in the East.
Late in 1887 he addressed the demise of western big game and its habitat
by organizing friends and associates to fight for wildlife protection. Wilderness destruction posed an intangible but important danger: He believed that the American character, forged in the wilderness, periodically
had to be renewed in the wilderness, which therefore had to be protected.

Roosevelt's view of the threat to wilderness was reinforced by declines he saw in the Badlands over the next few years. The buffalo were probably the most numerous big game along the Little Missouri up to 1880; by 1883 all but a few stragglers had been killed.[2] The second most abundant game was likely the mule deer, which was not hunted heavily until the buffalo began to nosedive. By 1896, Roosevelt estimated, not a twentieth, maybe not even a fiftieth, of the deer survived. Elk, plentiful in 1880, were reduced to stragglers by 1883; the last Roosevelt shot at the ranch was in 1886, though two or three were reportedly shot after that, and riders on the 1893 roundup nearly roped a cow and calf. Pronghorn were much reduced by 1894; only a few remained. Badlands mountain sheep soon would be exterminated. The Badlands around the Little Missouri in the mid-1890s could "hardly be called a game country."[3] Wyoming's Bighorn Mountains, where Roosevelt had hunted grizzlies, did not much survive his visit. In 1893 George Bird Grinnell wrote, "For years the Big Horn Mountains have been known as a gameless country; 'shot out' was the expressive phrase applied to them by hide and horn hunters."[4]

Part of the problem was frontier mentality. "Frontiersmen, always sensitive about their standing among male peers, could gain status through hunting. As with human enemies, the more they killed the better. Hunters often kept score, held contests, compared their prey, and, if they returned home laden with meat, had the satisfaction of being greeted as heroes."[5] Owen Wister, author of the archetypal western novel *The Virginian*, put the westerner's view of natural resources this way: "The pervading spirit of the far West as to game, as to timber, as to everything that a true American should feel it is his right to use and his duty to preserve for those coming after, is—'What do I care, so long as it lasts my time?'"[6]

Roosevelt drew support for conservation not only from friends but also from the nation's top wildlife experts. Among them was George Bird Grinnell, with whom Roosevelt had nurtured a friendship since the day they discussed *Hunting Trips of a Ranchman* in Grinnell's office. Grinnell had recently launched the National Audubon Society through *Forest and Stream* magazine to work for bird protection. Roosevelt suggested to Grinnell that they create an organization to promote big-game conservation.[7] In December 1887, they assembled a dinner meeting that included a selection of wealthy eastern hunters; the result was the Boone and Crockett

Club, named after Daniel Boone and Davy Crockett, the "tutelary deities of American hunting lore."[8] It was the first organization created explicitly to influence conservation legislation.[9]

The club elected Roosevelt president in January 1888. The members were determined to protect not just game animals but also wildlife habitat: "The preservation of the forests and of game go hand in hand. He who works for either works for both."[10] Club members also believed—here Roosevelt's voice dominates—that hunting was singularly important to creating sturdy citizens, "a vigorous and masterful people. The rifle-bearing hunter, whether he goes on foot or on horseback, whether he voyages in a canoe or travels with a dog-sled, must be sound of body and firm of mind, and must possess energy, resolution, manliness, self-reliance, and capacity for hardy self-help. In short, the big-game hunter must possess qualities without which no race can do its life-work well; and these are the very qualities which it is the purpose of this Club, so far as it may be, to develop and foster."[11]

No one was eligible for membership "who has not killed with the rifle in fair chase, by still-hunting or otherwise, at least one individual of one of the various kinds of American large game, including bear, bison, mountain sheep, caribou, cougar, musk-ox, mountain goat, elk, gray wolf, pronghorn, moose, and deer."[12] In language that smacks of its time, Roosevelt wrote, "The club is emphatically an association of men who believe that the hardier and manlier the sport is the more attractive it is, and who do not think that there is any place in the ranks of true sportsmen either for the game-butcher, on the one hand, or, on the other, for the man who wishes to do all his shooting in preserves, and to shirk rough hard work."[13]

The Boone and Crockett Club supported state laws to protect wildlife and was instrumental to passage of the 1891 federal Forest Reserve Act, which gave the president the authority to create federal forest reserves that protected timber from being sold or homesteaded.[14] Presidents Grover Cleveland, Benjamin Harrison, and William McKinley subsequently set aside forest reserves, protecting a total of forty-five million acres.[15] The club's work for forest protection was an extension of its advocacy for better protection of Yellowstone National Park—an effort that is a perfect bookend to Roosevelt's 1883 bison hunt, because a key factor in Yellowstone preservation was protection for bison.[16] The 1872 legislation that made the Yellowstone Plateau into the world's first national park failed to authorize punishment for those who violated park rules.[17] Souvenir hunters carved up rock formations, loggers cut trees, and market hunters slaughtered park wildlife, including the few score bison that survived there. Bison heads were selling for up to five hundred dollars apiece, far exceeding the few dollars that a buffalo robe had brought during the heyday of bison hunting.[18] The scarcer bison became, the more valuable they were to market hunters. Roosevelt, Grinnell, and their club worked for enactment of legislation that set punishment for poachers and other park violators, winning the battle in 1894 with enactment of the National Park Protective Act.[19] The club also was successful in stopping legislation that would have allowed the railroad industry to build a rail line across the northern reaches of the park.[20]

In addition to lobbying for conservation legislation, Roosevelt edited, with Grinnell, a series of annual books designed to share knowledge about animals and their need for protection. Roosevelt's own contributions to these volumes drew heavily on his western experiences. The books attracted attention across the Atlantic and advanced Roosevelt's concept of an organization designed to promote conservation laws. Grinnell: "Before very long, in the United States and in England, other clubs and associations were formed on the same model; so that in founding the club he organized, Roosevelt was directly responsible for the good work of each of these."[21] Years after Roosevelt's death, Grinnell would contend that "no single thing that he did for conservation has had so far-reaching an effect as the establishment of the Boone and Crockett Club."[22]

While working for wildlife protection, Roosevelt pursued his many other interests. In autumn 1888 he went to the Kootenai region of Idaho, near the British Columbia border, with Bill Merrifield and his cousin J. West Roosevelt to hunt woodland caribou—a species now practically extinct in the United States—and other high-country creatures, including mountain goats.[23] He visited what was left of Medora in late September 1888, then immersed himself in affairs back east. On October 5, at Sagamore Hill, he started planning a book on the history of New York City, a work-for-hire he took on because he needed money.[24] Two days later he headed with Edith to Illinois, Michigan, and Minnesota to campaign for Benjamin Harrison, the Republican presidential candidate.[25] To Roosevelt's joy, the Republican Party swept both Congress and the White House on November 5. Before Christmas, he finished Volume 1 of *The Winning of the West*, his history of the settlement of America by the British. At about that time, his *Century* magazine hunting articles, which he had revised the previous summer, appeared as the book *Ranch Life and the Hunting Trail*. Roosevelt took pride in the book's realism: "I have been a part of all that I describe; I have seen the things and done them; I have herded my own cattle, I have killed my own food; I have shot bears, captured horse thieves, and 'stood off' Indians. The descriptions are literally exact; few eastern men have seen the wild life for themselves."[26]

On April 1, 1889—the third anniversary of his capture of the boat thieves—he wrapped up Volume 2 of *The Winning of the West*. That spring he moved to Washington, D.C., as a civil service commissioner. In August—when Edith was seven months pregnant with his second son, Kermit, who would be born on October 10—he took off for the Rockies, where he stalked grizzly bears along the Wisdom River in Idaho but complained that he was getting fat and lazy.[27] He killed a mountain lion, two bull moose, and two grizzlies, one of which "made a most determined charge, but I stopped him with the old winchester."[28]

One day in Idaho, just south of Montana and twenty-five miles west of Wyoming, he found bison tracks a few hours old and trailed the animals to a glade near a fringe of timber where they were feeding—a cow, a calf, and a yearling.[29] These buffalo almost certainly had wandered out of nearby Yellowstone National Park and would have numbered among the animals the Boone and Crockett Club was laboring to save. They were soon joined by another cow and calf. Roosevelt waited for the bull he was sure was among them. "Mixed with the eager excitement of the hunter was a certain half melancholy feeling as I gazed on these bison, themselves part of the last remnant of a doomed and nearly vanished race. Few, indeed, are the men who now have, or evermore shall have, the chance of seeing the mightiest of American beasts, in all his wild vigor, surrounded by the tremendous desolation of his far-off mountain home."[30]

Finally, as Roosevelt grew increasingly alarmed that the cows might run off, the bull appeared on the edge of the glade. The animal stood with outstretched head as he rubbed his throat against a young tree, its branches shaking with his movement. Roosevelt aimed behind the bull's front leg and fired. "At the crack of the rifle all the bison, without the momentary halt of terror-struck surprise so common among game, turned and raced off at headlong speed. The fringe of young pines beyond and below the glade cracked and swayed as if a whirlwind were passing, and in another moment they reached the top of a very steep incline, thickly strewn with boulders and dead timber. Down this they plunged with reckless speed."[31] Minutes later, fifty yards beyond the border of the forest, Roosevelt found his buffalo dead on the ground, "a splendid old bull, still in his full vigor, with large, sharp horns, and heavy mane and glossy coat; and I felt the most exulting pride as I handled and examined him; for I had procured a trophy such as can fall henceforth to few hunters indeed."[32] The irony of killing a breeding bull in a shrinking bison population that he and his colleagues were trying to save apparently was lost on him.

In 1890 he took Edith and his sister Anna to the Elkhorn Ranch, where Edith rode a horse named Wire Fence and watched cowboys rope and brand calves.[33] Whitefoot, from Wilmot Dow's old string of ponies, tried to buck off Theodore. Sylvane Ferris and Bill Merrifield were managing his two cattle operations at this time. Theodore lamented losing money in cattle, but Edith mollified him: "As for the money you lost there we are far better off without it than we should be without what it brought you—your health and books."[34] Roosevelt wrote to Bill Sewall in October 1889 to say, "I still keep the Elkhorn ranch-house open, but will probably close it for good next year. I am picking up a little in the cattle business, branding a slightly larger number of calves each year, and putting back a few thousand dollars into my capital; but I shall never make good my losses."[35]

In the early 1890s, Roosevelt was spending more than he earned and was again thinking about selling Sagamore Hill. Still working for the Civil Service Commission, he also considered giving up his Washington townhouse and renting a room.[36] By October 1890 he had parted with Merrifield, who moved to Montana; all the Roosevelt cattle were now in Sylvane Ferris' care. "Merrifield has great hopes of striking something where he can get rich very fast. He may succeed—and then again he may not."[37] Roosevelt had once had dreams of a quick strike, so he knew the vagaries of financial ambition.

Roosevelt hunted in Wyoming's Shoshone Mountains in 1891, killing four elk in about as many days and a cow "for meat," along with at least four blue grouse; his hunting companion killed two bighorn rams and five elk—a cow "for meat" and four bulls.[38] The two cow elk alone represented a conservative estimate of four hundred pounds of meat and likely much more. About ten days later, moments after killing another bull elk, Roosevelt killed one more, its antlers "the finest I ever got"; a few minutes later, while skinning those elk, he shot a third.[39] "That evening my home-coming to camp, with three elk tongues and a brace of ruffed grouse hung on my belt, was most happy."[40] He took only the heads and tongues of the bulls because "the flesh was far too strong to be worth taking, for it was just the height of the rut."[41] In all, during this single hunt he killed nine elk with fifty-eight shots, seventeen grouse with twenty-two shots, and two ducks with ten shots.

Roosevelt visited the West again in 1892, later writing Sewall, "I spent three weeks out West this year; first at my ranch, and then on a wagon trip down to the Black Hills, during the course of which I shot a few antelope. My cattle are doing better than they were. The ranch-house is in good repair, but of course it is melancholy to see it deserted; I stayed there several days. One morning, as I was sitting on the piazza, I heard a splashing in the river . . . and there were three deer! They walked up along the sand to the crossing; and I picked up my rifle, leaned against one of the big cottonwoods, and dropped one in its tracks. We were out of meat and the venison tasted first rate. I never expected to shoot a deer from the piazza."[42]

That year he set up the Elkhorn Stock Company in partnership with his brother-in-law Douglas Robinson and two friends, including an Englishman with whom he had hunted elk in the Shoshones.[43] He transferred equity in the ranch to the corporation. By the early 1890s the open range was coming to an end. "Fences and sheep and settlers were coming in, and the old-time big cow outfits were going out, and nothing was like it used to be any more," wrote Teddy Blue Abbott.[44] Dakota Territory had entered the Union as two states late in 1889.

Roosevelt camped and hunted on the Little Missouri in autumn 1893.[45] Late in the year he published *The Wilderness Hunter*, a book that he liked "better than anything I have done."[46] He told his friend Owen Wister, "I wanted to make the book a plea for manliness and simplicity and delight in a vigorous outdoor life; as well as try to sketch the feeling that the wilderness, with its great rivers, great mountains, great forests, and great prairies, leaves on one."[47] At least one reviewer believed Roosevelt had achieved his goal: "The man of social position and culture who can tramp for days at a time in the uninhabited mountains, sleeping in the open air and depending for food solely upon his rifle . . . sets an example of simple, wholesome living which not everybody can imitate but which all must respect, and which is of high value in counteracting the tendency toward effeminateness so prevalent among many of the young men of the present."[48] The *New York Times* in an August 6 review concluded, "It is good reading for anybody, and people who never hunt and never will are sure to derive pleasure from its account of that part of the United States, relatively small, which is still a wilderness."

In December 1897 Roosevelt told Sylvane to dispose of all the Roosevelt cattle.[49] The driving force behind the decision was the impending Spanish-American War, in which Roosevelt served at the head of a group of mounted soldiers called the Rough Riders. He recruited cowboys and Ivy League men. As for ranching, "I shall get out if I possibly can. What price do you think I ought to put on the cattle?"[50] By then, according to his account ledgers, he had lost $20,292.63 in the Badlands, not including interest.[51] In the end, Ferris bought the cattle and buildings at both ranches.[52] Roosevelt's sojourn as a rancher was over.

By 1898 Roosevelt had completed four volumes of *The Winning of the West*, in addition to his other books. He had helped make the Civil Service Commission less partisan and had served as head of the New York City police commission from 1895 to 1897. As assistant secretary of the navy from 1897 to 1898, he had helped launch the United States into the Spanish-American War, the four-month conflict from which the nation emerged as a world power and Roosevelt as a popular hero after his famous charge in Cuba at the head of the Rough Riders.

Beguiled by his fame, New Yorkers elected him governor in 1898. Continuing his natural-resources agenda, he became the first governor to make conservation a part of his administrative policies. He launched an investigation into the conduct of state conservation work and planned to improve state protection of forests, water, and wildlife. However, his time in office was short. In 1900 he ran as the Republican vice presidential candidate under President William McKinley, who was seeking his second term in the White House.

Republicans and even Democrats in North Dakota vigorously supported Roosevelt's vice presidential nomination.[53] A typical newspaper endorsement made the connection between Theodore Roosevelt and the West: "The next vice-president of the United States is, in no small degree, a product of North Dakota. For several years, at the most impressionable period of his life, he was a North Dakota man. The young college graduate spurned the luxury and formality of the East, and sought in this state, the freedom and independence he craved, and he became as thorough a western man as ever bestrode a mustang. He himself states that next to his experience in the Spanish-American War, he values his schooling he received on the plains of North Dakota. North Dakota is young, but she has assisted in training a vice-president and a possible president."[54]

The Republican presidential ticket's combination of a young reform politician with a Civil War veteran won the election. When McKinley was assassinated in September 1901, Roosevelt at forty-two years old became, and remains, the youngest man to serve as president. From 1901 to 1908, he pursued conservation from the White House with unprecedented vigor, creating the first national wildlife refuge and then adding fifty more to it; quadrupling the size of the national forest system, from fifty million to two hundred million acres; and successfully urging Congress to create five more national parks.[55] He shepherded the creation of today's U.S. Forest Service.[56] In May 1908, he assembled the governors of several states and the heads of various national organizations concerned with natural resources for a White House conference on conservation. The meeting led to the appointment of thirty-six state conservation commissions and, the following June, to the formation of the first national conservation commission, tasked with providing a guide for future conservation measures by completing the first inventory of U.S. natural resources.[57]

To lay the credit for Roosevelt's conservation awareness exclusively on his ranching years would risk oversimplifying the effects of his innate inclinations. Had he not been the sort of man who would go west, live on a ranch, and hunt in the wilderness, he might never have developed his conservation ethic. Moreover, he was not the first in his family to work for conservation.[58] He had a model in Robert Roosevelt, his father's brother, who made fish conservation and the protection of state waterways a leading cause of his life; he persuaded the state legislature to create a three-member Fish Commission and then headed it for twenty years, using his authority to stock state rivers, create fish hatcheries, and fight the use of fish nets in the Hudson River, where commercial fishers were damaging fish populations—newspapers referred to him as the "Izaak Walton of America."[59]

Nevertheless, those who knew Theodore Roosevelt acknowledged the West's influence on his conservation activities. His cousin Nicholas Roosevelt, for example, wrote, "TR's interest in the conservation of natural resources was, of course, traceable to his first-hand knowledge of the West and its problems. None of his predecessors had had his keen awareness of the role of these resources—awareness based not alone on study but on having been through many of the remaining wilderness areas in the country and on experience as a frontier landowner in the last decade of the passing of the old West. As an avid hunter TR knew the need to save the nation's game. As a one-time cowpuncher he knew the value of being able to graze stock on public lands—especially if no fee was charged for the grazing right. But he was aware not only of the injustice in letting a few men have sole use of public lands for grazing but also of the destructive effects of overgrazing."[60]

Decades later, Roosevelt scholar and historian Robert J. Moore agreed that Roosevelt's concerns about wildlife and wilderness were "the direct outgrowth of having lived in the West and [having] observed the swift changes that were taking place at first hand. His commitment to conserving our natural resources was conceived and born during 3½ years (1884–1887) of ranching and traveling in the Dakota and Montana Territories."[61] Moore added, "Certainly, if the genesis of TR's thoughts about wilderness and his conversion to the idea that resources (land, water, wildlife) are finite occurred anywhere, if his notion that wilderness formed the collective character of Americans and America began at a specific location, if the idea that Americans need to periodically renew themselves in wilderness sprang from a location, it was from the prairie grasses and weird rock formations of the Badlands, the sites of TR's western ranches during the years 1883–1896."[62]

However much conservation loomed in Theodore Roosevelt's mind, that issue alone would not have ushered him into the White House. A complex of factors saw him through that door, but Roosevelt rated his Badlands experiences high among them. His friend John Burroughs, the naturalist, recalled that when the two traveled together in the West in 1903, Roosevelt—then in his first term as president—said that "his ranch life had been the making of him. It had built him up and hardened him physically, and it had opened his eyes to the wealth of manly character among the plainsmen and cattlemen. Had he not gone West, he said, he never would have raised the Rough Riders regiment; and had he not raised that regiment and gone to the Cuban War, he would not have been made governor of New York; and had not this happened, the politicians would not unwittingly have made his rise to the Presidency so inevitable."[63]

In later years Roosevelt would write of the Badlands, "I owe more than I can ever express to the West, which of course means to the men and women I met in the West. There were a few people of bad type in my neighborhood—that would be true of every group of men, even in a theological seminary—but I could not speak with too great affection and respect of the great majority of my friends, the hard-working men and women who dwelt for a space perhaps of a hundred and fifty miles along the Little Missouri."[64]

Carleton Putnam, one of the most thorough biographers of Roosevelt's early years, wrote that to evaluate accurately Roosevelt's statement about his political debt to the West is "impossible. But a few things are certain. The Bad Lands gave him his first sustained contact with the mood and physical impress of the American frontier. . . . If the saying be true that one finds in Rome only what one takes there, it is equally true that one responds to the West in proportion to one's appreciation of its symbolisms, and Roosevelt, by both temperament and knowledge of the Eastern woods, was now well conditioned to receive its inspiration."[65]

Roosevelt also benefited from the egalitarian nature of the West. Putnam: "If there was a democratic leveling in the Bad Lands, it was not a leveling in the realm of character or capacity but in detachment from the past. No man carried an advantage because of his father—nor a disadvantage. The 'freshness' of a Western morning symbolized each man's new start. Thereafter Western society held him as ruthlessly to account, valued strength as highly, condemned weakness as harshly, as any other. The frontier cared little about Roosevelt's antecedents. If anything, these were a handicap to him. But it cared greatly about his ability to meet its own standards, and this was a challenge he relished. In meeting it he gained not only a new respect for himself but for individual merit in others." Putnam concluded, "All of these elements contributed much to his future political success, and his own estimate of their importance may not be exaggerated."

One measure of the role that the Badlands played in Roosevelt's political success can be found in commentary left by his friends and relatives. Corinne Roosevelt Robinson wrote of her brother's ranching years, "No period of the life of Theodore Roosevelt seems to me quite as important, in the influence which it was to bear upon his future usefulness to his country, as was that period in which, as man to man, he shared the vigorous work and pastimes of the men of that part of our country [the West]."[66] Roosevelt's friend William Roscoe believed that the West "imparted to him also a knowledge which was to prove most precious to him in the unforeseen future. For it taught him the immense diversity of the people, and consequently of the interests, of the United States. It gave him a national point of view, in which he perceived that the standards and desires of the Atlantic States were not all-inclusive or final. Yet while it impressed on him the importance of geographical considerations, it impressed, more deeply still, the fact that there are moral fundamentals not to be measured by geography, or by time, or by race."[67]

George Shiras, a wildlife photographer who knew Roosevelt, backed Thayer's view when he wrote, "Under any ordinary environment Theodore Roosevelt, by reason of his mentality, character, and education, would have achieved success in almost any field of endeavor. The radical change, however, in his surroundings, when, as a young man, he became a western ranchman, undoubtedly affected his subsequent career to a marked degree."[68] Though he entered that life "with the shell broken, he emerged as the advocate of the strenuous life, and with a better and more sympathetic understanding of those influences affecting the American people in their widely separated homes and occupations." Bill Sewall expressed the role of the Badlands in Roosevelt's life succinctly: "I call the West God's Country, for it undoubtedly saved Theodore Roosevelt's life and reason."[69]

A final observation comes from Stefan Lorant, who spent seventeen years compiling and publishing a photo collection of Roosevelt's life. Lorant concluded, "The extent to which the West shaped Roosevelt's outlook on life is hard to overstate. It had vast influence on his development. It brought the successful culmination of his quest for extraordinary physical stamina. It gave him a profound appreciation of the importance of frontier life and frontier philosophy in the American character."[70]

Roosevelt kept the West in his heart to the end of his life. When the ranches were no longer his, he expressed regret to Sylvane, saying that he missed his Medora friends and that "I am not a little melancholy at having surrendered all my interests out there, but I am so very busy here that it would not be possible for me to get out, at any rate for two years to come."[71] But he did not lose interest in the more arcane aspects of ranch life, asking Sylvane in 1899 to have his old saddle sent to Oyster Bay and to take care of his horses: "As for Sorrel Joe, Muley, Wirefence and Spear Fish, I wish you or Joe would just keep them and use them. They are old now and I hate to sell them just to be knocked about and ridden to death."[72] Roosevelt wrote to Joe Ferris in 1905 from the White House, "Can't Muley be kept up during the winter? I feel that he is entitled to a pension. I will of course pay all expenses connected with it."[73] Muley— Roosevelt's favorite cutting horse in the 1885 roundup—lasted another two years.[74]

Roosevelt visited the Dakotas by rail while campaigning for the vice presidency in 1900. Drawing large crowds wherever he appeared, he extolled President McKinley and shook hands with small-town voters from the train's rear platform. On September 12, shortly after a campaign stop, he sat on the rear platform as the locomotive chuffed westward toward Medora and the Badlands. His arms rested on a brake handle, his chin on a wrist, and his gaze on the prairie that rolled gently to all horizons. At some point he asked a porter to ward off visitors, and he shut the platform door, remaining alone outside. A member of his campaign staff came looking for him and found the porter standing before the door, blocking the way. "The governor don't want to see nobody for a while," the porter said. For at least an hour, Roosevelt was left to solitude, to the West, and to whatever memories he found there.[75]

EPILOGUE

MANY WESTERNERS WERE PLEASED WHEN THEODORE ROOSEVELT BE-
came president in 1901 following the McKinley assassination, even if they
sorrowed over the method by which he came into office. He was of their
ilk. The National Live Stock Association, at a meeting in Chicago during
December of that year, observed with enthusiasm that the nation now
was led by a president "familiar with the industry we represent; who has
wielded a lariat and branding iron, and knows personally of the joys, the
hardships and the fatigues of the life on the ranch and the range. The cowboy on the range, and the stockman on the ranch all feel that in President
Roosevelt the nation has a loyal, honest and fearless ruler, and the livestock industry has a friend at court in the person of one who knows the
needs and necessities of that industry."[1]

The cowboys he had met in the Badlands became welcome guests at the
White House and benefited from their comradeship with the president.
Roosevelt commissioned Bill Merrifield as a U.S. marshal in Montana.
He appointed Joe Ferris postmaster in Medora and put Sylvane in charge
of the Land Office.[2] When Joseph W. Jackson, a cowboy Roosevelt had

known in the Badlands, came to Washington, D.C., as part of a committee seeking a million dollars for a North Dakota reclamation project, Roosevelt slapped him "vigorously" on the back upon meeting him, exclaiming, "Good old North Dakota. I owe my life to that State, and anything she is entitled to I'll see that she gets it." The committee got its million dollars.[3]

In 1904, Roosevelt ran for president in his own right. John Willis, his former Montana hunting guide and an avowed "very radical Democrat," told him, "Now anything I can do, I will do gladly for you, not for your party."[4] He said he believed Roosevelt's election "will come from the common people and not from the monied class." Roosevelt won all states west of the Mississippi except Arkansas, Louisiana, and Texas. His inaugural parade included a "cowboy brigade" of some fifty riders.[5] Among them was Tom Mix, who would be the nation's first major star of western movies. The whole retinue, along with a contingent of Rough Riders, attended a reception in their honor at the White House on the eve of the inauguration. The cowboys had carried firearms while riding; at the reception, Roosevelt autographed some of their holsters and gun belts.

When Roosevelt bolted the Republican Party to run as an independent presidential candidate in 1912 on the Progressive Party ticket, the Ferris brothers, Merrifield, and George Myers, another of Roosevelt's ranch hands, appeared as delegates at the first Progressive Party convention, held in Chicago. Sylvane was a member of the party's central committee, and Dr. V. H. Stickney was a county chairman.[6]

Among some of Roosevelt's Badlands colleagues, life followed a predictable trajectory. Gregor Lang, who counseled Roosevelt on buying cattle during the 1883 buffalo hunt, became county commissioner and owner of a profitable ranch. His son Lincoln moved to Illinois, became an engineer, invented a device for braking and reversing locomotives, and devised a plan for adapting the brakes to naval vessels. He sought and received Roosevelt's help in making contacts within the navy.[7] He also sought Roosevelt's advice on creating a game reserve in North Dakota.[8] Roosevelt expressed his sympathies to Lang when his father died in spring 1900.[9] Lang published a book about Roosevelt and the Badlands in 1926.

Jerry Paddock became a prosperous businessman in Dickinson. He retired to California, where he died in 1912 at the age of eighty. Sylvane Ferris lived in the Badlands until 1898, relocated to Dickinson, where he became a bank president, and then moved to California, where he died in 1933. Merrifield moved to Flathead County, Montana, in 1891 and died there in 1929, age seventy-four. Saloon owner Bob Roberts was said to have drifted to Bismarck, making a living as a gambler, where he killed a man in a barroom brawl and was acquitted of murder before disappearing in Alaska's Klondike gold rush.[10] Redhead Finnegan, the boat thief, returned to his life of crime after his release from prison and died at the end of a rope.[11] De Morès paid a final visit to Medora in December 1887, then left for Europe and then China, where he had plans to build a railroad.[12] He died in North Africa in 1896, shot by Tuareg guides he had hired to take him to Muslim leaders as part of a grandiose plan to initiate a holy war against Jews and the British and, along the way, put himself on a revived French throne.[13]

Wilmot Dow died young of natural causes in 1891. Roosevelt wrote to Sewall that May, "I cannot realize that he, so lusty and powerful and healthy, can have gone. You know how highly I esteemed Wilmot. . . . May we all do our duty as straightforwardly and well as he did his."[14] Roosevelt's feelings were not mere formality; the following August he wrote Sewall, "I think of Wilmot all the time; I can see him riding a bucker, or paddling a canoe, or shooting an antelope; or doing the washing for his wife, or playing with the children. If ever there was a fine, noble fellow, he was one."[15] He offered to buy Dow's .40-90 Sharps rifle for a hundred dollars, but Dow's wife wanted to give it to him as a gift.[16] Finally he agreed to accept it, but he mailed Mrs. Dow a check for a hundred dollars as "a Christmas present for the children." As late as October 1892 he was writing Sewall, "Be sure you let me know how Mrs. Dow is getting on, and how her children are."[17]

Roosevelt stayed in touch with Bill Sewall until the end, when Sewall's beard had grown white and Sewall felt that he had come to look like John Brown ("But I do not resent that because I always had quite an admiration for Old John Brown he had qualities that I admired I well remember when he took Harpers Ferry and was executed for the same but he showed no white feathers").[18] Sewall asked for and received Roosevelt's help in being appointed collector of customs in Maine and in garnering a postmastership.[19]

Sewall and his family visited Roosevelt in Washington in autumn

1902; Roosevelt greeted Sewall by coming down a long White House hallway "with jangling spurs just as he formerly had come down the hall at the ranch house."[20] Roosevelt even booked lodging for the Sewalls and detailed his personal messenger to pick them up at the train and show them around the city.[21] He discussed political issues with Sewall over the years, such as the difficulties of dealing with corporations and labor unions and the problems of putting a canal through Panama; they also discussed William Howard Taft as Roosevelt's presidential successor and the subsequent rise of the Progressive Party.[22]

Roosevelt commented to Sewall on his decision not to seek a third term in 1908: "I have thoroly enjoyed the job. I never felt more vigorous, so far as the work of the office is concerned (it is different from some of the work in the backwoods and on the plains that you and I have done together in the past), and if I followed my own desires I should have been only too delighted to stay as President. I had said that I would not accept another term, and I believe the people think that my word is good, and I should be mighty sorry to have them think anything else. Moreover, for the very reason that I believe in being a strong President and making the most of the office and using it without regard to the little, feeble, snarling men who yell about executive usurpation, I also believe that it is not a good thing that any one man should hold it too long. My ambition is, in however humble a manner and however far off, to travel in the footsteps of Washington and Lincoln."[23]

Sewall made at least one visit to Oyster Bay, in 1910.[24] Yearly he would send the Roosevelt family maple sugar, and sometimes he arranged for special stockings and other gear knitted by a local Maine woman.[25] He would prove instrumental to preserving the story of Roosevelt's ranching years, providing information for biographer Hermann Hagedorn, who in 1921 published a book on Roosevelt in the Badlands. Roosevelt urged Sewall to talk openly with Hagedorn about the early days. "I want you to tell him everything, good, bad and indifferent. Don't spare me the least bit. Give him the very worst side of me you can think of, and the very best side of me that is truthful."[26] As a source of information, Sewall was a safe bet for Roosevelt. Sewall once said of his former boss, "I consider there has never been a man who was his equal—since the days of our Savior—if not before."[27]

Roosevelt's attachment to the West extended to an attachment for artifacts from his Badlands years. At Sagamore Hill—now open to the public as a national historic site—are many game heads, including elk, that brought back to him the essence of western life. Roosevelt: "Whoever had hunted the wapiti, as he looks at his trophies will always think of the great mountains with the snow lying in the rifts in their sides; of the splashing murmur of rock-choked torrents; of the odorous breath of the pine branches; of tents pitched in open glades; of long walks through cool, open forests; and of great camp-fires, where the pitchy stumps flame like giant torches in the darkness."[28] While vice president, he wrote to Joe Ferris asking him if his buffalo-skin sleeping bag could be found, and Ferris responded a few days later that he had found two sleeping bags that he would send.[29] Roosevelt kept his much beloved buckskin suit, which is displayed today at Sagamore Hill, along with two bison heads.

Roosevelt kept the spirit of the West and the wilderness alive in his children, telling them tales of Davy Crockett and the Alamo, of Daniel Boone, and of Custer's final battle.[30] Alice recalled how her father played with her and her two younger brothers when she was about ten: "We were very fond of small toy animals, little skin horses, and cows. Father would heat a wire hairpin red hot and brand them for us with the brands of his three different ranches. . . . It made me feel as if I had actually been with him in his ranching days, and taken part in what went on at the round-ups that he used to tell us about."[31] Roosevelt sent his sons out west, lining them up to see roundups and to hunt.[32] In 1918 Theodore junior and Kermit were members of the Boone and Crockett Club.[33]

Like his friends from the Badlands, Roosevelt's closest relatives suffered mixed fates. His brother, Elliott—the father of Eleanor Roosevelt—died at age thirty-four from the effects of alcoholism and dissipation.[34] Anna, in 1895, married a navy commander—later an admiral—named William Sheffield Cowles.[35] She was forty, he was almost a decade older. At age forty-three she gave birth to a son. In midlife she became deaf but learned to read lips. After providing Roosevelt with political and personal advice throughout his life, she outlived him by twelve years, dying in 1931 at age seventy-six. Roosevelt's sister Corinne lived until 1933 and was, like Anna, a high-profile social figure and literary patron. She wrote poetry in Theodore's honor and published a book about him.[36]

With close friends Edith would sometimes discuss "with mingled humor and exasperation...the tribulations of being married to a Roosevelt—problems that other Roosevelt wives have faced in other generations, owing to the fact that most Roosevelt husbands have been, like Theseus in *A Midsummer Night's Dream*, 'over-full of self-affairs.'"[37] She bore the challenges well: "Edith's was not an easy life, even though it was rich and full. Ungregarious, she was married to a man who loved people and liked to be the center of attention. Where she was reserved he overflowed with exuberance and enthusiasm. Having early acquired the wisdom of maturity (a niece suggested that Edith had, in fact, been 'born mature') she yet was wife to a man who kept much of the boy in him to the end."[38] She lived until September 30, 1948.

Alice married a member of the House of Representatives and became a Washington, D.C., doyenne. In old age—she died on February 20, 1980—she would conclude, "I don't think I would have liked my mother very much. Maybe it has something to do with the attitude the Roosevelts—along with most Victorians—had about the Little Woman and Large Families and the frail, lovely wife, who had to be protected and looked after."[39] The house in which the younger Alice was born, and in which her grandfather, grandmother, and mother had died, fell to urban expansion. Bergdorf Goodman now stands where the "cursed house" once loomed over Fifty-seventh Street.

Roosevelt's conservation legacy continues. The Boone and Crockett Club still works on conservation issues and keeps data on record big-game animals bagged by hunters. The National Wildlife Refuge System includes some 540 refuges, as well as 3,000 smaller wetland areas set aside for waterfowl. National forests cover more than 190 million acres.

Medora still stands today, covering about half a square mile and housing a permanent population of about a hundred residents.[40] The town lies just outside the main gate to Theodore Roosevelt National Park, where the Maltese Cross ranch house is on display. During tourist season, the town features a play on the West of Theodore Roosevelt's time; it has run since the late 1950s, when it was called *Old Four Eyes*.[41] The Marquis' abattoir burned down in 1907, with all its machinery and equipment inside.[42] The tall brick chimney still stands.

The Elkhorn Ranch house was used into the 1890s by passing cowboys who needed a place to spend the night.[43] A member of one group of cowboys recalled that in 1895 or 1896 the house was still standing, with nothing inside but cupboards and a table. By 1901 the house and other buildings were gone, salvaged for lumber by locals.

During a final trip west, Roosevelt arrived in Billings, Montana, on October 6, 1918, and encountered George Myers, the ranch hand who had been his teamster on the bighorn hunt. The town was so packed with people eager to see the former president that, like many others, Myers was unable to get a room. Roosevelt, when he learned of this situation, asked Myers to share his room and talk about old times. By then, Roosevelt was suffering from chronic illness. Myers was the last of the Badlands folks to see him alive.

On the evening of January 5, 1919, Roosevelt complained that he felt as if his heart were about to stop beating, but a doctor who examined him said his pulse and heart were good. He went to bed at Sagamore Hill about midnight. At half past twelve, Edith looked in to see if he was okay. At two in the morning of January 6 she checked again and thought he was sleeping comfortably, but at four he had stopped breathing, dying of an embolism. "Death had to take him sleeping, for if Roosevelt had been awake, there would have been a fight," Vice President Thomas Marshall said.[44]

In the summer of that year, Bill McCarty of the Custer Trail Ranch held a Badlands "roundup" in memory of Theodore Roosevelt, branding 125 calves.[45] People showed up in forty or fifty cars to watch. Among those who came were Bill Merrifield and Joe and Sylvane Ferris. At the end of a day of reminiscing, Sylvane was struck with sadness, recalling that the previous October, during his final visit to North Dakota, Roosevelt had said he would be back in summer 1919 to go with Sylvane, Joe, and Bill over the old stomping ground.[46]

The day after Roosevelt's death, *Des Moines Register* editorial cartoonist J. N. "Ding" Darling, who would one day win a Pulitzer Prize for his cartoons, published a commemorative drawing of Roosevelt that ran in newspapers throughout the nation. Captioned "The long, long trail," it showed Roosevelt dressed as a cowboy, mounted on a horse, and waving farewell as he rode off into clouds leading to distant mountains.

ACKNOWLEDGMENTS

I owe special thanks to my former colleague at the National Audubon Society TV Department, Chris Palmer, now at American University. A conversation with Chris first brought the idea for this book out of the darkness of my subconscious and into the light of thought. Without that discussion at the Austin Grill in Bethesda, Maryland, this book about Roosevelt and the Badlands might never have come within my grasp.

I bow to Wallace F. Dailey, who administers the Theodore Roosevelt Collection at Harvard University, for his patient help in locating sources, offering advice, and guiding me through the process of securing rights and permission. I also developed great admiration for the staff of the Library of Congress Periodicals Room and the staff of the library's Manuscripts Division, who were always helpful. Similarly helpful and patient was the staff of the North Dakota Historical Society's archives and library.

Thanks for reading the manuscript and for offering comments and advice are owed to Tweed Roosevelt, current president of the Theodore Roosevelt Association; Doug Ellison, owner of the Western Edge bookstore in Medora, North Dakota; and Valerie Naylor, supervisor of Theodore Roosevelt National Park, which preserves a corner of the world much as it was in Roosevelt's time. Thanks also to friends who read the manuscript or in other ways encouraged me in this project, including Vincent Costino, my uncle Gerard Di Silvestro, Linda Gallagher, my cousin Geraldine Morley, Don Nelsen, Trish Pooley, Kathy Shay, and my old college friend Michael Pfeiffer, an archeologist with the U.S. Forest Service who provided me with an excellent source of information on western clothing in the 1880s

Badlands. Special thanks also go to Dan Smith of the Weider History Group, who has offered me advice on graphic design when I needed it and who kept me inspired through countless discussions of history and historical artifacts. And I want to tip my hat to Casey Borthelmess of Miles City, Montana, who made me aware of sources on Theodore Roosevelt that I might otherwise have missed.

I bow also to my editor, Jacqueline Johnson; my publisher, George Gibson; my agent, Gail Ross; and Gail's creative director, Howard Yoon, without whose efforts this book would not exist.

Finally, I owe inexpressible gratitude to my wife, Jeanne, for her encouragement during the grayer days, for her patience with my book-imposed absences, and for her understanding of the book's impact on our shared schedule and time.

NOTES

PREFACE
1. Theodore Roosevelt, *Ranch Life and the Hunting Trail* (New York: Bonanza Books, 1978), p. 24.

PROLOGUE
1. Frederick S. Wood, ed., *Roosevelt as We Knew Him: The Personal Recollections of One Hundred and Fifty of His Friends and Associates* (Philadelphia: The John C. Winston Company, 1927), p. 12.
2. James F. Vivian, *The Romance of My Life: Theodore Roosevelt's Speeches in Dakota* (Fargo, ND: Theodore Roosevelt Medora Foundation, 1989), p. 30.
3. Hermann Hagedorn files, Theodore Roosevelt Collection, Houghton Library, Harvard University.

I: THE BADLANDS RANCHER AS A YOUNG MAN
1. James D. McCabe, *New York by Sunlight and Gaslight: A Work Descriptive of the Great American Metropolis* (n.p.: Edgewood Publishing Company, 1881), p.165.
2. Luc Sante, *Low Life: Lures and Snares of Old New York* (New York: Farrar, Straus & Giroux, 2003), pp. 49–50.
3. McCabe, *New York by Sunlight and Gaslight*, p. 267.
4. McCabe, *New York by Sunlight and Gaslight*, pp. 57–58.
5. Henry Collins Brown, *Valentine's Manual of Old New York* (Hastings-on-Hudson, NY: Valentine's Manual Inc., 1927), p. 11.
6. Brown, *Valentine's Manual*, pp. 4–10.
7. Brown, *Valentine's Manual*, p. 10.
8. Corinne Roosevelt Robinson, *My Brother Theodore Roosevelt* (New York: Charles Scribner's Sons, 1921), pp. 10–12; David McCullough, *Mornings on Horseback: The Story of an Extraordinary Family, a Vanished Way of Life, and the Unique*

Child Who Became Theodore Roosevelt (New York: Simon and Schuster, 1981), pp. 42, 45.

9. Robinson, *My Brother Theodore Roosevelt*, p. 18.

10. Robinson, *My Brother Theodore Roosevelt*, p. 18.

11. Allen Churchill, *The Roosevelts: American Aristocrats* (New York: Harper & Row, 1965), p. 1.

12. McCabe, *New York by Sunlight and Gaslight*, pp. 196–197.

13. Churchill, *The Roosevelts*, p. 45.

14. Churchill, *The Roosevelts*, p. 45.

15. Churchill, *The Roosevelts*, p. 49.

16. Churchill, *The Roosevelts*, pp. 103–104.

17. Churchill, *The Roosevelts*, pp. 103–106, 113.

18. Paul Grondahl, *I Rose Like a Rocket: The Political Education of Theodore Roosevelt* (New York: Free Press, 2004), p. 227; *New York Times*, February 11, 1878.

19. Churchill, *The Roosevelts*, pp. 122–123.

20. Theodore Roosevelt, *An Autobiography* (New York: The Macmillan Company, 1913), pp. 13–14.

21. G. Edward White, *The Eastern Establishment and the Western Experience: The West of Frederic Remington, Theodore Roosevelt, and Owen Wister* (New Haven: Yale University Press, 1968), p. 12.

22. Churchill, *The Roosevelts*, p. 106.

23. A restoration of the house, administered by the National Park Service, stands on the site and is open to the public.

24. Edmund Morris, *The Rise of Theodore Roosevelt* (New York: Modern Library, 1979), pp. 183–184.

25. Roosevelt, *An Autobiography*, p. 17.

26. McCullough, *Mornings on Horseback*, p. 36.

27. McCullough, *Mornings on Horseback*, p. 36; for a detailed discussion of asthma and the Roosevelts' attempts to deal with it, see pp. 90–108.

28. Lincoln Steffens, *Autobiography* (New York: Harcourt Brace, 1936), pp. 349–350.

29. Carlton Putnam, *Theodore Roosevelt, Volume 1: The Formative Years, 1858–1886* (New York: Charles Scribner's Sons, 1958), pp. 71–72; Edmund Morris, *The Rise of Theodore Roosevelt* (New York: Modern Library, 2001), p. 32.

30. Robinson, *My Brother Theodore Roosevelt*, p. 50.

31. Morris, *The Rise of Theodore Roosevelt*, p. 33.

32. Roosevelt, *An Autobiography*, p. 33; Putnam, *Theodore Roosevelt*, pp. 71–75.

33. Roosevelt, *An Autobiography*, p. 33.

34. Theodore Roosevelt, *Theodore Roosevelt's Diaries of Boyhood and Youth* (New York: Charles Scribner's Sons, 1928), pp. 355–357.

35. Roosevelt, *An Autobiography*, pp. 47–48.

36. Robinson, *My Brother Theodore Roosevelt*, p. 89.

37. Robinson, *My Brother Theodore Roosevelt*, pp. 89–90.

38. Robinson, *My Brother Theodore Roosevelt*, pp. 102–103.

39. Mayne Reid, *The Boy Hunter, or Adventures in Search of a White Buffalo* (New York: Hurst and Company, 1889), pp. 125–127.

40. Roosevelt, *An Autobiography*, pp. 18–19.

41. Reid, *The Boy Hunter*, p. 20.

42. Reid, *The Boy Hunter*, pp. 11–12.

43. Grondahl, *I Rose Like a Rocket*, p. 28.

44. Roosevelt, *An Autobiography*, pp. 17–18.

45. McCullough, *Mornings on Horseback*, p. 128; Roosevelt, *An Autobiography*, p. 23.

46. Roosevelt, *An Autobiography*, p. 24.

47. Theodore Roosevelt, *Outdoor Pastimes of an American Hunter* (Mechanicsburg, PA: Stackpole Books, 1990 [1905]), p. 210.

48. Putnam, *Theodore Roosevelt*, p. 129.

49. Putnam, *Theodore Roosevelt*, p. 120; Morris, *The Rise of Theodore Roosevelt*, p. 60.

50. Theodore Roosevelt to Mittie Roosevelt, October 8, 1878, folder bMS Am 1540, "Letters to TR's Mother and Father," Theodore Roosevelt Collection, Houghton Library, Harvard University; *Boston Globe*, March 28, 1878.

51. Jacob A. Riis, *Theodore Roosevelt: The Citizen* (Washington, D.C.: Johnson, Wynne Company, 1904), p. 33.

52. Putnam, *Theodore Roosevelt*, p. 166; Morris, *The Rise of Theodore Roosevelt*, p. 83.

53. Morris, *The Rise of Theodore Roosevelt*, p. 59.

54. White, *The Eastern Establishment and the Western Experience*, pp. 20–26; quote from p. 26.

55. Owen Wister, *Roosevelt: The Story of a Friendship, 1880–1919* (New York: The Macmillan Company, 1930), p. 9.

56. Wister, *Roosevelt: The Story of a Friendship*, p. 9.

57. Roosevelt, *An Autobiography*, pp. 28–29.

58. Roosevelt, *An Autobiography*, p. 29.

59. Putnam, *Theodore Roosevelt*, pp. 146–148.

60. Corinne Roosevelt's diaries, Hermann Hagedorn files, Theodore Roosevelt Collection, Houghton Library, Harvard University.

61. Corinne Roosevelt's diaries, Hermann Hagedorn files, Theodore Roosevelt Collection, Houghton Library, Harvard University.

62. Elliott Roosevelt's diaries, Hermann Hagedorn files, Theodore Roosevelt Collection, Houghton Library, Harvard University.

63. Diary entry, February 9, 1878, Theodore Roosevelt Collection, Library of Congress Manuscript Division.

64. Theodore Roosevelt Collection, Library of Congress.

65. Theodore Roosevelt Collection, Library of Congress.

66. Theodore Roosevelt Collection, Library of Congress.

67. Brown, *Valentine's Manual of Old New York*, pp. 35–36.

68. Brown, *Valentine's Manual of Old New York*, pp. 124–125.

69. Brown, *Valentine's Manual of Old New York*, p. 315. A certain amount of risk went along with attending plays. Theaters in the 1880s were firetraps; wrote a

theater-goer, "One of the pleasure[s] of old time theater going was speculating on the chances of being incinerated before the close of the performance." Brown, p. 265.

70. The description of TR's meeting and courting of Alice draws from Putnam, *Theodore Roosevelt*, pp. 164–197, and from Morris, *The Rise of Theodore Roosevelt*, pp. 80–113.

71. Michael Teague, *Mrs. L: Conservations with Alice Roosevelt Longworth* (Garden City, NY: Doubleday & Company, 1981), p. 16.

72. Teague, *Mrs. L: Conservations with Alice Roosevelt Longworth*, p. 16.

73. Teague, *Mrs. L: Conservations with Alice Roosevelt Longworth*, pp. 15–16.

74. Teague, *Mrs. L: Conservations with Alice Roosevelt Longworth*, p. 18.

75. McCullough, *Mornings on Horseback*, p. 218.

76. Theodore Roosevelt to John Roosevelt, February 25, 1880, quoted in Morris, *The Rise of Theodore Roosevelt*, p. 80.

77. Putnam, *Theodore Roosevelt*, p. 167.

78. Putnam, *Theodore Roosevelt*, p. 168.

79. Morris, *The Rise of Theodore Roosevelt*, p. 82.

80. Morris, *The Rise of Theodore Roosevelt*, p. 79.

81. Putnam, *Theodore Roosevelt*, p. 172.

82. Morris, *The Rise of Theodore Roosevelt*, p. 82.

83. Putnam, *Theodore Roosevelt,*, p. 173.

84. Putnam, *Theodore Roosevelt*, p. 172.

85. Morris, *The Rise of Theodore Roosevelt*, p. 86.

86. Morris, *The Rise of Theodore Roosevelt*, p. 91.

87. Morris, *The Rise of Theodore Roosevelt*, p. 92.

88. Putnam, *Theodore Roosevelt*, p. 175.

89. Morris, *The Rise of Theodore Roosevelt*, p. 93.

90. Morris, *The Rise of Theodore Roosevelt*, p. 98.

91. Morris, *The Rise of Theodore Roosevelt*, p. 100.

92. Morris, *The Rise of Theodore Roosevelt*, p. 100.

93. Putnam, *Theodore Roosevelt*, p. 171.

94. McCullough, *Mornings on Horseback*, p. 223.

95. Morris, *The Rise of Theodore Roosevelt*, p. 102.

96. Putnam, *Theodore Roosevelt*, p. 188.

97. Alice (Roosevelt) Longworth [Family Papers], 1878–1918, Box 1 of 1, bMS Am 1541.9, Theodore Roosevelt Collection, Houghton Library, Harvard University.

98. Sixteen letters from Alice Lee Roosevelt to Theodore Roosevelt, bMS AM 1541.9 (26–41), Theodore Roosevelt Collection, Houghton Library, Harvard University.

99. Putnam, *Theodore Roosevelt*, p. 189.

100. Putnam, *Theodore Roosevelt*, p. 189.

101. Sixteen letters from Alice Lee Roosevelt to Theodore Roosevelt, bMS AM 1541.9 (26–41), Theodore Roosevelt Collection, Houghton Library, Harvard University.

102. Sixteen letters from Alice Lee Roosevelt to Theodore Roosevelt, bMS AM 1541.9 (26–41), Theodore Roosevelt Collection, Houghton Library, Harvard University.

103. Sixteen letters from Alice Lee Roosevelt to Theodore Roosevelt, bMS AM 1541.9 (26–41), Theodore Roosevelt Collection, Houghton Library, Harvard University.

104. Sixteen letters from Alice Lee Roosevelt to Theodore Roosevelt, bMS AM 1541.9 (26–41), Theodore Roosevelt Collection, Houghton Library, Harvard University.

105. Morris, *The Rise of Theodore Roosevelt*, p. 115.

106. Stefan Lorant, *The Life and Times of Theodore Roosevelt* (Garden City, NY: Doubleday & Company, 1959), p. 167.

107. Diary entries for dates given, Theodore Roosevelt Collection, Library of Congress Manuscript Division.

108. Putnam, *Theodore Roosevelt*, p. 178.

109. Roosevelt, *An Autobiography*, pp. 29–30.

110. William Wingate Sewall. "As I Knew Him." *Forum*, May 1919. The pages of the source copy used here, from a Library of Congress electronic archive, are unnumbered.

111. Morris, *The Rise of Theodore Roosevelt*, p. 107.

112. Roosevelt, *An Autobiography*, p. 62.

113. William Roscoe Thayer, *Theodore Roosevelt: An Intimate Biography* (New York: Grosset & Dunlap, 1919), p. 28.

114. Henry Cabot Lodge, *A Memorial to Theodore Roosevelt* (Albany: Authorized by the State Legislature, 1919), pp. 94–95.

115. McCabe, *New York by Sunlight and Gaslight*, p. 123.

116. Morris, *The Rise of Theodore Roosevelt*, p. 124.

117. Roosevelt, *An Autobiography*, p. 63.

118. Riis, *Theodore Roosevelt: The Citizen*, p. 47.

119. Churchill, *The Roosevelts*, pp. 107–108.

120. Churchill, *The Roosevelts*, p. 109.

121. Churchill, *The Roosevelts*, pp. 116–117.

122. McCabe, *New York by Sunlight and Gaslight*, pp. 54–55.

123. Thayer, *Theodore Roosevelt: An Intimate Biography*, p. 46–47.

124. Diary entry October 28, 1881, Theodore Roosevelt Collection, Library of Congress Manuscript Division.

125. Michael Teague, "Theodore Roosevelt and Alice Hathaway Lee: A New Perspective." *Harvard Library Bulletin* XXXII, 3 (Summer 1985): 234, in Sixteen letters from Alice Lee Roosevelt to Theodore Roosevelt, bMS AM 1541.9 (26–41), Theodore Roosevelt Collection, Houghton Library, Harvard University.

126. Diary entry for November 8, 1881, Theodore Roosevelt Collection, Library of Congress Manuscript Division.

127. Lodge, *A Memorial to Theodore Roosevelt*, p. 32.

128. Putnam, *Theodore Roosevelt*, p. 250.

129. Putnam, *Theodore Roosevelt*, p. 251.

130. Quoted, without date, in Riis, *Theodore Roosevelt: The Citizen*, pp. 54–55.

131. Sixteen letters from Alice Lee Roosevelt to Theodore Roosevelt, bMS AM 1541.9 (26–41), Theodore Roosevelt Collection, Houghton Library, Harvard University.

132. Morris, *The Rise of Theodore Roosevelt*, p. 162.

133. Frederick S. Wood, ed., *Roosevelt as We Knew Him: The Personal Recollections of One Hundred and Fifty of His Friends and Associates* (Philadelphia: The John C. Winston Company, 1927), p. 9.

134. Putnam, *Theodore Roosevelt*, pp. 279, 370–373; Morris, *The Rise of Theodore Roosevelt*, pp. 215–217.

135. Putnam, *Theodore Roosevelt*, pp. 221–227.

136. Morris, *The Rise of Theodore Roosevelt*, p. 136.

137. Roosevelt, *Hunting Trips*, pp. 244–245, 249–250.

138. Roosevelt, *Hunting Trips*, pp. 244, 550–563.

139. Mittie Roosevelt to Elliott Roosevelt, December 7, 1880, quoted in Edmund Morris, *The Rise of Theodore Roosevelt* (New York: Modern Library, 1979) p. 812.

2: THE LURE OF THE WEST

1. *New York Times*, May 29, 1883.

2. *New York Times*, May 29, 1883.

3. Hermann Hagedorn, *Roosevelt in the Bad Lands* (Boston: Houghton Mifflin Company, 1921), pp. 8–9; www.famousamericans.net.

4. Hagedorn, *Roosevelt in the Bad Lands*, p. 9.

5. James D. McCabe, *New York by Sunlight and Gaslight: A Work Descriptive of the Great American Metropolis* (n.p.: Edgewood Publishing Company, 1881), pp. 462–464.

6. Lincoln A. Lang, *Ranching with Roosevelt* (Philadelphia: J. B. Lippincott Company, 1926), p. 17.

7. Carlton Putnam, *Theodore Roosevelt, Volume One: The Formative Years, 1858–1886* (New York: Charles Scribner's Sons, 1958), p. 308.

8. David McCullough, *Mornings on Horseback: The Story of an Extraordinary Family, a Vanished Way of Life, and the Unique Child Who Became Theodore Roosevelt* (New York: Simon and Schuster, 1981), p. 317.

9. McCullough, *Mornings on Horseback*, pp. 278, 317–318; G. Edward White, *The Eastern Establishment and the Western Experience: The West of Frederic Remington, Theodore Roosevelt, and Owen Wister* (New Haven: Yale University Press, 1968), p. 127.

10. Hagedorn, *Roosevelt in the Bad Lands*, p. 8.

11. Game included deer, sheep, pronghorn, grizzlies, wolves, and mountain lions. A. C. Huidekoper, *My Experience and Investment in the Bad Lands of Dakota and Some of the Men I Met There* (Baltimore, Wirth Brothers, 1947) p. 18.

12. *Bismarck Tribune*, February 1880, quoted in Chester L. Brooks and Ray H. Mattison, *Theodore Roosevelt and the Dakota Badlands* (Washington, D.C.: National Park Service, 1958), p. 11.

13. Hagedorn, *Roosevelt in the Bad Lands*, p. 9; Putnam, *Theodore Roosevelt*, p. 308; Morris, *The Rise of Theodore Roosevelt*, p. 182.

14. Lang, *Ranching with Roosevelt*, pp. 35–36.

15. Theodore Roosevelt, *Ranch Life and the Hunting Trail* (New York: Bonanza Books, 1978), p. 111.

16. Dr. V. K. Stickney, "Early Days in North Dakota," *The Commercial West* 44, 2 (July 14, 1923): 23.

17. Roosevelt, *Ranch Life*, p. 101. Custer's wheel ruts remain to this day.

18. Hermann Hagedorn files, 332.H12p, files 705 and 709, Theodore Roosevelt Collection, Houghton Library, Harvard University; Donald Dresden, *The Marquis de Morès: Emperor of the Bad Lands* (Norman: University of Oklahoma Press, 1970), p. 30; Theodore Roosevelt, "Who Should Go West," *Harper's Weekly*, January 2, 1886, p. 7.

19. Hagedorn, *Roosevelt in the Bad Lands*, p. 48.

20. Hermann Hagedorn files, 332.H12p, files 29–45, Theodore Roosevelt Collection, Houghton Library, Harvard University.

21. Hermann Hagedorn files, 332.H12p, files 29–45, Theodore Roosevelt Collection, Houghton Library, Harvard University.

22. Lang, *Ranching with Roosevelt*, pp. 59–60.

23. Brooks and Mattison, *Theodore Roosevelt and the Dakota Badlands* (Washington, D.C.: National Park Service, 1958), p. 11.

24. Ernest Thompson Seton, *Lives of Game Animals* (Boston: Charles T. Branford Company, 1953), p. 655.

25. William T. Hornaday, *The Extermination of the American Bison* (Washington, D.C.: U.S. Government Printing Office, 1889), p. 504.

26. Steve Nicholls, *Paradise Found: Nature in America at the Time of Discovery* (Chicago: University of Chicago Press, 2009), p. 411.

27. Hornaday, *Extermination of the American Bison*, pp. 388–389.

28. E. C. Abbott and Helena Huntington Smith, *We Pointed Them North: Recollections of a Cowpuncher* (Norman: University of Oklahoma Press, 1955), p. 101.

29. Abbott and Smith, *We Pointed Them North*, p. 102.

30. Hornaday, *Extermination of the American Bison*, pp. 444–445.

31. Henry Collins Brown, *Valentine's Manual of Old New York* (Hastings-on-Hudson, NY: Valentine's Manual Inc., 1927), p. 142.

32. Hornaday, *Extermination of the American Bison*, pp. 444–445.

33. Interview with Joe Dietrich, April 29, 1922, L. F. Crawford Papers, North Dakota Historical Society.

34. Abbott and Smith, *We Pointed Them North*, p. 102.

35. Hornaday, *Extermination of the American Bison*, pp. 446–447.

36. Hornaday, *Extermination of the American Bison*, pp. 446–447.

37. Hornaday, *Extermination of the American Bison*, p. 497.

38. Hornaday, *Extermination of the American Bison*, p, 510.

39. Theodore Roosevelt and George Bird Grinnell, eds., *American Big-Game Hunting:*

The Book of the Boone and Crockett Club (New York: Forest and Stream Publishing Co., 1901), p. 193.

40. Hornaday, *Extermination of the American Bison*, p. 513.

41. James McLaughlin, *My Friend the Indian* (Lincoln: University of Nebraska Press, 1989), pp. 109, 114.

42. Putnam, *Theodore Roosevelt*, p. 317.

43. Hornaday, *Extermination of the American Bison*, p. 512.

44. Abbott and Smith, *We Pointed Them North*, p. 75.

45. Lang, *Ranching With Roosevelt*, p. 63.

46. Hornaday, *Extermination of the American Bison*, p. 520.

47. Hornaday, *Extermination of the American Bison*, pp. 513–519.

48. Hornaday, *Extermination of the American Bison*, p. 518.

49. Hornaday, *Extermination of the American Bison*, p. 521.

50. Hornaday, *Extermination of the American Bison*, p. 519.

51. Hornaday, *Extermination of the American Bison*, p. 520.

52. Abbott and Smith, *We Pointed Them North*, p. 102.

53. Lang, *Ranching with Roosevelt*, p. 23.

54. Hornaday, *Extermination of the American Bison*, p. 521.

55. Putnam, *Theodore Roosevelt*, pp. 117–118; Morris, *The Rise of Theodore Roosevelt*, p. 185; Natalie A. Naylor, "Understanding the Place: Theodore Roosevelt's Hometown of Oyster Bay and his Sagamore Hill Home," *Theodore Roosevelt Association Journal* XXX, 1–2, (Winter-Spring 2009): 7.

56. Naylor, "Understanding," p. 10.

57. Morris, *The Rise of Theodore Roosevelt*, p. 184.

58. Alice Roosevelt to Anna Roosevelt, July 22, 1883, bMS Am 1541.9 Alice (Roosevelt) Longworth [Family Papers], 1878–1918, Box 1 of 1, Theodore Roosevelt Collection, Houghton Library, Harvard University.

59. Hermann Hagedorn files, 332.H12p, files 300–332, Theodore Roosevelt Collection, Houghton Library, Harvard University. Late in August 1883 he paid ten thousand dollars for more land at Cove Neck and took on a twenty-thousand-dollar mortgage, bringing his holding to 155 acres, sixty of which he promptly sold to relatives to relieve some of his financial burden. Sylvia Jukes Morris, *Edith Kermit Roosevelt* (New York: Vintage Books, 1990), p. 73; Putnam, *Theodore Roosevelt*, p. 310; Theodore Roosevelt to Anna Roosevelt, September 3, 1883, *The Letters of Theodore Roosevelt*, ed. Elting E. Morison (Cambridge, MA: Harvard University Press, 1951), p. 62.

60. Theodore Roosevelt to Alice Roosevelt, September 2, 1883, Sixteen letters from Alice Lee Roosevelt to Theodore Roosevelt, bMS AM 1541.9 (26–41), Theodore Roosevelt Collection, Houghton Library, Harvard University.

3: THE BISON HUNT

1. Donald Dresden, *The Marquis de Morès: Emperor of the Bad Lands* (Norman: University of Oklahoma Press, 1970), p. 6.

2. Robert G. Athearn, *Westward the Briton* (New York: Charles Scribner's Sons, 1953), pp. 16–17.

3. Theodore Roosevelt to Mittie Roosevelt, September 4, 1883, folder bMS Am 1540, "Letters to TR's Mother and Father," Theodore Roosevelt Collection, Houghton Library, Harvard University.

4. Lincoln A. Lang, *Ranching with Roosevelt* (Philadelphia: J. B. Lippincott Company, 1926), p. 22.

5. Lang, *Ranching with Roosevelt*, p. 21.

6. Carlton Putnam, *Theodore Roosevelt, Volume One: The Formative Years, 1858–1886* (New York: Charles Scribner's Sons, 1958), p. 313.

7. William T. Hornaday, *The Extermination of the American Bison* (Washington, D.C.: U.S. Government Printing Office, 1889), pp. 507–508.

8. Various Texas cattle outfits moved into the northern range. Hughes and Simpson Company's Hash Knife set up on Box Elder Creek and ran Texas steers almost exclusively, shipping sixty thousand head from the Dickinson rail stop in 1884; W. A. Towers and Gudgell's OX ranch ran eight thousand to ten thousand cattle in the early 1880s; and the Berry, Boice Cattle Company's 777 ranch ran ten thousand to fifteen thousand. Interview with W. B. Galligan, a Hash Knife cowboy, L. F. Crawford Papers, North Dakota Historical Society; interview with John W. Goodall, L. F. Crawford Papers, North Dakota Historical Society.

9. Stefan Lorant, *The Life and Times of Theodore Roosevelt* (Garden City, NY: Doubleday & Company, 1959), p. 167.

10. Theodore Roosevelt to Alice Roosevelt, September 8, 1883, bMS AM 1541.9 (26–41), sixteen letters from Alice Lee Roosevelt to Theodore Roosevelt, Theodore Roosevelt Collection, Houghton Library, Harvard University. In his *Autobiography* he would write that he arrived at 3:00 a.m.

11. Lang, *Ranching with Roosevelt*, pp. 49–50.

12. Theodore Roosevelt to Alice Roosevelt, September 8, 1883, bMS AM 1541.9 (26–41), sixteen letters from Alice Lee Roosevelt to Theodore Roosevelt, Theodore Roosevelt Collection, Houghton Library, Harvard University; Theodore Roosevelt, *An Autobiography* (New York: The Macmillan Company, 1913), pp. 104–106.

13. Townsend Whelen of *Sports Afield* magazine to Carlton Putnam, August, presumably in the mid-1950s. Roosevelt was using a Sharp's .45, but his favorite rifle probably was a Winchester 1876 Centennial Model of fancy grade with piston grip. He probably used .45–75–350 Winchester cartridges. (.45 cal, 75 grains powder, 350-grain bullet). The 10-gauge shotgun Roosevelt indicated he had may have been a black powder double-barrel British No. 10 rifle designed for big game in Asia and Africa. The letter is in the Putnam Papers, Theodore Roosevelt Collection, Houghton Library, Harvard University.

14. Lang, *Ranching with Roosevelt*, p. 52.

15. Athearn. *Westward the Briton*, pp. 26–27.

16. Lang, *Ranching with Roosevelt*, p. 53.

17. Theodore Roosevelt to Alice Roosevelt, September 8, 1883, bMS AM 1541.9 (26–41), sixteen letters from Alice Lee Roosevelt to Theodore Roosevelt, Theodore Roosevelt Collection, Houghton Library, Harvard University; Roosevelt, *An Autobiography*, pp. 104–106.

18. Lang, *Ranching with Roosevelt*, p. 53.

19. Lang, *Ranching with Roosevelt*, pp. 53–54.

20. Theodore Roosevelt, *Hunting Trips of a Ranchman and The Wilderness Hunter* (New York: The Modern Library, 2004), pp. 16–17.

21. Lang, *Ranching with Roosevelt*, p. 48.

22. Dresden, *The Marquis de Morès*, pp. 16–17; Anonymous, *50 Years in the Saddle*, Vol. 1 (Watford City, ND: 50 Years in the Saddle Club, 1963), p. 287.

23. For de Morès background, see Dresden, *The Marquis de Morès*, pp. 17–20.

24. Putnam, *Theodore Roosevelt*, pp. 362–363.

25. Dresden, *The Marquis de Morès*, pp. 22–23.

26. Dresden, *The Marquis de Morès*, pp. 24–25.

27. Dresden, *The Marquis de Morès*, pp. 25–26.

28. Dresden, *The Marquis de Morès*, p. 14.

29. Dresden, *The Marquis de Morès*, p. 35.

30. Dresden, *The Marquis de Morès*, p. 43.

31. Interview with John W. Goodall, L. F. Crawford Papers, North Dakota Historical Society; also Crawford's notes from an interview with Goodall on February 8, 1913.

32. McCullough, *Mornings on Horseback*, p. 344.

33. Quoted from an undated copy of the *Dickinson Press* in Hermann Hagedorn, *Roosevelt in the Bad Lands* (Boston: Houghton Mifflin Company, 1921), pp. 79–80.

34. Putnam material, interview on September 16, 1952, with Mrs. George Pelissier, a resident of the Medora area in the 1880s, Theodore Roosevelt Collection, Houghton Library, Harvard University.

35. Roosevelt, *Hunting Trips and Wilderness Hunter*, p. 121.

36. Frank Wilkeson, "Cattle-raising on the Plains," *Harper's New Monthly Magazine*, April 1886, p. 789.

37. Lang, *Ranching with Roosevelt*, p. 71.

38. The story of the de Morès shootout has been told in and by many sources. Those used here in assembling the story are Lang, *Ranching with Roosevelt*, pp. 72–74; Hagedorn, *Roosevelt in the Bad Lands*, pp. 62–65; William Wingate Sewall, *Bill Sewall's Story of T.R.* (New York: Harper & Brothers, 1919), pp. 25–28; interviews with various Badlands contemporaries of de Morès cited individually below and found in the Hermann Hagedorn files, 332.H12p, file 512, Theodore Roosevelt Collection, Houghton Library, Harvard University.

39. Interview with Sylvane Ferris, April 2, 1918, L. F. Crawford Papers, North Dakota Historical Society.

40. Reuter's origins, comments from John Reuter in Hermann Hagedorn files, 332.H12p, file 489, Theodore Roosevelt Collection, Houghton Library, Harvard University.

41. Hermann Hagedorn files, 332.H12p, Theodore Roosevelt Collection, Houghton Library, Harvard University.

42. Putnam, *Theodore Roosevelt*, p. 323; Hermann Hagedorn files, 332.H12p, file 459, Theodore Roosevelt Collection, Houghton Library, Harvard University.

43. Interview with Mrs. George Pelissier, a resident of the Medora area in the 1880s, on September 16, 1952, Putnam files, Theodore Roosevelt Collection, Houghton Library, Harvard University; A. C. Huidekoper, in Hermann Hagedorn papers, Theodore Roosevelt Collection, Houghton Library, Harvard University.

44. Hermann Hagedorn files, 332.H12p, file 455, Theodore Roosevelt Collection, Houghton Library, Harvard University; Hagedorn, *Roosevelt in the Bad Lands*, pp. 49–50.

45. A. C. Huidekoper, in Hermann Hagedorn papers, Theodore Roosevelt Collection, Houghton Library, Harvard University.

46. Hagedorn, *Roosevelt in the Bad Lands*, p. 49.

47. Interview with Mrs. Elizabeth Roberts, a resident of the Medora area in the 1880s, on September 16, 1952, Putnam files, Theodore Roosevelt Collection, Houghton Library, Harvard University.

48. Hermann Hagedorn files, 332.H12p, files 1–28, Theodore Roosevelt Collection, Houghton Library, Harvard University.

49. Hermann Hagedorn files, 332.H12p, files 1–28, Theodore Roosevelt Collection, Houghton Library, Harvard University.

50. Hermann Hagedorn files, 332.H12p, file 569, Theodore Roosevelt Collection, Houghton Library, Harvard University.

51. Lang, *Ranching with Roosevelt*, p. 73; Anonymous, *50 Years in the Saddle*, pp. 286–287; quote is from an interview with Lincoln Lang in Hermann Hagedorn files, 332.H12p, files 330–332, Theodore Roosevelt Collection, Houghton Library, Harvard University.

52. Lang, *Ranching with Roosevelt*, pp. 72–73.

53. Interview with Mrs. Elizabeth Roberts, a resident of the Medora area in the 1880s, on September 16, 1952, Putnam files, Theodore Roosevelt Collection, Houghton Library, Harvard University.

54. Interview with Mrs. Elizabeth Roberts, a resident of the Medora area in the 1880s, on September 16, 1952, Putnam files, Theodore Roosevelt Collection, Houghton Library, Harvard University.

55. *St. Paul Pioneer Press*, June 28, 1883.

56. Hermann Hagedorn files, 332.H12p, file 578, Theodore Roosevelt Collection, Houghton Library, Harvard University; Hagedorn, *Roosevelt in the Bad Lands*, p, 63.

57. Hermann Hagedorn files, 332.H12p, files 1–28, Theodore Roosevelt Collection, Houghton Library, Harvard University.

58. Hermann Hagedorn files, 332.H12p, files 1–28, Theodore Roosevelt Collection, Houghton Library, Harvard University.

59. The consensus of reports on the shooting indicate that de Morès' men opened

fire first. However, the Marquis claimed that the hunters fired first. *St. Paul Pioneer Press*, June 28, 1883.

60. Hermann Hagedorn files, 332.H12p, file 512, Theodore Roosevelt Collection, Houghton Library, Harvard University.

61. Theodore Roosevelt to Alice Roosevelt, September 8, 1883, bMS AM 1541.9 (26–41), Sixteen Letters from Alice Lee Roosevelt to Theodore Roosevelt, Theodore Roosevelt Collection, Houghton Library, Harvard University.

62. Hermann Hagedorn files, 332.H12p, file 550, Theodore Roosevelt Collection, Houghton Library, Harvard University.

63. Interview with Joe Dietrich, April 29, 1922, L. F. Crawford Papers, North Dakota Historical Society.

64. Lang, *Ranching with Roosevelt*, p. 52.

65. Hermann Hagedorn files, 332.H12p, files 300–332, Theodore Roosevelt Collection, Houghton Library, Harvard University.

66. Hagedorn, *Roosevelt in the Bad Lands*, p. 21.

67. Lang, *Ranching with Roosevelt*, p. 76.

68. Lang, *Ranching with Roosevelt*, pp. 50–51.

69. Hermann Hagedorn files, 332.H12p, files 300–332, Theodore Roosevelt Collection, Houghton Library, Harvard University.

70. Hagedorn, *Roosevelt in the Bad Lands*, pp. 10–11; Hermann Hagedorn files, 332.H12p, file 713, Theodore Roosevelt Collection, Houghton Library, Harvard University.

71. Hagedorn, *Roosevelt in the Bad Lands*, pp. 14–15.

72. Putnam, *Theodore Roosevelt*, p. 321; Ray H. Mattison, *Roosevelt and the Stockmen's Association* (Theodore Roosevelt Nature and History Association, 1969), reprint from *North Dakota Historical Society Quarterly* 17, 2 (April 1950) and 17, 3 (July 1950), Theodore Roosevelt Collection, Harvard University, Houghton Library, pp. 4–5; interview with Sylvane Ferris, April 2, 1918, L. F. Crawford Papers, North Dakota Historical Society; interview with John W. Goodall, L. F. Crawford Papers, North Dakota Historical Society.

73. Morris, *The Rise of Theodore Roosevelt*, p. 191.

74. Hermann Hagedorn files, 332.H12p, file 412, Theodore Roosevelt Collection, Houghton Library, Harvard University.

75. Roosevelt, *Autobiography*, p. 110; Hermann Hagedorn files, 332.H12p, file 714, Theodore Roosevelt Collection, Houghton Library, Harvard University.

76. Theodore Roosevelt to Alice Roosevelt, September 8, 1883, bMS AM 1541.9 (26–41), Sixteen Letters from Alice Lee Roosevelt to Theodore Roosevelt, Theodore Roosevelt Collection, Houghton Library, Harvard University.

77. Hagedorn, *Roosevelt in the Bad Lands*, p. 11.

78. Hagedorn, *Roosevelt in the Bad Lands*, p. 16.

79. Hagedorn, *Roosevelt in the Bad Lands*, p. 12.

80. Theodore Roosevelt to Alice Roosevelt, September 8, 1883, bMS AM 1541.9

(26–41), Sixteen Letters from Alice Lee Roosevelt to Theodore Roosevelt, Theodore Roosevelt Collection, Houghton Library, Harvard University.

81. Hermann Hagedorn files, 332.H12p, file 1036, Theodore Roosevelt Collection, Houghton Library, Harvard University.

82. Hermann Hagedorn files, 332.H12p, file 1037 and 1037b, Theodore Roosevelt Collection, Houghton Library, Harvard University; Hermann Hagedorn files, 332. H12p, file 715, Theodore Roosevelt Collection, Houghton Library, Harvard University.

83. Most sources indicate that the hammer of the Winchester was broken, but a firearms expert whom Carlton Putnam consulted suggested that the broken part was more likely a firing pin. Townsend Whelen of *Sports Afield* magazine to Carlton Putnam, August 5, presumably in the mid-1950s, in the Theodore Roosevelt Collection, Houghton Library, Harvard University.

84. Hagedorn, *Roosevelt in the Bad Lands*, p. 12.

85. Theodore Roosevelt, *Ranch Life and the Hunting Trail* (New York: Bonanza Books, 1978 [1888]), p. 76.

86. Roosevelt, *Hunting Trips and Wilderness Hunter*, p. 20.

87. Roosevelt, *Hunting Trips and Wilderness Hunter*, p. 428.

88. Hagedorn, *Roosevelt in the Bad Lands*, p. 13.

89. Lang, *Ranching With Roosevelt*, p. 80; Roosevelt, *Autobiography*, pp. 104–106.

90. T. F. Roberts, "Pioneer Life in Western Dakota," *North Dakota Historical Society Quarterly* 15, 3 (Summer 1948): 226; Lang, *Ranching with Roosevelt*, pp. 49–50; Hagedorn, *Roosevelt in the Bad Lands*, pp. 15–16.

91. Hermann Hagedorn files, 332.H12p, file 743a, Theodore Roosevelt Collection, Houghton Library, Harvard University.

92. Lang, *Ranching with Roosevelt*, p. 77.

93. Lang, *Ranching with Roosevelt*, p. 67.

94. Hagedorn, *Roosevelt in the Bad Lands*, p. 14.

95. Hagedorn, *Roosevelt in the Bad Lands*, pp. 16–17.

96. Hagedorn, *Roosevelt in the Bad Lands*, pp. 17.

97. Lang, *Ranching with Roosevelt*, p. 100.

98. Lang, *Ranching with Roosevelt*, pp. 14–21.

99. Hermann Hagedorn files, 332.H12p, files 203–250, Theodore Roosevelt Collection, Houghton Library, Harvard University.

100. Lang, *Ranching with Roosevelt*, pp. 17–18.

101. Hermann Hagedorn files, 332.H12p, files 203–250, Theodore Roosevelt Collection, Houghton Library, Harvard University.

102. Lang, *Ranching with Roosevelt*, p. 100.

103. Lang, *Ranching with Roosevelt*, p. 101.

104. Lang, *Ranching with Roosevelt*, p. 101.

105. Phillip Ashton Rollins, *The Cowboy: An Unconventional History of Civilization on the Old-Time Cattle Range* (Norman: University of Oklahoma Press, 1997), pp. 166–167.

106. Abbott and Smith, *We Pointed Them North*, p. 126.

107. Abbott and Smith, *We Pointed Them North*, pp. 126–127.

108. Rollins, *The Cowboy*, p. 166.

109. Lang, *Ranching with Roosevelt*, p. 102.

110. After Gorringe fired Moore, Moore started a ranch on Gardner Creek, a couple miles above the mouth, that he later sold to the nephew of Lieutenant Edward Casey, who trained and led Cheyenne Indian scouts for the army and who ended his career as the last military fatality of the official Indian wars. Lang: "I believe in fact that Moore was backed in the ranch undertaking by Casey, at the outset, but am not sure." Lang interview in Hermann Hagedorn files, 332.H12p, file 547, Theodore Roosevelt Collection, Houghton Library, Harvard University. Lt. Casey lost both his own and his sister's money in cattle investments. For his story, see Roger Di Silvestro, *In the Shadow of Wounded Knee* (New York: Walker Books, 2006).

111. Lang, *Ranching with Roosevelt*, pp. 106–111. When president, Roosevelt wrote to a friend, "I am mighty glad you like what I have been doing in the governmental field. I do not have to tell you that my great hero is Abraham Lincoln, and I have wanted while President to be representative of the 'plain people' in the sense that he was—not, of course, with the genius and power that he was, but, according to my lights, along the same lines." Theodore Roosevelt to William Sewall, June 13, 1906, Theodore Roosevelt Collection, Library of Congress Manuscript Division.

112. Lang, *Ranching with Roosevelt*, p. 113.

113. Hagedorn, *Roosevelt in the Bad Lands*, pp. 23–24.

114. Hermann Hagedorn files, 332.H12p, file 420, Theodore Roosevelt Collection, Houghton Library, Harvard University; Theodore Roosevelt never cursed or swore: Wood, ed., *Roosevelt As We Knew Him*, pp. 20–22.

115. Hagedorn, *Roosevelt in the Bad Lands*, p. 27.

116. Lang, *Ranching with Roosevelt*, p. 113.

117. Hermann Hagedorn files, 332.H12p, file 412, Theodore Roosevelt Collection, Houghton Library, Harvard University.

118. Theodore Roosevelt to Alice Roosevelt, September 14, 1883, bMS AM 1541.9 (26–41), Sixteen Letters from Alice Lee Roosevelt to Theodore Roosevelt, Theodore Roosevelt Collection, Houghton Library, Harvard University.

119. Theodore Roosevelt to Alice Roosevelt, September 17, 1883, bMS AM 1541.9 (26–41), Sixteen Letters from Alice Lee Roosevelt to Theodore Roosevelt, Theodore Roosevelt Collection, Houghton Library, Harvard University.

120. Lang, *Ranching with Roosevelt*, p. 115.

121. Hermann Hagedorn, "Conversation at Dusk Along the Little Missouri," *Outlook*, September 24, 1919, pp. 137 ff. (the copy used as a source here is an electronic version from the Library of Congress that has no page numbers).

122. Putnam, *Theodore Roosevelt*, p. 198.

123. Jack Willis, *Roosevelt in the Rough* (New York: Ives Washburn, 1931), p. 237.

124. The description of the closing days of the bison hunt are from Roosevelt, *Hunting Trips and Wilderness Hunter*, pp. 251–261.

125. Theodore Roosevelt to Alice Roosevelt, September 8, 1883, bMS AM 1541.9 (26–41), Sixteen Letters from Alice Lee Roosevelt to Theodore Roosevelt, Theodore Roosevelt Collection, Houghton Library, Harvard University.

126. Theodore Roosevelt and George Bird Grinnell, eds. *American Big-Game Hunting: The Book of the Boone and Crockett Club* (New York: Forest and Stream Publishing Co., 1901), pp. 163–164.

127. Roosevelt, *Hunting Trips and Wilderness Hunter*, p. 254.

128. Hagedorn, *Roosevelt in the Bad Lands*, p. 36.

129. Roosevelt, *Hunting Trips and Wilderness Hunter*, p. 258.

130. Roosevelt, *Hunting Trips and Wilderness Hunter*, p. 258.

131. Roosevelt, *Hunting Trips and Wilderness Hunter*, pp. 259–260.

132. Lang, *Ranching with Roosevelt*, pp. 116–117.

133. Hagedorn, *Roosevelt in the Bad Lands*, pp. 42–44.

134. Hermann Hagedorn files, 332.H12p, file 723a, Theodore Roosevelt Collection, Houghton Library, Harvard University.

135. This is the story of the deal as told by Sylvane Ferris and Bill Merrifield to Hermann Hagedorn, who describes it this way in his book, *Roosevelt in the Bad Lands*, pp. 42–43. Lincoln Lang, in his book, *Ranching with Roosevelt*, p. 118, says that no check exchanged hands during Roosevelt's stay on the Lang cabin and that the money was given to them months later.

136. McCullough, *Mornings on Horseback*, p. 278.

137. Diary for 1881, closing page, Theodore Roosevelt Collection, Library of Congress Manuscript Division.

138. Hagedorn, *Roosevelt in the Bad Lands*, pp. 40–41.

139. Granville Stuart, *Forty Years on the Frontier, Part 2: Pioneering in Montana* (Lincoln: University of Nebraska Press, 1977), p. 175.

140. Hagedorn, *Roosevelt in the Bad Lands*, p. 44.

141. Roosevelt, *Hunting Trips and Wilderness Hunter*, p. 260.

142. Hagedorn, *Roosevelt in the Bad Lands*, p. 44.

143. Hagedorn, *Roosevelt in the Bad Lands*, p. 45.

144. Morris, *The Rise of Theodore Roosevelt*, p. 815

145. Theodore Roosevelt to Alice Roosevelt, September 20, 1883, bMS AM 1541.9 (26–41), Sixteen Letters from Alice Lee Roosevelt to Theodore Roosevelt, Theodore Roosevelt Collection, Houghton Library, Harvard University.

146. Hermann Hagedorn files, 332.H12p, file 1036, Theodore Roosevelt Collection, Houghton Library, Harvard University.

147. Hermann Hagedorn files, 332.H12p, file 715, Theodore Roosevelt Collection, Houghton Library, Harvard University.

148. Lang, *Ranching with Roosevelt*, p. 119.

149. Theodore Roosevelt to Alice Roosevelt, September 23, 1883, bMS AM 1541.9 (26–41), Sixteen Letters from Alice Lee Roosevelt to Theodore Roosevelt, Theodore Roosevelt Collection, Houghton Library, Harvard University.

150. Theodore Roosevelt to Alice Roosevelt, September 23, 1883, bMS AM 1541.9

(26–41), Sixteen Letters from Alice Lee Roosevelt to Theodore Roosevelt, Theodore Roosevelt Collection, Houghton Library, Harvard University.

4: LOVE AND LOSS

1. Sixteen Letters from Alice Lee Roosevelt to Theodore Roosevelt, bMS AM 1541.9 (26–41), Theodore Roosevelt Collection, Houghton Library, Harvard University.
2. Six Letters to Alice Lee Roosevelt 1878–1884, bMS A 1834 (954–959), Theodore Roosevelt Collection, Houghton Library, Harvard University.
3. Stacy A. Cordery, *Alice: Alice Roosevelt Longworth, from White House Princess to Washington Power Broker* (New York: Viking, 2007), p. 15.
4. Sixteen Letters from Alice Lee Roosevelt to Theodore Roosevelt, bMS AM 1541.9 (26–41), Theodore Roosevelt Collection, Houghton Library, Harvard University.
5. Cordery, *Alice*, p. 15.
6. Carlton Putnam, *Theodore Roosevelt, Volume One: The Formative Years, 1858–1886* (New York: Charles Scribner's Sons, 1958), pp. 382–383.
7. *New York Times*, February 13, 1884.
8. Putnam, *Theodore Roosevelt*, p. 386.
9. Putnam, *Theodore Roosevelt*, p. 386.
10. Cordery, *Alice*, pp. 15–16.
11. Diary entry February 14, 1884, Theodore Roosevelt Collection, Library of Congress Manuscript Division.
12. Anna Bulloch Gracie to Archibald Bulloch Sr., May 14, 1884 (reel 1), Theodore Roosevelt Collection, Library of Congress Manuscript Division.
13. Theodore Roosevelt, *In Memory of My Darling Wife Alice Hathaway Roosevelt and of My Beloved Mother Martha Bullock Roosevelt Who Died in the Same House and on the Same Day on February 14, 1884* (New York: G. P. Putnam's Sons, 1884), p. 28, Theodore Roosevelt Collection, Hougton Library, Harvard University. The *New York Times* editorial page on February 16, 1884, used the resolution to make a political statement on Roosevelt's behalf: "It is a tribute which is well deserved, and shows that more of the satisfying rewards of public life are to be won by fidelity to conviction than by the indirect methods that are too often considered necessary to political success."
14. James D. McCabe, *New York by Sunlight and Gaslight: A Work Descriptive of the Great American Metropolis* (n.p.: Edgewood Publishing Company, 1881), p. 625; *New York Times*, "Wife and Mother Buried Together," February 17, 1884, p. 3; Stacy A. Cordery, *Alice: Alice Roosevelt Longworth, from White House Princess to Washington Power Broker* (New York: Viking, 2007), p. 16.
15. Putnam, *Theodore Roosevelt*, pp. 387–389.
16. Roosevelt, *In Memory of My Darling Wife*, p. 7.
17. Roosevelt, *In Memory of My Darling Wife*, pp. 7–14.

18. Roosevelt, *In Memory of My Darling Wife*, pp. 22–23.

19. Roosevelt, *In Memory of My Darling Wife*, pp. 26–27. Funeral costs in the early 1880s in general were: rosewood coffin, $90 to $150, but if trimmed with velvet, could exceed $400. Eight coffin handles cost $10 to $20, and full-length handles along the sides cost $30. Engraved plates cost $1 to $12. A carriage ride to Green-Wood cost $7. A lot at Green-Wood, measuring 378 square feet, cost $500 to $1,000 but could be bought as half, third, or quarter lots; single graves cost $25. In all, with tombstone and other charges for church, undertaker, and cemetery, a funeral at Green-Wood might run $2,191. McCabe, *New York by Sunlight and Gaslight*, pp. 232–234.

20. Anna Bullock Gracie to Archibald Gracie, May 14, 1884 (reel 1), Theodore Roosevelt Collection, Library of Congress Manuscript Division.

21. Cordery, *Alice*, p. 17.

22. Theodore Roosevelt Collection, Houghton Library, Harvard University. The entry starts on the page for February 16 and extends to the page for February 17 and refers to the christening on that day. He may have written it over two days, or on the seventeenth, or even later in the week.

23. Theodore Roosevelt to Andrew Dickson White, February 18, 1884, *The Letters of Theodore Roosevelt*, ed. Elting E. Morison (Cambridge, MA: Harvard University Press, 1951), pp. 65–66.

24. Putnam, *Theodore Roosevelt*, p. 390.

25. Nicholas Roosevelt, *Theodore Roosevelt: The Man as I Knew Him* (New York: Dodd, Mead & Company, 1967), p. 29.

26. Roosevelt, *Theodore Roosevelt: The Man as I Knew Him*, p. 29.

27. Roosevelt, *Theodore Roosevelt: The Man as I Knew Him*, p. 33.

28. Roosevelt, *Theodore Roosevelt: The Man as I Knew Him*, p. 33. Corinne's close friend Fanny Parsons, on the way to dinner at Corinne's, told her husband, who had never met Corinne and her spouse, "Now, don't forget! Talk as loudly as you possibly can and answer your own questions!" (p. 34).

29. Roosevelt, *Theodore Roosevelt: The Man as I Knew Him*, p. 33.

30. Roosevelt, *Theodore Roosevelt: The Man as I Knew Him*, pp. 29–30.

31. Putnam, *Theodore Roosevelt*, p. 27. Fanny Parsons, perhaps five or six years younger than Anna, also as a child thought of Anna "only as a grownup, and remembered in particular 'a certain authoritative attitude which was never questioned.'" Roosevelt, *Theodore Roosevelt: The Man as I Knew Him*, p. 30.

32. Theodore Roosevelt to Corinne Roosevelt Robinson, July 1, 1888, *The Letters of Theodore Roosevelt*, ed. Elting E. Morison (Cambridge, MA: Harvard University Press, 1951), p. 61.

33. Cordery, *Alice*, p. 17.

34. Edmund Morris, *The Rise of Theodore Roosevelt* (New York: Modern Library, 2001), p. 237.

35. Sixteen letters from Alice Lee Roosevelt to Theodore Roosevelt, bMS AM 1541.9 (26–41), Theodore Roosevelt Collection, Houghton Library, Harvard University.

36. Hermann Hagedorn, *The Roosevelt Family of Sagamore Hill* (New York: The Macmillan Company, 1954), p. 9.

37. Cordery, *Alice*, p. 17.

38. Putnam, *Theodore Roosevelt*, p. 390.

39. Theodore Roosevelt to William Sewall, March 9, 1884, Theodore Roosevelt Collection, Library of Congress Manuscript Division.

40. Theodore Roosevelt to Carl Schurz, February 21, 1884, *The Letters of Theodore Roosevelt*, p. 66.

41. Putnam material, "Alice Lee" file, Theodore Roosevelt Collection, Houghton Library, Harvard University.

42. Morris, *The Rise of Theodore Roosevelt*, p. 238; Putnam, *Theodore Roosevelt*, p. 393.

43. Morris, *The Rise of Theodore Roosevelt*, p. 240; Putnam, *Theodore Roosevelt*, pp. 392–395.

44. *New York Times*, November 12, 1884. Roosevelt expressed these views in a speech at the Nineteenth Century Club after the presidential election and in part was justifying decisions he had made in support of the Republican candidate that year; consequently, his analysis of the party at that time might have been more moderate and even more reasoned than he might have expressed had he given a speech on the same subject in April 1884.

45. *New York Times*, November 12, 1884.

46. William Roscoe Thayer, *Theodore Roosevelt: An Intimate Biography* (New York: Grosset & Dunlap, 1919), pp. 46–47.

47. *New York Times*, November 12, 1884.

48. Putnam, *Theodore Roosevelt*, pp. 419–423.

49. Thayer, *Theodore Roosevelt: An Intimate Biography*, pp. 46–47.

50. Thayer, *Theodore Roosevelt: An Intimate Biography*, p. 51.

51. Theodore Roosevelt, *Ranch Life and the Hunting Trail* (New York: Bonanza Books, 1978), p. 59; Theodore Roosevelt to Simon Newton Dexter North, April 30, 1884, *The Letters of Theodore Roosevelt*, pp. 66–67.

52. Thayer, *Theodore Roosevelt: An Intimate Biography*, p. 45.

53. William Wingate Sewall. "As I Knew Him," *Forum* LXI, 5. (May 1919). The pages of the source copy used here, from a Library of Congress electronic archive, are unnumbered.

54. Frederick S. Wood, ed., *Roosevelt as We Knew Him: The Personal Recollections of One Hundred and Fifty of His Friends and Associates* (Philadelphia: The John C. Winston Company, 1927), p. 467.

55. Henry Collins Brown, *Valentine's Manual of Old New York* (Hastings-on-Hudson, NY: Valentine's Manual Inc., 1927), p. 16.

56. Corinne Roosevelt Robinson, *My Brother Theodore Roosevelt* (New York: Charles Scribner's Sons, 1921), pp. 124–126.

57. Putnam, *Theodore Roosevelt*, p. 414.

58. Theodore Roosevelt to Anna Roosevelt, June 8, 1884, *The Letters of Theodore Roosevelt*, p. 72.

59. Theodore Roosevelt to Anna Roosevelt, June 8, 1884, *The Letters of Theodore Roosevelt*, pp. 70–71.

60. Theodore Roosevelt to Anna Roosevelt, June 8, 1884, *The Letters of Theodore Roosevelt*, p. 71.

61. Theodore Roosevelt to Simon Newton Dexter North, April 30, 1884, *The Letters of Theodore Roosevelt*, pp. 66–67.

62. Morris, *The Rise of Theodore Roosevelt*, p. 259.

63. Theodore Roosevelt to Anna Roosevelt, June 8, 1884, *The Letters of Theodore Roosevelt*, p. 70.

5: UNDER WESTERN SKIES

1. Sean Dennis Cashman, *America in the Gilded Age* (New York: New York University Press, 1993), pp. 283–284.

2. G. Edward White, *The Eastern Establishment and the Western Experience: The West of Frederic Remington, Theodore Roosevelt, and Owen Wister* (New Haven: Yale University Press, 1968), p. 127.

3. Granville Stuart, *Forty Years on the Frontier*, Part 2: *Pioneering in Montana* (Lincoln: University of Nebraska Press, 1977), p. 188.

4. Phillip Ashton Rollins, *The Cowboy: An Unconventional History of Civilization on the Old-Time Cattle Range* (Norman: University of Oklahoma Press, 1997), pp. 21–22, 68–71.

5. Joseph Nimmo Jr., "The American Cowboy," *Harper's New Monthly Magazine*, (November 1886), p. 881.

6. David Dary, *Cowboy Culture: A Saga of Five Centuries* (Lawrence: University of Kansas Press, 1989), pp. 67–69.

7. Cashman, *America in the Gilded Age*, p. 286.

8. Dary, *Cowboy Culture* pp. 17, 18.

9. E. C. Abbott and Helena Huntington Smith, *We Pointed Them North: Recollections of a Cowpuncher* (Norman: University of Oklahoma Press, 1955), pp. 6–7.

10. Abbott and Smith, *We Pointed Them North*, pp. 5–6.

11. Abbott and Smith, *We Pointed Them North*, pp. 5–6.

12. Rollins, *The Cowboy*, p. 9.

13. Rollins, *The Cowboy*, p. 10.

14. Nimmo, "The American Cowboy," p. 881.

15. Nimmo, "The American Cowboy," p. 881.

16. Dary, *Cowboy Culture*, pp. 242–243.

17. Cashman, *America in the Gilded Age*, p. 286.

18. Rollins, *The Cowboy*, pp. 10–11.

19. David T. Courtwright, *Violent Land: Single Men and Social Disorder from the Frontier to the Inner City* (Cambridge, MA: Harvard University Press, 2000), p. 89.

20. Rollins, *The Cowboy*, p. 15.

21. Nimmo, "The American Cowboy," p. 883.

22. Abbott and Smith, *We Pointed Them North*, p. 191.

23. Robert G. Athearn, *Westward the Briton* (New York: Charles Scribner's Sons, 1953), p. 102; Nimmo, "The American Cowboy," p. 883.

24. Athearn, *Westward the Briton*, p. 103.

25. *New York Times*, "Paying Cattle Ranches," September 21, 1884.

26. *New York Times*, "Paying Cattle Ranches," September 21, 1884.

27. Abbott and Smith, *We Pointed Them North*, p. 4.

28. Athearn. *Westward the Briton*, p. 103.

29. Athearn. *Westward the Briton*, p. 105.

30. Hermann Hagedorn, *Roosevelt in the Bad Lands* (Boston: Houghton Mifflin Company, 1921) p. 254. The Badlands was a region of extremes, from summer heat waves reaching one hundred and twenty degrees in the shade to winter freezes down to sixty below zero, from prolonged droughts to flash floods. Lincoln A. Lang, *Ranching with Roosevelt* (Philadelphia: J. B. Lippincott Company, 1926), p. 41.

31. Frank Wilkeson, "Cattle-raising on the Plains," *Harper's New Monthly Magazine*, April 1886, p. 789.

32. Wilkeson, "Cattle-raising on the Plains," p. 789.

33. Wilkeson also noticed that the "cattle country" was not really the country of cattle. In 1880 the region encompassed by Montana, Wyoming, Colorado, New Mexico, Arizona, Utah, Idaho, Nevada, Oregon, and Washington held 1,786,262 cattle, which was 594,714 less than Illinois alone held. New York State in 1880 harbored 2,300,008 cattle—613,826 more than the western grazing grounds. Wilkeson, "Cattle-raising on the Plains," p. 790.

34. Lang, *Ranching with Roosevelt*, p. 338.

35. Theodore Roosevelt, *Ranch Life and the Hunting Trail* (New York: Bonanza Books, 1978), p. 18.

36. Wilkeson, "Cattle-raising on the Plains," p. 791.

37. Wilkeson, "Cattle-raising on the Plains," p. 792.

38. Courtwright, *Violent Land*, p. 95

39. Courtwright, *Violent Land*, p. 88.

40. Wallace Stegner, "Who Are the Westerners?" *American Heritage* 38, 8 (December 1987): 36.

41. Courtwright, *Violent Land*, p. 87.

42. Courtwright, *Violent Land*, p. 87.

43. Athearn, *Westward the Briton*, p. 114.

44. Courtwright, *Violent Land*, p. 47.

45. Courtwright, *Violent Land*, p. 48.

46. Courtwright, *Violent Land*, p. 48

47. Courtwright, *Violent Land*, pp. 2–3. "Nor is the carnage entirely in the past. Insofar as the frontier experience has become a foundation of the national self-image—that is, insofar as Americans continue to think a manly man is someone with a gun and

an attitude—it continues to influence the amount and type of violence in the United States, as well as our collective response to it." Courtwright, pp. 3–4.

48. Courtwright, *Violent Land*, p. 3.

49. Courtwright, *Violent Land*, p. 13.

50. Courtwright, *Violent Land*, pp. 3–4.

51. Abbott and Smith, *We Pointed Them North*, p. 26.

52. Hermann Hagedorn files, 332.H12p, file 734, Theodore Roosevelt Collection, Houghton Library, Harvard University.

53. Roosevelt, *Ranch Life*, p. 109.

54. Richard B. Townshend, *A Tenderfoot in Colorado* (Boulder: University of Colorado Press, 2008), pp. 16–17.

55. Courtwright, *Violent Land*, p. 34.

56. Hermann Hagedorn files, 332.H12p, files 1–28, Theodore Roosevelt Collection, Houghton Library, Harvard University.

57. Townshend, *A Tenderfoot in Colorado*, p. 216.

58. Courtwright, *Violent Land*, pp. 96–98.

59. Courtwright, *Violent Land*, pp. 151–150.

60. Abbott and Smith, *We Pointed Them North*, pp. 8, 188.

61. Townshend, *A Tenderfoot in Colorado*, p. 214.

62. William Hepworth Dixon, British traveler and historian, quoted in Athearn, *Westward the Briton*, p. 66.

63. Rollins, *The Cowboy*, pp. 83–84.

64. Rollins, *The Cowboy*, pp. 83–84.

65. Hagedorn, *Roosevelt in the Bad Lands*, pp. 326–27. Teddy Blue Abbott explained the cowboy's pragmatic outlook on religion: "You could pray all you damned pleased, but it wouldn't get you water where they wasn't water. Talk about trusting to Providence, hell, if I'd trusted to Providence I'd have starved to death." Abbott and Smith, *We Pointed Them North*, pp. 28–29.

66. Lang, *Ranching with Roosevelt*, pp. 161–162.

67. William Thompson Dantz, "Tales of the Roosevelt Country," *McClure's Magazine*, May 1925.

68. Hagedorn, *Roosevelt in the Bad Lands*, pp. 127–128.

69. Frank Greene to Hermann Hagedorn, July 18, 1916, Files 853–854, Hermann Hagedorn files, 332.H12p, Theodore Roosevelt Collection, Houghton Library, Harvard University.

70. Hermann Hagedorn files, 332.H12p, files 251–299, Theodore Roosevelt Collection, Houghton Library, Harvard University.

71. Hermann Hagedorn files, 332.H12p, files 251–299, Theodore Roosevelt Collection, Houghton Library, Harvard University.

72. Hagedorn, *Roosevelt in the Bad Lands*, pp. 128–129.

73. Hagedorn, *Roosevelt in the Bad Lands*, p. 129.

74. Hermann Hagedorn files, 332.H12p, file 734a, Theodore Roosevelt Collection, Houghton Library, Harvard University.

75. Hermann Hagedorn files, 332.H12p, files 1–28, Theodore Roosevelt Collection, Houghton Library, Harvard University.

76. *Bad Lands Cow Boy*, February 21, 1884.

77. Quoted in Hagedorn, *Roosevelt in the Bad Lands*, p. 65.

78. Lang, *Ranching with Roosevelt*, pp. 167–168.

79. *Bad Lands Cow Boy*, March 6, 1884, and March 27, 1884; subscription rate, February 21, 1884.

80. Lang, *Ranching with Roosevelt*, pp. 167–168.

81. *Bad Lands Cow Boy*, March 6, 1884, and March 27, 1884; subscription rate, February 21, 1884.

82. *Bad Lands Cow Boy*, February 28, 1884.

83. *Bad Lands Cow Boy*, February 28, 1884.

84. *Bad Lands Cow Boy*, March 27, 1884.

85. News of the association appeared in *Bad Lands Cow Boy*, March 6, March 13, and April 10, 1884.

86. *Bad Lands Cow Boy*, March 13, 1884.

87. Hagedorn, *Roosevelt in the Bad Lands*, p. 84.

88. Hagedorn, *Roosevelt in the Bad Lands*, pp. 93–92.

89. Hagedorn, *Roosevelt in the Bad Lands*, p. 84.

90. Hagedorn, *Roosevelt in the Bad Lands*, p. 84. The source for this story is Hagedorn, who routinely changed the names of characters Roosevelt knew or interacted with in the Badlands.

91. Hagedorn, *Roosevelt in the Bad Lands*, p. 86.

6: THE RANCHMAN

1. Hermann Hagedorn, *Roosevelt in the Bad Lands* (Boston: Houghton Mifflin Company, 1921), p. 90.

2. Hagedorn, *Roosevelt in the Bad Lands*, p. 136; Edmund Morris, *The Rise of Theodore Roosevelt* (New York: Modern Library, 2001), p. 266.

3. *Bad Lands Cow Boy*, June 26, 1884, and July 3, 1884.

4. Theodore Roosevelt, *An Autobiography* (New York: The Macmillan Company, 1913), p. 103.

5. Theodore Roosevelt, *Ranch Life and the Hunting Trail* (New York: Bonanza Books, 1978), p. 9.

6. Roosevelt, *Ranch Life*, pp. 9–10.

7. Dr. V. K. Stickney, "Early Days in North Dakota," *The Commercial West* 44, 2 (July 14, 1923): 24.

8. Interview on September 16, 1952, with Mrs. George Pelissier, a resident of the Medora area in the 1880s, Putnam material, Roosevelt Collection, Houghton Library, Harvard University.

9. Interview on September 13, 1952, with Ben Bird, who worked with Roosevelt on the 1885 autumn roundup, Putnam Material, Theodore Roosevelt Collection, Houghton Library, Harvard University.

10. Hermann Hagedorn files, 332.H12p, files 46–100, Theodore Roosevelt Collection, Houghton Library, Harvard University.

11. Margaret Roberts, "In the Bad Lands, When I Knew T.R.," *McCall's*, October 1919, p. 2.

12. Jack Willis, *Roosevelt in the Rough* (New York: Ives Washburn, 1931), p. 40. In what may have been an indirect comment on his childhood illnesses, Roosevelt, according to hunting guide Jack Willis, said one night at a campfire, "I don't know why it is but there is a quirk in all of us that makes us want to do the thing we are least fitted to do. Human nature seems to run that way. Many failures are attributable to that cause, which appears to be little understood. It takes a lot of grit and courage to overcome Nature's handicaps, but it can be done, sometimes. I have fewer qualifications for being a hunter than any man I know. Therefore I am determined to be a great hunter."

13. Hermann Hagedorn files, 332.H12p, file 1004a , Theodore Roosevelt Collection, Houghton Library, Harvard University.

14. Roberts, "In the Bad Lands, When I Knew T.R.," p. 2.

15. Interview with William Merrifield, June 1919, Hermann Hagedorn files, 332. H12p, Theodore Roosevelt Collection, Houghton Library, Harvard University; Bill Sewall, *Bill Sewall's Story of T.R.* (New York: Harper & Brothers, 1919), pp. 47–48.

16. Hagedorn, *Roosevelt in the Bad Lands*, p. 102.

17. Don Rickey Jr., *Cowboy Dress, Arms, Tools and Equipments as Used in the Little Missouri Range Country and the Medora Area, in the 1880s*, Theodore Roosevelt National Monument Park, File No. H2215, 1957, p. 28.

18. David McCullough, *Mornings on Horseback: The Story of an Extraordinary Family, a Vanished Way of Life, and the Unique Child Who Became Theodore Roosevelt* (New York: Simon and Schuster, 1981), p. 320 and personal observation of some of the items, which are on display at national park sites.

19. Phillip Ashton Rollins, *The Cowboy: An Unconventional History of Civilization on the Old-Time Cattle Range* (Norman: University of Oklahoma Press, 1997), pp. 103–105.

20. David Dary, *Cowboy Culture: A Saga of Five Centuries* (Lawrence: University of Kansas Press, 1989), p. 240; Rollins, *The Cowboy*, p. 106.

21. Rollins, *The Cowboy*, p. 157.

22. Rollins, *The Cowboy*, pp. 157–158.

23. Rickey, *Cowboy Dress*, p. 18.

24. Rickey, *Cowboy Dress*, pp. 20–21.

25. Rickey, *Cowboy Dress*, p. 9.

26. Rickey, *Cowboy Dress*, pp. 6, 10.

27. Rickey, *Cowboy Dress*, p. 10.

28. Rickey, *Cowboy Dress*, p. 13.

29. Rollins, *The Cowboy*, pp. 106–107.

30. Rollins, *The Cowboy*, p. 116.

31. Rickey, *Cowboy Dress*, p. 11.

32. *Bad Lands Cow Boy*, May 1, 1884.

33. Rickey, *Cowboy Dress*, p. 36.

34. Rickey, *Cowboy Dress*,, p. 26.

35. Richard B. Townshend, *A Tenderfoot in Colorado* (Boulder: University of Colorado Press, 2008), p. 84.

36. Putnam, *Theodore Roosevelt*, pp. 461–462.

37. Hermann Hagedorn files, 332.H12p, file 760, Theodore Roosevelt Collection, Houghton Library, Harvard University.

38. Donald Dresden, *The Marquis de Morès: Emperor of the Bad Lands* (Norman: University of Oklahoma Press, 1970), pp. 101–102.

39. Hagedorn, *Roosevelt in the Bad Lands*, p. 112; A. T. Packard. "Roosevelt's Ranching Days," *The Saturday Evening Post*, March 4, 1905, p. 13.

40. Interview with or letter from A. T. Packard, September 2, 1920, Hermann Hagedorn files, 332.H12p, file 861,Theodore Roosevelt Collection, Houghton Library, Harvard University; Packard. "Roosevelt's Ranching Days," p. 13; Hagedorn, *Roosevelt in the Bad Lands*, p. 112.

41. Dresden, *The Marquis de Morès*, p. 101–102.

42. *Bad Lands Cow Boy*, June 5, 1884, and March 20, 1884. In the barn Eaton planned to house registered Holstein milk cows he had bought for at least $250 each, making them the most valuable livestock in the area, as related in the *Cowboy* for April 24, 1884.

43. *Bad Lands Cow Boy*, June 5, 1884.

44. A. T. Packard. "Roosevelt's Ranching Days," p. 13; Hagedorn, *Roosevelt in the Bad Lands*, p. 112.

45. Hagedorn, *Roosevelt in the Bad Lands*, p. 91.

46. Hermann Hagedorn files, 332.H12p, file 469, Theodore Roosevelt Collection, Houghton Library, Harvard University.

47. Hagedorn, *Roosevelt in the Bad Lands*, pp. 93, 106.

48. Hagedorn, *Roosevelt in the Bad Lands*, p. 99.

49. Theodore Roosevelt to Henry Cabot Lodge, June 17, 1884, *The Letters of Theodore Roosevelt*, ed. Elting E. Morison (Cambridge, MA: Harvard University Press, 1951), p. 73. The St. Paul interview ran on June 10, and Roosevelt's reply to the *Evening Post* appeared on June 12. As he rode to the Langs' on the eleventh, it is difficult to sort out when the exchange of telegrams occurred between Roosevelt and the *Post*. Given that the Maltese Cross ranch was only a thirty-minute ride from Medora, one could speculate that he received the telegram and replied before leaving for the Langs'.

50. Theodore Roosevelt to Anna Roosevelt, June 17, 1884, *The Letters of Theodore Roosevelt*, p. 73.

51. Theodore Roosevelt to William Sewall, March 9, 1884, Theodore Roosevelt Collection, Library of Congress Manuscript Division.

52. Folder labeled "TR: Badlands, 1883–1886," boxed with the letters to Anna "Bamie" Roosevelt, Theodore Roosevelt Collection, Houghton Library, Harvard University.

53. Roosevelt's ranch ledger, Theodore Roosevelt Collection, Houghton Library, Harvard University.

54. Dary, *Cowboy Culture*, pp. 247–249.

55. T. F. Roberts, "Pioneer Life in Western Dakota," *North Dakota Historical Society Quarterly* 15, 2 (Spring 1948): 60–63.

56. Roosevelt's ranch ledger, Theodore Roosevelt Collection, Houghton Library, Harvard University.

57. Putnam, *Theodore Roosevelt*, pp. 337, 453.

58. Readers can see a facsimile of this contract in Stefan Lorant, *The Life and Times of Theodore Roosevelt* (Garden City, NY: Doubleday & Company, 1959), p. 212. The original is with the ranch ledger book at the Theodore Roosevelt Collection of Harvard University's Houghton Library.

59. Theodore Roosevelt, *An Autobiography* (New York: The Macmillan Company, 1913), p. 123; Lincoln A. Lang, *Ranching with Roosevelt* (Philadelphia: J. B. Lippincott Company, 1926), p. 151. The story of the hunt draws on Lang, pp. 150–160, except as otherwise noted.

60. The date on which the two departed for the Maddox ranch shortly after sunrise is uncertain; Roosevelt's diary suggests they may have left on Sunday, June 15, though Lang's memoir indicates the date was Saturday the fourteenth. Roosevelt, who was so precise in his recording of the killing of animals—he sometimes accounted not only for the number of animals killed but also for the type of ammunition used to do it—is strangely silent on the occasion of his first pronghorn kill. One might fear that Lang made up the story, were it not that Lang is otherwise a reliable source. Putnam, *Theodore Roosevelt*, p. 454; Roosevelt Diary, Theodore Roosevelt Collection, Library of Congress; diary transcript, Theodore Roosevelt Collection, Houghton Library, Harvard University; Lang, *Ranching with Roosevelt*, pp. 150–151.

61. Roger Di Silvestro, *The Endangered Kingdom: The Struggle to Save America's Wildlife* (New York: John Wiley and Sons, 1989), p. 54.

62. Lang, *Ranching with Roosevelt*, p. 156.

63. Roosevelt, *An Autobiography*, p. 123.

64. Theodore Roosevelt, *Outdoor Pastimes of an American Hunter* (Mechanicsburg, PA: Stackpole Books,), p. 142.

65. Hagedorn, *Roosevelt in the Bad Lands*, p. 96.

66. Theodore Roosevelt, *Ranch Life and the Hunting Trail* (New York: Bonanza Books, 1978), p. 81.

67. Mayne Reid, *The Boy Hunter, or Adventures in Search of a White Buffalo* (New York: Hurst and Company, 1889), pp. 36–37.

68. Hermann Hagedorn files, 332.H12p, file 769, Theodore Roosevelt Collection, Houghton Library, Harvard University.

69. Hermann Hagedorn files, 332.H12p, file 908, Theodore Roosevelt Collection, Houghton Library, Harvard University.

70. The *Bad Lands Cow Boy* would refer to Roosevelt showing up in full cowboy costume in the June 26, 1884, issue.

71. Roosevelt, *Ranch Life*, p. 59.

72. Theodore Roosevelt to Anna Roosevelt, June 17, 1884, *The Letters of Theodore Roosevelt*, p. 73.

73. Theodore Roosevelt to Anna Roosevelt, June 17, 1884, *The Letters of Theodore Roosevelt*, pp. 73, 74.

74. Theodore Roosevelt to Anna Roosevelt, June 17, 1884, *The Letters of Theodore Roosevelt*, p. 74.

75. Putnam, *Theodore Roosevelt*, p. 465.

76. *The New York Evening Post*, June 11, 1884.

77. Putnam, *Theodore Roosevelt*, p. 465.

78. Putnam, *Theodore Roosevelt*, p. 465.

79. Theodore Roosevelt to Henry Cabot Lodge, June 17, 1884, *The Letters of Theodore Roosevelt*, pp. 72–73.

80. Theodore Roosevelt to Henry Cabot Lodge, June 18, 1884, *The Letters of Theodore Roosevelt*, p. 74.

81. Theodore Roosevelt, *Hunting Trips of a Ranchman and The Wilderness Hunter* (New York: Modern Library, 2004), p. 193 (the following account of his trip is from this source, pp. 192–215, unless cited otherwise); Hagedorn, *Roosevelt in the Bad Lands*, pp. 98–99.

82. Theodore Roosevelt to Anna Roosevelt, June 23, 1884, *Letters from Theodore Roosevelt to Anna Roosevelt Cowles 1870–1918* (New York: Charles Scribner's Sons, 1924), p. 59.

83. Roosevelt, *Hunting Trips*, p. 193.

84. Roosevelt, *Ranch Life*, p. 40.

85. Roosevelt, *Hunting Trips*, p. 66. His diaries show that he nevertheless racked up a score against the birds, killing one curlew on June 13 and two on June 14. Diary, Theodore Roosevelt Collection, Library of Congress.

86. Roosevelt, *Hunting Trips*, p. 194.

87. Roosevelt, *Hunting Trips*, p. 195.

88. Roosevelt, *Hunting Trips*, pp. 195–196.

89. Roosevelt, *Hunting Trips*, p. 201.

90. The most common outer garment in the 1880s the Badlands area was a yellow slicker, called a "Fishbrand" or "Tower" slicker after the companies that made them, crafted from lightweight canvas or duck and waterproofed with linseed oil. Perhaps Roosevelt was carrying one of these. It would have had skirts that reached almost to the ankle, covering rider and saddle on horseback. The slickers cost up to four dollars. Rickey, *Cowboy Dress*, pp. 14–15.

91. Roosevelt, *Hunting Trips*, p. 203.

92. Roosevelt, *Hunting Trips*, p. 210.

93. Roosevelt, *Hunting Trips*, pp. 214–215.

94. Hermann Hagedorn files, 332.H12p, William Merrifield to Hermann Hagedorn, June 13, 1919, file 1060, Theodore Roosevelt Collection, Houghton Library, Harvard University; Hermann Hagedorn files, 332.H12p, file 760, Theodore Roosevelt Collection, Houghton Library, Harvard University.

95. *Bad Lands Cow Boy*, June 26, 1884.

96. Roberts, "Pioneer Life in Western Dakota," pp. 235–236.

97. This discussion of the vigilante episode draws from Putnam, *Theodore Roosevelt*, pp. 460–461. For details on the vigilantes and the events leading to their formation, see Granville Stuart, *Forty Years on the Frontier*, Part 2: *Pioneering in Montana* (Lincoln: University of Nebraska Press, 1977).

98. Roosevelt, *An Autobiography*, p. 124.

7: THE POLITICIAN

1. Theodore Roosevelt to William Sewall, July 6, 1884, Theodore Roosevelt Collection, Library of Congress Manuscript Division.

2. Phillip Ashton Rollins, *The Cowboy: An Unconventional History of Civilization on the Old-Time Cattle Range* (Norman: University of Oklahoma Press, 1997), pp. 208–209.

3. Interview with William Merrifield, June 1919, Hermann Hagedorn files, 332. H12p, Theodore Roosevelt Collection, Houghton Library, Harvard University.

4. Corinne Roosevelt Robinson, *My Brother Theodore Roosevelt* (New York: Charles Scribner's Sons, 1921), p. 44.

5. Robinson, *My Brother Theodore Roosevelt*, p. 44.

6. Sylvia Jukes Morris, *Edith Kermit Roosevelt* (New York: Vintage Books, 1990), pp. 41–42.

7. Morris, *Edith Kermit Roosevelt*, p. 9.

8. Morris, *Edith Kermit Roosevelt*, p. 13.

9. Morris, *Edith Kermit Roosevelt*, p. 12; Nicholas Roosevelt, *Theodore Roosevelt: The Man as I Knew Him* (New York: Dodd, Mead & Company, 1967), p. 21.

10. Hermann Hagedorn, *The Roosevelt Family of Sagamore Hill* (New York: The Macmillan Company, 1954), p. 10.

11. Morris, *Edith Kermit Roosevelt*, p. 20.

12. Morris, *Edith Kermit Roosevelt*, pp. 26–27.

13. Roosevelt, *Theodore Roosevelt: The Man as I Knew Him*, p. 21.

14. Morris, *Edith Kermit Roosevelt*, pp. 57–59.

15. Edmund Morris, *The Rise of Theodore Roosevelt* (New York: Modern Library, 2001), p. 74.

16. Morris, *The Rise of Theodore Roosevelt*, p. 74.

17. Anna Roosevelt Cowles letters, Theodore Roosevelt Collection, Houghton Library, Harvard University.

18. Morris, *Edith Kermit Roosevelt*, p. 64.

19. Carlton Putnam, *Theodore Roosevelt, Volume One: The Formative Years, 1858–1886* (New York: Charles Scribner's Sons, 1958), p. 210.

20. Morris, *Edith Kermit Roosevelt*, p. 69.

21. Morris, *Edith Kermit Roosevelt*, p. 69.

22. Morris, *Edith Kermit Roosevelt*, p. 70.

23. Morris, *Edith Kermit Roosevelt*, pp. 72–73.

24. Interview with William Merrifield, June 1919, Hermann Hagedorn files, 332. H12p, Theodore Roosevelt Collection, Houghton Library, Harvard University.

25. Michael Teague, *Mrs. L: Conversations with Alice Roosevelt Longworth* (Garden City, NY: Doubleday & Company, 1981), p. 5.

26. Teague, *Mrs. L: Conversations with Alice Roosevelt Longworth*, p. 10.

27. Teague, *Mrs. L: Conversations with Alice Roosevelt Longworth*, p. 22.

28. Teague, *Mrs. L: Conversations with Alice Roosevelt Longworth*, p. 4.

29. Teague, *Mrs. L: Convsersations with Alice Roosevelt Longworth*, p. 5.

30. Putnam, *Theodore Roosevelt*, pp. 390–391.

31. Putnam, *Theodore Roosevelt*, p. 391.

32. Teague, *Mrs. L: Conversations with Alice Roosevelt Longworth*, p. 16.

33. Putnam, *Theodore Roosevelt*, pp. 465–467.

34. Anonymous, "In the Public Eye," *Munsey's Magazine*, June 1897, p. 438.

35. Putnam, *Theodore Roosevelt*, p. 467.

36. Theodore Roosevelt to Henry Cabot Lodge, July 28, 1884, *The Letters of Theodore Roosevelt*, ed. Elting E. Morison (Cambridge, MA: Harvard University Press, 1951), p. 75.

37. Theodore Roosevelt to Henry Cabot Lodge, July 28, 1884, *The Letters of Theodore Roosevelt*, p. 75.

38. Putnam, *Theodore Roosevelt*, p. 464.

39. Owen Wister, *Roosevelt: The Story of a Friendship, 1880–1919* (New York: The Macmillan Company, 1930), p. 26.

40. William Roscoe Thayer, *Theodore Roosevelt: An Intimate Biography* (New York: Grosset & Dunlap, 1919), pp. 51–55.

41. Morris, *Edith Kermit Roosevelt*, p. 77; Henry Cabot Lodge, *A Memorial to Theodore Roosevelt* (Albany: Authorized by the State Legislature, 1919), p. 12.

42. Theodore Roosevelt, *Ranch Life and the Hunting Trail* (New York: Bonanza Books, 1978), p. 116.

43. Paul Russell Cutright, *Theodore Roosevelt: The Making of a Conservationist* (Urbana: University of Illinois Press, 1985), p. 125.

44. Putnam, *Theodore Roosevelt*, p. 154.

45. William Sewall, *Bill Sewall's Story of T.R.* (New York: Harper & Brothers, 1919), pp. 3–4.

46. Putnam files, "Sewall Correspondence," Theodore Roosevelt Collection, Houghton Library, Harvard University.

47. Putnam files, "Sewall Correspondence," Theodore Roosevelt Collection, Houghton Library, Harvard University.

48. Putnam files, "Sewall Correspondence," Theodore Roosevelt Collection, Houghton Library, Harvard University.

49. Theodore Roosevelt to William Sewall, July 14, 1884, Theodore Roosevelt Collection, Library of Congress Manuscript Division.

50. William Sewall, *Bill Sewall's Story of T.R.* (New York: Harper & Brothers, 1919), p. 14.

8: A TIME OF PREPARATION

1. *Bad Lands Cow Boy*, September 25, 1884.

2. William Sewall, *Bill Sewall's Story of T.R.* (New York: Harper & Brothers, 1919), p. 17.

3. Roosevelt may have resented Sewall's comment enough to remember it when writing his first book on ranching in the Badlands, in which he would declare, "A traveler seeing it for the first time is especially struck by its look of parched, barren desolation; he can with difficulty believe that it will support cattle at all." Theodore Roosevelt, *Ranch Life and the Hunting Trail* (New York: Bonanza Books, 1978), p. 2.

4. *Bad Lands Cow Boy*, July 31, 1884.

5. Hermann Hagedorn, *Roosevelt in the Bad Lands* (Boston: Houghton Mifflin Company, 1921), p. 162; Carlton Putnam, *Theodore Roosevelt, Volume One: The Formative Years, 1858–1886* (New York: Charles Scribner's Sons, 1958), p. 471, footnote.

6. William Sewall to Sam Sewall, August 17, 1884, in Ray H. Mattison, ed., "Life at Roosevelt's Elkhorn Ranch—the Letters of William W. and Mary Sewall," reprint of *North Dakota Historical Society Quarterly* 27, 3–4 (Summer and Fall 1960): 5, Theodore Roosevelt Collection, Harvard University, Houghton Library.

7. Theodore Roosevelt to Anna Roosevelt, August 12, 1884, file of Anna Roosevelt Cowles letters, Theodore Roosevelt Collection, Houghton Library, Harvard University.

8. Theodore Roosevelt to Anna Roosevelt, August 12, 1884, Anna Roosevelt Cowles, *Letters from Theodore Roosevelt to Anna Roosevelt Cowles 1870–1918* (New York: Charles Scribner's Sons, 1924), pp. 60–61.

9. Hagedorn, *Roosevelt in the Bad Lands*, p. 161.

10. William Sewall to Sam Sewall, August 17, 1884, Putnam Papers, Theodore Roosevelt Collection, Houghton Library, Harvard University.

11. William Sewall to Sam Sewall, August 17, 1884, Putnam Papers, Theodore Roosevelt Collection, Houghton Library, Harvard University.

12. Hagedorn, *Roosevelt in the Bad Lands*, pp. 163–164.

13. Hagedorn, *Roosevelt in the Bad Lands*, pp. 163–164.

14. *Bad Lands Cow Boy*, August 7, 1884.

15. Lincoln A. Lang, *Ranching with Roosevelt* (Philadelphia: J. B. Lippincott Company, 1926), p. 166.

16. Lang, *Ranching with Roosevelt*, p. 167.

17. Jerry Paddock was rumored to be on the Strangler hit list, but his current position with the Marquis de Morès protected him. Hagedorn, *Roosevelt in the Bad Lands*, pp. 157–158.

18. Clyde A. Milner II and Carol A. O'Conner, *As Big as the West: The Pioneer Life of Granville Stuart* (New York: Oxford University Press, 2009), p. 240. Roosevelt estimated that the Stranglers killed around sixty people—"not, however, with the best judgment in all cases" (Theodore Roosevelt, *Ranch Life and the Hunting-Trail* [New York: Bonanza Books, 1978], p. 14). Milner and O'Conner, p. 248, put the number at around twenty. The Stranglers expenses, estimated at $2,137, may have been paid in part by the Montana Stockgrowers Association (Milner and O'Conner, pp. 241–242). Vigilantism suffered from serious flaws. For example, if a man who killed someone was not lynched but allowed to stand trial in court, a presumption began to arise that the killer must not be guilty of murder, or the vigilantes would have hung him, a logic that "vastly increased the difficulty of getting juries to convict. Popular criminals are quite sure to get off, and the ordinary law becomes glaringly ineffective and sinks into something very like contempt, while the lynchers alone are dreaded. And this very dread increases crime, because horse-thieves and cattle-thieves, when pursued, know they will probably be lynched, and never hesitate to shoot, thinking they may as well be hanged for killing a man as for killing a calf. Every thief becomes a potential murderer, and goes armed. Peaceful citizens arm themselves in defence of their lives and property, and, as collisions will occur, crimes of violence naturally abound. The remedy is worse than the disease." Richard B. Townshend, *A Tenderfoot in Colorado* (Boulder: University of Colorado Press, 2008), p. 130.

19. Roosevelt, *Hunting Trips of a Ranchman and The Wilderness Hunter*, pp. 75–76.

20. Hagedorn, *Roosevelt in the Bad Lands*, p. 164.

21. Theodore Roosevelt, *Outdoor Pastimes of an American Hunter* (Mechanicsburg, PA: Stackpole Books, 1990 [1905]), p. 275.

22. Roosevelt, *Ranch Life and the Hunting Trail*, p. 150.

23. William Sewall to Sam Sewall, August 17, 1884, Putnam Papers, Theodore Roosevelt Collection, Houghton Library, Harvard University.

24. William Sewall to Sam Sewall, August 17, 1884, Putnam Papers, Theodore Roosevelt Collection, Houghton Library, Harvard University.

25. Putnam, *Theodore Roosevelt*, p. 472.

26. William Wingate Sewall, "As I Knew Him," *Forum* LXI, 5 (May 1919). The pages of the source copy used here, from a Library of Congress electronic archive, are unnumbered.

27. Roosevelt, *Outdoor Pastimes*, p. 147.

28. Hermann Hagedorn files, 332.H12p, file 406, Theodore Roosevelt Collection, Houghton Library, Harvard University.

29. Hermann Hagedorn files, 332.H12p, file 575, Theodore Roosevelt Collection, Houghton Library, Harvard University.

30. Hermann Hagedorn files, 332.H12p, file 575, Theodore Roosevelt Collection, Houghton Library, Harvard University.

31. Hagedorn, *Roosevelt in the Bad Lands*, pp. 164–165.

32. Theodore Roosevelt to Henry Cabot Lodge, August 12, 1884, *The Letters of Theodore Roosevelt*, p. 76.

33. Theodore Roosevelt to Anna Roosevelt, August 12, 1884, *Letters from Theodore Roosevelt to Anna Roosevelt Cowles*, p. 61.

34. Hagedorn, *Roosevelt in the Bad Lands*, pp. 165–166.

35. Hagedorn, *Roosevelt in the Bad Lands*, p. 169.

36. Theodore Roosevelt to Anna Roosevelt, August 12, 1884, *Letters from Theodore Roosevelt to Anna Roosevelt Cowles*, p. 60.

37. Theodore Roosevelt to Anna Roosevelt, August 12, 1884, *Letters from Theodore Roosevelt to Anna Roosevelt Cowles*, p. 61.

38. Roosevelt, *Hunting Trips*, p. 130.

39. Roosevelt, *Hunting Trips*, p. 42.

40. Roosevelt, *Hunting Trips*, p. 192. Roosevelt refers to riding Manitou in what can only be June 1884. Sewall told Hagedorn that Roosevelt bought the horse from Bill Jones; Files 251–299, Hermann Hagedorn files, 332.H12p, Theodore Roosevelt Collection, Houghton Library, Harvard University.

41. Roosevelt, *Hunting Trips*, pp. 41–42.

42. The date of the incident in Mingusville is unknown. Roosevelt is vague about it in his autobiography. Hagedorn thought it may have occurred in June 1884, which seems unlikely given the activities Roosevelt recorded in his diary for that month; Putnam thought it might have been in April 1885; Morris puts it in August 1884, which seems to make sense, because Roosevelt in the autobiography says he was looking for stray horses at the time, which, given Roosevelt's gift for putting a touch of rugged spin on his tales, suggests the incident may have occurred while he was trying to line up horses for the Bighorn Mountain hunt, especially as he was wandering widely at that time. The account here is drawn from Theodore Roosevelt, *An Autobiography* (New York: The Macmillan Company, 1913), pp. 135–136.

43. Roosevelt wrote in his autobiography that the incident took place in a saloon that occupied the ground floor of the hotel, but at least one Badlands resident said in later years that the hotel was only a one-and-a-half-story frame house that had no saloon; Frank Greene to Hermann Hagedorn, October 5, 1920, Files 851–852, Hermann Hagedorn files, 332.H12p, Theodore Roosevelt Collection, Houghton Library, Harvard University. Roosevelt may not have wanted to admit to going into a saloon—as president he was accused of drunkenness by various political enemies even though he never drank more than lightly—and may have finessed the issue by saying the bar was in the hotel; on the other hand, he actively avoided the saloons in Medora, so it seems unlikely he would enter one willingly in another town, especially after he heard shots inside.

44. Roosevelt, *An Autobiography*, p. 136.

45. Frank Greene to Hermann, October 5, 1920, Hermann Hagedorn files, 332.H12p, Files 851–852, Theodore Roosevelt Collection, Houghton Library, Harvard University.

46. *Bad Lands Cow Boy*, August 7, 1884; the item originally was published in the *New York Tribune*, July 28, 1884.

47. Theodore Roosevelt to Anna Roosevelt, August 12, 1884, *Letters from Theodore Roosevelt to Anna Roosevelt Cowles*, p. 61.

48. Roosevelt, *Hunting Trips*, pp. 35–36.

49. Frederick S. Wood, ed., *Roosevelt as We Knew Him: The Personal Recollections of One Hundred and Fifty of His Friends and Associates* (Philadelphia: The John C. Winston Company, 1927), p. 223.

50. Roosevelt, *Outdoor Pastimes*, p. 162.

51. Roosevelt, *Hunting Trips*, pp. 34–35.

52. *The Bad Lands Cow Boy*, July 17, 1884.

53. *Bad Lands Cow Boy*, August 21, 1884, and September 4, 1884.

54. Roosevelt, *Hunting Trips*, p. 759.

55. Roosevelt, *Hunting Trips*, pp. 242–243.

56. Roosevelt, *Hunting Trips*, p. 133.

57. Roosevelt, *Hunting Trips*, p. 134.

58. Roosevelt, *Hunting Trips*, p. 136.

59. Roosevelt, *Hunting Trips*, p. 286.

60. Roosevelt, *Hunting Trips*, p. 489. See also pp. 286–288.

61. Roosevelt, *Hunting Trips*, p. 54.

62. Roosevelt, *Hunting Trips*, p. 58.

63. Theodore Roosevelt and George Bird Grinnell, eds., *American Big-Game Hunting: The Book of the Boone and Crockett Club* (New York: Forest and Stream Publishing Co., 1901), p. 136.

64. Roosevelt, *Hunting Trips*, p. 348.

65. Roosevelt, *Outdoor Pastimes*, p. 238.

66. Roosevelt and Grinnell, eds., *American Big-Game Hunting*, pp. 129–130; Roosevelt, *Outdoor Pastimes*, p. 145.

67. Roosevelt, *Hunting Trips*, p. 71.

68. Roosevelt, *Outdoor Pastimes*, p. 239.

69. William Sewall to Sam Sewall, September 14, 1884, in Mattison, "Life at Roosevelt's Elkhorn Ranch," p. 7, Theodore Roosevelt Collection, Harvard University, Houghton Library.

70. Roosevelt, *Hunting Trips*, p. 163.

71. Roosevelt, *Outdoor Pastimes*, p. 255.

72. Sewall, *Bill Sewall's Story of T.R.*, pp. 47–48.

73. Edmund Morris, *The Rise of Theodore Roosevelt* (New York: Modern Library, 2001), p. 277.

74. Theodore Roosevelt, *In Memory of My Darling Wife Alice Hathaway Roosevelt and of My Beloved Mother Martha Bullock Roosevelt* (New York: G. P. Putnam's Sons, 1884), pp. 3–4, Theodore Roosevelt Collection, Houghton Library, Harvard University.

75. *Letters from Theodore Roosevelt to Anna Roosevelt Cowles*, p. 62.

76. *Letters from Theodore Roosevelt to Anna Roosevelt Cowles*, p. 62. Roosevelt seemed to delight in his cowboy garb. He wrote much the same description of himself to Henry Cabot Lodge in a letter dated August 12, 1884. *The Letters of Theodore Roosevelt*, ed. Elting E. Morison (Cambridge, MA: Harvard University Press, 1951), p. 77.

9: GRIZZLY HUNT

1. Wagon drivers were called "teamsters." A teamster who took a regular job driving freight wagons was called a "freighter." A man who drove mules was a mule "skinner," but a man who drove oxen was a "bull whacker." Phillip Ashton Rollins, *The Cowboy: An Unconventional History of Civilization on the Old-Time Cattle Range* (Norman: University of Oklahoma Press, 1997), p. 198.

2. T. F. Roberts, "Pioneer Life in Western Dakota," *North Dakota Historical Society Quarterly* 15, 3 (Summer 1948): 227–228.

3. Hermann Hagedorn, *Roosevelt in the Bad Lands* (Boston: Houghton Mifflin Company, 1921), p. 176.

4. Hagedorn, *Roosevelt in the Bad Lands*, p. 176.

5. Hermann Hagedorn files, 332.H12p, file 479, Theodore Roosevelt Collection, Houghton Library, Harvard University.

6. Theodore Roosevelt, *Hunting Trips of a Ranchman and The Wilderness Hunter* (New York: The Modern Library, 2004), p. 47.

7. Hermann Hagedorn files, 332.H12p, file 333, Theodore Roosevelt Collection, Houghton Library, Harvard University.

8. Carlton Putnam, *Theodore Roosevelt, Volume One: The Formative Years, 1858–1886* (New York: Charles Scribner's Sons, 1958), pp. 474, 489.

9. Theodore Roosevelt, *Outdoor Pastimes of an American Hunter* (Mechanicsburg, PA: Stackpole Books, 1990 [1905]), p. 157.

10. Roosevelt, *Outdoor Pastimes of an American Hunter*, p. 157.

11. Roosevelt, *Hunting Trips*, p. 40.

12. Private Diary, Theodore Roosevelt Collection, Houghton Library, Harvard University.

13. Private Diary, Theodore Roosevelt Collection, Houghton Library, Harvard University.

14. Private Diary, Theodore Roosevelt Collection, Houghton Library, Harvard University.

15. Roosevelt, *Hunting Trips*, pp. 119–120.

16. Roosevelt, *Hunting Trips*, p. 120.

17. Roosevelt, *Hunting Trips*, p. 120.

18. Lincoln A. Lang, *Ranching with Roosevelt* (Philadelphia: J. B. Lippincott Company, 1926), p. 168.

19. Roosevelt, *Hunting Trips*, pp. 118–119.

20. Private Diary and Herman Hagedorn files, 332.H12p, files 333–334, Theodore Roosevelt Collection, Houghton Library, Harvard University.

21. Roosevelt, *Hunting Trips*, p. 122.

22. Private Diary, Theodore Roosevelt Collection, Houghton Library, Harvard University.

23. Roosevelt, *Hunting Trips*, p. 122.

24. Hermann Hagedorn files, 332.H12p, files 333–334, Theodore Roosevelt Collection, Houghton Library, Harvard University.

25. Hermann Hagedorn files, 332.H12p, files 333–334, Theodore Roosevelt Collection, Houghton Library, Harvard University.

26. Putnam, *Theodore Roosevelt*, p. 476.

27. Roosevelt, *Hunting Trips*, p. 122.

28. Roosevelt, *Hunting Trips*, p. 123.

29. Jack Willis, *Roosevelt in the Rough* (New York: Ives Washburn, 1931), pp. 54–55.

30. Roosevelt, *Outdoor Pastimes*, p. 174.

31. Private Diary, Theodore Roosevelt Collection, Houghton Library, Harvard University.

32. Private Diary, Theodore Roosevelt Collection, Houghton Library, Harvard University.

33. Hermann Hagedorn files, 332.H12p, file 338, Theodore Roosevelt Collection, Harvard University, Houghton Library.

34. Rollins, *The Cowboy*, pp. 67–68.

35. Hermann Hagedorn files, 332.H12p, file 339, Theodore Roosevelt Collection, Houghton Library, Harvard University.

36. Private Diary, Theodore Roosevelt Collection, Houghton Library, Harvard University.

37. Roosevelt, *Hunting Trips*, p. 237.

38. Theodore Roosevelt to Anna Roosevelt, August 24, 1884, *Letters from Theodore Roosevelt to Anna Roosevelt Cowles 1870–1918* (New York: Charles Scribner's Sons, 1924), p. 63.

39. Theodore Roosevelt to Anna Roosevelt, August 24, 1884, *Letters from Theodore Roosevelt to Anna Roosevelt Cowles*, p. 65.

40. Theodore Roosevelt to Henry Cabot Lodge, August 24, 1884, *The Letters of Theodore Roosevelt*, ed. Elting E. Morison (Cambridge, MA: Harvard University Press, 1951), p. 80.

41. Hermann Hagedorn files, 332.H12p, file 335, Theodore Roosevelt Collection, Houghton Library, Harvard University.

42. Putnam, *Theodore Roosevelt*, p. 475. This chapter draws on descriptions of the expedition left by both Roosevelt and Merrifield. Merrifield's version usually leaves him looking quite heroic. But whether Roosevelt's accounts are any more accurate is hard to assess. He wrote his account within months of the expedition and kept a diary during the trip, while Merrifield gave his account to Hermann Hagedorn in interviews thirty-five years later. But Roosevelt also took literary license in his stories for the sake of narrative flow. For example, in *Hunting Trips of a Ranchman* he introduces the Wyoming hunt in this way (p. 268): "During last summer we found

it necessary to leave my ranch on the Little Missouri and take quite a long trip through the cattle country of Southeastern Montana and Northern Wyoming; and having come to the foot of the Bighorn Mountains, we took a fortnight's hunt through them after elk and bear." In this way, he gave the impression that he had hunted in the mountains opportunistically, because he just happened to be there on other business, when in fact he went there strictly to hunt. Such minor distortions appear throughout his accounts.

43. Roosevelt, *Outdoor Pastimes*, pp. 157–158.

44. Roosevelt, *Outdoor Pastimes*, p. 158.

45. Roosevelt, *Outdoor Pastimes*, p. 158.

46. Roosevelt, *Hunting Trips*, p. 174.

47. Roosevelt, *Hunting Trips*, pp. 60–61.

48. Roosevelt, *Hunting Trips*, p. 262.

49. Willis, *Roosevelt in the Rough*, p. 55.

50. Roosevelt, *Hunting Trips*, p. 272.

51. Private Diary, Theodore Roosevelt Collection, Houghton Library, Harvard University.

52. Private Diary, Theodore Roosevelt Collection, Houghton Library, Harvard University.

53. Roosevelt, *Hunting Trips*, p. 45.

54. Private Diary, Theodore Roosevelt Collection, Houghton Library, Harvard University.

55. Hermann Hagedorn files, 332.H12p, files 336–337, Theodore Roosevelt Collection, Houghton Library, Harvard University.

56. Private Diary, Theodore Roosevelt Collection, Houghton Library, Harvard University.

57. Hermann Hagedorn files, 332.H12p, file 344, Theodore Roosevelt Collection, Houghton Library, Harvard University.

58. Hermann Hagedorn files, 332.H12p, file 344, Theodore Roosevelt Collection, Houghton Library, Harvard University.

59. Private Diary, Theodore Roosevelt Collection, Houghton Library, Harvard University.

60. Hermann Hagedorn files, 332.H12p, file 352, Theodore Roosevelt Collection, Houghton Library, Harvard University.

61. Theodore Roosevelt Collection, Houghton Library, Harvard University, Hermann Hagedorn files, 332.H12p, file 353.

62. Private Diary, Theodore Roosevelt Collection, Houghton Library, Harvard University.

63. Hermann Hagedorn files, 332.H12p, file 357, Theodore Roosevelt Collection, Houghton Library, Harvard University.

64. Private Diary, Theodore Roosevelt Collection, Houghton Library, Harvard University; Roosevelt, *Hunting Trips*, p. 269.

65. Roosevelt, *Hunting Trips*, pp. 270–271.

66. Private Diary and Hermann Hagedorn files, 332.H12p, file 356, Theodore Roosevelt Collection, Houghton Library, Harvard University.

67. Roosevelt, *Hunting Trips*, p. 271.

68. Roosevelt, *Hunting Trips*, pp. 271–272.

69. Roosevelt, *Hunting Trips*, p. 274.

70. Hermann Hagedorn files, 332.H12p, file 360, Theodore Roosevelt Collection, Houghton Library, Harvard University.

71. Roosevelt, *Hunting Trips*, p. 282.

72. Private Diary, Theodore Roosevelt Collection, Houghton Library, Harvard University.

73. Private Diary, Theodore Roosevelt Collection, Houghton Library, Harvard University.

74. Private Diary, Theodore Roosevelt Collection, Houghton Library, Harvard University.

75. Roosevelt, *Hunting Trips*, p. 281.

76. Roosevelt, *Hunting Trips*, pp. 282–283.

77. Roosevelt, *Hunting Trips*, p. 281.

78. Private Diary, Theodore Roosevelt Collection, Houghton Library, Harvard University.

79. Private Diary, Theodore Roosevelt Collection, Houghton Library, Harvard University.

80. Hermann Hagedorn files, 332.H12p, file 351, Theodore Roosevelt Collection, Houghton Library, Harvard University.

81. Edmund Morris, *The Rise of Theodore Roosevelt* (New York: Modern Library, 2001), p. 280.

82. Interview with William Merrifield, June 1919, Hermann Hagedorn files, 332. H12p, Theodore Roosevelt Collection, Houghton Library, Harvard University.

83. Hermann Hagedorn files, 332.H12p, file 349, Theodore Roosevelt Collection, Houghton Library, Harvard University.

84. Roosevelt, *Hunting Trips*, pp. 283–284.

85. Roosevelt, *Hunting Trips*, p. 284.

86. Roosevelt, *Hunting Trips*, p. 285.

87. Roosevelt, *Hunting Trips*, p. 285.

88. Hermann Hagedorn files, 332.H12p, file 364, Theodore Roosevelt Collection, Houghton Library, Harvard University.

89. Roosevelt, *Hunting Trips*, pp. 299–300.

90. Roosevelt, *Hunting Trips*, p. 302.

91. Roosevelt, *Hunting Trips*, p. 303.

92. Roosevelt, *Hunting Trips*, p. 304.

93. Roosevelt, *Hunting Trips*, pp. 304–305.

94. Hermann Hagedorn files, 332.H12p, file 367, Theodore Roosevelt Collection, Houghton Library, Harvard University.

95. The following account of the killing of two grizzlies draws from Roosevelt, *Hunting Trips of a Ranchman*, pp. 309–310.

96. Hermann Hagedorn files, 332.H12p, files 368–369, Theodore Roosevelt Collection, Houghton Library, Harvard University.

97. Hermann Hagedorn files, 332.H12p, files 368–369, Theodore Roosevelt Collection, Houghton Library, Harvard University.

98. Roosevelt, *Hunting Trips*, pp. 306–307; private diary, Theodore Roosevelt Collection, Houghton Library, Harvard University.

99. Roosevelt, *Hunting Trips*, pp. 306–307.

100. Hermann Hagedorn files, 332.H12p, files 370–371, Theodore Roosevelt Collection, Houghton Library, Harvard University.

101. Private diary, Theodore Roosevelt Collection, Houghton Library, Harvard University.

102. Hermann Hagedorn files, 332.H12p, file 372, Theodore Roosevelt Collection, Houghton Library, Harvard University.

103. Hermann Hagedorn files, 332.H12p, file 345, Theodore Roosevelt Collection, Houghton Library, Harvard University.

104. Theodore Roosevelt to Anna Roosevelt, September 20, 1884, Anna Roosevelt Cowles letters, Theodore Roosevelt Collection, Houghton Library, Harvard University.

105. Theodore Roosevelt to Anna Roosevelt, September 20, 1884, Anna Roosevelt Cowles letters, Theodore Roosevelt Collection, Houghton Library, Harvard University.

106. Theodore Roosevelt to Anna Roosevelt, September 20, 1884, Anna Roosevelt Cowles letters, Theodore Roosevelt Collection, Houghton Library, Harvard University.

107. Private Diary, Theodore Roosevelt Collection, Houghton Library, Harvard University.

108. Private Diary, Theodore Roosevelt Collection, Houghton Library, Harvard University; Roosevelt, Roosevelt, *Hunting Trips*, p. 211.

109. Private Diary, Theodore Roosevelt Collection, Houghton Library, Harvard University

110. Roosevelt, *Hunting Trips*, p. 124.

111. Hermann Hagedorn files, 332.H12p, file 373, Theodore Roosevelt Collection, Houghton Library, Harvard University.

112. Roosevelt, *Hunting Trips*, pp. 125–126.

113. Putnam, *Theodore Roosevelt*, p. 489. A colorful though inaccurate account of the grizzly hunt appeared in the December 24, 1884, *New York Times*, saying Roosevelt had killed three grizzlies, six elk, and antelope too numerous to count (the *Times* should have said "too few to count," as he shot none). "Several buffaloes also fell before his rifle . . . Mr. Roosevelt was very proud of a twelve-hundred pound grizzly, whose skin will follow him in a few weeks to New-York. He is very nearsighted, and the bear approached within nine feet of him before he saw it. The animal had seen the

Assemblyman, and was doubtless preparing to embrace him in a brotherly fashion when a well-directed rifle ball struck him in the forehead and stretched his vigorous frame at full length on the ground."

114. Hermann Hagedorn files, 332.H12p, file 375, Theodore Roosevelt Collection, Houghton Library, Harvard University.

115. *Bad Lands Cow Boy*, October 23, 1884.

116. *Bad Lands Cow Boy*, November 27, 1884.

117. *Bad Lands Cow Boy*, November 13, 1884, December 4, 1884.

118. *Bad Lands Cow Boy*, November 13, 1884, October 30, 1884.

119. William T. Hornaday, *The Extermination of the American Bison* (Washington, D.C.: U.S. Government Printing Office, 1889), p. 520.

120. *Bad Lands Cow Boy*, December 18, 1884.

121. *Bad Lands Cow Boy*, January 22, 1885.

122. Wolves were not the only former bison predators to trouble ranchers. Roosevelt singled out former buffalo hunters as rough men readymade for crime once the buffalo were gone. "They were absolutely shiftless and improvident; they had no settled habits; they were inured to peril and hardship, but entirely unaccustomed to steady work; and so they afforded just the materials from which to make the bolder and more desperate kinds of criminals." Theodore Roosevelt, *Ranch Life and the Hunting Trail* (New York: Bonanza Books, 1978), p. 13.

123. Roosevelt, *Hunting Trips*, pp. 624–625.

124. Roosevelt, *Hunting Trips*, p. 283.

125. Hermann Hagedorn files, 332.H12p, file 348, Theodore Roosevelt Collection, Houghton Library, Harvard University.

126. Theodore Roosevelt to Anna Roosevelt, September 20, 1884, Anna Roosevelt Cowles letters, Theodore Roosevelt Collection, Houghton Library, Harvard University.

10: GUNFIGHTERS AND BLAINE

1. William Wingate Sewall, *Bill Sewall's Story of T.R.* (New York: Harper & Brothers, 1919), p. 20.

2. Ray H. Mattison, "Roosevelt's Elkhorn Ranch," *North Dakota Historical Society Quarterly* 27, 2 (Spring 1960): 61–62.

3. William Sewall to Sam Sewall, September 14, 1884, in Ray H. Mattison, "Life at Roosevelt's Elkhorn Ranch—the Letters of William W. and Mary Sewall," reprint of *North Dakota Historical Society Quarterly* 27, 3–4 (Summer and Fall 1960): 6–7, Theodore Roosevelt Collection, Harvard University, Houghton Library.

4. William Sewall to Sam Sewall, September 14, 1884, Mattison, "Life at Roosevelt's Elkhorn Ranch," p. 7.

5. William Sewall to Sam Sewall, September 14, 1884, Mattison, "Life at Roosevelt's Elkhorn Ranch," p. 10.

6. Carlton Putnam, *Theodore Roosevelt, Volume One: The Formative Years, 1858–1886* (New York: Charles Scribner's Sons, 1958), p. 490.

7. Sewall, *Bill Sewall's Story of T.R.*, p. 22.

8. Sewall, *Bill Sewall's Story of T.R.*, p. 21.

9. Hermann Hagedorn, *Roosevelt in the Bad Lands* (Boston: Houghton Mifflin Company, 1921), p. 208; Sewall, *Bill Sewall's Story of T.R.*, p. 21. Neither Hagedorn nor Sewall accuses Paddock by name; in his book, Hagedorn changed the names of various Roosevelt associates, calling Paddock "Maunders," apparently to avoid difficulties with people still alive. Sewall calls him "a man who was known as a trouble-maker and who worked on the ranch of a Frenchman named de Morès," which puts the finger on Paddock.

10. Hagedorn, *Roosevelt in the Bad Lands*, p. 208; Sewall, *Bill Sewall's Story of T.R.*, p. 21.

11. Sewall, *Bill Sewall's Story of T.R.*, pp. 21–22.

12. Sewall, *Bill Sewall's Story of T.R.*, p. 23.

13. Sewall, *Bill Sewall's Story of T.R.*, pp. 23–24.

14. Phillip Ashton Rollins, *The Cowboy: An Unconventional History of Civilization on the Old-Time Cattle Range* (Norman: University of Oklahoma Press, 1997), p. 54.

15. Putnam, *Theodore Roosevelt*, p. 490.

16. Putnam, *Theodore Roosevelt*, pp. 492–493.

17. Sean Dennis Cashman, *America in the Gilded Age* (New York: New York University Press, 1993), p. 261.

18. Henry Collins Brown. *Valentine's Manual of Old New York* (Hastings-on-Hudson, NY: Valentine's Manual Inc., 1927), p. 327.

19. *Sun*, October 12, 1884.

20. *New York Herald*, August 1, 1884.

21. Brown. *Valentine's Manual of Old New York*, p. 328; Putnam, *Theodore Roosevelt*, pp. 502–503.

22. Moses King, *King's Handbook of New York City* (Boston: Moses King, 1893), p. 238.

23. Luc Sante, *Low Life: Lures and Snares of Old New York* (New York: Farrar, Straus & Giroux, 2003), p. 55.

24. Brown, *Valentine's Manual of Old New York*, pp. 97, 99.

25. *New York World*, October 30, 1884, quoted in Putnam, *Theodore Roosevelt*, p. 503.

26. Putnam, *Theodore Roosevelt*, p.504.

27. Brown. *Valentine's Manual of Old New York*, p. 328.

28. Theodore Roosevelt to Henry Cabot Lodge, November 7, 1884, *The Letters of Theodore Roosevelt*, ed. Elting E. Morison (Cambridge, MA: Harvard University Press, 1951), p. 87.

29. Theodore Roosevelt to Henry Cabot Lodge, November 11, 1884, *The Letters of Theodore Roosevelt*, p. 88.

30. Putnam, *Theodore Roosevelt*, p. 500.

31. *New York Tribune*, November 12, 1885.

32. Theodore Roosevelt to Henry Cabot Lodge, November 11, 1884, *The Letters of Theodore Roosevelt*, p. 88.

II: WINTER, 1884–85

1. Private Diary, Theodore Roosevelt Collection, Houghton Library, Harvard University; Theodore Roosevelt, *Hunting Trips of a Ranchman* in *The Works of Theodore Roosevelt*, Volume I. (New York: Charles Scribner's Sons, 1926), p. 64.

2. Roosevelt, *Hunting Trips*, p. 64.

3. Roosevelt, *Hunting Trips*, p. 65.

4. Roosevelt, *Hunting Trips*, p. 66.

5. Roosevelt, *Hunting Trips*, p. 66.

6. Roosevelt, *Hunting Trips*, p. 67.

7. Theodore Roosevelt to Anna Roosevelt, November 23, 1884, *Letters from Theodore Roosevelt to Anna Roosevelt Cowles 1870–1918* (New York: Charles Scribner's Sons, 1924), pp. 69–70; Private Diary, Theodore Roosevelt Collection, Houghton Library, Harvard University. At this time Roosevelt, in the spirit of the moment, may have grabbed an axe and pitched in, though his skills at logging did not match those of the Maine woodsman—Sewall cut down fifty-three trees, Dow forty-nine, and Roosevelt "beavered down," as Dow put it, only seventeen. "Those who have seen the stump of a tree which has been gnawed down by a beaver will understand the exact force of the comparison," Roosevelt recalled. The date of this event is uncertain, but it is described in Theodore Roosevelt, *An Autobiography* (New York: The Macmillan Company, 1913), p. 108.

8. Private Diary, Theodore Roosevelt Collection, Houghton Library, Harvard University.

9. Theodore Roosevelt to Anna Roosevelt, November 23, 1884, *Letters from Theodore Roosevelt to Anna Roosevelt Cowles*, p. 69.

10. Roosevelt, *Hunting Trips*, p. 28.

11. Roosevelt, *Hunting Trips*, p. 80.

12. Don Rickey Jr., *Cowboy Dress, Arms, Tools and Equipments as Used in the Little Missouri Range Country and the Medora Area, in the 1880s*, Theodore Roosevelt National Monument Park, File No. H2215, 1957, pp. 14–15.

13. Private Diary, Theodore Roosevelt Collection, Houghton Library, Harvard University.

14. *Bad Lands Cow Boy*, September 25, 1884, and November 6, 1884.

15. *Bad Lands Cow Boy*, November 6, 1884.

16. Theodore Roosevelt to Anna Roosevelt, November 23, 1884, *Letters from Theodore Roosevelt to Anna Roosevelt Cowles*, pp. 69–70; Private Diary, Theodore Roosevelt Collection, Houghton Library, Harvard University; Ray H. Mattison, *Roosevelt and the Stockmen's Association* (Theodore Roosevelt Nature and History Association, 1969), p. 17, reprint from *North Dakota Historical Society Quarterly* 17, 2 (April 1950), and 17, 3 (July 1950), Theodore Roosevelt Collection, Harvard University, Houghton Library.

17. *Bad Lands Cow Boy*, December 4 and 11, 1884.

18. Mattison, *Roosevelt and the Stockmen's Association*, p. 8.

19. Lincoln A. Lang, *Ranching with Roosevelt* (Philadelphia: J. B. Lippincott Company, 1926), p. 168.

20. Theodore Roosevelt, *Ranch Life and the Hunting Trail* (New York: Bonanza Books, 1978) p. 18.

21. Roosevelt, *Ranch Life*, p. 21.

22. Roosevelt, *Ranch Life*, p. 24.

23. Hermann Hagedorn, *Roosevelt in the Bad Lands* (Boston: Houghton Mifflin Company, 1921), p. 225.

24. *Bad Lands Cow Boy*, October 30, 1884.

25. *Mandan Pioneer*, quoted in the *Bad Lands Cow Boy*, October 2, 1884.

26. Private Diary, Theodore Roosevelt Collection, Houghton Library, Harvard University.

27. Hagedorn, *Roosevelt in the Bad Lands*, p. 225.

28. Theodore Roosevelt, *Hunting Trips of a Ranchman and The Wilderness Hunter* (New York: The Modern Library, 2004), p. 13.

29. Roosevelt, *Hunting Trips of a Ranchman and The Wilderness Hunter*, p. 13.

30. Phillip Ashton Rollins, *The Cowboy: An Unconventional History of Civilization on the Old-Time Cattle Range* (Norman: University of Oklahoma Press, 1997), p. 156.

31. Theodore Roosevelt, *An Autobiography* (New York: The Macmillan Company, 1913), p. 109.

32. Rollins, *The Cowboy*, p. 163.

33. Rollins, *The Cowboy*, p. 86.

34. Theodore Roosevelt to Henry Cabot Lodge, May 15, 1885, *The Letters of Theodore Roosevelt*, ed. Elting E. Morison (Cambridge, MA: Harvard University Press, 1951), p. 90.

35. Hermann Hagedorn files, 332.H12p, file 869, Theodore Roosevelt Collection, Houghton Library, Harvard University.

36. Hermann Hagedorn files, 332.H12p, files 870 and 870a, Theodore Roosevelt Collection, Houghton Library, Harvard University.

37. Theodore Roosevelt, *An Autobiography* (New York: The Macmillan Company, 1913), p. 118.

38. Hermann Hagedorn files, 332.H12p, file 871, Theodore Roosevelt Collection, Houghton Library, Harvard University.

39. Hagedorn, *Roosevelt in the Bad Lands*, p. 226.

40. William Sewall to Sam Sewall, December 19, 1884, in Ray H. Mattison, "Life at Roosevelt's Elkhorn Ranch—the Letters of William W. and Mary Sewall," reprint of *North Dakota Historical Society Quarterly*, 27, 3–4 (Summer and Fall 1960): 11, in Theodore Roosevelt Collection, Harvard University, Houghton Library.

41. Roosevelt, *Hunting Trips*, p. 169. The account of the bighorn hunt is from the chaper, "A Trip After Mountain Sheep," in *Ranch Life*.

42. "George Myers"—Personal Diary, December 12, 1884, Theodore Roosevelt Collection, Houghton Library, Harvard University.

43. Roosevelt, *Hunting Trips*, pp. 169, 170.

44. Roosevelt, *Hunting Trips*, p. 171.

45. Roosevelt, *Hunting Trips*, p. 177.

46. Roosevelt, *Hunting Trips*, p. 179.

47. Roosevelt, *Hunting Trips*, p. 180.

48. Roosevelt, *Hunting Trips*, p. 184.

49. Theodore Roosevelt to Anna Roosevelt, December 14, 1884, *The Letters of Theodore Roosevelt*, p. 89.

50. Hagedorn, *Roosevelt in the Bad Lands*, p. 234; Mattison, *Roosevelt and the Stockmen's Association*, p. 18.

51. Hagedorn, *Roosevelt in the Bad Lands*, p. 233. Hagedorn interviewed many of Roosevelt's Badlands contemporaries and may have taken some of these words from their mouths.

52. Mattison, *Roosevelt and the Stockmen's Association*, p. 18.

53. Mattison, *Roosevelt and the Stockmen's Association*, p. 19.

54. *Bad Lands Cow Boy*, December 25, 1884.

55. Hagedorn, *Roosevelt in the Bad Lands*, p. 207.

56. Roosevelt, *Ranch Life and the Hunting Trail* (New York: Bonanza Books, 1978), p. 73.

57. *The Works of Theodore Roosevelt* (New York: Charles Scribner's Sons, 1926), 1:342.

58. *The Works of Theodore Roosevelt*, 1:343.

59. Hagedorn, *Roosevelt in the Bad Lands*, pp. 223–224.

60. Hagedorn, *Roosevelt in the Bad Lands*, pp. 224–225.

61. Hagedorn, *Roosevelt in the Bad Lands*, p. 228.

62. Hagedorn, *Roosevelt in the Bad Lands*, p. 228.

63. *The Works of Theodore Roosevelt*, p. 1:367.

64. *Bad Lands Cow Boy*, February 13 and 20, March 12 and 19, and May 7, 1885.

65. *Bad Lands Cow Boy*, March 26 and April 2, 1885.

66. Granville Stuart, *Forty Years on the Frontier*, Part 2: *Pioneering in Montana* (Lincoln: University of Nebraska Press, 1977), p. 212

67. *The Works of Theodore Roosevelt*, p. 1:341.

68. William Sewall to Sam Sewall, January 28, 1885, Putnam material, file "Sewall Correspondence," Theodore Roosevelt Collection, Houghton Library, Harvard University.

69. The source of the following story about trading with Indians: William Sewall to Sam Sewall, February 18, 1885, Putnam material, "Sewall Correspondence" file, Theodore Roosevelt Collection, Houghton Library, Harvard University.

70. Hagedorn, *Roosevelt in the Bad Lands*, p. 235.

71. Theodore Roosevelt to Anna Roosevelt, postcard, March 19, 1885, Theodore Roosevelt Collection, Houghton Library, Harvard University.

72. Theodore Roosevelt Collection, Houghton Library, Harvard University, Hermann Hagedorn files, 332.H12p, file 751d.

73. With *Hunting Trips*, Roosevelt established a pattern that would persist throughout his life of writing about his exploits as soon as, and sometimes before, they happened, inciting detractors to say that his motto was, "No sooner done than said." Frederick S. Wood, ed., *Roosevelt as We Knew Him: The Personal Recollections of One Hundred and Fifty of His Friends and Associates* (Philadelphia: The John C. Winston Company, 1927), p. 3.

74. Roosevelt, *Hunting Trips of a Ranchman and The Wilderness Hunter*, p. 250.

75. Roosevelt, *Hunting Trips of a Ranchman and The Wilderness Hunter*, pp. 129, 138–139.

76. Roosevelt, *Hunting Trips of a Ranchman and The Wilderness Hunter*, p. 286.

77. Roosevelt, *Hunting Trips of a Ranchman and The Wilderness Hunter*, p. 157.

78. Roosevelt, *Hunting Trips of a Ranchman and The Wilderness Hunter*, p. 70.

79. Carlton Putnam, *Theodore Roosevelt, Volume One: The Formative Years, 1858–1886* (New York: Charles Scribner's Sons, 1958), pp. 518–519.

80. Theodore Roosevelt to Henry Cabot Lodge, March 8, 1885, *The Letters of Theodore Roosevelt*, p. 89.

81. Theodore Roosevelt to Henry Cabot Lodge, March 8, 1885, *The Letters of Theodore Roosevelt*, p. 90.

82. Edmund Morris, *The Rise of Theodore Roosevelt* (New York: Modern Library, 2001), p. 293.

83. Hagedorn, *Roosevelt in the Bad Lands*, p. 239.

84. Hermann Hagedorn files, 332.H12p, file 613, Theodore Roosevelt Collection, Houghton Library, Harvard University.

12: ROUNDUP

1. Hermann Hagedorn, *Roosevelt in the Bad Lands* (Boston: Houghton Mifflin Company, 1921), p. 239; *Bad Lands Cow Boy*, April 23, 1885. The date of his arrival was April 17, 1885.

2. *Bad Lands Cow Boy*, April 23, 1885.

3. William T. Dantz, "Theodore Roosevelt—Cowboy and Ranchman," *Harper's Weekly*, August 6, 1904, pp. 1212–1215.

4. Hagedorn, *Roosevelt in the Bad Lands*, pp. 240–241.

5. Hagedorn, *Roosevelt in the Bad Lands*, p. 240.

6. William Sewall to Sam Sewall, May 17, 1885, Ray H. Mattison, *Life at Roosevelt's Elkhorn Ranch—the Letters of William W. and Mary Sewall*, p. 14, reprint of *North Dakota Historical Society Quarterly*, 27, 3 (Summer 1960) and 27, 4 (Fall 1960), Theodore Roosevelt Collection, Harvard University, Houghton Library.

7. Hagedorn, *Roosevelt in the Bad Lands*, p. 249.

8. This account of the river crossing is from Hagedorn, *Roosevelt in the Bad Lands*, pp. 249–252.

9. Hagedorn, *Roosevelt in the Bad Lands*, pp. 252–253.

10. Hagedorn, *Roosevelt in the Bad Lands*, p. 252.

11. Hermann Hagedorn files, 332.H12p, files 203–250, Theodore Roosevelt Collection, Houghton Library, Harvard University.

12. Hagedorn, *Roosevelt in the Bad Lands*, p. 258.

13. Hagedorn, *Roosevelt in the Bad Lands*, p. 257.

14. Hagedorn, *Roosevelt in the Bad Lands*, p. 258.

15. Theodore Roosevelt, *Hunting Trips of a Ranchman and The Wilderness Hunter* (New York: The Modern Library, 2004), p. 18.

16. Hagedorn, *Roosevelt in the Bad Lands*, p. 240.

17. Roosevelt, *Hunting Trips*, p. 24. Roosevelt details daily ranch work in *Ranch Life and the Hunting Trail* (New York: Bonanza Books, 1978 [1888]), pp. 27–36.

18. William Wingate Sewall, *Bill Sewall's Story of T.R.* (New York: Harper & Brothers, 1919), p. 43.

19. Hermann Hagedorn files, 332.H12p, file 1060a, Theodore Roosevelt Collection, Houghton Library, Harvard University.

20. Lincoln A. Lang, *Ranching with Roosevelt* (Philadelphia: J. B. Lippincott Company, 1926), p. 217.

21. Lang, *Ranching with Roosevelt*, pp. 217–218.

22. Ray H. Mattison, *Life at Roosevelt's Elkhorn Ranch*, p. 16. The story of the arrival of the cattle is from this source, pp. 16–18. Also, *Bad Lands Cow Boy*, May 7, 1885.

23. Roosevelt mentions having had lunch with the Marquis in a letter to Henry Cabot Lodge, dated May 15, 1885, *The Letters of Theodore Roosevelt*, ed. Elting E. Morison (Cambridge, MA: Harvard University Press, 1951), p. 90. As Roosevelt was in Medora on May 5 to meet his shipment of cattle, left that day for the Elkhorn, and arrived there on the eleventh, he may have lunched with the Marquis on the day he was in town to meet the shipment.

24. This account of the cattle drive is from Hagedorn, *Roosevelt in the Bad Lands*, pp. 268–270, and Roosevelt, *Ranch Life and the Hunting Trail*, pp. 67–68.

25. E. C. Abbott and Helena Huntington Smith, *We Pointed Them North: Recollections of a Cowpuncher* (Norman: University of Oklahoma Press, 1955), p. 58.

26. Granville Stuart, *Forty Years on the Frontier, Part 2: Pioneering in Montana* (Lincoln: University of Nebraska Press, 1977), p. 192.

27. Abbott and Smith, *We Pointed Them North*, p. 36.

28. Abbott and Smith, *We Pointed Them North*, p. 37.

29. Roosevelt, *Ranch Life and the Hunting Trail* p. 68.

30. Theodore Roosevelt to Henry Cabot Lodge, May 15, 1885, *The Letters of Theodore Roosevelt*, p. 90.

31. Lang, *Ranching with Roosevelt*, p. 176.

32. James Vance, a ranchman and former cowboy, quoted in the *Bad Lands Cow Boy*, September 4, 1884.

33. Ray H. Mattison, *Roosevelt and the Stockmen's Association* (Theodore Roosevelt

Nature and History Association, 1969), p. 25, reprint from *North Dakota Historical Society Quarterly* 17, 2 (April 1950) and 17, 3 (July 1950), Theodore Roosevelt Collection, Harvard University, Houghton Library.

34. Lang, *Ranching with Roosevelt*, pp. 195–196.

35. *Bad Lands Cow Boy*, April 30, 1885; Roosevelt, *Hunting Trips*, p. 22.

36. Roosevelt, *Ranch Life*, pp. 46–47.

37. Lang, *Ranching with Roosevelt*, pp. 183–185.

38. Roosevelt, *Ranch Life*, p. 48.

39. Edwin Tunis, *Frontier Living* (New York: The Lyons Press: 2000), p. 152.

40. Phillip Ashton Rollins, *The Cowboy: An Unconventional History of Civilization on the Old-Time Cattle Range* (Norman: University of Oklahoma Press, 1997), pp. 259–260.

41. Abbott and Smith, *We Pointed Them North*, pp. 136–138; interview with Mrs. George Pelissier, a resident of the Medora area in the 1880s, September 16, 1952, Putnam material, Theodore Roosevelt Collection, Houghton Library, Harvard University.

42. Tunis, *Frontier Living*, p. 152.

43. William Merrifield interview, Hermann Hagedorn files, 332.H12p, file 382a–382b, Theodore Roosevelt Collection, Houghton Library, Harvard University.

44. W. P. Sebens, executive secretary of the North Dakota State Soil Conservation Committee, "Roosevelt Recognized Conservation Values," Williams papers, file 6, Theodore Roosevelt Collection, Houghton Library, Harvard University. As Roosevelt "supplied" the game meat for the cowboys, he may have been leaping at a chance to make hunting part of his roundup "work."

45. Roosevelt, *Ranch Life*, p. 48.

46. Roosevelt, *Ranch Life*, p. 53.

47. Lang, *Ranching with Roosevelt*, pp. 182–183. Or perhaps he did not become Lord North; Lang was not certain of his source.

48. Roosevelt, *Hunting Trips*, pp. 22–23.

49. Roosevelt, *Hunting Trips*, pp. 23–24. Lincoln Lang disagreed: "Usually, it came closer to being 'Hell,' before we got through with it, as was the case on that particular round-up in 1885, when Mr. Roosevelt was along. Rained much of the time, and upon one occasion kept at it for a week on end. Tied the whole outfit up for several days at one point and I recall we had to wring the water out of our blankets every night before retiring. The boys liked to work on general round-ups, hard and all as they were, mainly because they had a chance to renew old acquaintances." Quoted in Hagedorn, *Roosevelt in the Bad Lands*, pp. 277–278, footnote.

50. Abbott and Smith, *We Pointed Them North*, p. 87.

51. David T. Courtwright, *Violent Land: Single Men and Social Disorder from the Frontier to the Inner City* (Cambridge, MA: Harvard University Press, 2000), p. 42.

52. Courtwright, *Violent Land*, p. 28.

53. Dantz, "Theodore Roosevelt—Cowboy and Ranchman," pp. 1212–1215; Hermann

Hagedorn files, 332.H12p, files 46–100, Theodore Roosevelt Collection, Houghton Library, Harvard University.

54. Theodore Roosevelt, *An Autobiography* (New York: The Macmillan Company, 1913), p. 110.

55. Interview with Frank Roberts, a cowboy and trapper in the Medora area in the 1880s, September 13, 1952, Putnam material, Theodore Roosevelt Collection, Houghton Library, Harvard University.

56. Interview with Frank Roberts, September 13, 1952, Putnam material, Theodore Roosevelt Collection, Houghton Library, Harvard University.

57. Hermann Hagedorn, "Conversation at Dusk Along the Little Missouri," *Outlook*, September 24, 1919, pp. 137 ff. (the copy used as a source here is an electronic version from the Library of Congress that has no page numbers).

58. Dantz, "Theodore Roosevelt—Cowboy and Ranchman," pp. 1212–1215.

59. Roosevelt, *An Autobiography*, p. 119.

60. Roosevelt, *Ranch Life*, p. 56.

61. Fred Badger, to his father, October 13 (no year, but certainly 1885), Fred Badger Letters, Folder 7, bMS Am 1454.50(4), Theodore Roosevelt Collection, Houghton Library, Harvard University.

62. Fred Badger, to his father, October 13 (no year, but certainly 1885), Fred Badger Letters, Folder 7, bMS Am 1454.50(4), Theodore Roosevelt Collection, Houghton Library, Harvard University.

63. Roosevelt, *Hunting Trips*, p. 23.

64. Roosevelt, *Outdoor Pastimes*, p. 176.

65. Rollins, *The Cowboy*, p. 162; Fred Badger, to his father, October 13 (no year, but certainly 1885), Fred Badger Letters, Folder 7, bMS Am 1454.50(4), Theodore Roosevelt Collection, Houghton Library, Harvard University.

66. Rollins, *The Cowboy*, p. 227.

67. Rollins, *The Cowboy*, p. 230.

68. Rollins, *The Cowboy*, pp. 228–229.

69. Fred Badger, to his father, October 13 (no year, but certainly 1885), bMS Am 1454.50(4), Folder 7, Theodore Roosevelt Collection, Houghton Library, Harvard University.

70. Hagedorn, *Roosevelt in the Bad Lands*, p. 314.

71. Richard B. Townshend, *A Tenderfoot in Colorado* (Boulder: University of Colorado Press, 2008), p. 236.

72. William Merrifield interview, Hermann Hagedorn files, 332.H12p, files 382c, Theodore Roosevelt Collection, Houghton Library, Harvard University.

73. William Merrifield interview, Hermann Hagedorn files, 332.H12p, files 382a, Theodore Roosevelt Collection, Houghton Library, Harvard University.

74. William Merrifield interview, Hermann Hagedorn files, 332.H12p, files 382b, Theodore Roosevelt Collection, Houghton Library, Harvard University. Sometimes Roosevelt's roping skills were just enough to get the job done. A day after a rain-

storm, Roosevelt was riding with Englishman Eric North, his erstwhile boxing partner and a guest of the Langs, when they crossed a makeshift bridge made of light logs that spanned a flooded wash. The timbers collapsed, dumping horses and riders into the torrent below. Roosevelt rode out of the water, but the young Englishman cried for help, shouting that he was drowning. Roosevelt quickly spun his lasso and, though not a skilled roper, snagged the man around the shoulders and pulled him ashore. Hagedorn, *Roosevelt in the Bad Lands*, pp. 297–298. On another occasion, Roosevelt tried to rope a nursing pronghorn doe, riding up to it on a swift former Indian pony named White Eye and throwing his lariat. "An expert with the rope would have captured her with the utmost ease; but I missed, sending the coil across her shoulders." He came close one more time before losing her, a process that could have been good neither for the doe nor her fawn, which "gave an agonized bleat, or bark." Roosevelt, *Outdoor Pastimes of an American Hunter*, pp. 151–152.

75. Interview with Frank Roberts, September 13, 1952, Putnam material, Theodore Roosevelt Collection, Houghton Library, Harvard University.

76. Interview with Frank Roberts, September 13, 1952, Putnam material, Theodore Roosevelt Collection, Houghton Library, Harvard University.

77. Interview with Frank Roberts, September 13, 1952, Putnam material, Theodore Roosevelt Collection, Houghton Library, Harvard University.

78. Roosevelt, *Ranch Life*, p. 54.

79. Roosevelt, *An Autobiography*, p. 116.

80. Abbott and Smith, *We Pointed Them North*, p. 66.

81. Abbott and Smith, *We Pointed Them North*, p. 66.

82. Rollins, *The Cowboy*, p. 267.

83. David Dary, *Cowboy Culture: A Saga of Five Centuries* (Lawrence: University of Kansas Press, 1989), pp. 195–196.

84. Putnam, *Theodore Roosevelt*, p. 526; the account of the story is based on Roosevelt, *An Autobiography*, pp. 116–117.

85. Roosevelt, *An Autobiography*, p. 116.

86. Roosevelt, *An Autobiography*, p. 116.

87. Abbott and Smith, *We Pointed Them North*, p. 67.

88. Abbott and Smith, *We Pointed Them North*, p. 68.

89. Build eagle nests: Local rancher quoted in Hermann Hagedorn files, 332.H12p, file 10–2, Theodore Roosevelt Collection, Houghton Library, Harvard University; Hagedorn, *Roosevelt in the Bad Lands*, p. 291.

90. Hagedorn, *Roosevelt in the Bad Lands*, p. 291; William Merrifield interview, Hermann Hagedorn files, 332.H12p, file 377, Theodore Roosevelt Collection, Houghton Library, Harvard University.

91. William Merrifield interview, Hermann Hagedorn files, 332.H12p, files 377, Theodore Roosevelt Collection, Houghton Library, Harvard University.

92. Contract between Theodore Roosevelt on the one hand and William Sewall

and Wilmot Dow on the other, dated June 20, 1885, Theodore Roosevelt Collection, Library of Congress Manuscript Division.

93. Hagedorn, *Roosevelt in the Bad Lands*, p. 307.

94. *Pioneer Press*, June 23, 1885, Theodore Roosevelt Collection, Houghton Library, Harvard University.

95. *Pittsburgh Dispatch*, August 23, 1885, quoted in Putnam, *Theodore Roosevelt*, p. 530, and in Edmund Morris, *The Rise of Theodore Roosevelt* (New York: Modern Library, 2001), p. 825.

96. *New York Daily Tribune*, July 8, 1885, quoted in Putnam, *Theodore Roosevelt*, p. 529.

97. *St. Paul Dispatch*, June 22, 1885, Theodore Roosevelt Collection, Houghton Library, Harvard University.

13: AT HOME IN EAST AND WEST

1. *New York Times* July 13, 1885. The book is still in print in several different editions. It also proved successful overseas—the January 16, 1886, issue of the *London Spectator* took up the *New York Times* anthem, calling the book "bright and fresh and full of good reading." Cited in Carlton Putnam, *Theodore Roosevelt, Volume One: The Formative Years, 1858–1886* (New York: Charles Scribner's Sons, 1958), p. 519.

2. Robert G. Athearn, *Westward the Briton* (New York: Charles Scribner's Sons, 1953), p. xv.

3. George Bird Grinnell, "Hunting Trips of a Ranchman," *Forest and Stream*, July 2, 1885, p. 451.

4. Albert Kenrick Fisher, "In Memoriam: George Bird Grinnell," *The Auk* 56 (January 1939): 1.

5. John F. Reiger, ed., *The Passing of the Great West: Selected Papers of George Bird Grinnell* (Norman: University of Oklahoma Press, 1985), p. 57.

6. Fisher, "In Memoriam: George Bird Grinnell," p. 2.

7. Fisher, "In Memoriam: George Bird Grinnell," pp. 8–10.

8. George Bird Grinnell, "Introduction," in *The Works of Theodore Roosevelt* (New York: Charles Scribner's Sons, 1926), 1: xiv.

9. Fisher, "In Memoriam: George Bird Grinnell," p. 3.

10. Fisher, "In Memoriam: George Bird Grinnell," p. 3; Michael Punke, *Last Stand: George Bird Grinnell, the Battle to Save the Buffalo, and the Birth of the New West* (New York: HarperCollins Publishers, 2007), p. 123.

11. George Bird Grinnell, writing as "Ornis," "Buffalo Hunt with the Pawnees," *Forest and Stream* 1, 20 (December 25, 1873): 305.

12. Grinnell, "Buffalo Hunt with the Pawnees," p. 305.

13. Grinnell, "Introduction," 1: xiv–xv.

14. Grinnell, "Introduction," 1: xiv–xv.

15. Grinnell, "Introduction," 1: xv.

16. Grinnell, "Introduction," 1: xvi.

17. Carlton Putnam, *Theodore Roosevelt, Volume One: The Formative Years, 1858–*

1886 (New York: Charles Scribner's Sons, 1958), p. 313.

18. Putnam, *Theodore Roosevelt*, p. 532.

19. Natalie A. Naylor, "Understanding the Place: Theodore Roosevelt's Hometown of Oyster Bay and His Sagamore Hill Home," *Theodore Roosevelt Association Journal* XXX, 1–2 (Winter-Spring 2009): 10.

20. Edmund Morris, *The Rise of Theodore Roosevelt* (New York: Modern Library, 2001), pp. 297–299.

21. Putnam, *Theodore Roosevelt*, p. 532.

22. Morris, *The Rise of Theodore Roosevelt*, pp. 297–299.

23. Putnam, *Theodore Roosevelt*, p. 532.

24. William Sewall to Sam Sewall, August 16, 1885, Ray H. Mattison, "Life at Roosevelt's Elkhorn Ranch—the Letters of William W. and Mary Sewall," p. 18, reprint of *North Dakota Historical Society Quarterly* 27, 3–4 (Summer and Fall 1960), Theodore Roosevelt Collection, Harvard University, Houghton Library.

25. William Wingate Sewall, *Bill Sewall's Story of T.R.* (New York: Harper & Brothers, 1919), p. 29.

26. Hermann Hagedorn, *Roosevelt in the Bad Lands* (Boston: Houghton Mifflin Company, 1921), p. 318.

27. Hagedorn, *Roosevelt in the Bad Lands*, pp. 318–321.

28. *Dickinson Press*, January 17, 1885. The building was insured for $2,200. De Morès had detractors, too. In the August 20, 1885, issue of the *Bad Lands Cow Boy*, "A Citizen" wrote, "Now, Mr. Editor, I would like to ask if there were hogs kept all over town and around it, would the stench be one-half as bad as that which we get from the offal that is carried away from the slaughter-house and left uncovered to taint the air and breed a pestilence among our citizens? It certainly would not cost much to have that pile covered up and not compel us to breathe air that is rotten."

29. Hagedorn, *Roosevelt in the Bad Lands*, p. 320. Sometimes the shooting was in earnest. In early November, Bob Roberts swapped bullets with a local named George Heywood in two separate shootouts in two different saloons. Total shots fired: about ten. Both men "had been drinking a little" and had exchanged words. Witnesses thought that Roberts' hitting George in the left breast and arm was an accident, in that Roberts was a good shot and had fired twice into the ceiling. "Roberts and Heywood are good citizens, and it is to be hoped that nothing serious will be the result of this little misunderstanding." No arrests were made. The shooting: *Bad Lands Cow Boy*, November 6, 1884, November 27, 1884, November 22, 1884.

30. This account of the Fourth of July is from Sewall, *Bill Sewall's Story of T.R.*, pp. 29–31.

31. Sewall, *Bill Sewall's Story of T.R.*, p. 30.

32. Sewall, *Bill Sewall's Story of T.R.*, p. 31.

33. Sewall, *Bill Sewall's Story of T.R.*, pp. 31–32. In the book, Sewall says they were looking for stolen livestock, but in a letter to his brother he indicates they were also

looking for the rustlers who stole the livestock and, had they found them, would have treated them predictably. William Sewall to Sam Sewall, August 16, 1885, Mattison, "Life at Roosevelt's Elkhorn Ranch," p. 18.

34. Hagedorn, *Roosevelt in the Bad Lands*, p. 324.

35. Sewall, *Bill Sewall's Story of T.R.*, p. 35.

36. Sewall, *Bill Sewall's Story of T.R.*, p. 36.

37. William Sewall to Sam Sewall, August 16, 1885, Mattison, "Life at Roosevelt's Elkhorn Ranch," pp. 17, 18.

38. William Sewall to Sam Sewall, August 16, 1885, Mattison, "Life at Roosevelt's Elkhorn Ranch," pp. 17, 19.

39. Sewall, *Bill Sewall's Story of T.R.*, p. 32.

40. William Sewall to Sam Sewall, August 16, 1885, Mattison, "Life at Roosevelt's Elkhorn Ranch," pp. 17–18.

41. William Sewall to Sam Sewall, August 16, 1885, Mattison, "Life at Roosevelt's Elkhorn Ranch," p. 19.

42. William Sewall to Sam Sewall, August 16, 1885, Mattison, "Life at Roosevelt's Elkhorn Ranch," p. 19.

43. *Bad Lands Cow Boy*, August 27, 1885.

44. Hermann Hagedorn, *Roosevelt in the Bad Lands* (Boston: Houghton Mifflin Company, 1921), p. 337.

45. Anonymous, *50 Years in the Saddle*, (Watford City, ND: 50 Years in the Saddle Club, 1963), 1: 286–287.

46. Hagedorn, *Roosevelt in the Bad Lands*, pp. 339–341.

47. Hagedorn, *Roosevelt in the Bad Lands*, p. 342.

48. Putnam, *Theodore Roosevelt* p. 536.

49. He made this statement to a reporter for the *New York Times* during a visit east the summer of 1885; quoted in Hagedorn, *Roosevelt in the Bad Lands*, p. 342. Jack Reuter, also called Dutch Wannegan, told Hagedorn that de Morès spent $286,000 paying off the jury, judge, and sheriff in his murder trial. Reuter said he "knew" he himself could have gotten at least $10,000, though he didn't say for what, from de Morès. Theodore Roosevelt Collection, Houghton Library, Harvard University, Hermann Hagedorn files, 332.H12p, files 29–45.

50. *Mandan Pioneer*, August 28, 1885, Theodore Roosevelt Collection, Houghton Library, Harvard University.

51. *Bad Lands Cow Boy*, August 27 and September 3, 1885.

52. Hagedorn, *Roosevelt in the Bad Lands*), p. 344; cryptically, Hagedorn says that the mob "bombarded" the jail but does not report what the mob used for its bombardment. Another source says that the mob, intent on lynching de Morès, shot at the jail and tried to burn it down, but was "thwarted." Donald Dresden, *The Marquis deMorès: Emperor of the Bad Lands* (Norman: University of Oklahoma Press, 1970), p. 166.

53. Theodore Roosevelt, *Outdoor Pastimes of an American Hunter* (Mechanicsburg, PA: Stackpole Books, 1990 [1905]), p. 149.

54. Theodore Roosevelt, *Ranch Life and the Hunting Trail* (New York: Bonanza Books, 1978), p. 26.

55. Roosevelt, *Ranch Life*, pp. 26–27.

56. Theodore Roosevelt, *Hunting Trips of a Ranchman and The Wilderness Hunter* (New York: Modern Library, 2004), p. 349.

57. Roosevelt, *Hunting Trips of a Ranchman and The Wilderness Hunter*, p. 226.

58. The following account of the elk hunt is from *The Works of Theodore Roosevelt* (New York: Charles Scribner's Sons, 1926), 1:226–227.

59. *Bad Lands Cow Boy*, September 3, 1885.

60. *Bad Lands Cow Boy*, September 3, 1885.

61. Theodore Roosevelt Collection, Hougton Library, Harvard University.

62. Hagedorn, *Roosevelt in the Bad Lands*, p. 347.

63. Interview with Joe Ferris, Hermann Hagedorn Papers, 322.H12p, File 735, Theodore Roosevelt Collection, Houghton Library, Harvard University. "Roosevelt put some money into my new place and helped me build the store which still stands. He had a room in the southeast corner of the second floor which we used to call the Roosevelt room, and whenever he came to town he spent the night there. I remember how he used to work nights, writing, after the rest of us went to bed. He would open the dining-room and parlor doors wide, throwing the three rooms, including his own, into one; and then we would hear him walking up and down, stopping a few minutes to write, and then walking up and down again, as though he was being paid for it."

64. Sewall, *Bill Sewall's Story of T.R.*, pp. 27–28.

65. Sewall, *Bill Sewall's Story of T.R.*, p. 28.

66. Theodore Roosevelt Collection, Hougton Library, Harvard University.

67. Sewall, *Bill Sewall's Story of T.R.*, p. 28.

68. Lincoln Lang, *Ranching with Roosevelt* (Philadelphia: J. B. Lippincott Co., 1926), p. 75.

69. A. C. Huidekoper, quoted in David McCullough, *Mornings on Horseback: The Story of an Extraordinary Family, a Vanished Way of Life, and the Unique Child Who Became Theodore Roosevelt* (New York: Simon and Schuster, 1981), p.407.

70. Hermann Hagedorn files, 332.H12p, file 511, Theodore Roosevelt Collection, Houghton Library, Harvard University.

71. Anonymous, *50 Years in the Saddle*, pp. 286–287.

72. Interview with Frank Roberts, a cowboy and trapper in the Medora area in the 1880s, September 13, 1952, Putnam material, Theodore Roosevelt Collection, Houghton Library, Harvard University. Roberts concluded, "So that's what there was about the duel." Roosevelt compares a recent political argument with the threat from the Marquis in a letter dated December 28, 1893, and quoted in Sewall, *Bill Sewall's Story of T.R.*, pp. 101–102.

73. Hagedorn, *Roosevelt in the Bad Lands*, pp. 351–352 and 357.

74. Hagedorn, *Roosevelt in the Bad Lands*, pp. 351–352 and 357; Frederick Badger to his father, Henry Clay Badger, October 13, 1885, Frederick Badger Letters Folder 7,

bMS Am 1454.50 (4),Theodore Roosevelt Collection, Houghton Library, Harvard University.

75. The damage could be extensive. Fred Badger and Wilmot Dow rode over one area of burned grass that was thirty miles long. Frederick Badger to his father, Henry Clay Badger, October 13, 1885, Frederick Badger Letters Folder 7, bMS Am 1454.50 (4),Theodore Roosevelt Collection, Houghton Library, Harvard University.

76. Roosevelt, *Hunting Trips of a Ranchman and The Wilderness Hunter*, p. 411.

77. Theodore Roosevelt, *An Autobiography* (New York: The Macmillan Company, 1913), pp. 121–122.

78. Hagedorn, *Roosevelt in the Bad Lands*, pp. 351–353.

79. Hagedorn, *Roosevelt in the Bad Lands*, p. 350.

80. Hermann Hagedorn files, 332.H12p, file 771, Theodore Roosevelt Collection, Houghton Library, Harvard University.

81. Theodore Roosevelt, *Ranch Life* in *The Works of Theodore Roosevelt*, Volume I, p. 372.

82. Roosevelt, *An Autobiography*, p. 125.

83. Roosevelt, *An Autobiography*, p. 126.

84. Roosevelt, *An Autobiography*, p. 126.

85. Hagedorn, *Roosevelt in the Bad Lands*, p. 352.

86. Hermann Hagedorn files, 332.H12p, files 300–332, Theodore Roosevelt Collection, Houghton Library, Harvard University.

87. Lincoln A. Lang, *Ranching with Roosevelt* (Philadelphia: J. B. Lippincott Company, 1926), p. 203.

88. Lang, *Ranching with Roosevelt*, p. 137.

89. Lang, *Ranching with Roosevelt*, p. 204.

90. Lang, *Ranching with Roosevelt*, p. 202.

91. Lang, *Ranching with Roosevelt*, pp. 136–141.

92. Lang, *Ranching with Roosevelt*, pp. 137–138.

93. Roosevelt, *Hunting Trips of a Ranchman and The Wilderness Hunter*, p. 25.

94. Roosevelt, *Hunting Trips of a Ranchman and The Wilderness Hunter*, pp. 25–26. He would return to this theme in a book he wrote in 1886: "Much maudlin nonsense has been written about the governmental treatment of the Indians, especially as regards taking their land. For the simple truth is that they had no possible title to most of the lands we took, not even that of occupancy, and at the most were in possession merely by virtue of having butchered the previous inhabitants. For many of its actions towards them the government does indeed deserve the severest criticism; but it has erred quite as often on the side of too much leniency as on the side of too much severity." Theodore Roosevelt, *Thomas Hart Benton* (Boston: Houghton, Mifflin Company, 1886), p. 57,

95. Roosevelt, *Hunting Trips of a Ranchman and The Wilderness Hunter*, p. 26.

96. Hagedorn, *Roosevelt in the Bad Lands*, p. 355.

97. Thomas G. Dyer, *Theodore Roosevelt and the Idea of Race* (Baton Rouge: Louisiana State University Press, 1980), p. 82.

98. Frederick S. Wood, ed., *Roosevelt as We Knew Him: The Personal Recollections of One Hundred and Fifty of His Friends and Associates* (Philadelphia: The John C. Winston Company, 1927), p. 313.

99. Dyer, *Theodore Roosevelt and the Idea of Race*, pp. 83–84.

100. Dyer, *Theodore Roosevelt and the Idea of Race*, pp. 98–100.

101. Dyer, *Theodore Roosevelt and the Idea of Race*, p. 105.

102. Quoted in Dyer, *Theodore Roosevelt and the Idea of Race*, p. 109.

103. Putnam, *Theodore Roosevelt*, pp. 544–545.

104. Putnam, *Theodore Roosevelt*, p. 545.

105. Putnam, *Theodore Roosevelt*, p. 548.

106. William Merrifield, with varying degrees of accuracy, told Hermann Hagedorn, "He was in love with his present wife before he was with the first one. They fell out over a little disagreement over something or other. She would visit Bamie and she would stay there at night and Theodore would stay some place else to avoid meeting her. He said they had been engaged before. They were friends from the time they were three years old. She used to visit some people there in New York and he'd avoid meeting her, and they kept that up for years. Then he met her in the hall one time. He met her there by accident. When he knew she was going to be there for dinner he would go some place else. She used to come there to visit a chum by the name of Annie. He never would meet her face to face until two years after." Interview with William Merrifield, June 1919, Hermann Hagedorn files, 332.H12p, Theodore Roosevelt Collection, Houghton Library, Harvard University.

107. Sylvia Jukes Morris, *Edith Kermit Roosevelt* (New York: Vintage Books, 1990), p. 79.

108. Putnam, *Theodore Roosevelt*, p. 555.

109. Morris, *Edith Kermit Roosevelt*, p. 80.

110. Roosevelt, *An Autobiography*, p. 34.

111. Roosevelt, *Hunting Trips of a Ranchman and The Wilderness Hunter*, p. 158.

112. Roosevelt, *An Autobiography*, p. 34.

113. Theodore Roosevelt to Henry Cabot Lodge, October 30, 1885, quoted in Putnam, *Theodore Roosevelt*, p. 553.

114. Roosevelt, *An Autobiography*, p. 35.

115. *New York Times*, October 27, 1885.

116. *New York Times*, October 27, 1885.

117. Michael Teague, *Mrs. L: Conservations with Alice Roosevelt Longworth* (Garden City, NY: Doubleday & Company, 1981), p. 42.

118. Theodore Roosevelt to Henry Cabot Lodge, October 30, 1885, quoted in Putnam, *Theodore Roosevelt*, p. 553.

119. Morris, *Edith Kermit Roosevelt*, p. 81.

120. Teague, *Mrs. L*, p. 5.

121. Teague, *Mrs. L*, pp. 5–6.

122. Putnam, *Theodore Roosevelt*, p. 559; Edmund Morris, *The Rise of Theodore Roosevelt* (New York: Modern Library, 2001), p. 315.

123. Putnam, *Theodore Roosevelt*, p. 558.

124. Morris, *Edith Kermit Roosevelt*, p. 82.

125. Putnam, *Theodore Roosevelt*, p. 559.

126. Putnam, *Theodore Roosevelt*, pp. 558–559.

127. *The Letters of Theodore Roosevelt*, ed. Elting E. Morison (Cambridge, MA: Harvard University Press, 1951), p. 94.

128. Putnam, *Theodore Roosevelt*, p. 549–551, 554, footnote p. 558; *Bad Lands Cow Boy*, February 4, 1886. The *Bismarck Daily Tribune* for December 1, 1885, gives something of the flavor of these talks: "Theodore Roosevelt lectured last week in New York on 'Hunting the Game of the Far West.' Mr. Roosevelt says the western frontiersmen and hunters are a healthy and robust lot of men, but the worst thing they have to contend with is the familiarity of skunks. Yet, says Mr. Roosevelt, this is not so bad as politics in New York."

129. Theodore Roosevelt, "Who Should Go West," *Harper's Weekly*, January 2, 1886, p. 7.

130. *The Letters of Theodore Roosevelt*, p. 94.

131. Morris, *Edith Kermit Roosevelt*, p. 83. These were much the same issues he was sorting out when married to Alice.

132. Putnam, *Theodore Roosevelt*, p. 559.

14: ON THE TRAIL OF OUTLAWS

1. Theodore Roosevelt to Anna Roosevelt, March 20, 1886, *Letters from Theodore Roosevelt to Anna Roosevelt Cowles 1870–1918* (New York: Charles Scribner's Sons, 1924), p. 71.

2. Hermann Hagedorn, *Roosevelt in the Bad Lands* (Boston: Houghton Mifflin Company, 1921), pp. 360, 363–364; *Bad Lands Cow Boy*, February 25, 1886.

3. Hagedorn, *Roosevelt in the Bad Lands*, p. 363.

4. Hagedorn, *Roosevelt in the Bad Lands*, p. 364.

5. Frederick Badger to Henry Clay Badger, March 20, 1886, Frederick Badger Letters Folder 2, bMS Am 1454.50 (4), Theodore Roosevelt Collection, Houghton Library, Harvard University.

6. William to Sam Sewall, February 28, 1886, Ray H. Mattison, "Life at Roosevelt's Elkhorn Ranch—the Letters of William W. and Mary Sewall," p. 26, reprint of *North Dakota Historical Society Quarterly* 27, 3–4 (Summer and Fall 1960), Theodore Roosevelt Collection, Harvard University, Houghton Library.

7. Frederick Badger to Henry Clay Badger, March 20, 1886, Frederick Badger Letters Folder 2, bMS Am 1454.50 (4), Theodore Roosevelt Collection, Houghton Library, Harvard University.

8. Joseph Henry Taylor, *Kaleidoscopic Lives* (Washburn, ND: author, 1902), p. 96.

9. Theodore Roosevelt to Anna Roosevelt, March 20, 1886, *Letters from Theodore Roosevelt to Anna Roosevelt Cowles*, p. 71.

10. Frederick Badger to Henry Clay Badger, March 9, 1886, Frederick Badger Letters Folder 2, bMS Am 1454.50 (4), Theodore Roosevelt Collection, Houghton Library, Harvard University.

11. Frederick Badger to Henry Clay Badger, June 18, 1886, Frederick Badger Letters Folder 2, bMS Am 1454.50 (4), Theodore Roosevelt Collection, Houghton Library, Harvard University.

12. Mary Sewall to Nancy Sewall (Mary addressed Nancy as "sister"; Nancy was married to Sewall's brother Sam, so would been Mary's sister-in-law if not her sibling), March 1, 1886, Mattison, "Life at Roosevelt's Elkhorn Ranch," pp. 24–25.

13. Mary Sewall to Nancy Sewall, March 1, 1886, Mattison, "Life at Roosevelt's Elkhorn Ranch," pp. 24–25.

14. Frederick Badger to Henry Clay Badger, March 9, 1886, Frederick Badger Letters Folder 2, bMS Am 1454.50 (4), Theodore Roosevelt Collection, Houghton Library, Harvard University.

15. William Sewall to Sam Sewall, February 25, 1886, Mattison, "Life at Roosevelt's Elkhorn Ranch," p. 25.

16. Theodore Roosevelt to Anna Roosevelt, March 20, 1886, *Letters from Theodore Roosevelt to Anna Roosevelt Cowles*, p. 72.

17. Frederick Badger to Henry Clay Badger, March 20, 1886, Frederick Badger Letters Folder 2, bMS Am 1454.50 (4), Theodore Roosevelt Collection, Houghton Library, Harvard University; Theodore Roosevelt to Anna Roosevelt, March 28, 1886, *Letters from Theodore Roosevelt to Anna Roosevelt Cowles*, p. 72.

18. Theodore Roosevelt to Anna Roosevelt, March 28, 1886, *Letters from Theodore Roosevelt to Anna Roosevelt Cowles*, p. 72.

19. Frederick Badger to Henry Clay Badger, March 20, 1886, Frederick Badger Letters Folder 2, bMS Am 1454.50 (4), Theodore Roosevelt Collection, Houghton Library, Harvard University.

20. William Sewall to Sam Sewall, February 25, 1886, Ray H. Mattison, "Life at Roosevelt's Elkhorn Ranch—the Letters of William W. and Mary Sewall," p. 25, reprint of *North Dakota Historical Society Quarterly* 27, 3–4 (Summer and Fall 1960), Theodore Roosevelt Collection, Harvard University, Houghton Library.

21. Theodore Roosevelt, *Ranch Life and the Hunting Trail* (New York: Bonanza Books, 1978, p. 114.

22. Frederick Badger to Henry Clay Badger, March 28, 1886, Frederick Badger Letters Folder 2. bMS Am 1454.50 (4), Theodore Roosevelt Collection, Houghton Library, Harvard University; William Sewall to Sam Sewall, June 27, 1886, Mattison, "Life at Roosevelt's Elkhorn Ranch," p. 36.

23. William Wingate Sewall, *Bill Sewall's Story of T.R.* (New York: Harper & Brothers, 1919), pp. 659–660.

24. Roosevelt, *Ranch Life*, p. 114.

25. Mike Finnegan to Theodore Roosevelt, January 1887(?), Reel 1, Theodore Roosevelt Collection, Library of Congress.

26. Hagedorn, *Roosevelt in the Bad Lands*, p. 369.

27. *Bad Lands Cow Boy*, December 24, 1885. Apologists said he would not have shot up the town if he had not been drunk, but Packard editorialized that drunkenness was no excuse: "He has repeatedly done the same thing previously and it is high time that he was made to feel that there can be some control over him. Mr. Willard did his duty both as a citizen and an officer in putting the quietus on Mr. B.M. Finnegan." Packard in press mockingly referred to Redhead as "Mr. Ba-a-ad Man Finnegan."

28. Roosevelt, *Ranch Life*, p. 115; Sewall, *Bill Sewall's Story of T.R.*, p. 64. The spelling of the men's names varies from one account to another.

29. Roosevelt, *Ranch Life*, p. 126; Sewall, *Bill Sewall's Story of T.R.*, p. 76.

30. Taylor, *Kaleidoscopic Lives*, p. 96.

31. Roosevelt, *Ranch Life*, p. 115; Sewall, *Bill Sewall's Story of T.R.*, p. 60.

32. Roosevelt, *Ranch Life*, p. 114; Sewall, *Bill Sewall's Story of T.R.*, p. 60; William Sewall to Sam Sewall, April 21, 1886, Mattison, "Life at Roosevelt's Elkhorn Ranch," p. 25. The following account of the pursuit of the thieves is taken from the Roosevelt and Sewall books except where otherwise cited.

33. Sewall, *Bill Sewall's Story of T.R.*, pp. 60–61.

34. Roosevelt, *Ranch Life*, p. 115.

35. Carlton Putnam, *Theodore Roosevelt, Volume One: The Formative Year, 1858–1886* (New York: Charles Scribner's Sons, 1958), pp. 569, 562.

36. Roosevelt, *Ranch Life and the Hunting Trail*, p. 115.

37. Putnam files, "Sewall Correspondence," Theodore Roosevelt Collection, Houghton Library, Harvard University. See chapter 7.

38. Frederick Badger to Henry Clay Badger, March 28, 1886, Frederick Badger Letters Folder 2, bMS Am 1454.50 (4), Theodore Roosevelt Collection, Houghton Library, Harvard University; *Bad Lands Cow Boy*, April 1, 1886; letter from William Sewall to his brother, April 21, 1886, Mattison, "Life at Roosevelt's Elkhorn Ranch," pp. 29–30.

39. Theodore Roosevelt to Henry Cabot Lodge, March 27, 1886, *The Letters of Theodore Roosevelt*, p. 95.

40. Roosevelt, *Ranch Life*, p. 116.

41. Sewall, *Bill Sewall's Story of T.R.*, p. 62.

42. Sewall, *Bill Sewall's Story of T.R.*, pp. 62–63.

43. Taylor, *Kaleidoscopic Lives*, pp. 96–97.

44. William Sewall to Sam Sewall, April 21, 1886, Mattison, "Life at Roosevelt's Elkhorn Ranch," p. 30.

45. William Sewall to Sam Sewall, April 21, 1886, Mattison, "Life at Roosevelt's Elkhorn Ranch," p. 30.

46. William Sewall to Sam Sewall, April 21, 1886, Mattison, "Life at Roosevelt's Elkhorn Ranch," p. 30. Roosevelt in his account of the capture in *Hunting Trails*

wrote that Finnegan and Burnsted were captured together, as did Sewall in his 1919 book; but in this letter to his brother, written immediately after the events, Sewall describes the men as coming into camp a half hour apart. The letter account is used here on the assumption that it was written when the story was fresher in mind; moreover Sewall, in his later account in his book, may have been influenced by Roosevelt's version, and Roosevelt's tendency to tamper with details makes that version dubious, though only in a minor detail—Roosevelt probably was seeking merely to streamline the narrative. Putnam in his Roosevelt biography also adopted the version of the story described in Sewall's letter.

47. William Sewall to Sam Sewall, April 21, 1886, Mattison, "Life at Roosevelt's Elkhorn Ranch," p. 31.

48. Roosevelt, *Ranch Life*, p. 120.

49. Roosevelt in his account does not mention Dow's interjection, but Sewall does both in his April 21, 1886, letter to his brother and in his book.

50. Taylor, *Kaleidoscopic Lives*, pp. 96–97.

51. William Sewall to Sam Sewall, April 21, 1886, Mattison, "Life at Roosevelt's Elkhorn Ranch," p. 31.

52. Mike Finnegan to Theodore Roosevelt, January 1887 (?), File 1, Theodore Roosevelt Collection, Library of Congress.

53. Roosevelt, *Ranch Life*, p. 124.

54. He later wrote to his sister Anna that he "read it through with much more interest than I have any other novel for I do not know how long. . . . Anna had a character so contradictory, unbalanced, melancholy and fiercely passionate that she can hardly be received as being other than partially insane." Theodore Roosevelt to Anna Roosevelt, April 12, 1886, *Letters of Theodore Roosevelt to Anna Roosevelt Cowles*, p. 74.

55. Roosevelt, *Ranch Life*, p. 125.

56. Sewall, *Bill Sewall's Story of T.R.*, p. 73.

57. Sewall, *Bill Sewall's Story of T.R.*, p. 73.

58. Sewall, *Bill Sewall's Story of T.R.*, p. 73.

59. Sewall, *Bill Sewall's Story of T.R.*, pp. 73–74.

60. Sewall, *Bill Sewall's Story of T.R.*, p. 74.

61. Roosevelt, *Ranch Life*, p. 127.

62. Quoted in Hagedorn, *Roosevelt in the Bad Lands*, pp. 382–383.

63. This account of Sewall and Dow's return trip is drawn from Sewall, *Bill Sewall's Story of T.R.*, pp. 76–85.

64. Sewall, *Bill Sewall's Story of T.R.*, p. 77.

65. Sewall, *Bill Sewall's Story of T.R.*, pp. 78–79.

66. Sewall, *Bill Sewall's Story of T.R.*, p. 84.

67. Sewall, *Bill Sewall's Story of T.R.*, p. 83. The *Bad Lands Cow Boy*, April 15, 1886, gave this account of the Roosevelt adventure: "Theodore Roosevelt returned Monday from a successful chase after the men who stole his boat about three weeks ago. Sewell and Dow accompanied him on the trip and they overtook the thieves about a hundred miles down river. Mr. Bad Man Finnegan tried some of his old tactics and

refused to return but such sound arguments were advanced that he concluded to change his mind. The prisoners were brought across the country to Dickinson and from there were sent to Mandan for trial. They will be sent up for as long a time as the law allows." The capture of the boat thieves raises questions about how Roosevelt might have functioned with the vigilantes had Granville Stuart permitted him to join the Montana Stranglers. His eagerness to sign up may have outstripped his facility for executing untried criminals when the time came actually to do it.

68. Putnam, *Theodore Roosevelt*, p. 570. The *Bad Lands Cow Boy*, April 15, 1886, again praised Roosevelt's leadership at the meeting: "There were numerous complimentary remarks at Mr. Roosevelt's method of conducting the stock meeting. Useless or irrelevant discussions were brought to a sudden stop and close attention was held on the business before the meeting."

69. Theodore Roosevelt to Corinne Roosevelt Robinson, April 15, 1886, *The Letters of Theodore Roosevelt*, p. 97.

70. This account of the organization draws from Hagedorn, *Roosevelt in the Bad Lands*, pp. 387–392. Voter turnout was less than enthusiastic; the April 15, 1886 *Bad Lands Cow Boy* reported that "on Monday the 12th, voters polled at Paddock's livery office, but owing to lack of interest and bad weather, only half of registered voters voted—122 votes."

71. Hermann Hagedorn files, 332.H12p, files 29–45, Theodore Roosevelt Collection, Houghton Library, Harvard University.

72. Roosevelt, *Ranch Life* p. 90.

73. Theodore Roosevelt to Anna Roosevelt, April 22, 1886, *The Letters of Theodore Roosevelt*, p. 99.

74. From an undated story from the *Minneapolis Tribune* quoted in Hagedorn, *Roosevelt in the Bad Lands*, p. 393.

75. From an undated story from the *Minneapolis Tribune* quoted in Hagedorn, *Roosevelt in the Bad Lands*, p. 393.

76. From an undated story from the *Minneapolis Tribune* quoted in Hagedorn, *Roosevelt in the Bad Lands*, p. 393.

77. Hagedorn, *Roosevelt in the Bad Lands*, pp. 394–395.

78. Theodore Roosevelt to Anna Roosevelt, April 22, 1886, *The Letters of Theodore Roosevelt*, p. 99.

79. Putnam, *Theodore Roosevelt*, pp. 572–573.

80. Theodore Roosevelt to Corinne Roosevelt Robinson, May 12, 1886, *The Letters of Theodore Roosevelt*, p. 99.

81. Theodore Roosevelt to Anna Roosevelt, May 15, 1886, *The Letters of Theodore Roosevelt*, p. 100.

82. William Sewall to Sam Sewall, February 28, 1886, Mattison, "Life at Roosevelt's Elkhorn Ranch," p. 27; Mary Sewall to her sister Annie [surname unknown], June 13, 1886, Mattison, "Life at Roosevelt's Elkhorn Ranch," p. 34.

83. Theodore Roosevelt to William Sewall, May 4, 1898, Theodore Roosevelt Collection, Library of Congress.

84. Theodore Roosevelt to Henry Cabot Lodge, June 7, 1886, *The Letters of Theodore Roosevelt*, p. 102.

85. Sewall describes this hunt in *Bill Sewall's Story of T.R.*, pp. 86–90, but in the book says the hunt took place in autumn; however, he described the same hunt in a June 27, 1886, letter to his brother Sam (see note 101), indicating it had just taken place. As the letter was written immediately after the hunt, presumably it had the correct date. Moreover, in this book, Sewall says his son and Dow's were born after the hunt; as they were born in August 1886, the hunt described in the book had to have been that summer.

86. William Sewall to Sam Sewall, June 27, 1886, Mattison, "Life at Roosevelt's Elkhorn Ranch," p. 36.

87. Theodore Roosevelt to Douglas Robinson, June 28, 1886, *The Letters of Theodore Roosevelt*, p. 106.

88. Theodore Roosevelt to Anna Roosevelt, June 7, 1886, and June 19, 1886, *Letters from Theodore Roosevelt to Anna Roosevelt Cowles*, p. 82 and pp. 83–84 respectively.

89. Mary Sewall to her sister Annie, June 13, 1886, Mattison, "Life at Roosevelt's Elkhorn Ranch," p. 34.

90. This account of the speech and surrounding events is from James F. Vivian, *The Romance of My Life* (Fargo, ND: Prairie House, 1989), pp. 3–12.

91. A. T. Packard interview, Hermann Hagedorn files, 332.H12p, file 878–878a, Theodore Roosevelt Collection, Houghton Library, Harvard University.

92. A. T. Packard interview, Hermann Hagedorn files, 332.H12p, file 878–878a, Theodore Roosevelt Collection, Houghton Library, Harvard University.

93. Vivian, *The Romance of My Life*, p. 9.

94. Vivian, *The Romance of My Life*, p. 9.

95. Vivian, *The Romance of My Life*, pp. 8–9.

96. Vivian, *The Romance of My Life*, p. 9.

97. Theodore Roosevelt to Corinne Roosevelt Robinson, July 5, 1886, *The Letters of Theodore Roosevelt*, p. 107.

98. Hagedorn, *Roosevelt in the Bad Lands*, pp. 394–405. Phillips (1811–1884) was an abolitionist and Indian rights activist noted for his oratory.

99. A. T. Packard interview, Hermann Hagedorn files, 332.H12p, file 878–878a, Theodore Roosevelt Collection, Houghton Library, Harvard University.

100. A. T. Packard interview, Hermann Hagedorn files, 332.H12p, file 878–878a, Theodore Roosevelt Collection, Houghton Library, Harvard University.

101. Hermann Hagedorn files, 332.H12p, file 738, Theodore Roosevelt Collection, Houghton Library, Harvard University.

102. Theodore Roosevelt to Corinne Roosevelt Robinson, July 5, 1886, *The Letters of Theodore Roosevelt*, pp. 106–107.

103. Theodore Roosevelt to Anna Roosevelt, June 28, 1886, *The Letters of Theodore Roosevelt*, p. 104; Edmund Morris, *The Rise of Theodore Roosevelt* (New York: Modern Library, 2001), p. 335.

104. *The Letters of Theodore Roosevelt*, p. 91, footnote.

105. Shaler's court defense was led by Elihu Root, who would serve as U.S. secretary of state under President Theodore Roosevelt. *The Letters of Theodore Roosevelt*, p. 91, footnote.

106. Theodore Roosevelt to Corinne Roosevelt Robinson, July 5, 1886, *The Letters of Theodore Roosevelt*, p. 107.

107. Theodore Roosevelt to Corinne Roosevelt Robinson, July 5, 1886, *The Letters of Theodore Roosevelt*, p. 107.

108. *Bad Lands Cow Boy*, July 22, 1886.

109. *Bad Lands Cow Boy*, July 15, 1886.

110. Ray H. Mattison, "Roosevelt's Elkhorn Ranch." *North Dakota Historical Society Quarterly* 27, 2 (Spring 1960): 55.

111. Lincoln A. Lang, *Ranching with Roosevelt* (Philadelphia: J. B. Lippincott Company, 1926), p. 220.

112. *Bismarck Daily Tribune*, July 9, 1886 ("Gatling gun"); the rest of the comments on the cattle business are from the *Mandan Pioneer*, July 16, 1886.

113. *Bismarck Daily Tribune*, July 9, 1886.

114. Lang, *Ranching with Roosevelt*, p. 221. What Lang more likely sensed was Roosevelt's growing interest in Edith and the East.

115. Lang, *Ranching with Roosevelt*, p. 222.

116. Lang, *Ranching with Roosevelt*, p. 222.

117. Lang, *Ranching with Roosevelt*, pp. 223–224.

118. Lang, *Ranching with Roosevelt*, p. 225.

119. William Sewall to Sam Sewall, April 21, 1886, Mattison, "Life at Roosevelt's Elkhorn Ranch," p. 33.

120. Shaler would hold on to the position until he was removed in 1891. *The Letters of Theodore Roosevelt*, p. 91, footnote.

121. Theodore Roosevelt to Anna Roosevelt, August 7, 1886, *The Letters of Theodore Roosevelt*, p. 107.

15: LOVE AND GUILT

1. Margaret Roberts, "In the Bad Lands, When I Knew T.R." *McCall's*, October 1919, p. 2.

2. Hermann Hagedorn files, interview with Mrs. William Merrifield, 332.H12p, file 1073, Theodore Roosevelt Collection, Houghton Library, Harvard University.

3. Edmund Morris, *The Rise of Theodore Roosevelt* (New York: Modern Library, 2001), p. 335; Sylvia Jukes Morris, *Edith Kermit Roosevelt* (New York: Vintage Books, 1990), p. 90.

4. Morris, *Edith Kermit Roosevelt*, p. 88.

5. Carlton Putnam, *Theodore Roosevelt, Volume One: The Formative Years, 1858–1886* (New York: Charles Scribner's Sons, 1958), p. 585.

6. William Wingate Sewall, *Bill Sewall's Story of T.R.* (New York: Harper & Brothers, 1919), p. 74.

7. Theodore Roosevelt to Anna Roosevelt Cowles, August 11, 1886, *Letters from Theodore Roosevelt to Anna Roosevelt Cowles 1870–1918* (New York: Charles Scribner's Sons, 1924), p. 88.

8. Theodore Roosevelt to Anna Roosevelt Cowles, August 11, 1886, *Letters from Theodore Roosevelt to Anna Roosevelt Cowles*, p. 88.

9. Theodore Roosevelt to Anna Roosevelt Cowles, August 11, 1886, *Letters from Theodore Roosevelt to Anna Roosevelt Cowles*, p. 88.

10. Theodore Roosevelt to Anna Roosevelt Cowles, August 11, 1886, Theodore Roosevelt Collection, Houghton Library, Harvard University; also published in *Letters from Theodore Roosevelt to Anna Roosevelt Cowles*, pp. 88–89.

11. Morris, *The Rise of Theodore Roosevelt*, pp. 335–336.

12. William Wingate Sewall, "As I Knew Him." *Forum* LXI, 5 (May 1919). The pages of the source copy used here, from a Library of Congress electronic archive, are unnumbered.

13. Putnam, *Theodore Roosevelt*, p. 585.

14. Theodore Roosevelt to Henry Cabot Lodge, August 10, 1886, *The Letters of Theodore Roosevelt*, ed. Elting E. Morison (Cambridge, MA: Harvard University Press, 1951), p. 108.

15. Theodore Roosevelt to Henry Cabot Lodge, August 10, 1886, *The Letters of Theodore Roosevelt*, p. 108.

16. Theodore Roosevelt to Henry Cabot Lodge, August 10, 1886, *The Letters of Theodore Roosevelt*, p. 108.

17. Theodore Roosevelt, *Ranch Life and the Hunting Trail* (New York: Bonanza Books, 1978), p. 109.

18. Theodore Roosevelt to Henry Cabot Lodge, August 20, 1886, *The Letters of Theodore Roosevelt*, p. 108.

19. Sewall, *Bill Sewall's Story of T.R.*, p. 91.

20. Sewall, *Bill Sewall's Story of T.R.*, p. 91.

21. Theodore Roosevelt to Anna Roosevelt, August 20, 1886, quoted in Morris, *The Rise of Theodore Roosevelt*, p. 335.

22. William Sewall to Sam Sewall, August 1, 1886, in Ray H. Mattison, "Life at Roosevelt's Elkhorn Ranch—the Letters of William W. and Mary Sewall," p. 38, reprint of *North Dakota Historical Society Quarterly* 27, 3–4 (Summer and Fall 1960), Theodore Roosevelt Collection, Houghton Library, Harvard University.

23. William Sewall to Sam Sewall, August 1, 1886, Mattison, "Life at Roosevelt's Elkhorn Ranch," pp. 38–39.

24. Roosevelt, *Ranch Life*, pp. 175–176.

25. Jack Willis, *Roosevelt in the Rough* (New York: Ives Washburn, 1931), p. 8.

26. Willis, *Roosevelt in the Rough*, p. 9.

27. Theodore Roosevelt, *Hunting Trips of a Ranchman and The Wilderness Hunter* (New York: Modern Library, 2004), p. 434.

28. Vesta O. Robbins, "'Making a Man of Roosevelt," *Outdoor Life and Recreation*, August 1928 (no page numbers on original), Series 16, Addition II, Theodore Roosevelt

Collection, Library of Congress Manuscript Division. Ironically, Willis had been born in 1857 on February 14—a day Roosevelt would associate with the deaths of his wife and mother.

29. Willis, *Roosevelt in the Rough*, p. 5.

30. Hermann Hagedorn files, 332.H12p, files 121–167, Theodore Roosevelt Collection, Houghton Library, Harvard University. In regard to this story, Roosevelt said to Willis that there were other fellows who ought to have been killed, but Willis "never took the hint."

31. Willis, *Roosevelt in the Rough*, p. 5. He wrote that deer skins sold for a dollar to a dollar and a quarter, though toward the end of his hunting career they were going for as much as five dollars.

32. Willis, *Roosevelt in the Rough*, p. 9.

33. Willis, *Roosevelt in the Rough*, p. 10.

34. Willis, *Roosevelt in the Rough*, p. 11.

35. Roosevelt, *Ranch Life*, p. 171.

36. Roosevelt, *Ranch Life*, p. 172.

37. Willis, *Roosevelt in the Rough*, pp. 13–14.

38. Willis, *Roosevelt in the Rough*, pp. 15–16.

39. Willis, *Roosevelt in the Rough*, p. 16.

40. Willis, *Roosevelt in the Rough*, p. 17.

41. Roosevelt, *Ranch Life*, pp. 179–182. In other particulars, the stories are not much different.

42. Roosevelt, *Ranch Life*, p. 179.

43. Willis, *Roosevelt in the Rough*, pp. 17–18.

44. Willis also told of another Roosevelt tumble during the hunt. According to Willis, Roosevelt wanted photographs of a tall waterfall and, to get the perspective he wanted, he had his two companions suspend him from a gorge wall in front of the waterfall, only to find, after he took his photos, that he could not be hauled back up. Willis wrote that eventually Roosevelt had to drop about thirty-five feet into the pool at the base of the falls. Roosevelt does not mention the incident in his account of the hunt. Willis, *Roosevelt in the Rough*, pp. 19–23.

45. Roosevelt, *Ranch Life*, pp. 181–182.

46. Roosevelt, *Ranch Life*, p. 182.

47. Roosevelt, *Ranch Life*, p. 178.

48. Roosevelt, *Ranch Life*, p. 182.

49. Willis, *Roosevelt in the Rough*, p. 4.

50. Willis, *Roosevelt in the Rough*, p. 19.

51. Willis, *Roosevelt in the Rough*, pp. 27–28.

52. Willis, *Roosevelt in the Rough*, p. 27.

53. Robbins, "'Making a Man' of Roosevelt." Evaluating the accuracy of Willis' claims is often difficult, however, because he seems to have been prone to exaggeration, especially in putting himself into a good light.

54. John Willis to Theodore Roosevelt, December 16, 1905, Series 16, Addition II, Theodore Roosevelt Collection, Library of Congress Manuscript Division.

55. Willis, *Roosevelt in the Rough*, pp. 40–41.

56. Willis claimed that when he realized how much Roosevelt had paid him, he wrote to Roosevelt, addressing the letter to "Theodore Roosevelt, in New York City," saying he could not accept the cash and would return all but $150 if Roosevelt would send him an office or home address. Roosevelt responded that *Century* magazine was going to pay him $2,500 for a story about the goat hunt, and as Willis had made it possible for him to write the story, it seemed fair he should get half the money. He also said that if Willis didn't keep the money and quit talking about it, he would withdraw his promise to pay Willis another visit. Willis kept the money. Willis, *Roosevelt in the Rough*, pp. 40–41.

57. Theodore Roosevelt to Anna Roosevelt, August 20, 1886, quoted in Morris, *The Rise of Theodore Roosevelt*, p. 336.

58. *New York Times*, August 29, 1886.

59. *New York Times*, September 5, 1886.

60. Theodore Roosevelt Collection, Houghton Library, Harvard University.

61. Nicholas Roosevelt, *Theodore Roosevelt: The Man as I Knew Him* (New York: Dodd, Mead & Company), p. 22.

62. Roosevelt, *Theodore Roosevelt*, pp. 22–23.

63. Sewall, *Bill Sewall's Story of T.R.*, p. 91.

64. Hermann Hagedorn, *Roosevelt in the Bad Lands* (Boston: Houghton Mifflin Company, 1921), p. 424.

65. Sewall, *Bill Sewall's Story of T.R.*, p. 92.

66. Sewall, *Bill Sewall's Story of T.R.*, p. 92.

67. Putnam discusses this point at some length and concludes that the price of the cattle was a flimsy reason for leaving. Putnam, *Theodore Roosevelt*, pp. 588–590.

68. Mattison, "Life at Roosevelt's Elkhorn Ranch," p. 39; Hagedorn, *Roosevelt in the Bad Lands*, p. 427; Bill Merrifield interview, Hermann Hagedorn files, 332. H12p, file 1078, Theodore Roosevelt Collection, Hougton Library, Harvard University.

69. Putnam, *Theodore Roosevelt*, p. 590.

70. Sewall, *Bill Sewall's Story of T.R.*, p. 93.

71. Sewall, *Bill Sewall's Story of T.R.*, pp. 94–95.

72. Hagedorn, *Roosevelt in the Bad Lands*, p. 431.

73. Granville Stuart, *Forty Years on the Frontier*, Part 2: *Pioneering in Montana* (Lincoln: University of Nebraska Press, 1977), p. 234.

74. Hagedorn, *Roosevelt in the Bad Lands*, p. 431.

75. Hagedorn, *Roosevelt in the Bad Lands*, pp. 412–413.

76. This general outline of Roosevelt's mayoral candidacy leans heavily on Morris, *The Rise of Theodore Roosevelt*, pp. 339–356.

77. *The Letters of Theodore Roosevelt*, p. 110.

78. Morris, *The Rise of Theodore Roosevelt*, p. 353.

79. Morris, *The Rise of Theodore Roosevelt*, pp. 339–341.

80. Henry F. Pringle, *Theodore Roosevelt* (New York: Harcourt, Brace & World, 1956), p. 78.

81. James D. McCabe, *New York by Sunlight and Gaslight: A Work Descriptive of the Great American Metropolis* (n.p.: Edgewood Publishing Company, 1881), pp. 308–310.

82. Morris, *The Rise of Theodore Roosevelt*, p. 346.

83. *The World*, "Rallying for Roosevelt," October 28, 1886.

84. Morris, *The Rise of Theodore Roosevelt*, p. 351.

85. "Roosevelt Is a Rustler," *The World*, October 30, 1886.

86. Morris, *The Rise of Theodore Roosevelt*, p. 351.

87. Theodore Roosevelt to Francis Theodora Smith Dana, October 21, 1886, *The Letters of Theodore Roosevelt*, p. 113.

88. Theodore Roosevelt to Francis Theodora Smith Dana, October 21, 1886, *The Letters of Theodore Roosevelt*, p. 113.

89. Theodore Roosevelt to Francis Theodora Smith Dana, October 21, 1886, *The Letters of Theodore Roosevelt*, p. 113.

90. Hermann Hagedorn files, 332.H12p, files 1086–1113, Theodore Roosevelt Collection, Houghton Library, Harvard University.

91. Quoted in Sylvia Jukes Morris, *Edith Kermit Roosevelt* (New York: Vintage Books, 1990), p. 93.

92. Morison, ed., *The Letters of Theodore Roosevelt*, p. 110.

93. Theodore Roosevelt, *An Autobiography* (New York: The Macmillan Company, 1913), p. 144.

94. Morris, *The Rise of Theodore Roosevelt*, p. 356.

95. Hermann Hagedorn files, 332.H12p, files 121–167, Theodore Roosevelt Collection, Houghton Library, Harvard University.

96. Morison, ed., *The Letters of Theodore Roosevelt*, p. 116.

97. Theodore Roosevelt to Anna Roosevelt, January 3, 1887, Theodore Roosevelt Collection, Houghton Library, Harvard University; also published in Morison, ed., *The Letters of Theodore Roosevelt*, p. 117.

98. Theodore Roosevelt to Anna Roosevelt, August 20, 1886, Theodore Roosevelt Collection, Hougton Library, Harvard University.

99. Theodore Roosevelt to Anna Roosevelt, January 3, 1887, Theodore Roosevelt Collection, Houghton Library, Harvard Univeristy; also published in *The Letters of Theodore Roosevelt*, p. 117.

100. *The Letters of Theodore Roosevelt*, p. 118.

101. *The Letters of Theodore Roosevelt*, p. 121.

102. Theodore Roosevelt to Corinne Roosevelt Robinson, January 22, 1887, *The Letters of Theodore Roosevelt*, p. 119; Theodore Roosevelt to Francis Theodora Smith Dana, October 21, 1886, *The Letters of Theodore Roosevelt*, p. 113.

103. Theodore Roosevelt to Corinne Roosevelt Robinson, February 27, 1887, *The Letters of Theodore Roosevelt*, p. 123.

104. Nicholas Roosevelt, *Theodore Roosevelt: The Man as I Knew Him* (New York: Dodd, Mead & Company), p. 24.

105. Letters of Anna Bamie Roosevelt, Theodore Roosevelt Collection, Houghton Library, Harvard University

106. Morris, *Edith Kermit Roosevelt*, p. 106.

107. Michael Teague, *Mrs. L: Conservations with Alice Roosevelt Longworth* (Garden City, NY: Doubleday & Company, 1981), p. 12.

108. Teague, *Mrs. L*, p. 18.

109. Alice Roosevelt Longworth, *Crowded Hours* (New York: Charles Scribner's Sons, 1933), pp. 8–9.

110. Teague, *Mrs. L*, pp. 36, 30.

111. Teague, *Mrs. L*, pp. 36–37.

112. Teague, *Mrs. L*, p. 37.

113. Morris, *Edith Kermit Roosevelt*, p. 107.

114. Morris, *Edith Kermit Roosevelt*, pp. 107–108.

115. Morris, *The Rise of Theodore Roosevelt*, p. 373.

116. Theodore Roosevelt to William Sewall, April 7, 1887, Theodore Roosevelt Collection, Library of Congress Manuscript Division.

16: THE BLIZZARDS OF 1886–87

1. Lincoln A. Lang, *Ranching with Roosevelt* (Philadelphia: J. B. Lippincott Company, 1926), p. 241. The tragic winter of 1886 to 1887 had its origins far across the globe. In August 1883, the Indonesian volcano Krakatoa erupted with an explosion that was heard three thousand miles away and that blasted out six cubic miles of ash and dust. Aside from the production of dazzling sunsets throughout the world, the atmospheric particulates blocked enough sunlight to cause bitter winters. "The legendary harsh winter of 1886–87 and the devastating blizzards of 1888—Krakatoa's unwelcome gifts to the struggling settlers and ranchers in the Great Plains— brought cattle-grazing on the open range of the United States to an end." Henry Pollack, *A World Without Ice* (New York: Avery, 2009), pp. 135–136.

2. Lang, *Ranching with Roosevelt*, pp. 234–235.

3. William T. Dantz, "Theodore Roosevelt—Cowboy and Ranchman." *Harper's Weekly*, August 6, 1904, pp. 1212–1215; Lang, *Ranching with Roosevelt*, p. 239.

4. *Bismarck Daily Tribune*, December 9, 1886.

5. The description of the early weather conditions and of the blizzard draw on Lang, *Ranching with Roosevelt*, pp. 241–243.

6. Lang, *Ranching with Roosevelt*, p. 242.

7. Dr. Stickney survived being lost in a blizzard. "During the late severe storm Dr. Stickney was called to the country to visit a patient and together with the person who came after him lost his way, wandering on the prairie all night." *Dickinson Press*, December 11, 1886.

8. Lang, *Ranching with Roosevelt*, p. 246.

9. Lang, *Ranching with Roosevelt*, p. 246.

10. Lang, *Ranching with Roosevelt*, p. 250.

11. Hermann Hagedorn files, 332.H12p, file 1079f, Theodore Roosevelt Collection, Houghton Library, Harvard University.

12. Lang, *Ranching with Roosevelt*, p. 247.

13. Hermann Hagedorn, *Roosevelt in the Bad Lands* (Boston: Houghton Mifflin Company, 1921), p. 436.

14. Theodore Roosevelt, *Ranch Life and the Hunting Trail* (New York: Bonanza Books, 1978), p. 22. This book was published in 1888, but Roosevelt wrote the content earlier as *Century* magazine stories.

15. *Dickinson Press*, March 7, 1887, Theodore Roosevelt Collection, Houghton Library, Harvard University.

16. Lang, *Ranching with Roosevelt*, pp. 250–251. Lang put a philosophical spin on the situation: "And watching it, too, in the mind of the man who knew, there was more than room for the thought, 'An eye for an eye and a tooth for a tooth.' The White Man had desecrated Nature's preserves. Had saturated the earth with the blood of her wild kinsfolk. Had replaced them with his herds. Nature had come back at him in full measure and had retaliated in her own peculiar way. Now she was sweeping out the carcasses as something obnoxious in her sight" (p. 251).

17. Howard Eaton to William Sewall, February 26, 1887, Sewall Correspondence, Putnam materials, Theodore Roosevelt Collection, Houghton Library, Harvard University.

18. Granville Stuart, *Forty Years on the Frontier* (Lincoln: University of Nebraska Press, 1977), pp. 236–237.

19. Interview with Sylvane Ferris, April 2, 1918, L. F. Crawford Papers, North Dakota Historical Society; Ray H. Mattison, *Roosevelt and the Stockmen's Association* (Theodore Roosevelt Nature and History Association, 1969), p. 4, reprint from *North Dakota Historical Society Quarterly* 17, 2 (April 1950) and 17, 3 (July 1950), Theodore Roosevelt Collection, Harvard University, Houghton Library.

20. Hermann Hagedorn files, 332.H12p, file 1079a, Theodore Roosevelt Collection, Houghton Library, Harvard University.

21. Roosevelt, *Ranch Life*, p. 79. In 1887 Roosevelt paid taxes on 60 percent fewer cattle than he had in 1886, according to the assessor's returns: Ray H. Mattison, "Roosevelt's Elkhorn Ranch," *North Dakota History* 27, 2 (Spring 1960): 56.

22. Theodore Roosevelt to Henry Cabot Lodge, April 20, 1887, *The Letters of Theodore Roosevelt*, ed. Elting E. Morison (Cambridge, MA: Harvard University Press, 1951), p. 127.

23. Theodore Roosevelt to Anna Roosevelt, April 16, 1887, *The Letters of Theodore Roosevelt*, pp. 126–127.

24. Lang, *Ranching with Roosevelt*, pp. 252–253.

25. T. F. Roberts, "Pioneer Life in Western Dakota." *North Dakota Historical Society Quarterly* 15, 3 (Summer 1948): 242.

26. Hagedorn, *Roosevelt in the Bad Lands*, p. 441.

27. Theodore Roosevelt to William Sewall, December 26, 1887, Theodore Roosevelt Collection, Library of Congress Manuscript Division. Married that year: Hagedorn, *Roosevelt in the Bad Lands*, p. 447.

28. Hagedorn, *Roosevelt in the Bad Lands*, p. 439.

29. Howard Eaton to William Sewall, February 26, 1887, Sewall Correspondence, Putnam materials, Theodore Roosevelt Collection, Houghton Library, Harvard University.

30. *Bismarck Daily Tribune*, December 9, 1886; Howard Eaton to William Sewall, February 26, 1887, Sewall Correspondence, Putnam materials, Theodore Roosevelt Collection, Houghton Library, Harvard University; Hagedorn, *Roosevelt in the Bad Lands*, p. 451.

31. *Dickinson Press*, February 12, 1887, Theodore Roosevelt Collection, Houghton Library, Harvard University.

32. A. C. Huidekoper, in Hermann Hagedorn papers, Theodore Roosevelt Collection, Houghton Library, Harvard University. Hermann Hagedorn offers details about the Marquis de Morès' failure in *Roosevelt in the Bad Lands* (Boston: Houghton Mifflin Company, 1921), pp. 447–451. John Goodall agreed that the Marquis was squeezed out: Anonymous, *50 Years in the Saddle*, (Watford City, ND: 50 Years in the Saddle Club, 1963), 1: 291.

33. Interview with John W. Goodall, L. F. Crawford Papers, North Dakota Historical Society.

34. Interview with John W. Goodall, L. F. Crawford Papers, North Dakota Historical Society.

35. *Dickinson Press*, June 4, 1887, and May 21, 1887, Theodore Roosevelt Collection, Houghton Library, Harvard University.

36. *Dickinson Press*, June 18, 1887, Theodore Roosevelt Collection, Houghton Library, Harvard University.

37. *Dickinson Press*, August 6, 1887, Theodore Roosevelt Collection, Houghton Library, Harvard University.

38. Quoted in Hagedorn, *Roosevelt in the Bad Lands*, p. 430.

39. Phillip Ashton Rollins, *The Cowboy: An Unconventional History of Civilization on the Old-Time Cattle Range* (Norman: University of Oklahoma Press, 1997), p. 31.

40. Rollins, *The Cowboy*, p. 30.

41. Sean Dennis Cashman, *America in the Gilded Age* (New York: New York University Press, 1993), p. 282.

42. Mattison, *Roosevelt and the Stockmen's Association*, p. 41.

43. Lang, *Ranching With Roosevelt*, p. 259.

44. Hagedorn, *Roosevelt in the Bad Lands*, pp. 444–446.

45. Mattison, *Roosevelt and the Stockmen's Association*, p. 41. Roosevelt, his time as

an active rancher over, stayed on the rolls of the Montana Stockgrowers Association until 1890, when he resigned as the only member of the executive committee from Dakota Territory. He reappeared on the rolls only once after that, in 1905, when he was running for president; Mattison, p. 51.

46. Edmund Morris, *The Rise of Theodore Roosevelt* (New York: Modern Library, 2001), p. 380.

47. Morris, *The Rise of Theodore Roosevelt*, p. 381.

48. Sylvia Jukes Morris, *Edith Kermit Roosevelt* (New York: Vintage Books, 1990), p. 112; Morris, *The Rise of Theodore Roosevelt*, p. 386.

49. Morris, *The Rise of Theodore Roosevelt*, p. 386.

50. A small bison herd made the local news when it showed up in autumn 1886 in McLean and Lamoure counties; *Bismarck Daily Tribune*, November 26, 1886.

51. Theodore Roosevelt, *Outdoor Pastimes of an American Hunter* (Mechanicsburg, PA: Stackpole Books, 1990 [1905]), p. 287.

52. Roosevelt, *Ranch Life*, p. 24.

17: BADLANDS LEGACY

1. Theodore Roosevelt to Jonas Van Duzer, January 15, 1888, *The Letters of Theodore Roosevelt*, ed. Elting E. Morison (Cambridge, MA: Harvard University Press, 1951), p. 136.

2. Theodore Roosevelt, *Outdoor Pastimes of an American Hunter* (Mechanicsburg, PA: Stackpole Books, 1990 [1905]), pp. 190–191 for all following estimates on game status.

3. Roosevelt, *Outdoor Pastimes*, p. 192.

4. Theodore Roosevelt and George Bird Grinnell, eds., *American Big-Game Hunting: The Book of the Boone and Crockett Club* (New York: Forest and Stream Publishing Co., 1901), pp. 245–246.

5. David T. Courtwright, *Violent Land: Single Men and Social Disorder from the Frontier to the Inner City* (Cambridge, MA: Harvard University Press, 2000), p. 125.

6. Roosevelt and Grinnell, eds., *American Big-Game Hunting*, p. 58.

7. Paul Russell Cutright, *Theodore Roosevelt: The Making of a Conservationist* (Urbana: University of Illinois Press, 1985), p. 169; Michael Punke, *Last Stand: George Bird Grinnell, the Battle to Save the Buffalo, and the Birth of the New West* (New York: HarperCollins Publishers, 2007), pp. 165–166; James B. Trefethen, *Crusade for Wildlife: Highlights in Conservation Progress* (Harrisburg, PA: The Stackpole Company; New York: Boone and Crockett Club, 1961), pp. 16–19.

8. Theodore Roosevelt, "The Boone and Crockett Club," *Harper's Weekly*, March 18, 1893, p. 267.

9. Punke, *Last Stand*, p. 166.

10. Roosevelt and Grinnell, eds., *American Big-Game Hunting*, p. 326.

11. Roosevelt and Grinnell, eds., *American Big-Game Hunting*, pp. 14–15.

12. Roosevelt, "The Boone and Crockett Club," p. 267.

13. Roosevelt, "The Boone and Crockett Club," p. 267; see also Roosevelt and Grinnell, eds., *American Big-Game Hunting*, pp. 10–11.

14. Trefethen. *Crusade for Wildlife*, p. 48.

15. Sean Dennis Cashman, *America in the Gilded Age* (New York: New York University Press, 1993), p. 311.

16. Trefethen, *Crusade for Wildlife*, p. 48.

17. George Bird Grinnell, "Our National Parks," *Forest and Stream*, December 3, 1891, p. [1?].

18. Punke, *Last Stand*, p. 139.

19. *Congregationalist*, August 24, 1893; George Bird Grinnell, "The Capture of Howell," *Forest and Stream* XLII, 18 (March 31, 1894): 270; Anonymous, "Park Poachers and Their Ways," *Forest and Stream* XLII, 21 (May 26, 1894): 444; George Bird Grinnell, "A Premium on Crime," *Forest and Stream* XLII, 12 (May 24, 1894); L. H. Pammel, ed., *Major John F. Lacey: Memorial Volume* (Cedar Rapids: Iowa Park and Forestry Association, 1915), p. 60; Punke, *Last Stand*, p. 216; George S. Anderson, *Report of the Superintendent of the Yellowstone National Park to the Secretary of the Interior* (Washington, D.C.: U.S. Government Printing Office, 1895), pp. 11–12.

20. Anderson, *Report of the Superintendent*, p. 9; Grinnell, "Our National Parks." Much of the account of the 1892 fight given here also is adapted from Punke, *Last Stand*, pp. 186–191.

21. George Bird Grinnell, introduction to *The Works of Theodore Roosevelt* (New York: Charles Scribner's Sons, 1929), 1: xvii.

22. Grinnell, introduction to *The Works of Theodore Roosevelt*, 1: xvii.

23. Theodore Roosevelt, *Hunting Trips of a Ranchman and The Wilderness Hunter* (New York: Modern Library, 2004), pp. 446–448, 454–477; Jack Willis, *Roosevelt in the Rough* (New York: Ives Washburn, 1931), pp. 42–53; Theodore Roosevelt to Anna Roosevelt, October 5, 1888, *The Letters of Theodore Roosevelt*, p. 146.

24. Edmund Morris, *The Rise of Theodore Roosevelt* (New York: Modern Library, 2001), p. 395.

25. Theodore Roosevelt to Anna Roosevelt, October 5, 1888, *The Letters of Theodore Roosevelt*, p. 146. He chortled that Edith would at last "see the wonderful Mrs. Selmes, for we will visit St. Paul, as well as Detroit and Chicago." He added that Alice was happy to see him when he returned and that, at about four and a half, "she is sunny and merry the whole day long," as befit the daughter of a woman called Sunshine.

26. Theodore Roosevelt to Richard Waston Gilder, July 19, 1888, *The Letters of Theodore Roosevelt*, pp. 143–144.

27. Sylvia Jukes Morris, *Edith Kermit Roosevelt* (New York: Vintage Books, 1990), p. 119.

28. Theodore Roosevelt to William Sewall, October 13, 1889, Theodore Roosevelt Collection, Library of Congress Manuscript Division.

29. Roosevelt, *Hunting Trips*, pp. 569–572; Sylvia Jukes Morris, *Edith Kermit Roosevelt* (New York: Vintage Books, 1990), p. 119.

30. Roosevelt, *Hunting Trips*, p. 571.

31. Roosevelt, *Hunting Trips*, p. 571.

32. Roosevelt, *Hunting Trips*, pp. 571–572. Wildlife conservation was in a strange state in the late 1800s, when one of the leading advocates of wildlife protection could with pride kill a healthy member of a vanishing species.

33. Theodore Roosevelt to William Sewall, October 20, 1890, Theodore Roosevelt Collection, Library of Congress Manuscript Division.

34. Edith Roosevelt to Theodore Roosevelt, August 15, 1889, quoted in Morris, *Edith Kermit Roosevelt*, p. 119.

35. Theodore Roosevelt to William Sewall, October 13, 1889, Theodore Roosevelt Collection, Library of Congress Manuscript Division.

36. Morris, *Edith Kermit Roosevelt*, pp. 138–140. See also pp. 88, 91, and 102.

37. Theodore Roosevelt to William Sewall, October 20, 1890, Theodore Roosevelt Collection, Library of Congress Manuscript Division.

38. Roosevelt, *Hunting Trips*, p. 517; details of the hunt are pp. 498–522.

39. Roosevelt, *Hunting Trips*, p. 517; details of the hunt are p. 518.

40. Roosevelt, *Hunting Trips*, p. 518.

41. Roosevelt, *Hunting Trips*, p. 518.

42. William Wingate Sewall, *Bill Sewall's Story of T.R.* (New York: Harper & Brothers, 1919), pp. 100–101.

43. Hermann Hagedorn, *Roosevelt in the Bad Lands* (Boston: Houghton Mifflin Company, 1921), p. 458.

44. E. C. Abbott and Helena Huntington Smith, *We Pointed Them North: Recollections of a Cowpuncher* (Norman: University of Oklahoma Press, 1955), p. 209.

45. Hagedorn, *Roosevelt in the Bad Lands*, pp. 458–459.

46. Owen Wister, *Roosevelt: The Story of a Friendship, 1880–1919* (New York: The Macmillan Company, 1930), p. 41.

47. Theodore Roosevelt to Owen Wister, April 20, 1894, quoted in Wister, *Roosevelt: The Story of a Friendship*, p. 36.

48. *Congregationalist*, August 24, 1893.

49. Theodore Roosevelt to Sylvane Ferris, December 7, 1897, reel 315, Theodore Roosevelt Collection, Library of Congress Manuscript Division.

50. Theodore Roosevelt to Sylvane Ferris, April 24, 1898, reel 316, Theodore Roosevelt Collection, Library of Congress Manuscript Division.

51. Hagedorn, *Roosevelt in the Bad Lands*, p. 482.

52. Ray H. Mattison, "Roosevelt's Elkhorn Ranch," *North Dakota Historical Society Quarterly* 27, 2 (Spring 1960): 57–58.

53. D. Jerome Tweton, "North Dakota Editors and the Presidential Candidates of 1900," *North Dakota Historical Society Quarterly* 27, 2 (Spring 1960): 37.

54. *Fessenden Advertiser*, June 25, 1900, cited in Tweton, "North Dakota Editors and the Presidential Candidates of 1900," 37.

55. Cutright, *Theodore Roosevelt: The Making of a Conservationist*, pp. 220, 223–224, and 225.

56. Theodore Roosevelt, *An Autobiography* (New York: The Macmillan Company, 1913), p. 437.

57. Roosevelt, *An Autobiography*, pp. 445–447. For details of the governors' conference, see Newton C. Blanchard et al., eds., *Proceedings of a Conference of Governors in the White House, Washington, D.C., May 13–15, 1908* (Washington, D.C.: U.S. Government Printing Office, 1909).

58. Allen Churchill, *The Roosevelts: American Aristocrats* (New York: Harper & Row, 1965), pp. 117–118.

59. Churchill, *The Roosevelts*, p. 117–118. Izaak Walton was a seventeenth-century English fishing enthusiast who wrote a classic book on the subject, *The Compleat Angler*.

60. Nicholas Roosevelt, *Theodore Roosevelt: The Man as I Knew Him* (New York: Dodd, Mead & Company, 1967), p. 128.

61. Robert J. Moore, quoted in Lowell E. Baier, "The Cradle of Conservation: Theodore Roosevelt's Elkhorn Ranch, An Icon of America's National Identity," *Theodore Roosevelt Association Journal*, XXVIII, 1 (Winter 2007): 16.

62. Robert J. Moore, quoted in Baier, "The Cradle of Conservation," p. 16.

63. John Burroughs, *Camping and Tramping with Roosevelt* (Boston and New York: Houghton Mifflin Company, 1907), pp. 14–15. Burroughs had reservations about Roosevelt's conclusion: "There is no doubt, I think, that he would have got there some day; but without the chain of events above outlined, his rise could not have been so rapid" (p. 15).

64. Roosevelt, *An Autobiography*, p. 132.

65. Carlton Putnam, *Theodore Roosevelt, Volume One: The Formative Years, 1858–1886* (New York: Charles Scribner's Sons, 1958), pp. 310–311.

66. Corinne Roosevelt Robinson, *My Brother Theodore Roosevelt* (New York: Charles Scribner's Sons, 1921), p. 150.

67. William Roscoe Thayer, *Theodore Roosevelt: An Intimate Biography* (New York: Grosset & Dunlap, 1919), p. 68.

68. Frederick S. Wood, ed., *Roosevelt as We Knew Him: The Personal Recollections of One Hundred and Fifty of His Friends and Associates* (Philadelphia: The John C. Winston Company, 1927), pp. 204–205.

69. William Wingate Sewall, "As I Knew Him," *Forum* LXI, 5, (May 1919). The pages of the source copy used here, from a Library of Congress electronic archive, are unnumbered.

70. Stefan Lorant, *The Life and Times of Theodore Roosevelt* (Garden City, NY: Doubleday & Company, 1959), p. 205.

71. Theodore Roosevelt to Sylvane Ferris, February 10, 1899, reel 320, Theodore Roosevelt Collection, Library of Congress Manuscript Division.

72. Theodore Roosevelt to Sylvane Ferris, November 27, 1899, reel 322, Theodore Roosevelt Collection, Library of Congress Manuscript Division.

73. Theodore Roosevelt to Joe Ferris, December 1, 1905, reel 343, Theodore Roosevelt Collection, Library of Congress Manuscript Division.

74. Joe Ferris to Theodore Roosevelt, October 26, 1907, Theodore Roosevelt Collection, Library of Congress Manuscript Division.

75. Henry F. Pringle, *Theodore Roosevelt* (New York: Harcourt, Brace & World, 1956), pp. 73–74; Roosevelt, *Theodore Roosevelt: The Man as I Knew Him*, pp. 136–137; Putnam, *Theodore Roosevelt*, p. 596.

EPILOGUE

1. Anonymous, "A rough rider in the White House," *Convergence*, Summer/Spring 2008, p. 19.

2. Theodore Roosevelt to Sylvane Ferris, September 28 [?], 1905, reel 339, Theodore Roosevelt Collection, Library of Congress Manuscript Division; Theodore Roosevelt, *An Autobiography* (New York: The Macmillan Company, 1913), p. 96.

3. Putnam material, "Misc. Correspondence," Theodore Roosevelt Collection, Houghton Library, Harvard University.

4. John Willis to Theodore Roosevelt, August 28, 1904, Series 16, Addition II, Theodore Roosevelt Collection, Library of Congress Manuscript Division.

5. Anonymous, "A Rough Rider in the White House," *Convergence*, Summer/Spring 2008, 21.

6. Sylvane Ferris to Frank Harper, December 10, 1912, Theodore Roosevelt Collection, Library of Congress Manuscript Division.

7. Lincoln Lang to Theodore Roosevelt, April 6, 1917, and Theodore Roosevelt to Lincoln Lang, January 23 [?], 1898, Theodore Roosevelt Collection, Library of Congress Manuscript Division.

8. Theodore Roosevelt to Lincoln Lang, February 21, 1909, Theodore Roosevelt Collection, Library of Congress Manuscript Division; Lincoln A. Lang, *Ranching with Roosevelt* (Philadelphia: J. B. Lippincott Company, 1926), pp. 363–364.

9. Theodore Roosevelt to Lincoln Lang, April 7, 1900, Theodore Roosevelt Collection, Library of Congress Manuscript Division.

10. Hermann Hagedorn papers, Theodore Roosevelt Collection, Houghton Library, Harvard University.

11. Hermann Hagedorn, *Roosevelt in the Bad Lands* (Boston: Houghton Mifflin Company, 1921), p. 457.

12. Donald Dresden, *The Marquis de Morès: Emperor of the Bad Lands* (Norman: University of Oklahoma Press, 1970), pp. 185, 190–197; Edmund Morris, *The Rise of Theodore Roosevelt* (New York: Modern Library, 2001), p. 379.

13. Dresden, *The Marquis de Morès*, pp. 231–249.

14. Theodore Roosevelt to William Sewall, May 26, 1891, Theodore Roosevelt Collection, Library of Congress Manuscript Division.

15. Theodore Roosevelt to William Sewall, August 5, 1891, Theodore Roosevelt Collection, Library of Congress Manuscript Division.

16. Theodore Roosevelt to William Sewall, August 5, 1891, October 20, 1891, and February 11, 1892, Theodore Roosevelt Collection, Library of Congress Manuscript Division.

17. Theodore Roosevelt Collection, Library of Congress Manuscript Division, letter from Theodore Roosevelt to William Sewall, October 11, 1892.

18. William Sewall to Theodore Roosevelt, December 11, 1911, reel 119, Theodore Roosevelt Collection, Library of Congress Manuscript Division.

19. Theodore Roosevelt to William Sewall, including November 17, 1904 (reel 336), December 26, 1904 (reel 333), December 4, 190[5?] (reel 339), May 13, 1901, November 17, 1904, December 4, 1905, December 15, 1905 (reel 340), September 30, 1908, December 18, 1908, May 9, 1911, and William Sewall to Theodore Roosevelt May 16, 1901, June 9, 1901, December 23, 1903, November 12, 1904, December 21, 1908, May 3, 1911, Theodore Roosevelt Collection, Library of Congress Manuscript Division.

20. Hagedorn Files, 332.H12p, files 121–167, Theodore Roosevelt Collection, Houghton Library, Harvard University.

21. Theodore Roosevelt to William Sewall, November 8, 1902, Theodore Roosevelt Collection, Library of Congress Manuscript Division.

22. Theodore Roosevelt to William Sewall, including September 22, 1903, December 26, 1903, reel 333, and William Sewall to Theodore Roosevelt, including December 23, 1903, June 24, 1908, August [11?], 1912, Theodore Roosevelt Collection, Library of Congress Manuscript Division.

23. Theodore Roosevelt to William Sewall, June 26, 1908, Theodore Roosevelt Collection, Library of Congress Manuscript Division.

24. William Sewall to Theodore Roosevelt, January 16, 1909; Theodore Roosevelt Collection, Library of Congress Manuscript Division; visit to Oyster Bay: William Sewall to Theodore Roosevelt, December 11, 1911, reel 119, Theodore Roosevelt Collection, Library of Congress Manuscript Division.

25. Theodore Roosevelt to William Sewall, May 22, 1888, April [17?], 1891, December 30, 1904 (reel 336), December 19, 1911 (reel 371), July 20, 1906, September 3, 1907, and William Sewall to Theodore Roosevelt, December 11, 1911 (reel 119), Theodore Roosevelt Collection, Library of Congress Manuscript Division. Knitting: Theodore Roosevelt to William Sewall, October 20, 1890, April [17?], 1891, September 11, 1902, September 17, 1908, November 8, 1908, December 18, 1908, July 16, 1909, and letter from William Sewall to Theodore Roosevelt November 5, 1902, November 4, 1908 (reel 85), December 21, 1908, Theodore Roosevelt Collection, Library of Congress Manuscript Division.

26. Theodore Roosevelt to William Sewall, October 8, 1917, Theodore Roosevelt Collection, Library of Congress Manuscript Division.

27. William Wingate Sewall, "As I Knew Him," *Forum* LXI, 5 (May 1919). The pages of the source copy used here, from a Library of Congress electronic archive, are unnumbered.

28. Theodore Roosevelt, *Outdoor Pastimes of an American Hunter* (Mechanicsburg, PA: Stackpole Books, 1990 [1905]), p. 274.

29. Theodore Roosevelt to Joe Ferris, December 31, 1900, and Joe Ferris to Roosevelt, January 11, 1900, reel 325, Theodore Roosevelt Collection, Library of Congress Manuscript Division.

30. Alice Roosevelt Longworth, *Crowded Hours* (New York: Charles Scribner's Sons, 1933), p. 12.

31. Longworth, *Crowded Hours*, p. 3.

32. Theodore Roosevelt to Seth Bullock, September 18, 1902 (reel 329); July 7, 1903 (reel 331); July 14, 1903; July 20, 1903 (reel 331); August 1, 1903 (reel 331); August 25, 1903 (reel 331); September 12, 1903 (reel 332); July 7, 1905 (reel 338); July 13, 1905 (reel 56); August 22, 1905 (reel 338); September 4, 1905 (reel 339); and letters from Seth Bullock to Theodore Roosevelt, July 14, 1903 (reel 35); September 12, 1903 (reel 37); August 22, 1905, (reel 58); August 31, 1905, (reel 59), Theodore Roosevelt Collection, Library of Congress Manuscript Division.

33. George Bird Grinnell to Theodore Roosevelt, October 29, 1918, reel 298, Theodore Roosevelt Collection, Library of Congress Manuscript Division.

34. David McCullough, *Mornings on Horseback: The Story of an Extraordinary Family, a Vanished Way of Life, and the Unique Child Who Became Theodore Roosevelt* (New York: Simon and Schuster, 1981), pp. 368–369.

35. McCullough, *Mornings on Horseback*, pp. 362–363.

36. McCullough, *Mornings on Horseback*, pp. 369–370.

37. Nicholas Roosevelt, *Theodore Roosevelt: The Man as I Knew Him* (New York: Dodd, Mead & Company), p. 27.

38. Roosevelt, *Theodore Roosevelt: The Man as I Knew Him*, pp. 23–24.

39. Michael Teague, *Mrs. L: Conservations with Alice Roosevelt Longworth* (Garden City, NY: Doubleday & Company, 1981), p. 5.

40. http://en.wikipedia.org/wiki/Medora,_North_Dakota.

41. Williams papers, file 6, Theodore Roosevelt Collection, Houghton Library, Harvard University.

42. Interview with John W. Goodall, March 9, 1923, L. F. Crawford Papers, North Dakota Historical Society.

43. Ray H. Mattison, "Roosevelt's Elkhorn Ranch," *North Dakota Historical Society Quarterly* 27, 2 (Spring 1960): 58.

44. William Roscoe Thayer, *Theodore Roosevelt: An Intimate Biography* (New York: Grosset & Dunlap, 1919), p. 450. Marshall also is known for the phrase, "What this country needs is a good five-cent cigar."

45. Hermann Hagedorn, "Conversation at Dusk Along the Little Missouri," *Outlook*, September 24, 1919, pp. 137 ff. (the copy used as a source here is an electronic version from the Library of Congress that has no page numbers).

46. Hagedorn, "Conversation at Dusk," pp. 137 ff.

INDEX

NOTE: Throughout the index, TR refers to Theodore Roosevelt

Abbott, Teddy Blue
  on buffalo hunters and hunters, 30, 32–33
  on cowboys and women/religion, 77, 287n65
  on driving cattle, 164–65
  on Easterners and Englishmen, 73
  on end of open range, 249
  on frontier violence, 76
  on roundups, 167–68
  in Texas, 72
Acton, Thomas C., 229–30
American bison. *See* bison
Arthur, Chester Alan, 66
asthma, 8–9, 33, 67
Astor, William Waldorf, 22
Audubon, Lucy, 178
Autobiography, An (Roosevelt)
  failure to mention Alice Lee, 104
  on novels of Mayne Reid, 10
  on NYC mayoral campaign, 231

Bad Lands Cow Boy newspaper
  on bison, 116
  bounty on wolves, 137–38, 304n122
  on cattle business, 73
  on cowboys and guns, 115
  on extermination of game, 116, 137
  overview, 80, 87–89

  on stockmen's association, 148, 155
  on TR's nomination for mayor of NYC, 230
  on TR's politics, 98–99
Bad Lands Gun Club, 156
Badlands of Dakota Territory
  descriptions of, 28–29, 36, 45–46, 51–52, 203–4
  deterioration of, 216
  expansion into, 70–71, 77–81, 286n30
  Gorringe's investments in, 27–29, 37–38
  hunting in, 115–19
  Sewall's first impression, 108, 112, 139–40, 295n3
  as "shot out," 244
  spring thaw, 162
  TR drifting away from, 228
Badlands stockmen's association. *See* Little Missouri River Stockmen's Association; Montana Stockgrowers' Association
Badlands weather
  blizzard of 1886–87, 234, 235–41, 331n1, 331n7, 332n16
  drought, 180, 215–16, 220–21
  harbingers of a bad winter, 228
  overview, 286n30
  rain, 49–50, 54, 98, 123–24

Badlands weather (*continued*)
  snow and wind, 157
  spring thaw, 162
  storms during roundup, 171–72, 173–74
  thawing and freezing, 199, 203–6
  TR on, 237
Baille-Grohman, William A., 177
bears, grizzly. *See* grizzly hunt in Bighorn
    Mountains
bears as entertainment at Roberts Saloon,
    Medora, 79, 148
beavers, 117, 216, 228
Bennett, Henry, 99
Benton, Thomas Hart, book by TR, 197,
    203, 215, 219
Berry-Boice Co. foreman, 168
Bighorn Mountains as "shot out," 244.
    See also grizzly hunt in Bighorn
    Mountains
bighorn sheep, 149, 152–54
Billings, Montana, 263
Billings County, Dakota Territory, 210
Bird, Ben, 84
Bismarck Daily Tribune, 216, 319n106
bison
  conservation attempts, 178–79, 245–46
  laws protecting, 32
  market hunters, 30, 31–32, 42, 246,
    304n122
  overview, 29–30, 71
  protection for, 245–47
  TR hunting for, 51–54, 56–57, 159,
    247–48, 336n32
  TR on slaughter of, 116–17
  uses for and waste of, 30–31
Blaine, James G., 66–69, 94–95, 105–6,
    142–43
blizzard of 1886–87, 234, 235–41, 331n1,
    331n7, 332n16
boat stolen from Elkhorn Ranch, 202–8,
    322n46, 323n67
Boone and Crockett Club, 244–46, 262
Boston Herald, 105
boxing, 9, 114, 167
branding cattle, 169–70

buffalo. *See* bison
Buffalo, Wyoming, 128
buffalo bag, 147–48
Burchard, Rev. Dr., 143, 144
Burnsted, Mr., 201–2, 204–8, 322n46,
    323n67
Burroughs, John, 253, 337n63

Carow, Charles, 101, 102, 103
Carow, Edith
  Merrifield on, 319n106
  New York Times report on engagement,
    226
  as TR's childhood friend, 101–3
  TR's courting and engagement, 194–95,
    210, 218, 225–27
  wedding to TR, 231
  See also Roosevelt, Edith Kermit
Casey, Edward, 280n110
cattle country, 72–73, 286n33
cattle drives, 164–65
cattle ranches, TR's. *See* Elkhorn Ranch;
    Maltese Cross Ranch
cattle ranching
  as character-building experience, 94,
    251–53, 254
  cowboys vs. cattlemen, 74–75
  depressed prices for beef, 216, 227
  disastrous winter, 234, 235–41
  eastern vs. longhorn cattle, 90
  effect on land, 238–39
  farmers requiring fencing, 240
  Ferris, Sylvane, and Merrifield, 44
  Lang and TR's discussions, 49, 50, 51
  lessons from blizzards, 237
  de Morés slaughterhouse, 39–41,
    315n28
  New Yorkers' investments in, 28, 73–74
  overstocking, 74, 80, 148–49, 211,
    216–17, 235–36
  overview, 36, 71–75, 275n8
  TR's investments in, 55–56, 90, 216, 227,
    250
  winter tasks, 155–56
  and wolves, 137–38, 304n122

See also cowboys; Elkhorn Ranch;
    Maltese Cross Ranch; West, the
Cheyenne Daily Leader on cowboys, 75
Cheyenne Indians in Wyoming, 127–28
Chimney Butte Ranch, 46, 108
chuck wagons, 166–67
citizenship, TR on, 213–14, 245
Civil Service Commission, 193, 247, 248
Civil War, 72
Cleopatra's Needle, 27
Cleveland, Grover, 142
Colt revolver, 87
Columbia College School of Law, 21
conservation
    development of TR's commitment to,
        251–55
    Grinnell's role in, 177–79, 244–46
    irony of TR's attitude toward, 247–48,
        336n32
    as New York governor, 250–51
    as president of the U.S., 251
    Roosevelt, Robert, on, 252
    TR and Grinnell's books on, 246
    TR decides in favor of, 242
    TR's fight for, 243–47
    of wildlife habitat, 31, 245–46, 247
Cooper Union, New York City, 229–30
Cope, E. D., 116
Courtwright, David, 74–75, 286n47
Cove Neck, Long Island, 33, 65, 180,
    274n59
Cowboy Candidate, TR as, 230
cowboys
    attire of, 85–87, 157–58
    and broncos, 151
    cattlemen vs., 74–75
    development of gear and techniques, 71–72
    enthusiasm for war, 220
    line riders, 155–56
    reputation of, 75–79, 114–15
    roping skills, 169, 170, 312n74
    and roundups, 165–74, 212–13, 311n49
    Sewall, Mary, on, 213
    songs for herding cattle, 171–73
    TR on, 83–84, 175–76

    and violence, 168
    wages, 100–101
    See also shootouts
"Cowboy's Dream, The" (night song), 172–73
Cowles, Anna Roosevelt, 261
Cowles, William Sheffield, 261
Crowded Hours (Roosevelt), 233
Custer Trail Ranch, 46
Cutler, Arthur, 63, 67

dairy farming, 88, 290n42
Dakota Territorial Governor's Report
    (1885), 74
Dana, Frances Theodora Smith, 230
deer market hunters, 225, 328n31
Delmonico's, New York City, 143–44, 241
Democratic Party
    Burchard's accusations against, 143
    Cleveland's illegitimate child, 142
    criticism of Blaine, 144
    election of 1912, 2
    leading Republicans switching to, 94–95
    mayoral election in NYC, 229, 231
    Roosevelt members of, 22–23
depression, Panic of 1873, 73
Des Moines Register, 263
Dickinson, Montana
    expansion of, 240, 258–59
    Independence Day celebration speech,
        213–14
    TR delivers boat thieves to, 207–8,
        323–324n54
Dickinson Press, 237, 240
digestive problems, 8
discrimination, TR's stance against, 193, 197
Dow, Lizzie, 183, 185, 199, 220
Dow, Wilmot
    boating down the river, 208–9
    death of, 259
    as nephew of Sewall, 90, 100
    return to Maine, 227–28
    on Sewall, 110
    TR's contracts with, 174
"duel" between TR and the Marquis,
    186–88, 317n72

Eaton, Alden, 167
Eaton, Howard, 88, 93, 148, 290n42
Edmunds, George F., 68–69
Egypt, 11
election of 1884, 65–69, 142–45, 284n44
election of 1912, 2
elk, 117, 129, 131–32, 159, 185–86, 212,
  325n85
Elkhorn Ranch
  boat stolen from, 202–8, 322n46, 323n67
  building a house on, 112, 139, 306n7
  depressed prices for beef, 227
  driving cattle to, 164–65
  Edith and Anna's visit to, 248
  end of, 262–63
  house on, 163
  hunter's shack, 112, 146–47
  as hunting lodge, 162
  ice gorge, 199
  routine, 163–64
  search for land, 98–99
  Sewall hired as foreman, 100–101, 109
  TR enjoying ride to, 184–85
  working with first 100 cattle, 111–12
  See also Maltese Cross Ranch
Elkhorn Stock Company, 249
English investors in cattle ranching, 73–74
Etruria (ocean liner), 231

fall roundup, 165–67
Federal Club speech, New York City, 241
Ferris, Joe
  as clerk of Billings County, 210
  as hunting guide for TR's first Badlands
    venture, 44–46, 47–54, 56–57
  as Medora postmaster, 257
  on de Morés, 188
  de Morés accusations against, 186–87
  TR and, 163, 198
  TR's room in his store building, 187,
    317n63
Ferris, Mrs. Joe, 198
Ferris, Sylvane
  biographical info, 44, 46–47
  on blizzard of 1886–87, 236–37
  career and death of, 258–59
  as clerk of Billings County circuit court,
    210
  contracts with TR, 55, 90–91, 227
  as Land Office commissioner, 257
  and de Morés, 81
  on politics, 112
  possessiveness of, 162–63
  purchasing TR's remaining stake,
    250
  TR and, on love, 218
  and TR's death, 263
  See also Maltese Cross Ranch
Finnegan, Mike "Redhead," 201–2, 204–8,
  259, 322n27, 322n46, 323n67
firearms for hunting, 37, 45, 118, 122–23,
  275n13, 279n83
fire fighting on the prairie, 188–89
Fish Commission of New York, 252
Fisher, J. C., 93
Florence, Italy, 232
Forest Reserve Act (1891), 245
Fort McKinney, Wyoming, 135
Fourth of July celebration, Medora,
  181–82
Fourth of July celebration, Dickinson,
  213–214
fox hunting, 194–95, 232
Free Trade Club annual dinner (1883),
  26–27, 229
frontiersmen, 76

game trophies at Sagamore Hill, 261
George, Henry, 229
goat hunt in Rocky Mountains
  Century magazine story, 329n56
  shooting a goat, 223–24
  sitting around the campfire, 224–25
  TR's serious falls during, 224, 328n44
  Willis as guide, 221–23, 225, 329n56
Goodall, John, 188
Gorringe, Henry Honeychurch
  Badlands investments, 27–29, 37–38
  biographical info, 27
  and Pender, 47–48

Gracie, Anna Bulloch (aunt), 61, 63
Great Northwest, The, 27–28
Grinnell, George Bird, 177–79, 244–46
grizzly hunt in Bighorn Mountains
  arrival in Buffalo, Wyoming, 128
  Cheyenne Indians, 127–28
  hunting for bears, 130–31, 132–35
  hunting game, 129–32
  pack horse problems, 128–29
  stories told about, 126, 134, 300*n*42,
    303*n*113
  travel to and from, 122–27, 135–36
  TR's companions, 121, 126–27
Gros Ventres Indians, 157–58
grouse, 118, 135, 147, 149, 224, 249
gun control vs. shootouts, 88

Hagedorn, Hermann, 3–4, 228, 260
Hall, Rev. John, 62–63
Halley, W. L., 44, 55
Harper's Weekly, 197
Harrison, Benjamin, 246–47
Harvard, 11–13, 21
Hasty Pudding Club, 12–13
Hewitt, Abram, 229
Hoffman, Medora von, 39
homestead acts, 240
Hornaday, William T., 30, 31, 32–33, 137
horses
  breaking, 150–52
  electric streetcars replacing, 240
  for fox hunting, 194–95, 232
  for hunting, 113–14
  for ranching, 149–50, 168–70
  survival in winter, 238–39
  TR on, 255
hospitality in cattle country, 48–49, 125,
    128, 141–42
Huggins, Bill, 160
hunter's shack at Elkhorn Ranch, 112,
    146–47
hunting
  in Adirondack Mountains, 11
  Badlands trip with Underhill and a
    cousin, 241–42

as character-building experience, 138,
    153, 245, 249–50
in Egypt, 11
Elliott's stories about, 25
firearms for, 37, 45, 118, 122–23, 275*n*13,
    279*n*83
as health-improvement plan, 84, 95–98,
    289*n*12
in Maine, 106
as male status symbol, 95, 118–19, 132,
    159, 194, 244
preparations, 33–34, 44–50, 113–14,
    119–20, 218
in Shoshone Mountains, 248–49
TR on, 115–19, 135, 225
hunting specific species
  beaver, 117
  bighorn sheep, 149, 152–54
  bison in Badlands, 51–54, 56–57,
    159
  bison market hunters, 30, 31–32, 42,
    304*n*122
  deer market hunters, 225, 328*n*31
  elk, 117, 129, 131–32, 159, 185–86, 212,
    325*n*85
  fox, 194–95, 232
  goats in Rocky Mountains, 221–25
  grouse, 118, 135, 147, 149, 224, 249
  mallard ducks, 111
  mountain lions, 200–201
  mule deer, 117, 127
  pronghorn antelope, 91–94, 97–98, 118,
    291*n*60
  woodland caribou, 246
  See also grizzly hunt in Bighorn
    Mountains; wildlife
Hunting Trips of a Ranchman (Roosevelt),
    159, 177–79, 199, 309*n*73, 314*n*1

ice gorge in Little Missouri River, 199
Independent Republicans (Mugwumps),
    66–68, 144–45
Indians
  and bison destruction, 31
  blaming for prairie fires, 180, 188

Indians (*continued*)
  Cheyennes in Wyoming, 127–28
  cowboys' fear of, 189
  Sewall, Dow, and, 209
  TR on bison slaughter and, 117
  TR on rights of, 191–93, 318n94
  TR's encounter with, 189–91
  Watts and Elkhorn men's shopping
    spree, 157–58
  white men's attacks, 191
Institute of 1770 social club, 12

Jackson, Joseph W., 257–58

"Kansas Line, The" (night song), 172
Krakatoa volcano, Indonesia, 331n1

Lang, Gregor, 47–50, 51, 54–55, 57,
    258
Lang, Lincoln
  biographical info, 47–49
  on blizzard of 1886–87, 235, 236, 237,
    332n16
  as engineer in Chicago, 258
  on Indians, 191
  on de Morés, 188
  on roundups, 311n49
  TR and, 91–94, 111
  on TR's awareness of Badlands deteriora-
    tion, 216
  on women in the West, 78
law of hospitality in cattle country, 48–49,
    125, 128, 141–42
Lebo, Norman, 121, 126–27
Lebo, Schuyler, 191
Lee, Alice Hathaway "Sunshine," 15,
    16–20. *See also* Roosevelt, Alice
    Hathaway
Lee, George Cabot (father-in-law), 15–16
Lee, Henry, 105
Leeholm, Cove Neck, New York, 33, 65,
    179–80, 274n59. *See also* Sagamore
    Hill
Lincoln, Abraham, 49, 60, 193, 280n111
line riders, 155–56

Little Missouri, Badlands
  founding of, 29, 43–44
  Morés, Marquis de, 38–41, 42–43
  shootout in Little Missouri/Medora,
    41–43, 277n59
  TR's arrival in, 36–38, 82
Little Missouri River
  dead cattle from winter blizzards, 237,
    332n16
  descriptions of, 38
  ice gorge in, 199
  overview, 28
  slaughtering animals near, 117, 137, 160
  spring thaw, 162, 173
  traveling along, 123, 146–47, 162
  traveling on, 202–9
Little Missouri River Stockmen's
    Association
  closing the range to new outfits,
    235–36
  meetings, 148–49, 154–55, 183, 186, 210,
    241
  de Morés as driving force, 80
  vigilantes, 182–83, 315n33
livestock associations. *See* Little Missouri
    River Stockmen's Association;
    Montana Stockgrowers' Association
Lodge, Henry Cabot
  and American Statesman Series, 197
  and Blaine's nomination, 94–95, 105,
    144–45
  loss in 1884 House race, 142–43, 144
  TR and, 113, 125, 126, 197
  TR's support for, 142, 159–60
  on Twenty-first District group, 22
Lorant, Stefan, 255
Luffsey, Riley, 41, 43, 184, 316n49

Maddox, "Old Lady," 91, 92
Maltese Cross Ranch
  as cattle headquarters, 162–63
  de Morés attempt to claim land, 80–81
  as display at Theodore Roosevelt
    National Park, 262
  original Ferris/Merrifield ranch, 46

TR learning the ropes, 89–90, 168–69, 170–71

TR partners with Sylvane and Merrifield, 55–56, 58, 90–91

TR waiting for news of cattle purchase, 57

winter tasks, 155–56

See also Elkhorn Ranch

Mandan, Badlands, 209

Mandan Pioneer newspaper, 181, 216

market hunters
of bison, 30, 31–32, 42, 246, 304n122
of deer, 225, 328n31

Marsh, O. C., 178

Marshall, Thomas, 263

Massiter, Mr., 111

mavericking, 170

McCarty, Bill, 263

McKinley, William, 251

McShane, "Dynamite Jimmie," 187

Meadowbrook Hunt Ball, 194–95

Medora, Dakota Territory
cowboy domination, 77, 78–79
current events in, 262
decline of, 239–40
expansion of, 79–80, 82–84, 181
overview, 38–40
and Redhead Finnegan, 201, 322n27, 323n67
TR's acceptance in, 84
See also Bad Lands Cow Boy newspaper

Medora Gun Club, 156

Merrifield, William "Bill"
biographical info, 46–47, 121
on cattle dead from blizzards, 237
contracts with TR, 55, 90–91, 227
on cutting cattle and TR, 170
deputy of Billings County, 210
as Elkhorn Ranch foreman, 239, 248
on grizzly bears, 128
hunting with TR, 126, 134, 152–54
leaving TR's employ, 248
on Little Missouri outlaws, 29
and de Morés, 81
possessiveness of, 162–63

on Rocky Mountain goat hunt, 222–25
as U.S. Marshal, 257
See also Maltese Cross Ranch

Mexico, impending war with, 220

Miles City, Montana, 210–11, 241

Mingusville, Montana, 114–15, 297nn42–43

Mix, Tom, 258

Montana Stockgrowers' Association
annual meeting, 210–11, 241
de Morés as liaison from Badlands, 154
TR as delegate from Badlands, 210
TR's resignation from, 333–334n45
vigilantes hanging thieves and murderers, 99, 111, 295n17, 296n18

Moore, Captain, 37

Moore, Frank, 43–44, 48, 280n110

Moore, Robert J., 252

Morés, Marquis de
attempts to claim Roosevelt land, 80–81, 113, 140–42
biographical info, 38–40
death of, 259
failure of businesses, 239–40
Luffsey shooting and trial, 43, 184, 316n49, 316n52
and Medora, 181
and Montana Stockgrowers' Assn. vigilantes, 99
and Paddock, 42–43
ranch and slaughterhouse, 39–41
reputation among ranchers, 40–41
TR and, 149, 183–84, 186–88, 212–13, 317n72

Morris, Gouverneur, 241

Morton, Levi P., 229

mountain lions, 200–201

Mount Rushmore, 1

Mrs. L: Conversations with Alice Roosevelt Longworth (Longworth), 233

mule deer, 117, 127, 159

Myers, George, 89, 151, 263

National Audubon Society, 178–79, 244

national conservation commission, 251

National Livestock Association, 257
National Park Protective Act
    (1894), 246
National Wildlife Refuge System, 262
Native Americans. *See* Indians
nature
    Badlands, 28–29, 36, 45–46, 51–52,
        203–4
    buffalo trails and carcasses, 125
    call of the bull elk, 130
    dawn at Elkhorn Ranch, 184–85
    hunter as lover of, 138
    plains, 95–97, 98
    and ranch life, 115
    westerner's view of, 244
    in winter, 156–57
Naval War of 1812, The (Roosevelt), 18, 25
New York Assembly
    and Alice's death, 60, 62, 282n13
    Roosevelt's acceptance of Blaine, 106
    serving in, 23–25
    TR after Alice's death, 65–67, 106
    TR's campaign, 22, 23
New York City
    City Investigating Committee, 65
    cost of living, 14–15, 283n19
    Delmonico's, 143–44
    electricity and telephones in, 21
    Federal Club speech, 241
    fog in, 60–61
    and politics, 22, 23
    presidency of the city board of health
        offer to TR, 215, 326n105, 326n120
    theater-going, 15, 269n69
    TR's homes in, 5–7, 8–9, 19–20, 25, 65,
        268n23
    TR's mayoral candidacy, 228–31
New York Evening Post, 89
New-York Free Trade Club annual dinner
    (1883), 26–27, 229
New York State convention (1885), 193
New York State Fish Commission, 252
New York State governorship, 193,
    250–51
New York Sun interview, 142–43

New York Times
    review of *Hunting Trips*, 177
    review of *The Wilderness Hunter*, 250
    on suicidal weather, 60–61
    on TR's engagement to Carow, 226
    on TR's political success, 282n13
New York World newspaper, 144
Nineteenth Century Club speeches, 66,
    145, 284n44
Nobel Peace Prize, 1–2
North, Eric, 167

obelisk from Pasha of Egypt, 27
O'Donald, Frank, 41, 42–43
Old Four Eyes (play), 262
Osterhaut, W. P., 182–83

Packard, A. T.
    biographical info, 87–89
    leaving the Badlands, 239
    shooting competition winner, 156
    TR and, 183
    on TR's July 4th speech, 214
    See also Bad Lands Cow Boy newspaper
Paddock, Eldridge G. "Jerry"
    arrest for Luffsey shooting, 184
    biographical info, 41–42, 258, 305n9
    and growth of Medora, 80
    and de Morés, 42–43, 140–42, 295n17
    move to Dickinson, 240
    and O'Donald, 41, 42–43
    and Sewall, 140–42
    shooting contest, 156
    and stockmen's association, 148, 154
    and TR's firearms, 45
Panic of 1873, 73
Parsons, Fanny, 282n28, 282n31
Pasha, Ismail, 27
Pender, Sir John, 47–48
Pfaffenbach, Chris, 201–2, 204–8, 219,
    322n46, 323n67
philanthropic causes of TR's father, 7–8
politics
    corruption reform, 24–25, 142–43
    election of 1888, 246–47

New Yorkers' aversion to, 22, 23
New York State convention of 1885, 193
TR on maintaining public usefulness, 105
TR's decision to pursue, 21–23
TR's plans for presidency, 131, 214–15
TR's retirement from, 106, 112, 126, 135, 176, 211
Young Republican Club speech, 197
Porcellian club, 12–13
pornography, 76
Powder River, Montana, 127
prairie fires, 188–89, 318n75
presidency of TR, 251–55, 258, 260
Progress and Poverty (George), 229
Progressive Party (Bull Moose Party), 2, 193, 258
pronghorn antelope, 91–94, 97–98, 118, 291n60
Putnam, Carleton, 104, 253–54
Putnam, George, 24

railroad
    and cattle ranching, 72, 73
    cowboys shooting at trains, 78–79
    and Little Missouri, Badlands, 29, 36–37
    traveling on, 35–37
ranching. *See* cattle ranching
Ranch Life and the Hunting Trail (Roosevelt), 242, 247
Reid, Whitelaw, 144
religion in the Wild West, 78, 287n65
Republican Party
    county convention in Brooklyn, 228–29
    election of 1884, 65–69, 142–45, 284n44
    election of 1888, 246–47
    New York State convention of 1885, 193
    split over Blaine nomination, 68–69, 94–95
    TR in New York Assembly, 2, 23–25
    TR lobbying for black vote, 193
    TR on Blaine candidacy, 105–6, 112–13
    TR on defeat in 1884 election, 144–45
    Twenty-first Assembly District Republican Association, 21–22, 23

Reuter, J. "Dutch Wannegan," 41, 113, 162–63, 187, 316n49
Roberts, Bob, 181, 259, 315n29. *See also* Roberts Saloon, Medora
Roberts, Elizabeth, 42
Roberts, Frank, 170–71
Roberts Hall, Medora, 154, 181
Roberts Saloon, Medora
    bears as entertainment, 79, 148
    cowboy pranks, 79, 201
    destroyed by fire, 181, 315n28
    meeting hall, 154, 181
Robins, Captain, 110
Robinson, Corinne Roosevelt (sister), 103, 215, 254, 261. *See also* Roosevelt, Corinne
Robinson, Douglas, 103, 215, 249
Rocky Mountains. *See* goat hunt in Rocky Mountains
Roosevelt, Alice Hathaway (wife)
    courtship, 15, 16–19
    courtship and wedding, 15, 16–20
    death and funeral, 61–63, 84, 131, 283n19
    Edith's caustic remarks about, 233
    engagement and wedding, 19–20
    love letters from and to TR, 20, 34, 45, 50–51, 59, 60
    pregnancy of, 33, 59–60
    TR's memorial to, 119, 219–20
Roosevelt, Alice Lee (daughter)
    baptism, 63
    biographical info, 262
    birth of, 60
    Edith as Mother, 232–33
    living with Aunt Anna, 63–64, 103–4
    and maternal grandparents, 104–5
    on TR, 261
    TR caring for, 158, 180
    TR's attitude toward, 94, 101, 104, 135, 147, 212, 217, 335n25
    TR's treatment of, 195
Roosevelt, Anna "Bamie" (sister)
    biographical info, 64, 261, 283n31
    at Elkhorn Ranch, 248

Roosevelt, Anna "Bamie" (continued)
  and New York Times report on TR's
    engagement, 226
  and Theodore, 63–65
  on TR's run for mayor of NYC, 230–31
  at TR's wedding to Edith Carow, 231
Roosevelt, Corinne (sister), 6, 13, 63–64,
    104, 282n28. See also Robinson,
    Corinne
Roosevelt, Cornelius Van Schaak (grand-
    father), 7, 8
Roosevelt, Edith Kermit (wife)
  at Elkhorn Ranch, 248
  pregnancies and children's births, 241, 247
  on TR, 261–62
  wedding and honeymoon, 231
  See also Carow, Edith
Roosevelt, Elliott (brother), 13–14, 25, 261
Roosevelt, Jacobus, 7
Roosevelt, James (uncle), 7, 55–56
Roosevelt, James West (cousin), 18–19
Roosevelt, Johannes, 7
Roosevelt, J. West (cousin), 226–27,
    241–42
Roosevelt, Kermit (son), 247, 261
Roosevelt, Martha "Minnie" (mother), 6–7,
    61
Roosevelt, Nicholas (cousin), 252
Roosevelt, Quentin, 2
Roosevelt, Robert (uncle), 23, 252
Roosevelt, Theodore
  ancestors, 6–8, 252, 254
  childhood, 5–6, 8–10
  Columbia College School of Law, 21
  death of, 263
  fathering skills, 158, 180, 261
  father's death, 13–15
  Harvard, 11–13, 21
  health from living in the Badlands,
    57–58, 94, 174–75, 248
  illnesses of, 8–9, 33, 51, 67, 84, 131, 160,
    161
  overview, 1–2
  roping skills, 312n74
  See also Roosevelt, Theodore, opinions

Roosevelt, Theodore, attire
  for Bighorn Mountain grizzly hunt, 122
  buckskin suit, 92–93
  cowboy splendor, 85, 86–87
  glasses, 24, 44–45, 48, 93, 114, 124, 168
  hats in Medora, 79
  hunting, 97, 120, 147–48, 299n76
  in New York, 85
  slicker, 292n90
Roosevelt, Theodore, diary entries
  on Alice Lee, 16–20, 63, 283n22
  on death of his father, 14, 15
  on Edith Carow, 196, 197
  failure to mention his daughter, 101
  on hunting, 115–16, 127, 130
  on making money, 21
  on politics, 21
Roosevelt, Theodore, opinions
  on deer at Elkhorn Ranch, 249
  on family life, 243
  on life in the West, 249–50, 253
  love letters from and to Alice, 20, 34, 45,
    50–51, 59, 60
  the past as past, 104
  on writing, 243
Roosevelt, Theodore, Sr. (father), 6, 7–9,
    13–15
Roosevelt, Theodore, Jr. (son), 241, 261
Roosevelt's outfit. See Maltese Cross Ranch
Root, Elihu, 229
roping skills, 169, 170, 312n74
Roscoe, William, 254
Rough Riders, 250, 258
roundups, 165–74, 212–13, 241, 311n49
Rowe, Bill, 170

Sagamore Hill (formerly Leeholm), Cove
    Neck, New York, 180, 194–95, 232, 261
Saltonstall, Richard, 15
Saturday Evening Post, 24
scalps, 157, 158
Selmes, Mr. and Mrs. Tilden, 219
Sewall, Bill
  biographical info, 106–8
  boating down the river, 208–9

and boat thieves, 203–7, 322n46, 323n67
and broncos, 151
and Captain Robins, 110–11
contracts with TR, 174
on cows' need for extra feed in winter,
    155, 161–62, 199–200
discovery of missing boat, 202
as foreman for TR's 2nd ranch, 100–101,
    109
Fourth of July celebration in Medora,
    181–82
on hunting with TR, 212
learning to ride a horse, 110
on life in the Badlands, 108, 112, 139–40,
    157, 180–81, 183, 295n3
return to Maine, 227–28
on role of the Badlands in TR's life, 255
on TR, 119, 163, 260
and TR as president, 259–60
and TR's family's worries, 161
TR's letters to, 90, 100–101, 108
as TR's second in duel with Marquis, 187
as vigilante, 182–83, 315n33
Sewall, Lucretia "Kitty," 212
Sewall, Mary, 183, 185, 199, 213, 220
Shaler, Alexander, 215
sheep ranching, 40, 113
Shiras, George, 254–55
shootouts
    assertion of rights vs., 114–15
    cowboy pranks, 78–79
    gun control vs., 88
    in Little Missouri/Medora, 41–43, 184,
        277n59
    Luffsey shooting and trial, 43, 184,
        316n49, 316n52
    overview, 75–76
    Roberts and Heywood, 315n29
Shoshone Mountains, Wyoming,
    248–49
Sioux Falls Press newspaper, 230–31
songs for herding cattle, 171–73
Spanish-American War, 250
spring roundup, 165–74, 212–13, 241,
    311n49

spring thaw in the Badlands, 162
Stalwart Republicans, 66
stampede, nighttime, 173
Stegner, Wallace, 75
Stickney, Victor, 84, 208, 213, 331n7
stockmen's associations. See Little Missouri
    River Stockmen's Association;
    Montana Stockgrowers' Association
St. Paul Dispatch interview, 175–76
St. Paul Pioneer Press interview, 69, 89,
    98–99, 290n49
Stranglers (vigilantes), 99, 111, 295n17,
    296n18
Stuart, Granville, 70–71, 99, 111
Sweet family, 240

Taft, William Howard, 2, 260
tariffs, TR's argument against, 26–27
teamsters, 299n1
Texas, 71–73
Texas longhorns, 71, 90
Thayer, William Roscoe, 66–67, 106
Theodore Roosevelt National Park, 262
Thomas Hart Benton book by TR, 197,
    203, 215, 219
Thompson Falls, Montana, 221–22, 225
Tolstoy, Leo, 206, 213, 323n54
Tompkins, W. J., 200–201
Townshend, Richard, 77–78, 87
Tranquillity, Oyster Bay, Long Island,
    9–10, 33, 102, 180
Twenty-first Assembly District Republican
    Association, 21–22, 23

Underhill, Frank, 242
U.S. Forest Service, 251

Vanderbilt, Mrs. Cornelius, 103
Vanderbilt, William H., 27
vigilantes
    Little Missouri River Stockmen's
        Association, 182–83, 315n33
    Montana Stranglers, 99, 111, 295n17,
        296n18
vigilantism, 296n18

Wadsworth, H. B., 44, 55
Wallop, Mr., 128
Walton, Izaak, 252, 337n59
Wannegan, Dutch (J. Reuter), 41, 113,
    162–63, 187, 316n49
Watts, James, 157–58
West, the
    egalitarian nature in, 253–54
    expansion into, 70–78
    farmers moving in, 240
    influence on TR, 253–55, 337n63
    law of hospitality, 48–49, 125, 128,
        141–42
    religion in, 78, 287n65
    support for TR's political career, 251,
        255, 257–58
    TR on, 197, 320n128
    violence in, 75–77
    women in, 77–78
    See also cowboys; shootouts; vigilantes
Wibaux, Pierre, 237
Wilderness Hunter, The (Roosevelt), 249–50

wildlife
    slaughter of, 116–17, 137–38, 179, 225,
        242, 244, 248–49
    TR saves a rabbit from a snake, 91
    TR's childhood interest in, 10–11
    See also conservation; hunting specific
        species
Wilkeson, Frank, 74, 286n33
Willard, Fred, 201
Willis, John, 221–25, 258
Wilson, Woodrow, 2
Winning of the West, The (Roosevelt), 197,
    247, 250
winter entertainment and ranch tasks,
    155–56. See also Badlands weather
Wister, Owen, 244
wolves, 137–38
woodland caribou, 246
Wright, W. R., 43

Yellowstone National Park, 31, 245–46,
    247

A NOTE ON THE AUTHOR

Roger Di Silvestro is a senior editor at *National Wildlife* magazine and author of *In the Shadow of Wounded Knee* and several nature books, including *The Endangered Kingdom* and *Reclaiming the Last Wild Places*. His article in *Wild West* magazine about Theodore Roosevelt in the Badlands won the 2010 Western Writers of America Spur Award for short nonfiction. He lives in Virginia, near Washington, D.C.